FINANCING GOVERNMENT IN A METROPOLITAN AREA:
THE CLEVELAND EXPERIENCE

THE STUDY GROUP

ON GOVERNMENTAL COSTS

Financing government in a metropolitan area

THE CLEVELAND EXPERIENCE

by Seymour Sacks
and William F. Hellmuth, Jr.

WITH LEO M. EGAND AND OTHERS

FOREWORD BY JAMES A. NORTON

The Free Press of Glencoe, Inc.
A DIVISION OF THE CROWELL-COLLIER PUBLISHING COMPANY

Foreword

COMPLEXITY HAUNTS THE PERSON WHO BECOMES aware of metropolitan urbanism. Throughout the nation civic, business, and political leaders are increasingly concerned with finding solutions to the problems created by this complexity. From a continuing discussion of these metropolitan problems came the idea in Cleveland of a major effort which would "get the facts" on which solutions could be based. The idea became the Cleveland Metropolitan Services Commission, incorporated in 1955 as a non-profit research organization. Political, civic, and business leaders were on its Executive Committee; business furnished the funds for its operation, and a professional staff working with Greater Clevelanders provided its competence.

The first chairman of METRO, as the newspapers soon named

it, was Dr. T. Keith Glennan, president of the Case Institute of Technology, respected by the community for his objectivity. While he presided the first suspicions of hidden bias were vocalized and substantially allayed. When he left his post for an appointment in Washington, the unanimous choice for his successor was Dr. John S. Millis, president of Western Reserve University, who also represented leadership.

Many of the questions posed could not be answered with absoluteness by researchers. Most of the important ones demanded an evaluation of alternatives in the light of the particular traditions and goals of Greater Clevelanders. To strengthen the research staff and draw conclusions from its fact-finding, special Study Groups of citizens and government officials were established. These Study Groups worked with the staff in establishing the aims of the research, looked over its shoulder while the work was underway, and made a summary report of their own with recommendations for community action.

During the period of its active research, November, 1956-June, 1959, the Cleveland Metropolitan Services Commission published twenty-nine reports. Some of these were staff reports only; some were reports of the Study Groups made after they had read the staff findings; some reports combined both.

This study is the thirtieth publication of METRO, a report by a section of the staff under the leadership of Dr. Seymour Sacks and Dr. William F. Hellmuth with Dr. Leo M. Egand. The questions to which they had addressed themselves are not new; they have risen from every intensive look at metropolitan government, and they came to the forefront when METRO began its studies.

What is new is the thorough and imaginative way the answers have been sought. The universe under study could be limited rationally to Cuyahoga County. Within that area the property tax assessments were made by a single agency and the comprehensive financial reports were more nearly comparable or could be made comparable with a higher degree of reliability than is usually the case. Some outstanding fiscal officers, members of this Study Group on Government Costs, and two capable consultants of long standing were available and gave their time to improve the data with which the staff worked. The intensity of the study was further facilitated by a grant from the Ford Foundation which made it possible to employ a staff worthy of the material and consultants with whom to whet the research instruments.

This Study Group deserves particular recognition. Among its members were both "experts" and laymen. Both groups asked critical, prying questions and were not satisfied with easy answers. The report of the Study Group, made when only the rough drafts of this report were at hand, is entitled *Government Costs: Questions for Community Decisions*. In it one will find more questions than answers probably, but there can be no doubt that the right questions are asked and evidence presented which should be a firm foundation for action.

Greater Cleveland is one of the great metropolitan complexes of the United States comprising over one million seven hundred thousand persons in several counties and scores of cities and villages in northeastern Ohio. The heart of this population agglomeration is Cuyahoga County, designated in our study as the Cleveland Metropolitan Area, a geographic description that included in 1959 twenty-two cities, thirty-six villages, four townships, thirty-two school districts, nine library districts, and the Metropolitan Park District as well as the county government itself—one hundred five separate governments.

For many years leaders in Cuyahoga County have recognized community-like bonds permeating this complexity. In 1917 the Metropolitan Park District was founded indicating the common concern with rapidly dwindling open spaces and forest lands. Since that time an "Emerald Necklace" of park lands has been acquired and preserved surrounding almost the entire county and extending beyond it into Summit County to the south and Lake County to the east. Its public acceptance is shown time and again as electors throughout the district vote in favor of continuing tax levies for its support. The parks are truly metropolitan in the loyalties which they incite.

In the nineteen-twenties, planning was first accepted as a county-wide function, and as the years have gone by, civic and political groups have sanctioned a "metropolitan" outlook on problems in the area. In 1928 a Regional Government Committee of 400 appointed by the mayor of the City of Cleveland held hearings and early the next year published its report stating:

Various tangible bonds have been pointed out which unite Cleveland and its ever outward spreading population. But even more potent than these is the fact that this whole population depends essentially upon the technological and economic practices which characterize our urban industrial and commercial civilization. This civilization rests upon integration, co-operation, and interdependence. Those metropolitan populations which most quickly and deeply grasp the implications of the economic and technological basis of urban civilization will be the first to square their governmental arrangements and practices with the premises which will in the long run control. Will Cleveland and her neighbors ignore what the moving finger of destiny has already written upon her scroll?

To the observers who saw only the major efforts to "square governmental arrangements" with the premises of metropolitan integration, it appeared that Greater Cleveland was indeed ignoring its common bonds when crucial tests arose. The electors of the county voted overwhelmingly for an amendment to the state constitution which would permit a more advanced home rule county government; and with just a little less enthusiasm then supported the choice of a charter commission. The charter itself received a majority vote in the central city and the county as a whole, but not in the suburbs. The State Supreme Court however voided the charter as not receiving the required majority. In 1936 and 1941 the voters refused to elect new charter commissions. After World War II the community tried again. This time the charter commission was elected with strong support, but when the charter was submitted to the voters in 1950, it was turned down.

This story was repeated in 1958. Sixty-one per cent of the voters in the City of Cleveland favored creation of a charter commission; sixty-nine per cent of the suburban voters wanted the commission to go to work. A charter was submitted which would streamline the county government and transfer many municipal functions in their metropolitan aspects to the county. When the voters looked the charter over, however, there were too many points which found their disfavor. Only forty-two per cent of the city voters approved the charter; forty-seven per cent in the suburbs voted for it, for an overall total of forty-five per cent. This charter has received the most stunning defeat of all.

When one looks only at these efforts to make great changes in government organization, however, he is apt to miss specific developments that add up over a period of years to important revisions of municipal parochialism. In almost every area of governmental service, accommodations have been worked out which involve co-operation among municipalities or with other governments and which serve to "solve" or at least to mitigate one or another of the metropolitan problems.

Public health is a good field for co-operation. In the southwestern part of the county two hospitals each serve several communities. But the largest steps forward are those in which City of Cleveland facilities and operations were recognized as being truly metropolitan in scope and were transferred to county-wide control and support. In 1953 the County opened a 452-bed hospital (later 775 beds) for the chronically ill following a co-operative study with the City of Cleveland, and purchase of the City Infirmary for one dollar. In 1957, sixty-seven per cent of the voters approved the transfer of the City Hospital to county ownership and financing. The most recent step toward a metropolitan program was the creation in 1959 of the post of County Coordinator of Chronic Illnesses under the County Commissioners. The physician appointed to this post has also been appointed as assistant health commissioner by each of the health departments in the county, and is working with them and the county chronic disease hospital to strengthen the program in prevention, early detection, and treatment of chronic diseases.

There are six public health units in the county and seven independent school health programs which, experts agree, could be more effective if they were combined. Nevertheless, this enumeration should not obscure the fact that seventeen cities which might, under state law, maintain their own health departments contract with the county general health district, which also serves the thirty-six villages. Similarly, twenty-five school districts contract with the same county district; this not only makes for a unit of more productive size but also eliminates many problems of co-ordination between municipal and school health agencies.

Under the state law the county department of public welfare handles categorical programs such as Aid for Disabled or Aid for Dependent Children, and also general relief for the villages and townships. Eleven of the cities administer their own general relief programs, but the others contract with the county department for services to their needy. Among the contracting group is the City of Cleveland which has the largest group of welfare recipients. Each city pays the costs for its own clients, but has available the professionalism of the large county department.

Numerous services under the aegis of the City of Cleveland have developed as truly metropolitan without transfer to the County. In some instances the areas outside the central city pay their own way or more, as in the supplying of water. The utilities department of the city supplies over fifty-five municipalities outside of Cleveland at rates that at least compensate for the costs of service. Indeed, some of the most bitter disagreements arise over the question of whether in water and sewer services the suburban areas do not actually subsidize the City. In the field of public transportation, the Cleveland Transit System, whose operations are paid for from the fare box, goes into many suburban communities. In other activities the financial return is absent, and the values of improved services to the entire area are the recompense for the City. Thus the Commissioner of Recreation for Cleveland and his staff serve many of the recreation boards of the smaller communities as unpaid consultants.

Mutual aid pacts in the field of public safety breach the splendid isolation one would expect from extreme municipal parochialism. Many fire departments are pledged to help another; some villages have no fire equipment of their own, but depend entirely on the services of a neighbor with whom they have a contract. Among police departments co-operative techniques have been developed to a high degree. Common communications stations help blanket the county with only eight radio frequencies; one base station actually dispatches the cars in twelve other municipalities. An "all-car" system which gave Cuyahoga County the first completely integrated police net in the nation (1950) prorated the initial costs among the municipalities on the basis of the number of mobile units, but all the maintenance is entirely at the expense of the City of Cleveland. Police training for all suburban departments is provided by an arrangement among the municipalities, the County Commissioners, the County Coroner, and Western Reserve University.

In the fields of construction and maintenance of highways, refuse disposal, assessment and collection of taxes, regional and community planning—and in almost every other governmental service—steps have been taken, some well planned and some haltingly and almost at random, to provide metropolitan co-operation where it was needed.

There is an untidiness about the plethora of governmental units and a malaise about the way decisions are made or left unmade, however, that is not assuaged by a recitation of contracts or mutual aid pacts or special service arrangements. If some decisions affect the metropolis, why is there no governmental arrangement for making the decision. If co-operation is good, why should it depend on the whims of personalities that change from day to day? If some municipal corporations are too small, and they obviously are, why should they not be combined with others to make stronger units? If professional administration gets more government service for each tax dollar, why should amateurs—often not even well intentioned—predominate in government after government? Should not the tax burden be distributed as the taxable wealth is distributed? Or should not the agency that creates a service problem also be in the jurisdiction where the problem has to be solved?

These questions, and others like them, were the *raison d'être* for METRO and the reports it published. This book is offered as a basis for further exploration. For the Cleveland area some questions are laid to rest, but the boundaries of what social scientists have yet to explore, like the boundaries of the modern metropolis, continue to expand.

Dr. Sacks has listed in his preface some persons who have our special thanks for this study. We would also like to acknowledge our indebtedness to Greater Clevelanders—the ones who created METRO and worked with it, and the ones whose contributions supported it financially. The grant from the Ford Foundation for this study, and the interest and confidence which that grant indicated and inspired, was a special contribution that can never be fully evaluated.

James A. Norton
EXECUTIVE DIRECTOR
CLEVELAND METROPOLITAN SERVICES COMMISSION

January, 1961

Preface

$\mathbb{T}$HE PURPOSE OF THIS BOOK IS TO ANALYZE THE fiscal operations of the governments that comprise the Cleveland Metropolitan Area in order to determine the impact of metropolitan growth on local government finances. The fiscal impact of the metropolitanization of the Cleveland area is viewed both in cross-section and over a period of time, not only in order to understand past behavior, but also to be prepared for future developments.

The interaction between metropolitan growth and local fiscal operations has been recognized as an important subject of discussion and inquiry for many years, but the concomitant expansion of metropolitan communities and local finances has resulted in a heightened interest in these problems. Primary, but not exclusive emphasis, up metropolitan communities, i.e., standard metropolitan areas, or between central cities, rather than within the metropolitan community. This has often been the result of the fact that fiscal data of many smaller governments are difficult to accumulate or, after they are accumulated, difficult to compare. This has been the case in this study in spite of the manifold efforts of many people of good will. We have persisted, however, and feel that the data in this and its companion volume *The Cleveland Metropolitan Area—A Fiscal Profile* are as comprehensive as any available for a single metropolitan area.

Because the major emphasis of this inquiry has been on the impact of the metropolis on local government finance, the effects of local finance on metropolitan growth have not been considered in detail and await further study. A number of conclusions are, however, implicit in the analysis of the fiscal operations, especially the relationship between school and municipal expenditures and growing government.

This study is based primarily on such statistical data and factual information as were available during 1957 and early 1958. It has been possible, in some instances, to take account of more recent developments, but it has not been possible to bring the material up to date. Moreover, there has been little reason for believing that the picture drawn on the basis of the final 1956 data has been modified by developments since then.

Inasmuch as this study is the product of many hands, it is necessary to try to sort out and acknowledge the particular contributions made by various individuals. The sections on taxation are the work of William F. Hellmuth. In addition to his many contributions to the study as a whole, Leo M. Egand contributed greatly to those sections involving statistical and metropolitan analysis. Michael Gomez collaborated in the initial preparation of the section involving capital outlays and Peter Max collaborated in those sections involving debt.

James A. Norton, Executive Director, and Oliver Brooks and John H. Romani, Associate Directors of the Cleveland Metropolitan Services Commission, gave us the benefits of their knowledge and advice in the preparation of the manuscript. Odell N. Waldby and Seymour Z. Mann also gave much useful advice and help.

I would like to give our most cordial thanks to the staff of the Government Cost Analysis Project, Barbara J. Haley, Eugenie Bolshakov, James Urban, Carol James, and Richard Boeckl, who gave us the best of their not inconsiderable talents.

Poestenkill, New York
January, 1960

Seymour Sacks

Contents

Tables

Tables

Charts

Maps

I

Introduction

SINCE THE END OF WORLD WAR II, TWO INTERRE-
lated developments have become the direct concern of approximately 100 million Americans and the indirect concern of the rest
of the nation's population. These are: greatly accelerated urban
growth in metropolitan communities, and provision of adequate
public services to these communities. The resultant problem of
financing local governments in metropolitan areas has assumed
critical importance.

The Cleveland Metropolitan Area, with its highly urbanized
population, has a long tradition of public interest in metropolitan
growth and its effects on local finances. In the last decade, however,
the magnitude of growth has been so pronounced, and its nature
so different from earlier periods that it has been considered neces-

1

sary to attempt a new and comprehensive analysis of the problems involved.

Because of its comprehensive nature, it is felt that the present study with its companion volume, *The Cleveland Metropolitan Area: A Fiscal Profile,*[1] will be of general use not only to those concerned with Cleveland directly but also to those concerned with metropolitan problems in general, and with the relationship between the metropolis and local public finances.

The metropolitan problem has many aspects—political, economic, fiscal, and social—and a successful analysis of any one aspect (in this case, the fiscal) requires a detailed knowledge of the metropolitan community as a whole, and a realization of the complexities involved. This is especially true of the present study, since demographic, economic, and social movements within the Cleveland Metropolitan Area are the generators of the multiplicity of financial problems of the constituent governments.

The main emphasis of this study then will be on those fiscal problems which are metropolitan in nature rather than those which concern urban finance of several cities and villages. This will be the case even though it is impossible at times to separate the purely local fiscal problems from those of a metropolitan nature. The individual governments which constitute the Cleveland Metropolitan Area will be considered primarily insofar as they influence and are influenced by the existence of the metropolitan community.

The Metropolitan Community

Before beginning our analysis proper, it might be best at this point to assay an adequate working definition of the term "metropolitan community." The word *adequate* is used advisedly, since no precise, universally agreed upon definition appears to exist.

Although the metropolitan community presents great definitional difficulties it has, nevertheless, generally been recognized that it is a natural socio-economic unit. It usually, but not necessarily, con-

---

1. Seymour Sacks, Leo M. Egand, and William Hellmuth, Jr.; Cleveland Metropolitan Services Commission, 1958. (Subsequent references refer to this study as *A Fiscal Profile.*)

sists of a single large nucleus (its central city), around which are clustered other smaller urbanized units of varying densities, and all of which are functionally interdependent. Perhaps Amos Hawley described the essential element best when he said that the metropolitan community is ". . . that area, the resident population of which is interrelated and integrated with reference to its daily requirements, whether contacts be direct or indirect." [2]

The metropolitan community is usually envisioned as having reached a certain size and having certain characteristics. Using the county as its unit, the Bureau of the Census has established formal criteria for what it calls Standard Metropolitan Areas.

As Reiss has abstracted these standards, a Standard Metropolitan Area consists of:

. . . a county or group of counties which contain at least one city of 50,000 inhabitants or more. Counties contiguous to the county with the central city of 50,000 or more are included in an SMA if they are considered metropolitan in character and if they are judged to be socially and economically integrated with the central city.

The operational criteria of the metropolitan character of a contiguous county relate primarily to the county as a place of work or residence for nonagricultural workers.

The extent of communication between the outlying counties and the central city is the major criterion of metropolitan integration.[3]

According to the Census criteria, the Cleveland Standard Metropolitan Area includes not only Cuyahoga County in which Cleveland is located, but Lake County to the east as well.

On the other hand, the Census Bureau has also developed an "urbanized" concept for metropolitan areas. This concept would necessitate the inclusion of the bulk of Cuyahoga County, a small part of Lake County, and part of Lorain County as well, in the make-up of the Cleveland Metropolitan Area. This concept does not depend on the county, and probably more accurately delimits the boundaries of a metropolitan community. But adherence to this concept would present almost insurmountable technical difficulties for purposes of fiscal analysis. The relationship between these vari-

---

2. Amos Hawley, *Human Ecology: A Theory of Community Structure* N. Y., Ronald Press (1950) pp. 257-58.

3. Albert J. Reiss, "The Community and the Corporate Area," *University of Pennsylvania Law Review*, February, 1957, p. 456.

ous concepts is shown in Map I-1, with some additional information on the growth of the urbanized area between 1950 and 1956 and the location of nearby Standard Metropolitan Areas.

In original intent the metropolitan concept was designed to show the natural boundaries of a functionally integrated community; but in actual fact it is found more convenient and even necessary to make the metropolitan area's boundary lines coterminous with the boundary lines of corporate areas.[4] This is so mainly because data is usually available for corporate units in their entirety only.

Because it is both a comprehensive corporate unit in itself and a good approximation of the metropolitan community, Cuyahoga County alone provides an excellent framework for the analysis of the financing of governments in the metropolitan area. Throughout this study the designation "Cleveland Metropolitan Area" will refer to Cuyahoga County in and of itself. Whatever slight advantages might be lost by thus limiting the area are more than compensated for by the availability of data on a uniform basis within the county. The principal advantage gained derives from the fact of county-wide assessment in Ohio. Exclusion of any area outside of Cuyahoga County would appear to involve little distortion in the picture of the Cleveland metropolitan community in 1959. But the fiscal problems that arise from the existence of county boundaries will have to be faced in the not-too-distant future.

Metropolitan Financial Problems

Basically, metropolitan financial problems are the result of a "disjuncture between the metropolitan community and the corporate areas which serve it in part."[5] The financial resources and requirements are distributed in such manner as to intensify the financial problems of the Cleveland Metropolitan Area, as well as of virtually every other metropolitan area in the United States. In addition to its fiscal implications, the metropolitan financial problem is of great interest because it mirrors many, if not most,

---

4. The corporate area is an area "created to develop and/or apply a policy or law, carry on public services, or enforce or adjudicate laws." *Ibid.*, p. 466.
5. *Ibid.* p. 448.

of the public and private problems confronting the metropolitan community.

The postwar economic growth of the Cleveland Metropolitan Area has been marked by an increased demand for urban services by a larger population. The demand for most traditional governmental services has expanded in terms of both amount and quality. New services are also being introduced as a result of public consensus.

These problems are faced by the existing local governments with their different requirements and capacities. Traditionally, the local community has been viewed as being sufficiently isolated or sufficiently large to guide its own fiscal decisions without significant effects on other communities. Each local government viewed its own fiscal requirements in terms of its own fiscal resources. At least for larger metropolitan areas this viewpoint must be profoundly modified. While in theory, and sometimes in practice, the traditional local finance, with its emphasis on local assumption of responsibility, still retains much of its importance, certain functions have been almost universally recognized as transcending local boundaries. Transportation, water, sewerage, air pollution, and health protection have been recognized as metropolitan or even regional in nature.

The Cleveland experience supports the generalization of Lyle C. Fitch that:

Metropolitan financial problems arise primarily from the lack of adequate machinery rather than from any lack of capacity. Presumptively, today's large urban communities, being typically the focal points of wealth and income, have the resources to meet their urban needs.[6]

In particular, it can be said that:

1. Existing revenue-producing machinery is generally inadequate for the task of financing local government functions; this is true both of functions appropriate for the conventional (metropolitan) local government and functions which can best be handled by metropolitan jurisdictions.

2. The extension of activities across jurisdictional lines makes it more and more difficult to relate benefits and taxes at the local government level. In the modern metropolitan community, a family may reside in one jurisdiction, earn its living in one or more others, send children

---

6. Lyle C. Fitch, "Metropolitan Financial Problems," *Annals of the American Academy of Political and Social Science*, November, 1957, p. 67.

to school in another, and shop and seek recreation in still others. But to a considerable extent, the American local financial system still reflects the presumption that these various activities are concentrated in one governmental jurisdiction.

3. In many areas, there are great discrepancies in the capacities of local government jurisdictions to provide needed governmental services. At one extreme are the communities which have not sufficient taxable capacity for essential services. The most common case is the bedroom community of low- and middle-income workers which has little industry or commerce. At the other extreme are the wealthy tax colonies, zoned to keep out low-income residents.[7]

The understanding of, and the solution to, metropolitan fiscal problems ultimately depends on knowledge of the relationship of expenditures and tax capacity in the area involved, as well as knowledge of the determinants of each individually.

The report which follows is divided into three sections, each designed to illuminate the problems involved in financing local governments in a metropolitan area, using the Cleveland Metropolitan Area as our case study. In Section One, the Cleveland Metropolitan Area is analyzed with particular attention to those developments which have impact on the over-all, but not individual, demand for government services and fiscal capacity. This is followed by a discussion of local government finances in the light of historical developments and in comparison with other related or like governments.

Section Two is devoted to an analysis of the expenditures, revenues, and borrowing operations of the several governments that comprise the Cleveland Metropolitan Area. The discussion of expenditures is considered in two parts: first, current operating expenditures and second, capital outlays. Interest is considered in its borrowing context.

The third and final Section of this report contains a summary along with staff recommendations which are phrased in terms of projections of local fiscal needs and resources made to determine the aggregate relationship between government costs and capacity in the Cleveland Metropolitan Area in 1965. Two critical concepts are developed with reference to the metropolitan financial problem;

---

7. *Ibid.*, p. 67.

first, the concept of the "fiscal gap," and second that of "fiscal imbalance." Concerning the former, alternatives for financing projected levels of expenditures are compared; concerning the latter, the underlying imbalance between the jurisdictions that comprise the Cleveland Metropolitan Area is considered.

Fiscal imbalance is a current problem which threatens to get worse for many jurisdictions over the next few years, as the responsibility of a government to perform functions, which require spending, outruns the ability of that government to raise the required revenues. The problem of revenue capacity is considered in detail in Chapter VI, the problem of responsibility for functions, in Chapters IV and V. The general problem is considered in Chapter IX.

II

The Historical

Perspective

THE RISE OF THE INTEGRATED METROPOLITAN COM-
munity has been characteristic of many areas in the United States.
This growth has not been uniform, since it has reflected differences
in local and regional conditions. In the evolution of the various
jurisdictions into a metropolitan community, many of the characteristics of earlier periods of their development are retained. It is
impossible, in fact, to analyze the financial problems of any metropolitan community without an understanding of the factors responsible for its development. Each stage in the development of the
modern metropolitan community has been accompanied by its own
characteristic fiscal problems and its own characteristic solutions. It
may be observed that solutions appropriate to one period of fiscal
development are often singularly inappropriate to another.

8

The evolution of the Cleveland Metropolitan Area can be divided into four main periods, as follows:

1. The era of independent communities—1801-60.
2. The dominance of the central city—1860-1910.
3. The movement to the suburbs—1910-45.
4. The metropolitan community—1945 to the present.

The Era of Independent Communities

Cuyahoga County, in which Cleveland is situated, was originally part of the Western Reserve of Connecticut which became part of the Ohio Territory in 1801. The land was divided into townships which were five miles, rather than the traditional six miles, square. The township was more important for the settling of land and for a rural society, than for the provision of municipal services. The twenty townships of the county, which were laid out in regular rectangular fashion, provided the framework within which later changes in local boundaries took place. The regularity of the township ignored natural features which, although relatively unimportant during this early period, were to have important effects with the expansion of the urban community.

Where urban settlement did take place, and villages and even cities were created, the provision of local services became essential. At this time, these communities were essentially independent communities surrounded by a rural countryside. In addition to Cleveland (and before 1854 Ohio City), there were a number of such communities which were located on an arc eleven to thirteen miles from downtown Cleveland along natural transportation routes. These included Chagrin Falls, Bedford, Berea, and Olmsted Falls. A considerable proportion of the population was rural.

The Historical Perspective

Table II-1—Actual and Estimated Population and Rate of Population Growth Cleveland and Cuyahoga County, 1810-1970

YEAR	POPULATION				RATE OF GROWTH (Per Cent)		
	Cuyahoga County	Cleveland	County Excluding Cleveland	Cleveland as per cent of County	Cuyahoga County	Cleveland	County Excluding Cleveland
1810	1,459	547	912	37.5			
					333.7	10.8	527.4
1820	6,328	606	5,722	9.6			
					63.9	77.6	62.5
1830	10,373	1,076	9,297	10.4			
					155.5	464.2	119.8
1840	26,506	6,071	20,435	22.9			
					81.5	180.6	52.0
1850	48,099	17,034	31,065	35.4			
					62.2	154.9	11.4
1860	78,034	43,417	34,617	55.6			
					69.2	113.8	13.2
1870	132,010	92,829	39,181	70.3			
					49.2	72.5	—6.1
1880	196,943	160,146	36,797	81.3			
					57.4	63.2	32.1
1890	309,970	261,353	48,617	84.3			
					41.7	46.1	18.0
1900	439,120	381,768	57,352	86.9			
					45.2	50.3	10.8
1910	637,425	573,872	63,553	90.0			
					48.0	40.5	115.8
1920	943,495	806,368	137,127	85.5			
					27.3	11.9	118.0
1930	1,201,455	902,471	298,984	75.1			
					1.3	—2.7	13.4
1940	1,217,250	878,336	338,914	72.2			
					14.2	4.2	40.1
1950	1,389,532	914,808	474,724	65.8			
					20.9	0.8	59.7
* 1960	1,680,400	922,418	757,982	54.9			
					16.0	2.6	32.2
‡ 1970	1,950,000	946,000	1,004,000	48.5			
* 1956	1,580,553	926,052	757,982	58.6			
					15.8	2.1	16.8
† 1965	1,830,000	945,000	885,000	51.6			

* Cleveland Real Property Inventory.
† Cleveland Electric Illuminating Company Area and Population by Communities, Cleveland Northeast Ohio, (Cleveland, Ohio, July 1, 1958).
‡ Cleveland Regional Planning Commission, Population Study—Second Report. Distribution and Characteristics. (Cleveland, 1958).
Sources: United States Census, 1810-1950.

The Dominance of the Central City

The period 1860-1910 was characterized by the overwhelming dominance of the central city over the area. During this period the City of Cleveland grew at a more rapid rate than the rest of the county chiefly because of immigration, natural growth, and annexation of contiguous communities.

By 1860, nothing in the area could compare in size or growth with Cleveland. And population growth proceeded at such a rapid pace that, although aggregate public expenditures and revenues increased dramatically in Cleveland, the per capita amounts remained virtually unchanged for a long period of time. The concentration of such large numbers of people and industry brought about a vast increase in the demands for local public services, including water, sewage disposal, and police and fire protection. The provision of public education began to assume a greater importance as compulsory education laws were enacted. As late as 1890, Cuyahoga County contained ten villages, nineteen townships, and one city, Cleveland. Since city status required only a population of 5,000, the dominance of Cleveland is clearly evident. The advent of independent school districts during this period further increased the number of separate government units.

The Movement to the Suburbs

By 1910, 90 per cent of the population of Cuyahoga County was located within the boundaries of the City of Cleveland. The next thirty-five years were characterized by a more rapid rate of growth within Cuyahoga County outside the limits of the City of Cleveland. Legal, as well as economic and social factors were responsible for the emergence of suburban communities clustering around and focussing on the central city. The number of cities had increased from one to four between 1890 and 1910; the number of villages from ten to nineteen, while the number of townships decreased slightly from nineteen to seventeen. The enactment of Constitutional Home Rule in 1912, combined with large population growth outside of Cleveland, provided the impetus for a large increase in the number of municipalities within the county. In 1930, there were still only four cities, but there were then fifty-two villages, and the number of townships had been reduced to six. The number of municipal corporations providing some public services was greatly increased. If to the number of municipalities were added the number of school districts (which reached thirty-six in 1925), the contemporary interest during the 1920's in reducing the number of governments in Cuyahoga County is readily understood.[1] This period also witnessed the final consolidation of the central city into its present shape. While there have been important changes within Cleveland since 1930, there has been little population increase. Growth occurred during this period primarily along a series of spokes on which rapid transit moved to and from the central city.

In terms of its fiscal development, the period 1910-45 was marked by the fact that population increase did not keep pace with the increases in the amount and quality of public services. The result was that per capita expenditure grew in spite of the unprecedented population increase. Furthermore, there was the great proliferation of the number of governments spending and raising money, with their markedly different resources and requirements.

Since 1930, although there has been little change in the total number of municipal governments in the Cleveland Metropolitan Area, there have been a large number of changes in status. By 1956, which is the base year of this study, there were twenty cities, thirty-eight villages and four townships; the changes in status being the product of changes in population. Since then, two new cities have come into existence, and it is further assumed that in 1960 the number of cities will have increased to thirty-three plus or minus two, depending on the exact Census counts in April, 1960. Detailed population estimates are shown in Table II-5.

---

1. *93 Governments or 1?* Cleveland Chamber of Commerce, A Report of the Committee on City Finances, 1925.

The Metropolitan Community

The expansion that has characterized Cuyahoga County since 1945 has been responsible for its metamorphosis into a truly metropolitan community with its peculiar attendant problems. Certainly the period 1940-45 was one of marking time for the community, as young men went off to war, families doubled up, and the building of private homes and automobiles was sharply curtailed. However, the population in the Cleveland Metropolitan Area remained high because of the attraction of war jobs there. If anything, the war years were responsible for movement back to the core area (the older, more built-up communities of Cleveland, Lakewood, East Cleveland, and Cleveland Heights), where both housing and transportation were available. Since 1945, however, there has been a vast movement outward, greatly increasing population density outside the core area and rapidly filling in most of the remaining non-urban areas of Cuyahoga County. As in most metropolitan areas, a new type of demographic, economic, and social balance has emerged between the central city and the area which surrounds it.[2] Population has been redistributed and circulated within the metropolitan community. And even if there has been little growth in population within the central city, there have been very large population movements within its borders; movements into the city have been offset by movements of approximately equal magnitude out of it.

The growth of population in the Cleveland Metropolitan Area may be compared with that of other metropolitan areas as well as with non-metropolitan and state and national growth. As shown in Table II-2, during the first part of the twentieth century, the Cleveland Metropolitan Area grew at a more rapid rate than that of the nation as a whole; but since 1930, the growth appears to have been less rapid. The Cleveland Metropolitan Area shows the same pat-

---

2. Raymond Vernon, *The Changing Economic Function of the Central City*, Committee for Economic Development (New York; January, 1959) *passim.*

Table II-2—Per Cent Change in Population in the Cleveland Metropolitan Area and Other Areas in the United States, Selected Years

Area	1900-10	1910-20	1920-30	1930-40	1940-50	1950-56
Cuyahoga County (CMA)	45.2	48.0	27.3	1.3	14.2	13.7
City of Cleveland	50.3	40.5	11.9	—2.7	4.2	1.2
CMA Less Cleveland	10.8	115.8	118.0	13.4	40.1	37.9
United States	21.0	14.9	16.1	7.2	14.5	19.8
Standard Metro. Areas	34.6	26.9	28.3	8.1	22.0	14.8
Central Cities	33.6	25.2	22.3	5.1	13.9	4.7
Satellite Cities	38.2	32.0	44.0	15.1	35.6	29.3
Outside Metro. Areas	16.4	9.6	7.9	6.5	6.1	3.4
Ohio	14.7	20.8	15.4	3.9	15.0	13.9
East North Central U.S.	14.2	17.7	17.8	5.3	14.2	11.1

Sources: Amos H. Hawley, *The Changing Shape of Metropolitan America: Deconcentration Since 1920*, p. 2. "U.S. Statistical Abstract," p. 13. U.S. Census Population Reports—Series p. 20, N 71.

tern of growth that Standard Metropolitan Areas in general have shown, namely the general redistribution of population outside the central city, but within the metropolitan area, which occurred during the first half of the twentieth century. Annexation (which simultaneously reduced growth outside the central city and increased it inside) became less effective as first rapid transit and then the automobile destroyed the dependence on the central city, and as home rule allowed municipalities adjacent to the central city to maintain their independence.

The concentration of population in urban centers which subsequently assumed metropolitan form, although nation-wide in nature, was a phenomenon especially characteristic of the northeast portion of this country, particularly along the coastal plain from Boston to Washington, and from Pittsburgh to Cleveland.

The Cleveland Metropolitan Area is a major metropolitan community containing a major metropolitan city, Cleveland. Its problems are not only quantitatively greater than those of other metropolitan areas in Ohio, but qualitatively different as well. According to the 1950 Census, the twelve Standard Metropolitan Areas in Ohio consist of eighteen Ohio counties. As shown in Table II-3, they

Table II-3—Twelve Standard Metropolitan Areas in Ohio,*
Population 1900-1950; Number of Local
Governments, 1957

Standard Metropolitan Area	1900	1910	1920	1930	1940	1950	Number of Govern- ments †
TOTAL OHIO	4,157,545	4,767,121	5,759,394	6,646,697	6,907,612	7,946,627	3,667
CLEVELAND	460,800	660,352	972,162	1,243,129	1,267,270	1,465,511	134
Cincinnati	527,293	590,456	628,999	756,281	787,044	904,402	133
Youngstown	174,112	246,616	364,018	458,451	473,605	528,498	209
Columbus	164,460	221,567	283,951	361,055	388,712	503,410	67
Dayton	161,759	193,496	240,753	306,740	331,343	457,333	88
Akron	71,715	108,253	286,065	344,131	339,405	410,032	54
Toledo	153,559	192,728	275,721	347,709	344,333	395,551	41
Canton	94,767	122,987	177,218	221,784	234,887	283,194	60
Lorain-Elyria	54,857	76,037	90,612	109,206	112,390	148,162	55
Hamilton-Middletown	56,870	70,271	87,025	114,084	120,249	147,203	42
Springfield	58,939	66,435	80,728	90,936	95,647	111,661	31
Lima	47,976	56,580	68,223	69,419	73,303	88,183	39

* These twelve Standard Metropolitan Areas consisted of eighteen Ohio counties in 1950.
† U.S. Bureau of the Census Classification.
Sources: Cleveland Real Property Inventory, Sheet-A-Week, Bureau of Census; Census of Governments, 1957. Vol. 1, No. 2.

ranged in size in 1950 from the Lima Standard Metropolitan Area with 88,183 persons to the Cleveland Standard Metropolitan Area with 1,465,511. These twelve Standard Metropolitan Areas are of only limited value comparison-wise for the present study. With the possible exception of the bi-state Cincinnati area, comparisons are limited by the absence of information and by the disparate natures of Cleveland and the state's other metropolitan areas. Despite the foregoing disclaimer, fiscal comparisons with other metropolitan areas in Ohio, to the extent that they are possible, are necessary and desirable.

For really extensive comparisons it is necessary to look further afield for other metropolitan communities whose characteristics approximate those of Cleveland. The populations of the nation's fifteen major metropolitan areas are shown in Table II-4. In terms of size, the most readily comparable areas would be those of Detroit, Boston, Pittsburgh, St. Louis, Baltimore, Buffalo, and Cincinnati. Similarity in size would tend to dictate a considerable similarity in fiscal and economic problems for these various areas, even without all

Table II-4—Fifteen Largest Standard Metropolitan Areas in the United States, Population 1900-50, Number of Local Governments, 1957

Standard Metropolitan Area	1900	1910	1920	1930	1940	1950	Number of Governments, 1957 †
United States	75,994,575	91,972,266	105,710,620	122,775,046	131,669,275	151,132,000	102,279
New York-N.E.N.J.	5,048,750	7,049,047	8,490,694	10,859,443	11,660,839	12,911,994	1,074
Chicago	2,092,883	2,752,820	3,521,789	4,675,877	4,825,527	5,495,364	954
Los Angeles	189,994	538,567	997,830	2,327,166	2,916,403	4,367,911	319
Philadelphia	1,892,128	2,268,209	2,714,271	3,137,040	3,199,637	3,671,048	705
Detroit	426,829	613,773	1,305,798	2,177,343	2,377,329	3,016,197	250
Boston-Lawrence-Lowell *	1,685,682	2,025,286	2,315,111	2,611,926	2,656,131	2,875,876	112+
San Francisco-Oakland	542,964	773,975	1,009,467	1,347,772	1,461,804	2,240,767	414
Pittsburgh	1,083,846	1,471,800	1,759,989	2,023,269	2,082,556	2,213,236	612
St. Louis	801,131	1,003,858	1,139,877	1,399,512	1,432,088	1,681,281	400
Cleveland	460,800	660,352	972,162	1,243,129	1,267,270	1,465,511	134
Washington D. C.	378,605	445,401	571,882	672,198	967,985	1,464,089	67
Baltimore	639,332	720,387	852,051	984,606	1,083,300	1,337,373	10
Minneapolis-St. Paul	431,940	594,819	704,566	857,513	940,937	1,116,509	222
Buffalo	508,647	621,021	753,393	911,737	958,487	1,089,230	155
Cincinnati	527,293	590,456	628,999	756,281	787,044	904,402	133

* Based on area consisting of the Counties of Essex, Middlesex, Norfolk, and Suffolk in Massachusetts. This differs slightly from the corresponding town-delimited Standard Metropolitan Areas.

† U.S. Bureau of the Census Classification.

Sources: Cleveland Real Property Inventory, Sheet-A-Week, June 9, 1955, Vol. XXII, No. 40 and Bureau of Census, Census of Governments, 1957, Vol. I, No. 2.

other things being equal. It should be noted that the fiscal problems of some of the major areas are of great and unwieldy magnitude as in the case of the New York, Chicago, and Los Angeles Standard Metropolitan Areas. Many tend to go beyond state borders, and in the instance of Detroit and Buffalo even beyond international borders, thus creating additional analytical problems. The Cleveland Metropolitan Area is in many ways ideal for purposes of analysis, since it is neither interstate nor of the international variety.

The Cleveland Metropolitan Area in Detail

Up to this point, principal emphasis has been placed on the over-all growth of the Cleveland Metropolitan Area, with little attempt to consider the area in detail. As of 1956, the Cleveland Metropolitan Area (as herein defined) consisted of one county, the Cleveland Metropolitan Park District (which extends beyond the borders of the county), twenty cities, thirty-eight villages, four townships, thirty-two school districts, and nine library districts.

Population data have been available for municipalities, townships, and counties, but not, unfortunately, for school and library districts. The absence of good comparable population data has proven a serious handicap in the detailed analysis of school and other local non-municipal fiscal problems. Even in its limited form, detailed information available on past population, as well as the estimates of present and future population, is an essential element in the analysis of local fiscal problems. In Ohio, a Census population of at least 5,000 or an election registration of at least the same number will automatically dictate that an incorporated municipality is a city rather than a village, having, therefore, different financial responsibilities and problems. There is no such relationship between population and status in the case of townships, which are unincorporated.

Knowledge of the distribution and of changes in the distribution of population in individual jurisdictions is necessary but not, of course, sufficient information for an understanding of the fiscal problems involved. Population may or may not be closely correlated with

Table II-5—Cleveland Metropolitan Area Population and Population Density, by Governmental Unit,[1] 1940, 1950, Estimated 1956, 1960, 1965

GOVERNMENTAL UNIT	POPULATION					POPULATION DENSITY				
	1940	1950	1956	1960	1965	1940	1950	1956	1960	1965
Cuyahoga County	1,217,250	1,389,532	1,580,553	1,654,407	1,815,000	2,656	3,032	3,449	3,611	3,993
Cities										
Bay Village	3,356	6,917	11,271	13,222	16,000	730	1,504	2,450	2,874	3,478
Bedford	7,390	9,105	12,721	15,564	18,000	1,524	1,877	2,623	3,209	3,711
Berea	6,025	12,051	13,368	15,399	18,700	1,287	2,575	2,856	3,290	3,996
Brooklyn	1,108	6,317	7,935	10,519	14,000	267	1,522	1,912	2,535	3,373
Cleveland	878,336	914,808	926,052	909,584	930,000	12,002	12,220	12,370	12,150	12,624
Cleveland Heights	54,992	59,141	61,845	62,316	65,000	6,731	7,239	7,570	7,627	7,956
East Cleveland	39,495	40,047	39,679	39,085	42,000	13,078	13,261	13,139	12,943	13,907
Euclid	17,866	41,396	59,645	66,338	78,000	1,657	3,840	5,533	6,154	7,236
Fairview Park	4,700	9,311	13,211	14,892	18,000	1,291	2,558	3,629	4,091	4,945
Garfield Heights	16,989	21,662	32,740	37,957	42,000	2,444	3,117	4,711	5,461	6,043
Lakewood	69,160	68,071	68,007	66,424	68,000	12,219	12,027	12,015	11,736	12,014
Lyndhurst	2,391	7,359	13,672	16,986	20,000	514	1,583	2,940	3,653	4,301
Maple Heights	6,728	15,586	27,227	31,888	38,000	1,212	2,808	4,906	5,746	6,847
Mayfield Heights	2,696	5,807	10,438	12,550	15,000	648	1,396	2,509	3,017	3,606
North Olmsted	3,487	6,604	12,151	15,147	18,500	303	574	1,057	1,317	1,609
Parma	16,365	28,897	62,587	77,676	92,000	815	1,439	3,117	3,882	4,582
Rocky River	8,291	11,237	15,256	17,938	20,000	1,753	2,376	3,225	3,792	4,228
Shaker Heights	23,393	28,222	34,770	37,456	40,000	3,577	4,315	5,317	5,727	6,116
South Euclid	6,146	15,432	25,149	28,424	30,000	1,299	3,263	5,317	6,009	6,342
University Heights	5,981	11,566	15,274	17,026	19,000	3,323	6,426	8,486	9,459	10,556

Villages										
Beachwood	372	1,073	4,133	5,821	8,000	82	235	906	1,277	1,754
Bedford Heights	*	*	4,415	5,052	7,000	*	*	950	1,086	1,505
Bentleyville	117	152	255	300	400	43	56	94	111	148
Bratenahl	1,350	1,240	1,275	1,315	1,500	1,286	1,181	1,214	1,252	1,429
Brecksville	1,900	2,664	4,269	5,300	8,000	96	134	215	267	403
Broadview Heights	1,141	2,279	4,166	5,546	7,000	88	175	321	427	539
Brooklyn Heights	496	931	1,319	1,444	2,000	270	506	717	785	1,087
Brook Park	1,122	2,725	2,665	6,459	8,000	116	342	335	811	1,005
Chagrin Falls	2,505	3,035	3,395	3,524	4,300	1,199	1,452	1,624	1,686	2,057
Cuyahoga Heights	674	713	785	834	1,200	201	213	234	249	358
Gates Mills	906	1,056	1,194	1,273	2,000	100	116	131	140	220
Glenwillow	218	257	315	306	500	75	89	109	105	172
Highland Heights	356	762	1,979	2,661	4,000	71	153	397	533	802
Hunting Valley	336	430	451	452	750	48	61	64	64	107
Independence	1,815	3,105	5,668	6,896	10,000	201	343	626	762	1,105
Linndale	445	399	394	376	400	4,450	3,990	3,940	3,760	4,000
Mayfield	448	805	1,616	1,983	3,000	114	204	410	503	761
Middleburg Heights	1,225	2,299	5,280	6,905	10,000	150	281	645	843	1,221
Moreland Hills	561	1,040	1,688	2,036	3,000	78	144	234	282	416
Newburgh Heights	3,830	3,689	3,621	3,626	3,600	6,964	6,707	6,584	6,593	6,545
North Randall	92	178	292	461	800	118	228	374	591	1,026
North Royalton	2,559	3,939	6,010	7,819	9,500	121	186	284	370	450
Oakwood	*	*	3,743	3,940	6,000	*	*	967	1,013	1,550
Olmsted Falls	754	1,137	1,759	2,019	2,500	527	795	1,230	1,412	1,748

(Continued on next page)

Table II-5 (Continued)

	POPULATION					POPULATION DENSITY				
	1940	1950	1956	1960	1965	1940	1950	1956	1960	1965
Villages										
Orange	492	897	1,629	1,945	3,500	142	259	470	561	1,009
Parkview	208	661	1,739	2,122	2,700	196	624	1,641	2,002	2,547
Parma Heights	1,330	3,901	11,552	15,592	20,000	331	970	2,874	3,879	4,975
Pepper Pike	423	874	2,133	3,004	5,000	57	119	289	408	678
Richmond Heights	507	891	3,365	4,803	7,000	113	220	748	1,067	1,556
Seven Hills	555	1,350	3,550	4,845	7,000	108	262	689	941	1,359
Solon	1,508	2,570	5,112	6,475	10,000	74	127	252	319	493
Strongsville	2,216	3,504	5,341	7,065	10,000	89	140	214	283	400
Valley View	753	998	1,127	1,197	1,400	122	162	183	195	228
Walton Hills	*	*	1,486	1,859	3,500	*	*	210	263	494
Warrensville Heights	1,175	4,126	7,583	9,910	12,000	295	1,037	1,905	2,490	3,015
Westlake	3,200	4,912	9,710	12,236	16,000	196	300	594	748	979
West View	407	625	1,070	1,259	1,500	186	285	489	575	685
Woodmere	**	419	433	430	500	**	1,048	1,083	1,075	1,250
Townships										
Chagrin Falls	24	55	89	91	80	45	104	168	172	151
Olmsted	1,585	2,562	4,278	4,882	6,000	149	241	402	459	564
Riveredge	76	6	92	436	170	123	10	177	838	274
Warrensville	2,291	1,877	2,093	2,360	3,000	759	622	693	781	993

1. Municipalities are classified according to States in 1956.
Sources: Area and Population by Communities, Cleveland-Northeast Ohio, The Cleveland Elec. Illuminating Co., July, 1958, Cleveland Real Property Inventory, Population Study—Second Report, Distribution and Characteristics, Cleveland Regional Planning Commission.
* Bedford Hts., Oakwood, & Walton Hills incorporated in 1951.
** Woodmere incorporated in 1944.

per capita expenditures, but it is an important determinant of total expenditures.

When combined with area figures the population figures provide measures of density. Even as gross figures (i.e., without taking into account land that is not available for residential purposes) densities provide measures of the degree of urbanization of an area. And to the extent that density is responsible for higher or lower per capita costs of government, the information is of great importance. No single set of figures can bring out the increasing urbanization of the Cleveland Metropolitan Area as vividly as the density figures; they show the disappearance of low density jurisdictions in the period 1940-56, and the filling up of most of the remaining land, which is expected by 1965. If data on net density were available, it would provide an even clearer measure of the degree of urbanization.

In Map II-2, the major changes in density between 1940 and 1956 are shown in terms of localities where the density rose or fell by over 20 percentage points relative to the average density of Cuyahoga County. The resulting picture shows a decline in the core area, and a growth immediately outside the core area. Although the rates of growth have been great beyond the inner ring, the *amount* of growth around the perimeter of the county has not been great, except in Bay Village.

The density data show the existence of a number of different kinds of communities, ranging from East Cleveland with a gross density of 13,139 per square mile, Cleveland with 12,370, and Lakewood with 12,015, to Hunting Valley with its density of 64 persons per square mile. The estimated densities for 1956 are shown in Map II-1. It can be observed that a new kind of municipality, the low density city, is now emerging, the first example of which is Westlake; others in this group will be Brecksville, Broadview Heights, North Royalton, Solon, and Strongsville. These cities will be confronted with the peculiar problems of providing urban services to low density communities.

Changes in the age distribution of population will have important effects on the demands for government service. If the population pyramid grows, but with greater relative change in the old at the top and the young at the bottom, expenditures on education and hospitals are also expected to grow relatively. Population pyramids

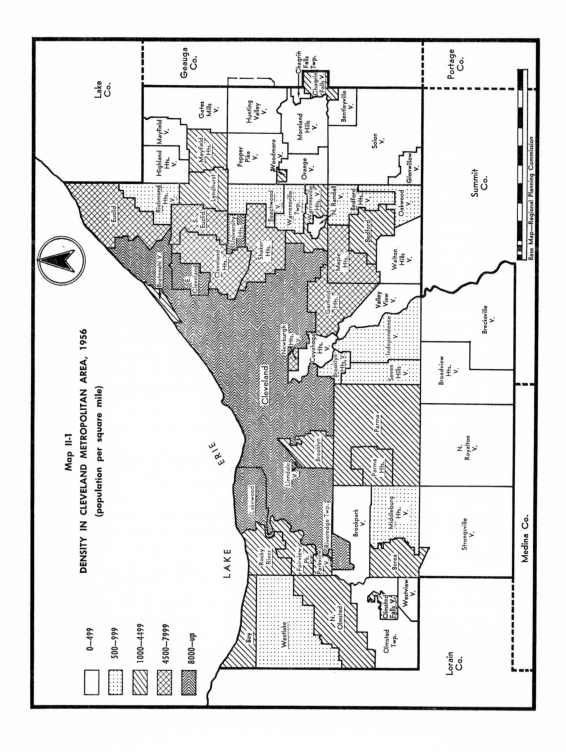

Map II-1

DENSITY IN CLEVELAND METROPOLITAN AREA, 1956

(population per square mile)

0—499
500—999
1000—4499
4500—7999
8000—up

Base Map—Regional Planning Commission

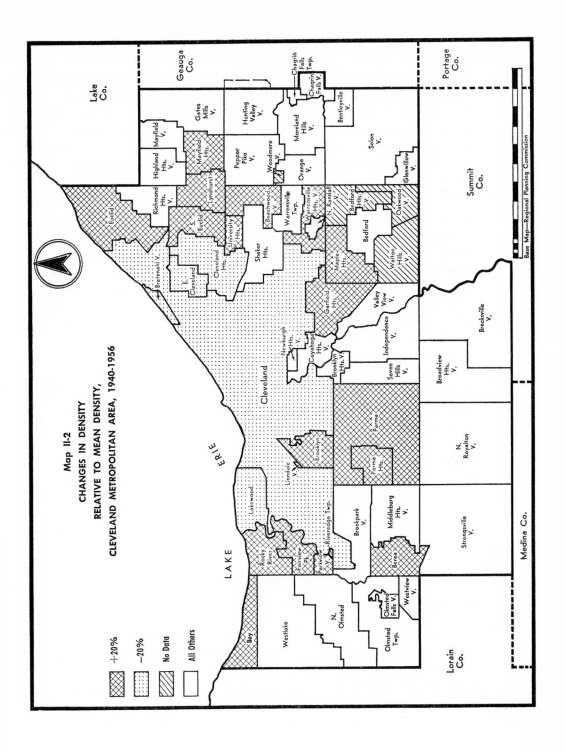

Map II-2

CHANGES IN DENSITY
RELATIVE TO MEAN DENSITY,
CLEVELAND METROPOLITAN AREA, 1940-1956

+20%
-20%
No Data
All Others

(Chart II-1) have been constructed by the Cleveland Regional Planning Commission based on the Census of 1950 and estimates for 1970, with a breakdown between the city of Cleveland and the suburbs. The data on population distributions provide an important benchmark for understanding present expenditure requirements and for planning for those of the future. It should be noted that we anticipate that many suburbs will have population pyramids more closely resembling Cleveland's than other suburbs', and that consequently the remaining suburban pyramid will be altered.

No analysis of population in the Cleveland Metropolitan Area would be complete without mention of the changing income and ethnic composition of the City of Cleveland, a phenomenon which has its parallel in other major cities throughout the United States. The tremendous absolute and relative growth of the Negro community in the City of Cleveland between 1940 and 1956 shows no sign of abating. It has risen from 9 per cent of the total population in 1940, to an estimated 25 per cent, in 1956, and is expected to rise further by 1965. The concentration of lower-income groups in the central city will not only have important and undesirable social effects, but it will also have important effects on expenditure requirements and taxable capacity of the central city.

In addition to knowledge of the age and ethnic and religious composition of the population, knowledge of the school age population in the various school districts is of importance, particularly in estimating public school educational requirements for any future period. The ratios of public school population to total population are shown in Table II-9.

The Economic Structure of the
Cleveland Metropolitan Area

Before we consider the individual communities in detail, a brief outline of the economic structure of the Cleveland Metropolitan Area, with particular emphasis on the movements that occurred since World War II, is of importance. The Cleveland Metropolitan Area is one of the outstanding manufacturing centers in the United States. Its industrial community is distinguished by the fact that it

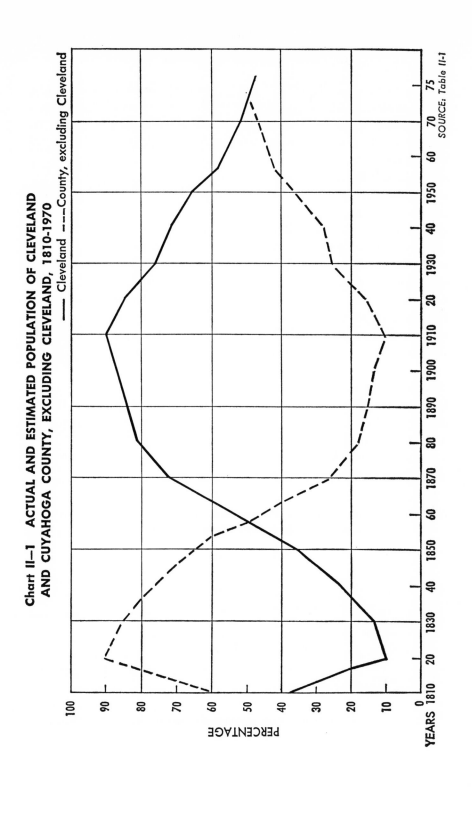

Chart II—1 ACTUAL AND ESTIMATED POPULATION OF CLEVELAND
AND CUYAHOGA COUNTY, EXCLUDING CLEVELAND, 1810-1970

—— Cleveland ---County, excluding Cleveland

SOURCE: Table II-1

PERCENTAGE

YEARS 1810   20   1830   40   1850   60   1870   80   1890   1900   1910   20   1930   40   1950   60   70   75

0   10   20   30   40   50   60   70   80   90   100

"has grown as a collection of many small or medium-sized plants, many under local ownership." [3] Machinery, especially precision metal working, is the leading industrial classification in the area; other important classifications are equipment, primary metals, and metal products.

Although there are many plants, they are concentrated in a few areas, both inside and outside of the central city. The original industrial center was along the flats of the Cuyahoga River. As late as 1919, 94.1 per cent of all manufacturing employees in Cuyahoga County were employed within Cleveland City. Between 1919 and 1939, the percentage of those employed within Cleveland declined only slightly. Cuyahoga Heights and Newburgh Heights along the flats, and Euclid located along the railroad right of way and close to Lake Erie were the only other highly industrialized areas in this county. Then, between 1939 and 1954, there was a major shift outside of the city of Cleveland, as communities like the aforementioned grew and were supplemented by newer industrial locations along existing railroads and highways—Brooklyn, Brook Park, Bedford Heights, and Walton Hills. The share of manufacturing employees in the area outside of Cleveland grew from 11 per cent to 27 per cent. The rate of change was accelerated between 1947 and 1954 as employment fell within Cleveland, while it rose by more than 50 per cent outside of Cleveland.

Table II-6—Manufacturing Production Workers, Cuyahoga County, 1919-54

(IN THOUSANDS)

Year	County	Cleveland	County Excluding Cleveland	Cleveland as per cent of County
1919 *	167.6	157.7	9.9	94.1
1929 *	161.3	146.9	14.4	91.1
1939 *	125.9	112.1	13.8	89.0
1947	259.0	211.5	47.5	81.7
1954	279.1	204.8	74.3	73.3

* Wage Earners.
Source: U. S. Census of Manufactures.

---

3. Cleveland Federal Reserve Bank, *Monthly Business Review*, March, 1957, p. 4.

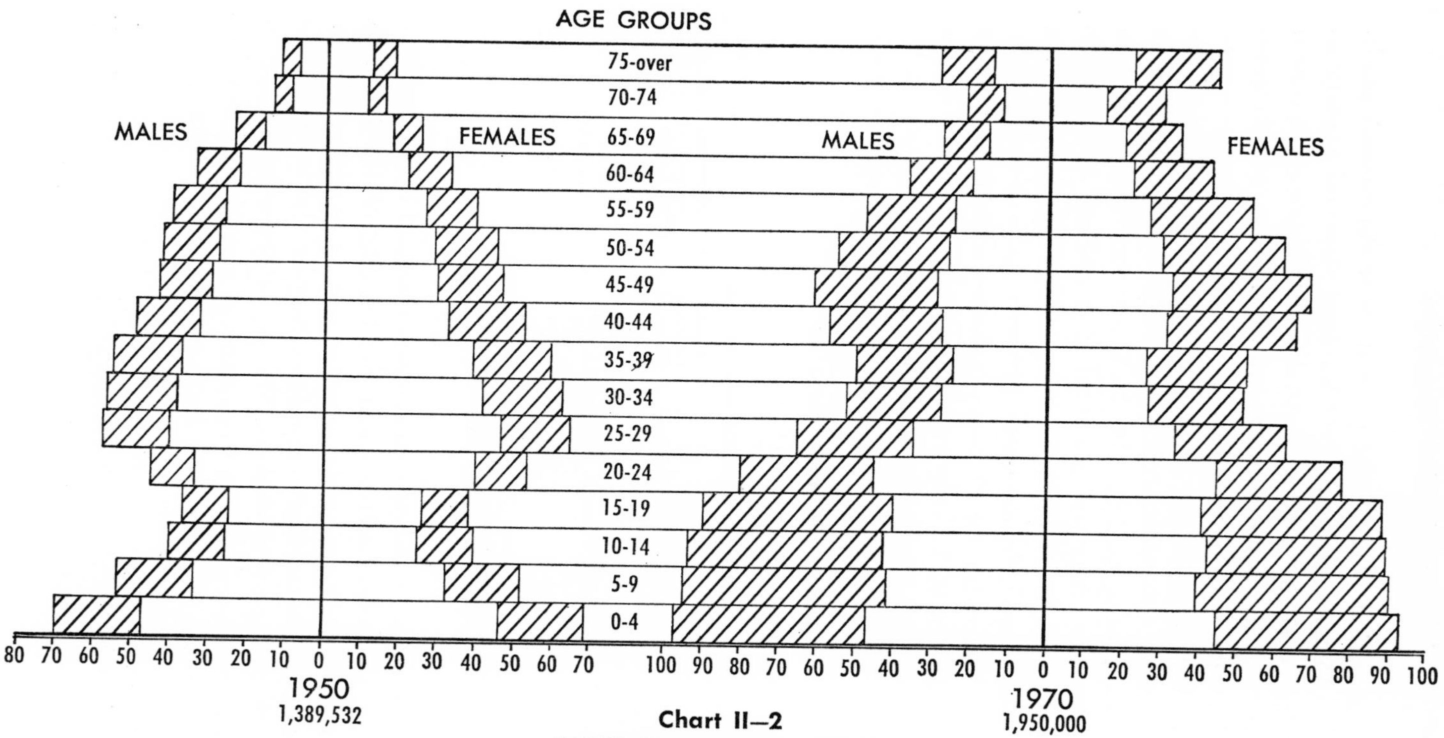
AGE GROUPS
MALES
FEMALES
MALES
FEMALES
75-over
70-74
65-69
60-64
55-59
50-54
45-49
40-44
35-39
30-34
25-29
20-24
15-19
10-14
5-9
0-4
80 70 60 50 40 30 20 10 0 10 20 30 40 50 60 70
100 90 80 70 60 50 40 30 20 10 0 10 20 30 40 50 60 70 80 90 100
1950
1,389,532
1970
1,950,000

Chart II—2
POPULATION "PYRAMIDS"
CUYAHOGA COUNTY—CITY OF CLEVELAND

City of Cleveland
Suburbs

SOURCE OF DATA—United States Census
Estimates by staffs of R.P.C. and Metro

During the period 1947-54, the percentage of the nation's workers engaged in manufacturing in the Cleveland Standard Metropolitan Area dropped slightly. Exactly parallel developments occurred in value added by the manufacturing industry. There was an interesting development with potentially important fiscal consequences—namely, that the 8.3 per cent decline in Cleveland's share of the area's employment was associated with a 9.9 per cent decline in its relative share in value added. This indicates that the changes in industry within the Cleveland Standard Metropolitan Area outside of Cleveland itself involved more value added per worker than within Cleveland and, hence more property subject to taxation. However, the concentration of heavy industry within the City of Cleveland continues to be relatively high, higher than any of the thirteen central cities studied by Raymond Vernon.[4]

Table II-7—Value Added by Manufacturing Cuyahoga County,* 1919-54

(IN MILLIONS OF CURRENT DOLLARS)

Year	County	Cleveland	County Excluding Cleveland	Cleveland as per cent of County
1919	509	478	31	93.95
1929	672	617	55	91.84
1939	489	434	56	88.62
1947	1,486	1,219	267	82.03
1954	2,297	1,656	641	72.10

* Figures do not necessarily add because of rounding.
Source: U. S. Census of Manufactures

The movements in industry have had important effects on both the demand for public services and the location of the tax base. Industry usually requires public services just as would residential development. Industry needs vary depending on the type of plant and the ratio of capital to workers. The public services required by an industrial community differ from those of a residential development; there would, for example, be a greater emphasis on public

4. Vernon, *op. cit.*, Appendix Table 4, pp. 74-75. Included in this study of central cities in addition to Cleveland were Baltimore, Boston, Lawrence, Lowell, Buffalo, Chicago, Cincinnati, Detroit, Los Angeles, New York City-Jersey City-Newark, Philadelphia, Pittsburgh, St. Louis, San Francisco-Oakland.

safety and utilities, and a lesser on education. Insofar as an industrialized jurisdiction can keep its tax base from being diluted by
large residential population, it can afford either very great services
at low tax rates, or normal services at extremely low rates. While
this dilution has been preserved in the case of municipalities, it has
not been so true in the case of school districts, where each of the
wealthy industrial communities has shared its tax capacity with one
or more of its poorer neighbors.

Retail trade has also moved outside of the City of Cleveland following the nation-wide trend of building huge suburban shopping
centers (although the proportion of retail trade employment in
Cleveland was exceeded only by that of Baltimore in the Vernon
study of central cities).[5] These are divided among a large number
of communities and are often located in residential areas. The
erection of a shopping center usually has effects on the demand for
government services, and quite often in a community other than
where its tax base is located.

The Individual Governments

The result of all these movements in population, industry, and
commerce is a diversity in the economic characteristics of the governmental jurisdictions involved. These movements influenced not
only the taxable resources, but also the demands for government
services. To permit a more detailed analysis of the nature of the
metropolitan area, individual governments have been classified into
a number of socio-economic categories, enumerated below, based
on a number of fiscally oriented variables. Where possible the
same criteria were applied to both municipalities and school districts.
It should be noted, however, that no attempt was made to analyze
variation within the boundaries of any jurisdiction.

The following variables were utilized to classify governmental
jurisdictions: a) assessed valuation, b) personal wealth as measured
by the Ohio Intangibles Tax Levy, c) industrial and commercial
establishment as measured by the Tangible Personal Property Assess-

---

5. Vernon, *op. cit.*, Appendix Table 2, pp. 66-67.

Table II-8—Indicators Used in Classifying Municipalities; Intangibles, Assessed Valuation, and Estimated Tangibles per Square Mile and per Capita, 1956

Governmental Unit	Assessed Valuation per sq. mile	Est. Tang. per sq. mile	Intangible Valuation per sq. mile	Assessed Valuation per capita	Est. Tang. per capita	Intangible Valuation per capita	Per Cent of Total Area	Density (Persons per sq. mile)	Residential Property as Per Cent of all Real Property	Classification in 1956	Classification in 1940
	(Thousands of dollars)			(Dollars)	(Dollars)	(Dollars)	(458.25 sq. mi. = 100)				
Cuyahoga County	10,258	2,263	16	2,974	656	4.51		3,449			
Cities											
Bay Village	6,654	80	12	2,716	33	4.87	1.0	2,450	97.5	D	D Vil
Bedford	7,188	1,140	3	2,740	435	1.28	1.1	2,623	71.4	B	D
Berea	6,227	548	5	2,180	192	1.70	1.0	2,856	81.8	D	D
Brooklyn	8,681	2,574	2	4,540	1,346	.94	.9	1,912	54.8	B	D Vil
Cleveland	35,274	9,355	27	2,852	761	2.22	16.3	12,370	42.0	B	B
Cleveland Heights	20,962	547	119	2,769	72	15.73	1.8	7,570	83.2	D	D
East Cleveland	30,614	3,301	44	2,330	251	3.35	.7	13,139	52.7	D	D
Euclid	20,292	6,727	8	3,668	1,216	1.48	2.4	5,533	58.2	B	B
Fairview Park	11,129	1,028	14	3,066	283	3.90	.8	3,629	75.8	D	D
Garfield Heights	8,751	738	2	1,858	157	.37	1.5	4,711	86.1	D (P)	D (P)
Lakewood	28,196	2,808	82	2,347	234	6.88	1.2	12,015	68.6	D	D
Lyndhurst	6,917	97	27	2,351	33	9.02	1.0	2,940	93.9	D	D Vil
Maple Heights	10,967	1,601	2	2,236	326	.35	1.2	4,906	81.4	D	D
Mayfield Heights	5,962	305	3	2,376	122	1.24	.9	2,509	86.0	D	D Vil
North Olmsted	2,465	102	1	2,336	96	.99	2.5	1,057	89.8	D	D Vil
Parma	7,694	1,283	2	2,469	411	.63	4.4	3,117	82.1	D	D
Rocky River	10,680	339	40	3,311	105	12.27	1.0	3,225	84.6	D	D
Shaker Heights	22,627	588	268	4,256	111	51.42	1.4	5,317	79.6	D (W)	D (W)
South Euclid	13,745	707	17	2,585	133	3.20	1.0	5,317	86.7	D	D
University Heights	26,861	644	63	3,165	78	7.43	.4	8,486	91.7	D	D

Villages

Villages											
Beachwood	4,470	26	17	4,932	29	19.19	1.0	906	96.9	D (W)	D (W)
Bedford Heights	3,966	1,924	1	4,177	2,072	.97	1.0	950	41.5	–	‡
Bentleyville	322	*	*	3,243	4	3.89	.6	94	100.0	D	
Bratenahl	5,110	72	123	4,208	60	101.66	.2	1,214	95.2	D (W)	D (W)
Brecksville	916	43	1	4,255	207	6.29	4.3	215	79.8	D	D
Broadview Heights	816	14	*	2,544	43	.21	2.8	321	91.0	D	D
Brooklyn Heights	2,107	201	1	2,939	281	1.08	.4	717	61.6	D	D
Brook Park	9,829	6,155	*	29,359	18,383	.71	1.7	335	19.5	–	D
Chagrin Falls	4,925	875	44	3,032	538	27.36	.5	1,624	72.8	D	D
Cuyahoga Heights	28,644	18,273	3	122,237	77,982	12.57	.7	234	4.3	–	–
Gates Mills	899	13	23	6,858	95	173.12	2.0	131	97.1	D (W)	D (W)
Glenwillow	478	82	*	4,403	752	.47	.6	109	80.5	D	D
Highland Heights	1,043	17	*	2,631	44	.92	1.1	397	96.0	D	D (W)
Hunting Valley	724	4	22	11,264	62	350.88	1.5	64	99.3	D (W)	D
Independence	2,059	19	1	3,288	300	2.31	2.0	626	87.6	D	D
Linndale	6,730	870	*	1,708	221	.08	†	3,940	70.0	D	D
Mayfield	1,076	36	1	2,623	87	3.33	.9	410	96.3	D	D
Middleburg Heights	2,304	233	1	3,573	361	1.20	1.8	645	78.1	D	D
Moreland Hills	953	10	1	4,070	44	5.57	1.6	234	93.4	D	D
Newburgh Heights	15,985	2,435	2	2,428	370	.25	.1	6,584	60.8	D	D
North Randall	6,874	736	2	18,363	1,966	5.29	.2	374	20.9	–	–
North Royalton	739	16	*	2,600	56	.64	4.6	284	90.8	D	D
Oakwood	1,264	22	*	1,307	23	.26	.8	967	88.9	D (P)	‡
Olmsted Falls	3,092	145	4	2,514	118	3.35	.3	1,230	91.4	D	D
Orange	1,481	12	*	3,154	26	.96	.8	470	92.9	D	D
Parkview	4,129	17	2	2,517	10	1.16	.2	1,641	97.2	D	D
Parma Heights	6,807	98	3	2,369	34	.92	.9	2,874	95.1	D	D
Pepper Pike	1,943	6	5	6,715	21	15.75	1.6	289	90.6	D (W)	D (W)

(Continued on next page)

Table II-8 (Continued)

Governmental Unit	Assessed Valuation per sq. mile	Est. Tang. per sq. mile	Intangible Valuation per sq. mile	Assessed Valuation per capita	Est. Tang. per capita	Intangible Valuation per capita	Per Cent of Total Area	Density (Persons per sq. mile)	Residential Property as Per Cent of all Real Property	Classification in 1956	Classification in 1940
	(Thousands of dollars)			(Dollars)	(Dollars)	(Dollars)					
Richmond Heights	1,732	30	2	2,316	40	2.27	1.0	748	95.1	D	D
Seven Hills	1,953	35	1	2,833	51	.75	1.1	689	97.1	D	D
Solon	953	78	1	3,784	311	2.76	4.4	252	80.9	D	D
Strongsville	566	32	*	2,649	147	1.12	5.5	214	67.8	D	D
Valley View	573	62	*	3,130	337	.44	1.3	183	55.2	D	D
Walton Hills	5,318	3,169	*	25,336	15,100	.73	1.5	210	28.4	—	‡
Warrensville Heights	4,680	336	2	2,457	176	1.09	.9	1,905	84.8	D	D
Westlake	1,725	54	1	2,905	91	2.45	3.6	594	89.7	D	D
West View	1,225	91	*	2,507	187	.22	.5	489	64.8	D	D
Woodmere	2,300	20	*	2,125	18	.05	.1	1,083	96.5	D	‡
Townships											
Chagrin Falls	872	11	1	5,191	64	7.13	.1	168	100.0	D	D
Olmsted	663	22	*	1,648	54	.37	2.3	402	70.6	D	D
Riveredge	124	55	—	837	370	—	.1	177	—	D	D
Warrensville	432	9	1	623	12	.07	.7	693	82.9	D	D

* less than $500.
† less than 0.1%.
‡ not in existence in 1940.
Classification: Dormitory—D; Dormitory (Poor)—D (P); Dormitory (wealthy)—D (W); Balanced—B;
Industrial—I; Village—Vil.

ment, d) population, and e) area. Where relevant, each of these variables was measured primarily in terms of population, and secondarily in terms of area. Each jurisdiction, municipal and school, can thus be described in terms of its density, assessed valuation per person, wealth per person, and an index of industrial and/or commercial establishment per person. Assessed valuation, wealth, and industrial valuation per square mile as well as commercial establishments and the number of miles per person (being simply another measure of density) were used as secondary criteria. In every instance except one, the two sets of data give parallel results; and in that one instance, Newburgh Heights, the additional knowledge showed the classification could be ambiguous, and was in the case of this very densely populated, very poor, highly industrialized jurisdiction.

Table II-8 summarizes the distribution of these variables by municipality, and Table II-9 by school district. In the case of school districts, data are presented not only in terms of population, but also in terms of the more relevant variable, the number of students in average daily membership. No attempt was made to calculate the variables per square mile for the school district.

The data show striking differences among governments, both in the case of municipalities and school districts, with less variation in the latter for reasons indicated below.

The data show that the municipalities seem to fall into several commonly used fiscal categories: [6] a) balanced municipalities characterized by industry and commerce as well as residence, with none predominating; b) dormitory municipalities, characterized by almost complete dependence on residential tax base, which may be divided into the very wealthy, average, and poor; c) industrial enclaves which specialize in providing non-residential community services, and which do not depend on a residential tax base. In the case of the balanced municipalities, the daytime population is roughly equal to the nighttime population; in the case of the dormitory municipalities, the nighttime population decidedly exceeds that of the daytime; and in the case of the industrial enclaves, the daytime

---

6. Julius Margolis, "Municipal Fiscal Structure in a Metropolitan Region," *Journal of Political Economy,* LXV No. 3, June, 1957, pp. 225-36.

Table II-9—Indicators Used in Classifying School Districts, 1956

School Districts	Assessed Valuation per ADM	Assessed Valuation per capita	Intangible Valuation per ADM	ADM (Average Daily Membership)	Population	Ratio of ADM to Population (Per Cent)
	(Thousands of Dollars)		(Dollars)			
Bay Village	13.0	2.7	23.40	2,349	11,300	20.8
Bedford	22.7	5.0	5.37	3,911	17,600	22.2
Berea	32.7	5.9	7.99	3,879	21,600	17.9
Brooklyn	21.8	4.5	4.24	1,650	7,900	20.8
Cleveland	22.4	2.9	17.29	117,730	915,300	12.9
Cleveland Heights	17.8	2.8	90.17	12,044	75,300	16.0
East Cleveland	19.3	2.4	24.18	5,417	43,500	12.5
Euclid	21.0	3.7	8.44	10,421	59,600	17.5
Fairview Park	16.0	2.6	22.87	2,361	14,300	16.5
Garfield Heights	12.7	1.8	2.78	4,322	31,200	13.9
Lakewood	21.6	2.3	63.23	7,401	68,000	10.9
Maple Heights	12.5	2.2	2.06	4,853	27,200	17.8
North Olmsted	13.0	2.3	5.48	2,191	12,200	18.0
Parma	14.3	2.5	3.95	13,418	77,700	17.3
Rocky River	21.8	3.6	70.83	2,640	15,900	16.6
Shaker Heights	26.0	3.7	275.65	6,570	45,600	14.4
So. Euclid-Lyndhurst	13.7	2.6	30.64	6,625	35,100	18.9
Local & Exempted						
Beachwood	43.6	4.9	169.17	467	4,100	11.3
Bratenahl	35.8	4.2	866.67	150	1,300	11.8
Brecksville	14.3	3.6	14.78	1,895	7,600	25.0
Chagrin Falls Ex.	10.8	2.4	89.93	1,201	5,400	22.1
Cuyahoga Heights	136.2	32.0	15.81	759	3,200	23.5
Independence	23.9	3.3	16.69	779	5,700	13.7
Mayfield (City)	14.2	2.8	76.00	2,987	15,200	19.6
North Royalton	12.5	2.5	2.91	1,375	6,900	20.0
Olmsted Falls	8.8	1.9	5.22	1,532	7,000	22.0
Orange	26.0	8.0	132.08	1,484	4,800	30.9
Richmond Heights	18.8	2.3	20.00	350	2,900	12.1
Solon	18.7	3.8	13.01	1,076	5,300	20.4
Strongsville	12.2	2.6	5.17	1,161	5,300	21.7
Warrensville Heights	17.0	2.3	6.75	1,482	11,000	13.5
Westlake Ex.	17.6	2.9	14.96	1,604	9,700	16.5
Total	20.8	3.0	31.54	226,084	1,574,700	14.4

population is far in excess of the nighttime population. Cleveland, as central city, is assumed to be *sui generis;* this is only partly reflected by the criteria utilized, for, unlike the other communities, it specializes not only in residence, industry, and commerce, but as the central city of a major metropolitan area it provides financial services, culture, education, and recreation to all parts of the metropolitan area and beyond.

As indicated by the figures in Tables II-8 and II-9, municipalities and school districts differ in the amount of assessed valuation per person (or per student). The range from $122,237 per person in Cuyahoga Heights to $1,307 per person in Oakwood is certainly very great. Since the average for the county as a whole is $2,974, the first step was to determine the characteristics of those communities which have assessed valuations far in excess of, or far below, the average. Those that exceeded the mean fell into two categories, the industrial enclaves and the very small but very wealthy dormitory communities. The jurisdictions that fell into these categories were determined by looking at the amount of industry and commerce (tangible personal property) and amount of wealth (intangible levy) per person. Included in the wealthy domitory category were Hunting Valley, Gates Mills, Beachwood, Bratenahl, and Pepper Pike; Moreland Hills was excluded as the marginal wealthy community. Primarily because of its population size and because the city could be unambiguously classified as wealthy, Shaker Heights was included in this category. In the analysis of Chapter IV, however, it was not treated separately from other cities. The industrial enclaves included Cuyahoga Heights, Brook Park, the race track jurisdiction of North Randall, and Walton Hills; Bedford Heights was excluded as the marginal industrial community.

At the other extreme were the communities which were poor, with the possibility that part of the poverty of the community might be hidden by the existence of industry. Three municipalities appear poor relative to the overall county averages—Garfield Heights, Oakwood, and Linndale.

The remaining communities fall either into the balanced or average dormitory category. Where there exists a substantial non-residential, as well as residential, tax base, the community is assured

of being a balanced jurisdiction, since there is little likelihood of a
marked surfeit or deficiency in tax resources.

The balanced city category includes Bedford, Brooklyn and
Euclid, with only the latter two being unambiguously placed there.
It is possible to consider the City of Cleveland as a balanced city,
but with its great concentration of people, industry, and commerce,
for most purposes it is in a class by itself, as the data indicate.

There are, of course, other fiscally important criteria for dis-
tinguishing among jurisdictions (e.g. the age of the municipality),
but no attempt is made here to categorize them according to such
criteria.

As presented on Map II-3, the classifications assume a definite
geographic pattern within the Cleveland Metropolitan Area. While
the balanced cities hug the core area, the industrial enclaves are
distributed throughout the entire area on various railroad rights
of way. And the wealthy jurisdictions are almost all found east of
the City of Cleveland. They embrace the real estate holdings
originally opened by the Van Sweringen brothers. To put the data
in historical perspective, analysis comparable with 1956 is made of
the Cleveland Metropolitan Area for the year 1940 and the results
are summarized in Table II-8. These show the changing nature of
the areas which make up the municipalities under consideration.
The major changes from 1940 to 1956 involve the opening up of
new industrial areas in Brook Park and Walton Hills and the rise of
new balanced communities in Euclid and Brooklyn.

Detailed maps using the measures of wealth, and assessed
valuation will be presented later in this study, because they indicate
the problems that arise because of differences in the resources
and requirements within the Cleveland Metropolitan Area.

Because of its fiscal importance, our final step will be to apply
the same kind of analysis to the school districts as to the municipalities. The results, from the point of view of resources and requirements, show far less variation, as many of the wealthier and fiscally
stronger areas are found in combination with poorer communities
in the make-up of the school districts.

What would be extreme cases vanish as Newburgh Heights and
Linndale fall into the Cleveland School District; Oakwood is in a
district which includes Bedford, Bedford Heights, and Walton

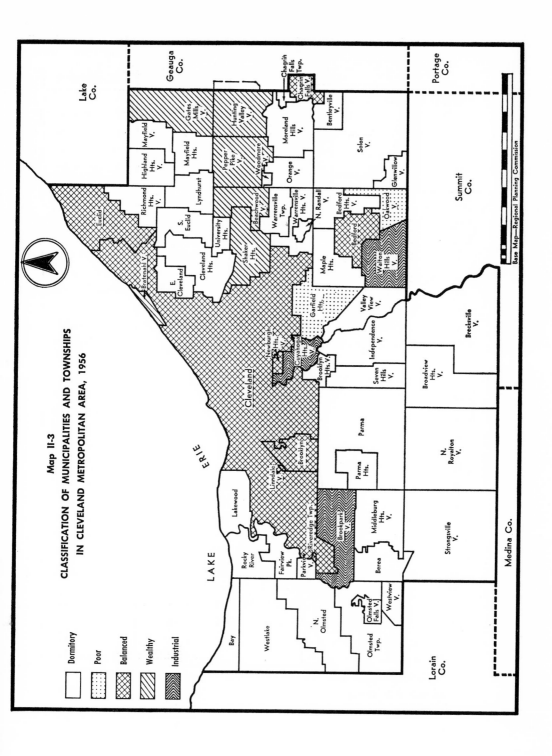

Map II-3

CLASSIFICATION OF MUNICIPALITIES AND TOWNSHIPS
IN CLEVELAND METROPOLITAN AREA, 1956

Dormitory
Poor
Balanced
Wealthy
Industrial

Base Map—Regional Planning Commission

Lake Co.

Geauga Co.

Portage Co.

Summit Co.

Medina Co.

Lorain Co.

ERIE

LAKE

Euclid

Bratenahl V.

E. Cleveland

Lakewood

Rocky River

Bay

Westlake

N. Olmsted

Olmsted Twp.

Olmsted Falls V.

Westview V.

Berea

Middleburg Hts. V.

Strongsville V.

N. Royalton V.

Brookpark V.

Parkview V.

Riveredge Twp.

Fairview Pk.

Linndale V.

Brooklyn

Parma Hts.

Parma

Cleveland

Brooklyn Hts. V.

Cuyahoga Hts. V.

Newburgh Hts. V.

Seven Hills V.

Independence V.

Broadview Hts. V.

Brecksville V.

Valley View V.

Garfield Hts.

Maple Hts.

Walton Hills V.

Bedford Hts.

Bedford

Oakwood V.

Glenwillow V.

Solon V.

N. Randall V.

Warrensville Hts. V.

Warrensville Twp.

Beachwood V.

Shaker Hts.

Cleveland Hts.

University Hts.

S. Euclid

Lyndhurst

Richmond Hts. V.

Highland Hts. V.

Mayfield Hts.

Mayfield V.

Woodmere V.

Pepper Pike V.

Orange V.

Moreland Hills V.

Hunting Valley V.

Gates Mills V.

Bentleyville V.

Chagrin Falls Twp.

Chagrin Falls V.

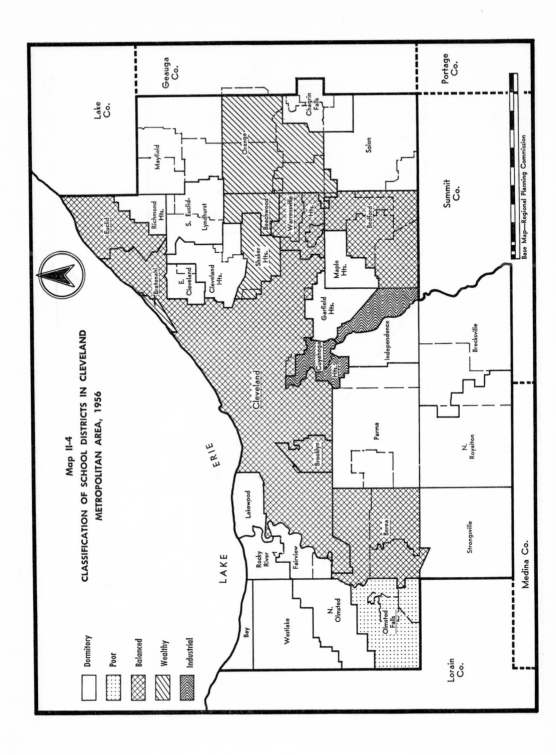

Map II-4

CLASSIFICATION OF SCHOOL DISTRICTS IN CLEVELAND
METROPOLITAN AREA, 1956

Dormitory
Poor
Balanced
Wealthy
Industrial

Base Map—Regional Planning Commission

Hills. The Cuyahoga Heights school district includes Valley View and Brooklyn Heights; Brook Park is included in the Berea school district; and North Randall is included in the Warrensville Heights school district. In the case of the school districts, the ratio of balanced areas to the total number is increased. Some of the wealthier communities such as Hunting Valley, Gates Mills, and Pepper Pike also share their resources with some of their fiscally poorer neighbors. Beachwood and Bratenahl continue as independent school districts without sharing their resources, and hence appear as relatively wealthy districts.

Thus, while there still remains great variation among the various school districts of the area, the variation is generally within a context of an upward leveling of the ratios of the resources to the requirements. There is only one school district, the Cuyahoga Heights School District, which is still completely dominated by its industrial tax base relative to its requirements. This school district very noticeably stands out not only when it is compared to its neighbors in the Cleveland Metropolitan Area, but also when compared to other school districts throughout the state. The wealthy areas remain in the eastern part of the county, while the balanced areas spread out from the core areas farther in the school districts than they do as municipalities. Only one school district, Olmsted Falls, appears as poor relative to the average for the county, but not poor by state-wide standards.

III

Trends in Fiscal Activity:

An Overview

AFTER REACHING A LOW POINT IMMEDIATELY AFTER World War II, government fiscal activity has expanded, until today expenditures, taxes, and debt outstanding approximate and exceed in absolute amounts their wartime peaks. This upward movement has occurred on the state and local as well as on the federal level. Fiscal activity in the Cleveland Metropolitan Area has followed the nationwide pattern of growth occasioned by expanded needs and demands for public services. Post World War II developments in governmental fiscal activity reflect the existence of a number of long-term underlying trends: a) an increase in governmental fiscal activity regardless of index used or government considered; b) an increase in the real amount and cost of government activity; c) an increase in the public sector relative to the private sector.

40

The over-all long term growth has been caused a) by the growth in population and economic activity; b) by the changing location of population, commerce and industry, c) by the upward movement in the price level; d) by the increase in the demand for greater amounts of public services of better quality; and e) by national defense considerations. As shown in Table III-1, total expenditures, excluding debt retirement, by all governments in the United States

Table III-1—Expenditures, Tax Receipts, and Gross Debt All Governments, United States, 1902-58

(In Millions of Current Dollars)

Fiscal Year	Total Expenditures	Tax Receipts	Gross Debt at End of Fiscal Year
1902	1,564	1,377	3,285
1913	2,960	2,263	5,607
1922	8,829	7,499	33,072
1927	10,531	9,424	33,393
1932	12,971	7,971	38,692
1936	15,044	10,577	53,253
1940	19,895	14,282	63,251
1944	103,501	52,082	218,482
1946	74,950	48,811	285,339
1948	55,893	54,507	270,948
1950	68,567	54,630	281,472
1952	99,840	84,796	289,205
1954	109,403	90,915	310,191
1956	113,505	100,025	321,912
1958	131,000	108,859	332,543

Source: Tax Foundation, *Facts and Figures on Government Finance, 1958-1959.*

which were approximately $1.6 billions in 1902 rose to $8.8 billions in 1922.[1] Expenditures continued to grow. Reaching a figure of $13.0 billions in 1932, they grew until they reached the figure of $19.9 billions on the eve of World War II in 1940. During World War II, expenditures reached a peak in terms of both real cost to society and relative share of the public sector which has still not been matched, although the absolute amounts have since been exceeded. Expenditures dropped sharply after the war, falling to a figure of

---

1. Tax Foundation, *Facts and Figures on Government Finance, 1958-1959.* Tenth Edition, New York, 1958, is the invaluable source for these and other historical figures on government finance.

$55.9 billions in 1948, as compared to $103.5 billions in 1944. This figure, although considerably higher than the pre-war level, was a good deal lower than the wartime peak. Since 1948, there has been a noticeable upward drift, as total expenditures, tax receipts, and debt have climbed beyond the World War II peak as the forces mentioned above—population growth, movement of population, industry and commerce, inflation, the growth in the amount and quality of federal, state and local public services, and continued world tensions—have continued in operation with no sign of abatement.

As a percentage of the Gross National Product the government sector of the economy has grown more rapidly than the private sector. In 1929, government expenditures were 8.17 per cent of the Gross National Product; as private production declined and government expenditures remained constant the percentage rose to 18.1 per cent in 1932. Thereafter during the 1930's and 1940's, except during actual war years, the government share of the GNP did not reach 20 per cent, although it did reach 19.2 per cent in 1936. Since 1950, however, there has been a distinct upward movement in the government share of the GNP, the figure having grown to 24.8 per cent in 1956 and 28.6 per cent in 1958.

This growth has been associated with a redistribution of functions among the various levels of government as well as with an expansion of traditional governmental functions. At the same time, intergovernmental fiscal relations have become more complex, and it has become more difficult to determine actual responsibility for governmental expenditures. For the period for which data are available—that is, after 1929—there can be discerned an underlying upward trend in federal expenditures relative to the GNP, influenced in large measure since 1940 by the extent of our national security commitment. During periods of actual involvement in war the percentage has gone up relatively sharply. On the other hand, state and local expenditures, after reaching a peak relative to the federal government and the GNP in 1932, declined relative to both up to 1945. Since then, even though the GNP and federal expenditures have grown, state and local expenditures have also grown relative to each of the other categories. The state and local growth has occurred partly because of the need to catch up with expenditures deferred during the war, partly because of increased urbanization, partly because of explicit expansion of certain state and local functions relative to those of the federal government and the private sector.

Table III-2—Gross National Product and Government Expenditures, All Governments, United States, Selected Years, 1929-58

(In Current Dollars)

Year	Gross National Product (Billions of Dollars)	Total Government Expenditures * (Billions of Dollars)	(Per Cent of GNP)	Federal Expenditures (Billions of Dollars)	(Per Cent of GNP)	State and Local Expenditures (Billions of Dollars)	(Per Cent of GNP)
1929	104.4	10.2	9.8	2.6	2.5	7.6	7.3
1932	58.4	10.6	18.1	3.2	5.5	7.4	12.7
1936	82.7	15.9	19.2	8.5	10.3	7.4	8.9
1940	100.6	18.5	18.4	10.1	10.0	8.4	8.3
1944	211.4	103.0	48.8	95.6	45.2	7.5	3.9
1946	210.7	47.0	22.3	37.0	17.6	10.0	4.7
1948	259.4	51.0	19.7	35.4	13.7	15.6	6.0
1950	284.6	61.0	21.5	41.0	14.4	20.1	7.1
1952	347.0	94.4	27.2	71.6	20.6	22.8	6.6
1954	363.1	96.7	27.9	69.6	21.3	27.2	6.7
1956	419.2	104.1	24.8	71.9	17.2	32.2	7.7
1958	436.7	124.5	28.6	87.0	19.9	37.5	8.8

* National income concept. This differs from the total in Table III-1, which is computed on a different basis.
Source: Tax Foundation, *Facts and Figures on Government Finance, 1958-1959; Economic Report of the President, 1959.*

The real value of state and local expenditures considered above are computed in terms of dollars of constant purchasing power. Because of its importance in the analysis of past changes in expenditures, and because it is valuable in projecting future trends, an index of "state and local purchasing power" based on the Commerce Department's "Implicit Deflator for State and Local Goods and Services" was constructed. This index, Chart III-1, shows what a dollar of state and local expenditure would purchase at yearly intervals since 1929. Thus, in 1940 a dollar of state and local expenditure would have purchased the equivalent of what $1.647 would have purchased in 1947. In like manner, one dollar in 1956 would have purchased the equivalent of what state and local governments would have received for $.682 in 1947. These figures are shown in Table III-4.

In addition to a knowledge of the real value of government expenditures, it is essential also to determine the direct real costs of financing in terms of the loss of consumer's purchasing power of the taxes, special assessments, fees, charges, etc., used to pay for the expenditures. Since the Consumer Price Index moves at a different rate from that of the "Implicit Price Deflator" for state and local expenditures on goods and services, the differences in rates have posed, and will continue to pose, a major problem in the financing of government expenditures. This problem is considered in detail in Chapter VIII.

The expansion of fiscal activity in the Cleveland Metropolitan Area reflects a nation-wide trend modified by local and state conditions. The growth in aggregate fiscal activity has been accompanied by increasingly complex relations between federal, state, and local governments. Intergovernmental programs, especially those involving matching funds or efforts, have had a direct impact on local fiscal activity, while changes in fiscal policy on the federal and state levels certainly have indirect, if not direct, effects on local fiscal policy.

Table III-3—Per Capita Amounts and Per Cent Distribution of Federal, State, and Local Government Expenditures, Selected Years, 1902-58

YEAR	PER CAPITA EXPENDITURES (In Current Dollars)				PER CENT DISTRIBUTION			
	Total	Federal	State	Local	Total	Federal	State	Local
1902	20	6	2	12	100	30.4	11.4	58.1
1913	31	8	4	20	100	24.2	12.6	63.3
1922	81	30	12	39	100	37.2	14.4	48.4
1927	90	24	16	49	100	26.9	17.9	55.1
1932	105	39	21	45	100	37.0	19.8	43.2
1940	152	73	34	44	100	48.3	22.5	29.2
1944	771	700	31	40	100	90.8	4.0	5.2
1946	566	466	47	53	100	82.4	8.3	9.4
1948	390	254	66	69	100	65.3	16.9	17.8
1950	461	290	85	86	100	62.9	18.5	18.6
1952	651	467	87	97	100	71.7	13.4	15.0
1954	691	479	100	113	100	69.3	14.4	16.3
1956	691	449	112	130	100	64.9	16.2	18.9
1958	769	493	129	147	100	64.1	16.8	19.1

Source: Tax Foundation, *Facts and Figures on Government Finance, 1958-1959.*

The Cleveland Metropolitan Area in Perspective

Total expenditures by all governments in the Cleveland Metropolitan Area, excluding expenditures on public services and debt retirement, grew from $88.2 millions in 1940, to $151.6 millions in 1950 and then to $270.6 millions in 1956. At the same time, all local expenditures in the United States rose from $5.8 billions in 1940, to $12.8 billions in 1950, and then to $21.4 billions in 1956. General fund expenditures by the Ohio state government increased from $156.8 millions in 1940, to $357.8 millions in 1950, to $505 millions in 1956. Expenditures by all states increased from $4.5 billions in 1940, to $12.7 billions in 1950, to $18.4 billions in 1956. If account is taken of changes in the price level and the appropriate indexes are utilized, the relative positions are unchanged although the amount of growth is considerably reduced.

A number of very interesting conclusions emerge from a close analysis of these figures. First and foremost, a good part of the increase in expenditures on all levels of government over the period 1940-56 was the result of the increase in population, and, if our index is correct, of the increased cost of providing the same amount of services. Although we know that very great growth occurred on the state and local levels commencing in 1946, we know also that the initial effects reflected deferred demand, the suburbanization of tremendous new tracts of land, and the generally excellent financial condition of most state and local governments in the immediate post World War II period. What is surprising is the fact that real per capita expenditure went up so little. The 23.9 per cent increase in per capita real estate expenditures between 1940 and 1956 does not resemble the 282.8 per cent increase in aggregate expenditures. In the case of all local expenditures, there was only a 22.6 per cent increase in per capita expenditures. For the State of Ohio and the Cleveland Metropolitan Area, there was virtually no change in per capita expenditures, while in the Cleveland Metropolitan Area, there was a decline not only in per capital real expenditures between 1940 and 1956, but also in total real expenditures, for the period 1940-50 at least.

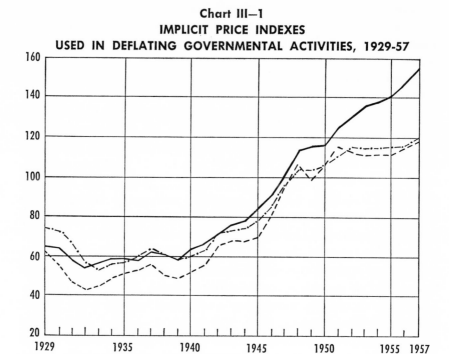

Chart III—1
IMPLICIT PRICE INDEXES
USED IN DEFLATING GOVERNMENTAL ACTIVITIES, 1929-57

———— Implicit price deflator, state & local purch. goods & service, 1947 = 100
--- - Wholesale price index, 1947-49 = 100
—·—·— Consumer price index, 1947-49 = 100

SOURCE: *Economic Report of the President,*
Jan. 1958, pp. 122, 156, 160

The decline in real per capita expenditures in the Cleveland Metropolitan Area and the much smaller-than-expected growth on the local level nationally is a reflection of the decline in local welfare payments as a result of improved economic conditions and shifting responsibility for welfare payments to the state and federal governments. If welfare expenditures are excluded, the decline in per capita real expenditures in the Cleveland Metropolitan Area for the period 1940-56 is changed to a net increase of 6.2 per cent for the period 1940-50, and there is an increase in total real expenditures.

The trend in revenues shows approximately the same pattern as that of expenditures on the state and local levels; but with a much more consistent growth on the federal level.

Long before there was, strictly speaking, a Cleveland Metropolitan Area, local government finance attracted interest as inhabitants began to demand government services, and argued about the methods of their financing. The latter part of the nineteenth century and earlier part of the twentieth was a period when local finances

Table III-4—Purchasing Power of Consumer and State and Local Government Dollars, 1929-57

Year	Purchasing Power of the Consumer Dollar * (1947-49 = 100)	Purchasing Power of Local Government Dollar † (1947 = 100)
1929	136.4	156.7
1930	140.1	160.3
1931	153.8	169.8
1932	171.2	183.5
1933	180.8	176.4
1934	174.8	170.6
1935	170.4	168.9
1936	168.6	171.2
1937	162.9	165.0
1938	165.8	166.4
1939	168.4	169.5
1940	166.9	164.7
1941	159.0	155.5
1942	143.5	142.9
1943	135.1	133.7
1944	133.0	128.5
1945	130.0	122.2
1946	119.9	112.6
1947	104.7	100.0
1948	97.3	90.3
1949	98.2	88.0
1950	97.3	86.7
1951	90.1	80.5
1952	88.1	76.6
1953	87.4	74.3
1954	87.1	72.8
1955	87.3	71.3
1956	86.1	68.2
1957	83.2	64.7

* Based on the Consumer Price Index.
† Based on the Implicit Deflator for State and Local Expenditures.
Source: *Economic Report of the President, 1958.*

were generally more important than either state or federal finances. This was reflected in the importance of Cleveland as compared to the state government at the time. It is estimated that, as late as 1905, expenditures of Cleveland exceeded those of the State of Ohio; total disbursement by the State of Ohio in that year for all purposes was some $8.7 millions, and, according to C. C. Williamson, total expenditures of Cleveland, including education, amounted to $11.4 millions.[2] Indeed, it was not until the mid-1930's that state expenditures exceeded those of Cleveland by any considerable margin.

For Cuyahoga County as a whole, the total current tax levy exceeded the revenues collected by the state as late as 1930. Although these fiscal operations do not compare in magnitude with those of a New York City or Chicago, they still indicate the scope of local finances during the period chosen. And when state finances began to exceed those of the governments that comprise the Cleveland Metropolitan Area, it was due to an expansion of state operations rather than to a decline of local operations.

Despite their importance compared to state expenditures, local expenditures prior to 1920 were low, viewed against post World War II levels. Williamson estimated that, in 1841 for instance, with total expenditures of $20,047, per capita governmental expenditure for Cleveland was $2.78, of which $2.22 was spent on current expenditures and the remainder on capital outlay and interest. Per capita expenditures on the protection of life and property, i.e., police and fire expenditure, were $.27 per person. Excluding capital expenditures, the cost of education per student in 1837 was $1.36 if the figures for costs and attendance are reliable.

By 1900, per capita expenditures in Cleveland for municipal, school, and library purposes had risen to $22.03 per person. Per capita operating costs, however, were $11.76, or approximately half the total cost. The cost of educating each pupil had risen to $42.50 by 1901. Comparable developments took place in revenues, as they rose from $3.20 in 1841 to $14.30 in 1871, and then to $17.70 per capita in 1901.

As in the case of almost all local governments in the United

---

2. C. C. Williamson, *The Finances of Cleveland,* New York, Columbia University Press, 1907, pp. 2-3.

Chart III—2
COMPARATIVE GROWTH OF EXPENDITURES in 1940, 1950, and 1956, in Current, Real, and Per Capita Real Terms. The Cleveland Metropolitan Area, All Local Governments, Ohio and All States. (1940 = 100)

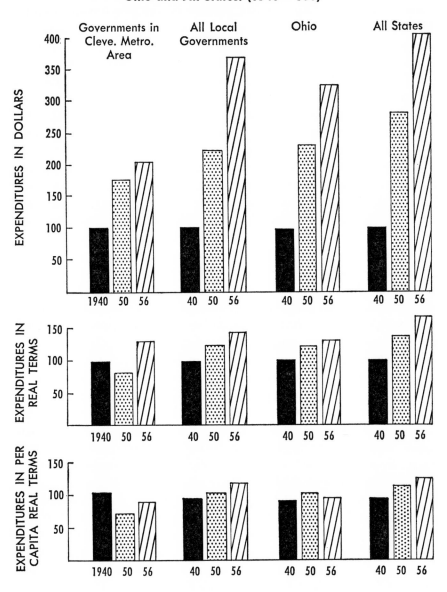

States, major reliance for tax revenues during this period was placed upon the general property base. General property taxes supplemented by special assessments were utilized almost exclusively prior to 1890. During the last decade of the nineteenth century, however, municipal public service enterprises (municipal industries as they were then called) began to contribute revenues through the utilization of user charges on water, sewerage, and the like.

There is little detailed financial information available on Cuyahoga County or any of the other local governments within the county, during this early period, apart from assessment data; but it is doubtless true that Cleveland dominated the fiscal picture as it dominated the economic picture.

Between 1900 and 1930, local government expenditures and revenues in the Cleveland Metropolitan Area increased very rapidly if Cleveland is considered as a bellwether; however, there were very broad cyclical swings. The principal changes occurred immediately after World War I and during the Great Depression. Deferred expenditures for municipal and school capital outlay accounted for a very large part of the increase in local expenditures that occurred during the 1920's. Special note should be made of the 60 per cent increase in general property tax collections between 1919 and 1920. Although complete information is not available, it appears that total expenditures and revenues reached a peak in the late 1920's and early 1930's. As the tax base was reduced during the 1930's, revenues contracted at the same time as governments tried to provide funds for the needy and unemployed. Real expenditures remained very high although they were low in current dollars. The manner in which the various governments in the Cleveland Metropolitan Area dealt with their fiscal problems during the 1930's is worthy of a separate and detailed treatment which is, however, outside the scope of the present study.

The remainder of this chapter is devoted to a description of the scope of fiscal activity in the Cleveland Metropolitan Area for the period since 1940. This is shown by means of a group of process tables for the years 1940, 1950, and 1956. For the years 1940 and 1950, brief summary tables are constructed for all the governments in the Cleveland Metropolitan Area. For the year 1956, detailed analytical tables are also included. These tables cross-classify the sources and uses of funds by the governments which comprise the Cleveland Metropolitan Area and, depending on the extent to which detailed data are available, these tables become more comprehensive and meaningful. Their particular value is that they show the interrelationships, a knowledge of which is essential to an understanding of the fiscal processes. Although they have been used for predictive purposes elsewhere, no such attempt is made here, since the several elements involved do not show stability when compared to available time series data. As Eugene Kramer pointed out in a study of the Chicago area, "the heart of the process approach is the use of a single table as an indicator of the flow of funds from revenue source to expenditure." [3]

However, in the case of governments such as municipalities and other multi-purpose jurisdictions, a large share of revenues goes into a general fund which serves a variety of expenditures, and hence it is impossible to segregate the sources of funds for many expenditures except in the most general way. Another complicating factor involves practically all governments, whether they are multi-purpose or single-purpose (like school districts); this involves the fact that there is no exact segregation of the extent to which current levies or previously accumulated cash balances are used

Table III-5—Expenditures, Receipts, Total Debt, Current Assessed Valuation, and Population, Cleveland, 1841-1901

(In Thousands of Dollars)

Year	Expenditures	Receipts	Debt	Assessed Valuation	Population
1841	20	23	20	1,509 *	7,167
1851	48 ‡	52 ‡	......	4,465 †	19,714
1861	224	237	706	18,210	48,756
1871	1,526	1,421	2,486	57,842	99,780
1881	2,025	2,581	8,067	79,586	170,263
1891	4,723	4,357	9,016	117,833	273,394
1901	8,410	6,951	17,054	196,453	392,400

* 1840, Data not available for 1841.
† 1947, Data not available for any closer year.
‡ 1852, Data not available for 1851.
Source: C. C. Williamson: *The Finances of The City of Cleveland.*

---

3. See Eugene Kramer, *The Scope of Chicago Area Fiscal Activities: A Process Approach,* Chicago Area Transportation Study No. 1 (December 10, 1957), p. 3.

for capital outlays and debt service charges as well as for current operating expenditures. In this case, however, it is possible to make reasonable approximations. Within these limitations, the data presented provide a variety of insights into the nature of the fiscal processes which are not otherwise available.

During 1956, a total of $359 millions was spent by all governments in the Cleveland Metropolitan Area for all purposes, including public service enterprises; total receipts amounted to $364 millions and as a result cash balances increased by $5 millions. Long term borrowing during the year was $60 millions and the long term debt retirement was $34 millions, or a net increase in long term debt of $26 millions. These figures are summarized in a table of cash flows and changes in long term debt for 1956.

The sources and uses of funds for all governments and for all purposes in 1956 are summarized in Table III-6. Expenditures are broken down into current and capital, and revenues into their major sources. This table permits a comparison of municipalities as well as the County and the Metropolitan Park District with the school and library districts. Expenditures on the three main public service enterprises, namely mass transit, water, and electricity, are segregated for individual consideration.

Excluding public service enterprises, municipal expenditures including the County and Metropolitan Park District amounted to 62.5 per cent of the total, school expenditures to 35.2 per cent and libraries 2.3 per cent. On the revenue side, almost identical ratios were found—municipalities receive 61.5 per cent of the total, schools 35.7 per cent, and libraries 2.8 per cent. Both of these ratios differ considerably from the state-wide ratios for schools and municipalities including the County.

The share going to municipal expenditures is considerably higher than that for the state as a whole (and perhaps higher than for other metropolitan areas in the state).

The division of expenditures among operating, capital, interest, and debt service, differs considerably among municipalities, school districts, and libraries. In 1956, a much higher proportion of school expenditures was for current purposes than was the case for municipal expenditures; the libraries spent an even greater proportion on current expenditures.

Table III-6—Receipts and Disbursements by Function and Source, All Governments, Cleveland Metropolitan Area, 1956

(In thousands of dollars. Public Service Enterprises segregated except in Totals.)

	DISBURSEMENTS						RECEIPTS							
	Current	Capital	Interest	Sub-total	Debt Retirement	TOTAL	Gen. Property Tax	Fees & Misc. Charges (Exhibit)	Other Local	State Aid	Fed. Aid	SUB-TOTAL (Revenues)	Borrowing	TOTAL
Municipal Functions														
General Government	14,804	2,588		17,392		17,392		(2,223)	2,224					
Police	16,542	830		17,372		17,372		(180)	180					
Fire	9,695	627		10,322		10,322		(2)	2					
Other Public Safety	4,467	251		4,718		4,718		(840)	840	68				
Public Health	1,845	12		1,857		1,857		(264)	264	1				
Hospital	12,201	1,479		13,680		13,680		(6,413)	6,413					
Public Welfare	21,178	40		21,218		21,218				9,291	3,147		NOT	
Streets & Highways	14,504	12,276		26,780		26,780		(580)	1,385	13,301			ALLOCATED	
Misc. Comm. Activity	12,826	14,603		27,429	497	27,926		(5,313)	6,630				BY	
Rec. & Culture	5,071	2,369		7,440		7,440	972	(822)	940	46			FUNCTION	
Land Use & Devel.	521	1,210		1,731		1,731					1,764			
Pensions	6,210			6,210		6,210				532				
Misc. & Unallocable	982	26	4,943	5,951	23,570	29,521	72,158	(1,533)	20,070	13,133	5			
Municipal Sub-Total	120,846	36,312	4,943	162,101	24,067	186,168	73,130	(18,170)	39,030	36,372	4,916	153,443	39,070	192,513
School Districts	78,511	18,147	2,047	98,704	6,227	104,933	68,553	(1,498)	5,915	14,561	176	89,205	12,392	101,597
Library Districts	6,364	658		7,022		7,022	108		6,874			6,982	0	6,982
Mass Transit	25,902	2,413	1,215	29,530	816	30,346		(32,025)				32,025	0	32,025
Water	8,406	10,772	1,315	20,493	2,568	23,061		(14,445)				14,445	9,000	23,446
Electricity	6,187	729	271	7,187	430	7,617		(7,318)				7,318		7,318
TOTAL	246,215	69,032	9,791	325,038	34,108	359,146	141,791		51,819	50,933	5,093	303,421	60,468	363,889

There are very considerable differences in the ratio of current to capital expenditures for the various municipal functions, ranging from miscellaneous commercial activity, where capital expenditures exceeded current expenditures, to those on pensions, public welfare, and public health where the ratio of capital to current expenditures was either zero or negligible. If the County is considered as a municipality, then over two thirds of total municipal capital expenditures were on streets and highways.

The sources of funds for the various classes of jurisdictions are shown in Tables III-6 to III-9. An attempt was made to go beyond the broad classification of revenues, however, by allocating wherever possible, revenue sources to the specific functions. This was done for local sources as well as for intergovernmental sources. Fees and miscellaneous charges were almost completely allocated as between functions such as hospitals, miscellaneous commercial activities, and general government. Wherever possible, special assessments were also segregated, but it was not possible to allocate them as specifically as was done in the case of fees and miscellaneous charges. In general, it did not prove feasible to allocate the bulk of municipal government revenues to specific functions, because taxes *per se* were not dedicated to specific functions. In the case of schools and libraries, the problem is somewhat simpler because of the limited number of functions which they perform. It should be noted, however, that insofar as each of these performs more than a single function, the problem of allocation becomes accordingly more difficult.

Intergovernmental revenues, in contrast to revenues from local sources, are usually dedicated to specific functions, although there are occasional exceptions, notably the Local Government Fund.[4] As shown in Tables III-6 thru III-9, intergovernmental revenues were primary revenue sources in the financing of public welfare and streets and highways as well as for schools. These tables also point out the relative importance of the public service enterprises and various other public enterprises where fees are utilized.

The relative importance of the various governments that com-

---

4. See H. Odell Waldby and Arlene A. Theuer, *Problems of Financial Management in Cuyahoga County* (Cleveland Metropolitan Services Commission, 1959) Chapter 2, *passim.*

Table III-7—Receipts and Disbursements by Function and Source, Cuyahoga County and the Cleveland Metropolitan Park District, 1956

(In thousands of dollars. Public Service Enterprises segregated except in Totals.)

	DISBURSEMENTS						RECEIPTS							
	Current	Capital	Interest	Sub-total	Debt Retirement	TOTAL	Gen. Property Tax	Fees and Misc. Charges (Exhibit)	Other Local	State Aid	Fed. Aid	SUB-TOTAL (Revenues)	Borrowing	TOTAL
Municipal Functions														
General Government	8,274	1,827		10,101		10,101		(2,170)	2,170					
Police	659	17		676		676		(79)	79					
Fire														
Other Public Safety	1,578	77		1,655		1,655		(383)	383	64				
Public Health	6			6		6								
Hospital	4,004	741		4,745		4,745								
Public Welfare	19,637	32		19,669		19,669				9,291	3,147			
Streets & Highways	3,090	3,189		6,279		6,279				4,661				
Misc. Comm. Activity	630	1,512		2,142		2,142		(210)	210					
Rec. & Culture	851	327		1,178		1,178		(61)	179	46				
Land Use & Devel.	256			256		256	972							
Pensions	784			784		784								
Misc. & Unallocable	96	0	496	592	2,056	2,648	14,778	(278)	3,871	3,422	0			
Municipal Sub-Total	39,865	7,722	496	48,083	2,056	50,139	15,750	(3,181)	6,892	17,484	3,147	43,273	8,849	52,122
School Districts														
Library Districts														
Mass Transit		37		37		37								
Water														
Electricity														
TOTAL	39,865	7,759	496	48,120	2,056	50,176	15,750		6,892	17,484	3,147	43,273	8,849	25,122

Table III-8—Receipts and Disbursements by Function and Source, Cleveland, Municipality, School District and Public Library, 1956

(In thousands of dollars. Public Service Enterprises segregated except in Totals.)

	DISBURSEMENTS						RECEIPTS							
	Current	Capital	Interest	Sub-total	Debt. Retirement	TOTAL	Gen. Property Tax	Fees & Misc. Charges (Exhibit)	Other Local	State Aid	Fed. Aid	Sub-Total (Revenues)	Borrow-ing	TOTAL
Municipal Functions														
General Government	3,496	33		3,529		3,529		(53)	54					
Police	10,958	449		11,407		11,407		(101)	101					
Fire	6,618	227		6,845		6,845		(2)	2					
Other Public Safety	2,370	165		2,535		2,535		(457)	457	4				
Public Health	1,541	12		1,553		1,553		(264)	264	1				
Hospital	5,671	713		6,384		6,384		(3,900)	3,900					
Public Welfare	1,424	8		1,432		1,432								
Streets & Highways	6,640	4,890		11,530		11,530		(580)	1,385	4,920				
Misc. Comm. Activity	8,656	7,638		16,294	497	16,791		(4,705)	4,979					
Rec. & Culture	3,152	1,313		4,465		4,465		(761)	761					
Land Use & Devel.	232	1,210		1,442		1,442					1,764			
Pensions	3,700			3,700		3,700				532				
Misc. & Unallocable	493		3,094	3,587	8,064	11,651	41,563	(0)	6,120	7,153	0			
Municipal Sub-Total	54,950	16,658	3,094	74,703	8,561	83,264	41,563	(10,832)	18,023	12,610	1,764	73,960	14,634	88,694
School Districts	39,039	2,768	24	41,831		41,831	31,625	(452)	1,884	7,503		41,012		41,012
Library Districts	4,229	19		4,248		4,248			4,525			4,525		4,525
Mass Transit	23,559	2,080	1,186	26,825	695	27,520		(29,451)				29,451		29,451
Water	6,855	8,703	1,287	16,845	2,126	18,971		(12,864)				12,864	9,006	21,870
Electricity	6,187	729	271	7,187	430	7,617		(7,318)				7,318		7,318
TOTAL	134,819	30,957	5,862	171,639	11,812	183,451	73,188		24,432	20,113	1,764	169,130	23,640	192,770

Table III-9—Receipts and Disbursements by Function and Source, All Governments Excluding Cleveland, the County, and Cleveland Metropolitan Park District, 1956

(In thousands of dollars. Public Service Enterprises segregated except in Totals.)

	DISBURSEMENTS						RECEIPTS							
	Current	Capital	Interest	Sub-Total	Debt Retirement	TOTAL	Gen. Property Tax	Fees & Misc. Charges (Exhibit)	Other Local	State Aid	Fed. Aid	Sub-Total (Revenues)	Borrowing	TOTAL
Municipal Functions														
General	3,033	738		3,761		3,761								
Police	4,925	364		5,289		5,289								
Fire	3,077	400		3,477		3,477								
Other Public Safety	519	9		528		528								
Public Health	298			298		298								
Hospital	2,526	25		2,551		2,551		(2,513)	2,513					
Public Welfare	117			117		117								
Streets & Highways	4,774	4,197		8,971		8,971				3,720				
Misc. Comm. Activity	3,540	5,453		8,993		8,993		(398)	1,441					
Rec. & Culture	1,068	729		1,797		1,797								
Land Use & Devel.	33			33		33								
Pensions	1,728			1,728		1,728								
Misc. & Unallocable	393	26	1,353	1,772	13,450	15,222	15,817	(1,255)	10,161	2,558	0			
Municipal Sub-Total	26,032	11,931	1,353	39,315	13,450	52,765	15,187	(4,166)	14,115	6,278	(5)	36,210	15,587	51,797
School Districts	39,471	15,381	2,023	56,875	6,227	63,102	36,928	(1,046)	4,031	7,058	176	48,193	12,392	60,585
Library Districts	2,134	639		2,773		2,773	108		2,348			2,457		2,457
Mass Transit	2,343	296	29	2,668	121	2,789		(2,574)				2,574		2,574
Water	1,551	2,069	28	3,648	442	4,090		(1,581)				1,581		1,581
Electricity														
TOTAL	71,531	30,316	3,443	105,279	20,240	125,519	52,853		20,495	13,336	176	91,015	27,979	118,994

prise the Cleveland Metropolitan Area may be calculated in many ways. In terms of dollars spent, the process tables provide a useful approximation of the fiscal importance of each class of jurisdiction. In accordance with the breakdown used elsewhere in this study, jurisdictions will be divided into three categories: Cuyahoga County and the Cleveland Metropolitan Park District—"County"; the City of Cleveland, Cleveland School District, and Cleveland Public Library—"Cleveland"; and all other governments excluding the "County" and "Cleveland"—"All Other." This breakdown highlights differences among the county, the central city, and the remaining governments that constitute the Cleveland Metropolitan Area. The tables show the relative importance within each category of the particular sources and uses of funds. And for "Cleveland" and "All Other" they provide a detailed breakdown among municipal, school, and library functions. In terms of aggregate fiscal activity it may be noted that 14 per cent was spent by the "County," 51 per cent by "Cleveland," and 35 per cent by "All Other" in 1956.

Slightly more than 50 per cent of the fiscal activity in the Cleveland Metropolitan Area was carried on by "Cleveland" in 1956, but if public service enterprises are excluded, the figure is reduced to somewhat less than 50 per cent. The "Cleveland" share of total fiscal activity in 1956 represents a considerable decline from 1940, and even from 1950.

The special characteristics of each category can be seen in its appropriate table. In the case of the "County," the concentration of a limited number of functions is immediately evident, as are the sources of funds. The largest single expenditure is for public welfare, the second largest for general government, with streets and highways and hospitals right behind. It may be noted that the transfer of hospitals from "Cleveland" to the "County," effected in 1958, will henceforth probably place hospital expenditures second in importance only to public welfare insofar as the "County" is concerned. In 1956, "County" functions were financed almost equally by local and intergovernmental sources with borrowing making up the remaining 15 per cent. Intergovernmental sources provided over 50 per cent of the revenues for both public welfare and street and highway expenditures. In fact, 82 per cent of all intergovernmental revenue received by the "County" was devoted to these two functions. Local sources were necessary to finance the remaining functions as well as to make up for the difference between total public welfare expenditures and total intergovernmental welfare sources. "County" public welfare expenditures were exceeded only by general government expenditures insofar as they were financed out of local sources.

Compared to the "County," "Cleveland" shows a great variety of expenditures. Unlike the "County," there are school and library expenditures, expenditures on public service enterprises, and a very large number of miscellaneous commercial activities. The greater variety of activities has resulted in a much more diversified pattern of expenditures than is true of the "County," with no single activity or group of activities dominating the picture.

Municipal current, capital, and interest expenditures exceed their school counterparts in "Cleveland." The ratio of total expenditures of the City of Cleveland to total school district expenditures is two to one. The principal state aid is for streets and highways, school expenditures and the Local Government Fund. The fiscal activities of the Cleveland Transit System and water and electric utilities are also shown in detail.

Although the City of Cleveland's expenditures are twice those of the Cleveland School District, the latter's dependence on the general property tax is far greater than that of the City. The Cleveland Public Library, not hitherto mentioned, does not use the general property tax at all, but depends on the Intangibles Tax.

The "All Other" government category contrasts with both the "County" and "Cleveland," both in amounts spent and variety of functions. If both current operating and capital expenditures are included, then the two principal expenditures of the municipalities involved were on streets and highways and on miscellaneous commercial activities (primarily sanitation and sewerage). In contrast with "Cleveland," school districts outside of Cleveland spent more for all purposes than their municipal counterparts. The great dependency on the general property tax by the school districts as contrasted with the municipalities is evident throughout the Cleveland Metropolitan Area.

Changes in Expenditures 1940-1956

As happened elsewhere in the United States between 1940 and 1956, current operating expenditures in the Cleveland Metropolitan Area rose by a larger absolute amount but by a smaller percentage than capital expenditures. While the pattern of expenditures, as measured by the relative share of current operating expenditures devoted to each function, was not the same in 1950 as in 1940, there were no major differences between the 1950 and 1956 patterns.

At best the term "current operating expenditures" (or "operating expenditures" or "current expenditures") is an ambiguous one. In principle these involved expenditures that do not result in a new fixed governmental asset or the major repair of an old one. Unfortunately, the dividing line between maintenance, which is an operating expenditure, and a major repair is often difficult to define in practice. Because the Cleveland Metropolitan Area embraces a single county in a single state and because detailed financial reports were available in which distinction was made between current and capital expenditures, the latter were more consistently treated than would ordinarily be the case. Nevertheless, any analysis of governmental expenditure depends ultimately on the manner of reporting, which in turn involves differences in judgment by a great number of officials with different backgrounds. It is felt, however, that while differences in reporting are important in the case of the individual function in the individual government, they are not important in the aggregate.

In 1956, current operating expenditures were 76.0 per cent of total expenditures; in 1950, they were 78.4 per cent of the total, and in 1940 78.6 per cent. Even in the peak years of locally financed capital activity, 1954 and 1955, the proportion did not fall to less than 72.4 per cent of the total. Although there is no such thing as a normal ratio between operating and total expenditures, the figure of 76.0 per cent in 1956 does not seem unduly high or low. There are, of course, important differences between governments, but this problem will be considered in more detail in Chapter V. There is some indication that this ratio of current operating to total expenditures will tend to fall, as both capital outlays and interest charges will rise in the future.

If operating expenditures by function are compared, then a more complete picture may be drawn. Operating expenditures grew from $69.3 millions in 1940 to $205.7 millions in 1956.[5] The growth occurred not only in the aggregate, but also in every single functional category herein considered, although it was not of uniform rate or amount as between functions.

As a result of this growth, the pattern of operating expenditures shown in Table III-10 emerges. Of the $205.7 millions spent on operating expenditures in 1956, 38.2 per cent was spent by school districts; the sixty-two municipalities, Cuyahoga County, the Cleveland Metropolitan Park District, and all the libraries accounted for the remaining 61.2 per cent. No single other function bulks large in expenditure terms compared with the schools. The next largest category, welfare, made up only 10.3 per cent of total expenditures, or a little more than one-fourth that of schools. This is considerably different from 1940 when local welfare expenditures were almost two thirds of school operating expenditures. In each year since 1940 for which detailed data have been collected, school and welfare expenditures amounted to less than 50 per cent of the total operating budgets of all the jurisdictions that comprise the Cleveland Metropolitan Area. Comparing 1956 to 1940, the increase in the share of school expenditures almost equals the decline in the share of welfare expenditures.

A number of other expenditure categories of approximately equal magnitude follow welfare expenditures in importance; these include police, general government, hospitals, streets and highways, and miscellaneous commercial activities. Although they differ slightly in their relative order, only schools, miscellaneous commercial activities, and pensions significantly increased their share of total operating expenditures in 1956 as compared to 1940.

These expenditures are not, of course, evenly distributed among governments. While some governments show great stability over time in the share devoted to individual functions, others do not. In almost all instances, these latter cases occurred as a result of a

---

5. See Table III-10.

Table III-10—Aggregate and Per Capita Expenditures by Purpose in Current Dollars, All Governments, Cleveland Metropolitan Area, 1940, 1950, and 1956

EXPENDITURE CATEGORY	AGGREGATE EXPENDITURES (In Thousands of Current Dollars)			PER CAPITA EXPENDITURES (In Current Dollars)			DISTRIBUTION (Per Cent)		
	1940	1950	1956	1940	1950	1956	1940	1950	1956
Total Current Operating	69,345	118,828	205,721	56.97	85.52	130.16	78.60	78.40	76.00
County, Municipalities & Metropolitan Park District	46,343	73,710	120,846	38.07	53.05	76.51	66.83	62.03	58.75
General Government	5,768	8,700	14,804	4.74	6.26	9.37	8.32	7.32	7.19
Police	5,693	10,918	16,542	4.68	7.86	10.47	8.21	9.19	8.04
Fire	3,585	6,071	9,695	2.95	4.37	6.13	5.17	5.11	4.72
Other Public Safety	947	2,675	4,467	.78	1.93	2.83	1.37	2.26	2.17
Public Health	646	1,455	1,845	.53	1.05	1.17	.93	1.23	.90
Hospital	4,605	5,774	12,201	3.78	4.16	7.72	6.64	4.86	5.93
Public Welfare	13,319	13,089	21,178	10.94	9.42	13.40	19.21	11.02	10.30
Streets & Highways	6,437	9,843	14,504	5.29	7.08	9.18	9.28	8.28	7.05
Misc. Comm. Activity	2,704	8,053	12,826	2.22	5.80	8.11	3.90	6.77	6.24
Recreation & Culture	1,027	3,082	5,071	.84	2.22	3.21	1.48	2.59	2.47
Land Use & Development	35	401	521	0.03	0.29	0.33	0.05	0.34	.25
Misc. & Unallocable	497	377	982	0.89	2.35	3.93	1.56	2.75	2.98
Pensions	1,080	3,272	6,210	0.41	0.27	0.67	0.72	0.32	.52
School Districts	20,771	40,625	78,511	17.06	29.24	49.67	29.95	34.19	38.16
Library Districts	2,231	4,492	6,364	1.83	3.23	4.03	3.22	3.78	3.09
Total Interest Payments	9,426	5,415	9,791	7.74	3.90	6.19	10.70	3.60	3.60
Total Capital Outlays	9,414	27,396	55,118	7.73	19.71	34.87	10.60	18.10	20.40
Total Expenditures	88,184	151,639	270,630	72.45	109.13	171.22	100.0	100.0	100.0

change in the nature of the community, from a small village to a city, or from a residential to an industrial community (such as Brook Park or Brooklyn), or of the assumption of a new function (such as the introduction of a full-time Fire Department in Middleburg Heights), or of a major expansion of an old function (such as the Lakewood Hospital). Stability in the percentage devoted to each function was, in fact, characteristic of all municipalities in the Cleveland Metropolitan Area from 1950 through 1956.

The distribution of expenditures by functions, as noted in Table III-10, does not take into account either the changes in cost of providing government services (i.e., the governments' cost of living), or the changes in population. The picture of expenditures in constant dollars that emerges function by function is quite different from that in current dollars.[6] In aggregate terms, the level of operating expenditures as a percentage of 1956 expenditures declined from 81.4 per cent in 1940 to 73.4 per cent in 1950. Almost all the decrease is, however, due to the decline in welfare expenditures, which declined from 151.8 per cent of its 1956 level, in 1940, to 78.6 per cent of that level, in 1950.

The decrease of $16.4 millions in 1956 dollars between 1940 and 1950 for all operating expenditures was mainly the result of a decrease of $15.5 millions in welfare expenditures. Hospital expenditures also decreased, as did expenditures for general government and streets and highways. Other expenditures remained constant, such as school district expenditures, or rose slightly.

From 1950 to 1956, however, the general movement of expenditures was upward, with the largest single absolute increase in school operating expenditures, followed by a large increase in welfare expenditures. Public health expenditures alone showed no upward movement.

If account is taken of the growth in population as well as the changes in the cost of providing particular government services as shown in Table III-11, there was a general decline in per capita real expenditures from 1940 to 1950. The decline was pervasive, involving all the more highly developed older functions. Newer activities which fall into the Miscellaneous Commercial Activity,

---

6. See Table III-11.

Table III-11—Aggregate and Per Capita Expenditures by Purpose in 1956 Dollars, All Governments, Cleveland Metropolitan Area, 1940, 1950 and 1956

Expenditure Category	Aggregate Expenditures					Per Capita Expenditures				
	IN THOUSANDS OF 1956 DOLLARS			AS PER CENT OF 1956		IN 1956 DOLLARS			AS PER CENT OF 1956	
	1940	1950	1956	1940	1950	1940	1950	1956	1940	1950
Total Current Operating	167,468	151,030	205,721	81.4%	73.4%	137.58	108.70	130.16	105.7%	83.5%
County, Municipalities & Metropolitan Park Districts	111,918	93,685	120,846	92.6	77.5	91.94	67.43	76.51	120.2	88.1
General Government	13,930	11,058	14,804	94.1	74.7	11.45	7.96	9.37	122.2	85.0
Police	13,749	13,877	16,542	83.1	83.9	11.30	9.99	10.47	107.9	95.4
Fire	8,658	7,716	9,695	89.3	79.6	7.12	5.55	6.13	116.2	90.5
Other Public Safety	2,287	3,400	4,467	51.2	76.1	1.88	2.45	2.83	66.4	86.6
Public Health	1,560	1,849	1,845	84.6	100.2	1.28	1.33	1.17	109.4	113.7
Hospital	11,121	7,339	12,201	91.1	60.2	9.13	5.29	7.72	118.3	68.5
Public Welfare	32,156	16,636	21,178	151.8	78.6	26.42	11.97	13.40	197.2	89.3
Streets & Highways	15,545	12,510	14,504	107.2	86.3	12.78	9.00	9.18	139.2	98.0
Misc. Comm. Activity	6,530	10,235	12,826	50.9	79.8	5.36	7.37	8.11	66.1	90.9
Recreation & Culture	2,480	3,917	5,071	48.9	77.2	2.03	2.82	3.21	63.2	87.9
Land Use Development	85	510	521	16.3	97.9	.07	.37	0.33	21.2	112.1
Pensions	2,608	4,159	6,210	42.0	67.0	2.15	2.99	3.93	54.7	76.1
Misc. & Unallocable	1,200	479	982	122.2	48.8	.99	.34	0.68	147.8	50.7
School Districts	50,162	51,636	78,511	63.9	65.8	41.20	37.16	49.67	82.9	74.8
Library Districts	5,388	5,709	6,364	84.7	89.7	4.42	4.11	4.03	109.7	102.0
Total Interest Payments	22,764	6,882	9,791	232.5	70.3	18.69	4.96	6.19	301.9	80.1
Total Capital Outlays	22,735	34,820	55,118	41.2	63.2	18.67	25.05	34.87	53.5	71.8
Total Expenditures	212,964	192,733	270,630	78.7	71.2	174.97	138.70	171.23	102.2	81.0

Recreation and Culture, and other Public Safety and Pension Categories moved against the trend from 1940 to 1950.

From 1950 to 1956, there was a general upward trend in per capita real expenditures, both in the aggregate and by functions. The only exceptions were public health, land use and development, and operating expenditures of libraries. Again these changes are summarized in Table III-11.

In 1940, total operating expenditures were divided as follows: 20.2 per cent by the County and Cleveland Metropolitan Park District; 46.7 per cent by municipalities; 29.9 per cent by the school districts; and 3.2 per cent by the library district. The percentage of Cuyahoga County, after dipping during the intervening years, reached 19.4 per cent, in 1956. City operating expenditures declined from 46.7 per cent of the total, in 1940, to 39.4 per cent, in 1956. Operating expenditures of school districts rose from 29.9 per cent, in 1940, to 38.2 per cent of a much larger total, in 1956.

The growth of government by class is shown in Table III-12. Although the growth was pervasive it was not uniform. Some governments grew absolutely and/or relatively more rapidly than their neighbors. The breakdown and fiscal activity by individual government will be considered in Chapters IV-VII.

Conclusion

The growth in aggregate fiscal activity since 1940 is the outstanding development which must be taken into account in any analysis of government finance within this period. Nevertheless, the growth was not uniform as between levels of government. Moreover, if both population and price changes are taken into account, the picture of fiscal activity on the state and local levels (including that of the Cleveland Metropolitan Area) is altered in magnitude and in some instances reverse trends are indicated. Thus, the increase in expenditure from 1940 to 1956 before adjustment may be transformed into a decrease after correcting for changes in population and prices. These developments are described in Chapter IV and subsequent chapters.

Table III-12—Expenditures of All Governments, Cleveland Metropolitan Area; Including and Excluding City of Cleveland, Cleveland Board of Education and Cleveland Public Library, 1940, 1950, 1956

(In Thousands of Dollars)

YEAR	GOVERNMENTAL UNIT	CURRENT OPERATING			INTEREST			CAPITAL			TOTAL		
		Total	Cleveland	Excluding Cleveland	Total	Cleveland	Excluding Cleveland	Total	Cleveland	Excluding Cleveland	Total	Cleveland	Excluding Cleveland
1940	County & Metropolitan Park District	13,973	—	13,973	1,688	—	1,688	2,347	—	2,347	18,008	—	18,008
	Cities, Villages & Townships	32,371	27,042	5,329	6,359	4,900	1,460	6,290	5,714	576	45,020	37,655	7,365
	School Districts	20,771	13,906	6,864	1,378	423	955	765	541	224	22,913	14,870	8,044
	Library Districts	2,231	1,878	393	1	0	1	11	6	5	2,243	1,844	399
	Total	69,345	42,786	26,559	9,426	5,323	4,104	9,414	6,261	3,153	88,184	54,369	33,816
1950	County & Metropolitan Park District	18,937	—	18,937	644	—	644	4,029	—	4,029	23,610	—	23,610
	Cities, Villages & Townships	54,775	41,596	13,179	4,025	3,184	841	15,276	10,317	4,959	74,075	55,097	18,978
	School Districts	40,625	24,094	16,531	746	80	666	7,705	1,371	6,334	49,076	25,545	23,531
	Library Districts	4,492	3,391	1,101	0	0	0	386	41	345	4,878	3,432	1,446
	Total	118,828	69,081	49,747	5,415	3,264	2,151	27,396	11,729	15,667	151,639	84,074	67,565
1956	County & Metropolitan Park District	39,865	—	39,865	496	—	496	7,722	—	7,722	48,083	—	48,083
	Cities, Villages & Townships	80,982	54,950	26,032	7,248	5,838	1,410	28,590	16,652	11,938	116,820	77,440	39,380
	School Districts	78,511	39,039	39,471	2,047	24	2,023	18,149	2,768	15,381	98,705	41,831	56,874
	Library Districts	6,364	4,229	2,135	0	0	0	658	19	639	7,021	4,248	2,773
	Total	205,721	98,218	107,503	9,791	5,862	3,929	55,118	19,439	35,679	270,630	123,519	147,111

Note: Because of rounding, detail may not add to total.

Table III-13—Per Cent Distribution of Expenditures and Revenues by Type of Government, Cleveland Metropolitan Area, 1940, 1950, 1956

YEAR	GOVERNMENTAL UNIT	EXPENDITURES				REVENUES		
		Current Operating	Interest	Capital	Total	Local	Intergovern-mental Revenue	Total
1940	County & Metropolitan Park District	20.2	17.9	25.0	20.4	18.2	21.3	18.9
	Cities, Villages & Townships	46.7	67.5	66.8	51.1	48.2	44.8	47.3
	School Districts	29.9	14.6	8.1	26.0	30.1	33.9	31.1
	Library Districts	3.2	0.0	0.1	2.5	3.5	0.0	2.7
	Total	100.0	100.0	100.0	100.0	100.0	100.0	100.0
1950	County & Metropolitan Park District	15.9	11.9	14.7	15.6	13.4	28.6	16.7
	Cities, Villages & Townships	46.1	74.3	55.8	48.9	52.4	42.8	50.3
	School Districts	34.2	13.8	28.1	32.4	30.4	28.6	30.0
	Library Districts	3.8	0.0	1.4	3.1	3.8	0.0	3.0
	Total	100.0	100.0	100.0	100.0	100.0	100.0	100.0
1956	County & Metropolitan Park District	19.4	5.1	14.0	17.8	11.7	36.8	17.4
	Cities, Villages & Townships	39.4	74.0	51.9	43.2	46.2	37.0	44.1
	School Districts	38.2	20.9	32.9	36.5	38.5	26.2	35.7
	Library Districts	3.0	0.0	1.2	2.5	3.6	0.0	2.8
	Total	100.0	100.0	100.0	100.0	100.0	100.0	100.0

IV

Current Operating
Expenditures
in the Cleveland
Metropolitan Area

A̲s IN THE CASE OF MOST OTHER METROPOLITAN
areas, expenditures in the Cleveland Metropolitan Area (regardless
of their classification) show great variation among governments.
The first major purpose of this chapter is to show the pattern of
local operating expenditures in cross-section for the year 1956, and
in terms of the changes that occurred between 1950 and 1956.
Expenditures are analyzed primarily in total and per capita terms
for the various kinds of governments. In the case of the municipalities, this involves a further functional breakdown of operating
expenditure by purpose. The second major purpose of this chapter
is to explain the observed variations in expenditures, both in cross-
section and over time, with the emphasis on the former.

The obvious variation in the pattern of local government finances is in total expenditures. If governments are ranked in descending order, then at the top would be the City of Cleveland, which in 1956 spent $128.3 millions excluding debt retirement, and at the other end of the scale would be Riveredge Township, which spent nothing that same year. The remaining governments fall into definite categories between these two extremes.

If only operating expenditures are considered (and that is the major emphasis of this chapter) then the range is reduced, but there is still very considerable variation between governments, as is shown in Tables IV-20 (municipalities and county), IV-21 (schools), and 1V-22 (libraries). The variation exists regardless of the class of government considered. Finally, it might be noted that Cuyahoga County unquestionably spends far more for operating purposes than any of the other eighty-seven counties in the state.

Although no attempt will be made to analyze in detail the geographical distribution of total operating expenditures within the Cleveland Metropolitan Area, their heavy concentration in the core area should at least be noted. The largest single operating expenditure of the County—welfare—also happens to be concentrated in the core area. However, the overwhelming financial dominance of the core area, so obvious in the 1940 and 1950 data, has been distinctly modified by 1956, due to increased population growth of the outlying areas within the boundaries of the area.

Operating Expenditures

Operating expenditures are incurred for a variety of purposes. In accordance with Ohio practice and the suggested classifications of the Bureau of the Census, municipal operating expenditures have been broken down into the following categories: General Government (executive, legislative, and judicial functions); Police; Fire; Other Public Safety; Hospital; Public Welfare; Streets and Highways; Miscellaneous Commercial Activity (sewerage, rubbish disposal); Recreation and Culture; Land Use and Development; Pensions (reflecting mainly Police and Fire expenditures); Public Health; Miscellaneous and Unallocable. The inclusion of sanitation expenditures in the Miscellaneous Commercial Activity category

Table IV-1—Per Cent Distribution of Current Operating Expenditures by Purpose; County and Municipal Governments, Cleveland Metropolitan Area, 1956

Governmental Unit	General Govt.	Police	Fire	Other Public Safety	Hospital	Public Welfare	Streets & Highways	Misc. Comm. Activity	Recreation & Culture	Land Use & Development	Pensions	Misc. & Unallocable	Total
Cuyahoga County	21.2	1.7	0.0	4.0	10.3	50.3	7.9	1.6	.1	.1	2.0	2.5	100.0
Cities													
Bay Village	12.4	14.3	11.1	3.2	0.0	0.0	26.1	16.1	7.6	.4	6.7	1.2	100.0
Bedford	8.6	13.1	.9	2.5	27.5	.3	16.9	17.5	3.1	0.0	7.8	1.2	100.0
Berea	10.5	15.3	11.9	2.5	3.3	0.0	19.7	21.6	6.9	.4	5.5	1.1	100.0
Brooklyn	21.4	20.8	18.1	.8	0.0	0.0	15.6	11.5	.7	.1	7.9	1.9	100.0
Cleveland	6.4	19.9	12.0	4.3	10.3	2.6	12.1	15.8	5.7	.4	6.7	.9	100.0
Cleveland Heights	11.2	16.2	12.4	1.4	0.0	.6	16.1	22.6	9.4	.1	6.6	1.6	100.0
East Cleveland	9.3	27.2	14.4	1.4	0.0	.7	15.4	16.5	4.6	.2	7.3	1.2	100.0
Euclid	11.2	20.0	12.8	1.9	0.0	.5	20.0	14.0	6.7	.1	10.6	1.2	100.0
Fairview Park	10.1	17.9	12.3	1.2	0.0	0.0	26.0	17.9	6.0	0.0	6.0	1.6	100.0
Garfield Heights	14.6	20.7	17.7	2.3	0.0	.4	20.7	13.2	0.0	.1	6.7	1.9	100.0
Lakewood	5.1	9.4	7.9	.5	46.8	.7	10.0	11.0	2.4	0.0	4.7	.4	100.0
Lyndhurst	14.0	20.1	11.7	3.6	0.0	0.0	20.7	14.1	8.6	0.0	2.3	3.7	100.0
Maple Heights	13.5	22.3	14.0	.3	0.0	1.4	19.0	20.5	1.6	.1	4.9	1.2	100.0
Mayfield Heights	17.0	21.9	11.7	2.1	0.0	0.0	24.1	10.9	1.4	.1	6.0	3.7	100.0
North Olmsted	11.3	16.4	10.2	3.7	5.1	0.0	26.9	8.7	4.8	0.0	10.3	1.6	100.0
Parma	17.1	20.3	13.9	4.6	0.0	1.9	27.5	4.4	2.8	0.0	3.5	3.1	100.0
Rocky River	9.9	14.2	11.1	1.3	0.0	0.0	34.6	16.4	4.4	0.0	6.4	1.0	100.0
Shaker Heights	12.5	18.2	17.0	1.9	0.0	.2	17.5	15.1	4.6	.2	9.1	2.7	100.0
South Euclid	13.3	19.9	15.8	2.4	0.0	0.0	17.4	14.7	5.3	.4	7.0	2.1	100.0
University Heights	15.4	23.9	20.2	2.2	0.0	0.0	14.7	13.6	.8	.2	6.3	1.3	100.0

Mean	100.0	NC	6.6	NC	4.4	14.8	20.0	NC	NC	2.2	12.8	18.6	12.2
Median	100.0	NC	6.6	NC	4.6	14.9	19.3	NC	NC	2.2	12.4	19.9	11.9
Villages													
Beachwood	100.0	3.0	.7	.6	5.9	13.5	23.1	0.0	0.0	7.2	2.4	27.2	15.6
Bedford Heights	100.0	2.6	.9	0.0	1.7	4.9	27.2	0.0	0.0	2.4	3.5	27.9	27.4
Bentleyville	100.0	.9	0.0	0.0	0.0	0.0	9.2	0.0	0.0	.9	6.4	58.7	22.9
Bratenahl	100.0	3.5	3.4	.1	4.5	6.4	21.8	0.0	0.0	.5	5.3	45.5	8.8
Brecksville	100.0	1.8	6.0	0.0	3.7	8.9	25.5	0.0	0.0	3.4	6.5	28.5	14.8
Broadview Heights	100.0	5.3	0.0	0.0	0.0	13.3	19.4	0.0	0.0	8.1	4.3	33.0	16.4
Brooklyn Heights	100.0	7.0	2.5	.5	3.9	6.8	17.0	0.0	0.0	1.8	4.8	23.4	31.7
Brook Park	100.0	1.9	9.9	.1	1.9	10.0	11.3	0.0	11.7	2.3	18.5	22.1	9.1
Chagrin Falls	100.0	2.2	1.2	1.0	1.0	28.9	22.6	0.0	0.0	1.2	2.8	26.0	12.8
Cuyahoga Heights	100.0	1.7	14.1	0.0	.2	2.8	6.7	0.0	0.0	2.1	33.2	22.3	15.1
Gates Mills	100.0	6.1	0.0	.7	6.6	5.0	31.7	0.0	0.0	1.4	1.9	29.4	16.7
Glenwillow	100.0	0.0	0.0	0.0	0.0	0.0	11.3	0.0	0.0	5.7	11.3	11.3	58.5
Highland Heights	100.0	1.3	0.0	.3	1.0	.8	29.0	0.0	0.0	4.8	5.3	28.0	28.7
Hunting Valley	100.0	1.7	2.9	.1	.9	0.0	34.9	0.0	0.0	.1	1.4	40.9	16.6
Independence	100.0	7.3	4.2	.1	1.1	2.7	38.2	0.0	0.0	1.7	2.4	29.1	13.2
Linndale	100.0	6.3	0.0	0.0	0.0	4.2	54.7	0.0	0.0	0.0	0.0	11.6	23.2
Mayfield	100.0	1.3	0.0	.2	0.0	3.8	16.5	0.0	0.0	8.5	5.6	40.4	23.1
Middleburg Heights	100.0	4.4	8.5	0.0	.6	8.7	13.4	0.0	8.9	3.0	16.1	21.5	13.1
Moreland Hills	100.0	2.8	2.9	.3	.1	1.7	24.9	0.0	0.0	4.9	2.0	40.8	18.9
Newburgh Heights	100.0	2.2	4.2	0.0	0.0	11.1	25.4	0.0	0.0	.7	3.4	29.2	23.2
North Randall	100.0	1.3	0.0	0.0	0.0	3.6	25.5	0.0	0.0	1.7	3.2	40.9	22.9
North Royalton	100.0	6.0	1.0	0.0	1.0	14.3	20.4	0.0	0.0	5.7	3.6	34.5	12.9
Oakwood	100.0	2.3	0.0	.6	0.0	2.5	39.2	0.0	0.0	5.5	4.1	25.8	19.3
Olmsted Falls	100.0	1.1	.9	.2	5.4	11.7	26.7	0.0	6.3	1.7	7.6	23.6	14.3

(Continued on next page)

Table IV-1 (Continued)

Governmental Unit	General Govt.	Police	Fire	Other Public Safety	Hospital	Public Welfare	Streets & Highways	Misc. Comm. Activity	Recreation & Culture	Land Use & Development	Pensions	Misc. & Unallocable	Total
Orange	13.3	56.1	0.0	.5	0.0	0.0	25.2	0.0	0.0	1.6	.8	1.6	100.0
Parkview	31.7	34.7	9.1	2.1	0.0	0.0	9.7	6.9	1.2	0.0	.3	3.3	100.0
Parma Heights	16.7	23.5	8.8	4.0	0.0	0.0	17.8	13.4	1.4	0.0	5.9	8.2	100.0
Pepper Pike	18.9	29.1	3.2	1.3	0.0	0.0	20.6	18.8	0.0	0.0	5.9	1.4	100.0
Richmond Heights	25.1	43.5	5.6	2.3	0.0	0.0	12.3	4.3	0.0	1.1	3.2	1.8	100.0
Seven Hills	14.0	32.7	3.3	10.7	0.0	0.0	18.4	8.7	5.6	.1	3.6	2.3	100.0
Solon	20.1	27.0	5.1	5.1	0.0	0.0	27.0	5.5	.5	2.3	5.6	.9	100.0
Strongsville	15.7	31.7	4.1	2.2	6.0	0.0	28.5	1.9	3.0	0.0	4.2	2.1	100.0
Valley View	30.8	38.8	7.8	1.1	0.0	0.0	9.3	5.8	.4	.7	0.0	3.5	100.0
Walton Hills	16.4	44.0	3.3	1.2	0.0	0.0	31.1	3.9	0.0	0.0	0.0	.2	100.0
Warrensville Heights	14.9	22.7	15.9	3.9	0.0	0.0	26.0	12.3	0.0	.4	1.6	1.6	100.0
Westlake	11.3	28.6	9.8	3.9	0.0	0.0	19.3	9.3	5.0	0.0	5.6	6.2	100.0
West View	17.5	27.5	5.8	5.0	7.9	0.0	18.3	11.7	0.0	0.0	.4	5.0	100.0
Woodmere	18.2	54.2	5.9	2.0	0.0	0.0	10.8	3.0	0.0	.5	3.0	2.0	100.0
Mean	19.7	32.0	6.4	N C	N C	N C	22.4	7.1	N C	N C	N C	N C	100.0
Median	16.7	29.1	5.2	N C	N C	N C	22.2	6.6	N C	N C	N C	N C	100.0
Townships													
Chagrin Falls	47.7	0.0	3.4	.6	0.0	0.0	46.0	1.1	0.0	0.0	0.0	1.1	100.0
Olmsted	16.0	30.3	10.7	0.0	23.4	0.0	.8	13.1	0.0	1.6	1.6	.8	100.0
Riveredge	0.0	0.0	0.0	0.0	0.0	0.0	0.0	0.0	0.0	0.0	0.0	0.0	0.0
Warrensville	40.5	23.8	0.0	0.0	0.0	0.0	16.7	16.7	0.0	0.0	0.0	7.1	100.0

NC—Not Computed. 0.0 less than 0.05 per cent, or none recorded.

represents the only major departure from usual practices, but differences in financing and the lack of universality of the function make the Ohio classification more appropriate than that of the Bureau of the Census.

While there is a bewildering diversity of local municipal expenditures on individual functions, with some municipalities maintaining services that others do not, definite patterns and regularities do emerge if operating expenditures are distributed on a percentage basis by municipality. Distinctly different patterns emerge in the case of cities, on the one hand, and in the case of villages, on the other. As can be seen in Table IV-1 exceptions emerge in both cases; but they are generally explicable by the existence of a publicly supported hospital (as in Bedford and Lakewood), in the cities, and the existence of a full-time fire department, and the provision of public rubbish and garbage collection in the villages.

As would be expected, the importance of individual functions diminishes as the number of functions increases. Thus, in 1956, using the unweighted mean, 78.4 per cent of city operating expenditures were concentrated on five functions: streets and highways, police, miscellaneous commercial activity, fire, and general government; 74.1 per cent of village operating expenditures were on three functions: police, streets and highways, and general government. While a full-time fire department and such miscellaneous commercial activities as rubbish and garbage collection are characteristic of cities in the Cleveland Metropolitan Area, they are exceptions in the villages. Stability of the percentage distribution of operating expenditures over time is characteristic of a large proportion of municipalities. Between 1940 and 1956, the addition of new functions or changes in the importance of existing functions are immediately noticeable in only a limited number of governments. But the impression has been gained from a detailed study of these patterns over time that city and village patterns tend to grow more similar as governments change their functions with increased size.

The pattern of county expenditures stands in contrast to municipalities. The special character of the county in Ohio is reflected in the relative importance of public welfare expenditures in its operating budget. In 1956, welfare expenditures made up slightly more than 50 per cent of Cuyahoga County's operating budget as compared with the next largest case, Cleveland, which devoted 2.6 per cent of its operating budget to it. The high percentage of operating expenditures devoted to general government by the County is a positive reflection of its various executive and judicial functions, rather than of the small amount devoted to other purposes, as is true in the case of every other government where general government expenditures are high.

Although it would be of considerable interest, no attempt has been made to depict these budgetary patterns geographically because of the complexities involved.

Per Capita Operating Expenditures

That the large differences in total operating expenditures are primarily the result of population and assessed valuation has usually been assumed and, as will be shown later in this study, is generally the case. The factors that determine the total operating expenditures will be considered in detail for all functions and for the important individual functions—general government, police, fire, and streets and highways. Miscellaneous commercial activity is excluded because of its heterogeneous nature.

The aggregate expenditure on any individual function or for all functions does not measure the amount of expenditure per person or per unit of property. Totals inevitably hide vast differences in the amount of services per person or per student or per unit of property. The question of the relationship between the amount of money spent and differences in service levels is one of great importance. Expenditures per capita and per $1,000 of assessed valuation provide a preliminary or very first approximation for an exact analysis of service levels. However, if broad gauge comparisons of service levels are desirable, then the expenditure data can prove very useful.

The distribution of school operating expenditures has been presented mainly on the basis of students in average daily membership, rather than on a per capita basis, because of the obvious advantages of the former. However, estimates of school district population have been formulated to permit the computation of the per capita costs of education—figures comparable to the per capita costs of municipal services. The operating expenditures of both municipalities and school districts have also been computed on the basis of assessed valuation.

The computation and interpretation of per capita costs and expenditures per $1,000 of assessed valuation are facilitated by two sets of circumstances for which the Cleveland Metropolitan Area is especially fortunate. The first is the existence of the Cleveland Real Property Inventory, which has formulated population estimates based on an annual census of occupied family units by municipality for *all* inter-census years. The availability of these data removes the problem of dependence on Census Year data, which in the case of rapidly growing governments with rapidly growing problems may be virtually obsolete by the time they are utilized. The second fortunate circumstance is the existence of county-wide assessment, which is mandatory under Ohio law. Although this does not iron out all the problems in assessment, as shown in Chapter VI and in *Problems in Financial Management in Cuyahoga County*,[1] it does permit interjurisdictional comparison of property values, something which would be almost impossible otherwise. The calculated figures of expenditures per $1,000 assessed valuation for Cuyahoga County governments are directly comparable with each other. Unfortunately, they are not necessarily comparable with those of other governments in other neighboring counties because of different assessment ratios.

The picture that emerges from Table IV-2 (showing per capita municipal operating expenditures) is that of the central area having higher per capita expenditures than the outer ring with the exception of the three industrial enclaves and the very wealthy communities of Hunting Valley, Gates Mills, and Bratenahl. Low-expenditure communities tend to be located next to other low-expenditure communities, and high-expenditure communities next to high-expenditure communities.

In Map IV-2 expenditures per student in average daily member-

---

1. *Op. Cit.*

Table IV-2—Per Capita Current Operating Expenditures by Purpose; County and Municipal Governments, Cleveland Metropolitan Area, 1956

(In Dollars)

Governmental Unit	General Govt.	Police	Fire	Other Public Safety	Hospital	Public Welfare	Streets & Highways	Misc. Comm. Activity	Recreation & Culture	Land Use & Development	Pensions	Misc. & Unallocable	Total Current Expenditures
Cuyahoga County	5.20	0.40	0.00	1.00	2.50	12.40	2.00	0.40	0.00	0.20	0.50	0.10	24.70
Cities													
Bay Village	4.60	5.30	4.10	1.20	0.00	0.00	9.60	5.90	2.80	0.20	2.40	0.40	36.80
Bedford	5.20	8.00	0.60	1.50	16.70	0.20	10.30	10.70	1.90	0.00	4.80	0.70	60.80
Berea	4.90	7.20	5.60	1.20	1.60	0.00	9.20	10.10	3.20	0.20	2.60	0.50	46.80
Brooklyn	8.70	8.40	7.30	0.30	0.00	0.00	6.30	4.70	0.30	0.00	3.20	0.80	40.40
Cleveland	3.80	11.80	7.10	2.60	6.10	1.50	7.20	9.30	3.40	0.30	4.00	0.50	59.30
Cleveland Heights	5.00	7.30	5.60	0.60	0.00	0.30	7.20	10.10	4.20	0.00	3.00	0.70	44.80
East Cleveland	3.30	9.50	5.00	0.50	0.00	0.30	5.40	5.80	1.60	0.10	2.50	0.40	34.90
Euclid	3.70	6.60	4.30	0.60	0.00	0.20	6.60	4.60	2.20	0.00	3.50	0.40	33.20
Fairview Park	4.00	7.10	4.90	0.50	0.00	0.00	10.30	7.10	2.40	0.00	2.40	0.60	39.70
Garfield Heights	2.80	4.00	3.40	0.40	0.00	0.10	4.00	2.50	0.00	0.00	1.30	0.40	19.10
Lakewood	3.50	6.40	5.40	0.40	32.00	0.50	6.80	7.50	1.60	0.00	3.20	0.30	68.40
Lyndhurst	3.60	5.20	3.00	0.90	0.00	0.00	5.40	3.70	2.20	0.00	0.60	1.00	25.90
Maple Heights	3.30	5.50	3.50	0.10	0.00	0.30	4.70	5.10	0.40	0.00	1.20	0.30	24.70
Mayfield Heights	5.00	6.40	3.40	0.60	0.00	0.00	7.00	3.20	0.40	0.00	1.80	1.10	29.20
North Olmsted	3.70	5.40	3.40	1.20	1.70	0.00	8.80	2.90	1.60	0.00	3.40	0.50	32.80
Parma	4.20	5.00	3.40	1.10	0.00	0.50	6.70	1.10	0.70	0.00	2.20	0.80	25.60
Rocky River	5.20	7.40	5.80	0.70	0.00	0.00	18.10	8.50	2.30	0.00	3.30	0.50	52.20
Shaker Heights	7.30	10.60	9.90	1.10	0.00	0.10	10.20	8.80	2.70	0.10	5.30	1.60	58.10
South Euclid	4.50	6.70	5.30	0.80	0.00	0.00	5.80	4.90	1.80	0.10	2.30	0.70	33.50
University Heights	5.50	8.50	7.20	0.80	0.00	0.00	5.20	4.80	0.30	0.10	2.20	0.50	35.60

Mean	4.60	7.10	4.90	0.90	2.90	0.20	7.70	6.10	1.80	0.10	2.80	0.60	40.00
Median	4.30	6.90	5.00	0.80	6.10	0.20	6.90	5.40	1.80	NC	2.60	0.50	36.20
Villages													
Beachwood	6.60	11.40	1.00	3.00	0.00	0.00	9.70	5.70	2.50	0.30	0.30	1.30	42.00
Bedford Heights	5.90	6.00	0.70	0.50	0.00	0.00	5.90	1.10	0.40	0.00	0.20	0.60	21.60
Bentleyville	9.80	25.10	2.70	0.40	0.00	0.00	3.90	0.00	0.00	0.00	0.00	0.40	42.70
Bratenahl	10.70	55.50	6.50	0.50	0.00	0.00	26.60	7.80	5.50	0.10	4.20	4.30	122.10
Brecksville	4.70	9.00	2.00	1.10	0.00	0.00	8.00	2.80	1.20	0.00	1.90	0.60	31.50
Broadview Heights	3.20	6.50	0.80	1.60	0.00	0.00	3.80	2.60	0.00	0.00	0.00	1.00	19.70
Brooklyn Heights	10.60	7.80	1.60	0.60	0.00	0.00	5.70	2.30	1.30	0.20	0.80	2.40	33.40
Brook Park	17.50	42.60	35.60	4.40	22.60	0.00	21.70	19.20	3.60	0.20	19.10	3.70	192.70
Chagrin Falls	5.50	12.20	1.20	0.50	0.00	0.00	9.80	12.50	0.40	0.40	0.50	0.90	43.20
Cuyahoga Heights	79.40	117.60	175.30	11.10	0.00	0.00	35.30	14.70	1.10	0.00	74.10	9.20	527.30
Gates Mills	17.40	30.70	2.00	1.40	0.00	0.00	33.20	5.30	6.70	0.80	0.00	6.40	104.50
Glenwillow	9.80	1.90	1.90	1.00	0.00	0.00	1.90	0.00	0.00	0.00	0.00	0.00	16.80
Highland Heights	5.70	5.60	1.10	1.00	0.00	0.00	5.80	0.20	0.20	0.10	0.00	0.30	19.90
Hunting Valley	28.20	69.40	2.40	0.20	0.00	0.00	59.20	0.00	1.60	0.20	4.90	2.90	169.80
Independence	3.90	8.60	0.70	0.50	0.00	0.00	11.30	0.80	0.30	0.00	1.20	2.20	29.60
Linndale	5.60	2.80	0.00	0.00	0.00	0.00	13.20	1.00	0.00	0.00	0.00	1.50	24.10
Mayfield	6.70	11.70	1.60	2.50	0.00	0.00	4.80	1.10	.000	0.10	0.00	0.40	29.00
Middleburg Heights	4.00	6.60	4.90	0.90	2.70	0.00	4.10	2.70	0.20	0.00	2.60	1.30	30.60
Moreland Hills	7.70	16.60	0.80	2.00	0.00	0.00	10.10	0.70	0.10	0.10	1.20	1.10	40.70
Newburgh Heights	6.20	7.90	0.90	0.20	0.00	0.00	6.80	3.00	0.00	0.00	1.10	0.60	27.00
North Randall	41.80	74.70	5.80	3.10	0.00	0.00	46.60	6.50	0.00	0.00	0.00	2.40	182.50
North Royalton	2.90	7.70	0.80	1.30	0.00	0.00	4.60	3.20	0.20	0.00	0.20	1.30	22.30
Oakwood	2.60	3.50	0.60	0.70	0.00	0.00	5.40	0.30	0.00	0.10	0.00	0.30	13.70
Olmsted Falls	4.40	7.20	2.30	0.50	1.90	0.00	8.20	3.60	1.60	0.10	0.30	0.30	30.60

(Continued on next page)

Table IV-2 (Continued)

(In Dollars)

Governmental Unit	General Govt.	Police	Fire	Other Public Safety	Hospital	Public Welfare	Streets & Highways	Misc. Comm. Activity	Recreation & Culture	Land Use & Development	Pensions	Misc. & Unallocable	Total Current Expenditures
Orange	3.00	12.70	0.00	0.10	0.00	0.00	5.70	0.00	0.00	0.40	0.20	0.40	22.70
Parkview	6.00	6.60	1.70	0.40	0.00	0.00	1.80	1.30	0.20	0.00	0.10	0.60	19.00
Parma Heights	5.20	7.30	2.70	1.20	0.00	0.00	5.50	4.10	0.40	0.00	1.80	2.50	31.00
Pepper Pike	10.50	16.10	1.80	0.70	0.00	0.00	11.40	10.40	0.00	0.00	3.30	0.80	55.20
Richmond Heights	4.10	7.20	0.90	0.40	0.00	0.00	2.00	0.70	0.00	0.20	0.50	0.30	16.50
Seven Hills	3.90	9.20	0.90	3.00	0.00	0.00	5.20	2.40	1.60	0.00	1.00	0.60	28.00
Solon	6.10	8.10	1.50	1.50	0.00	0.00	8.10	1.60	0.20	0.70	1.70	0.30	30.10
Strongsville	5.00	10.10	1.30	0.70	1.90	0.00	9.00	0.60	1.00	0.00	1.30	0.70	31.80
Valley View	12.30	15.50	3.10	0.40	0.00	0.00	3.70	2.30	0.20	0.30	0.00	1.40	40.00
Walton Hills	5.40	14.50	1.10	0.40	0.00	0.00	10.20	1.30	0.00	0.00	0.00	0.10	32.90
Warrensville Heights	4.20	6.40	4.50	1.10	0.00	0.00	7.30	3.40	0.00	0.10	0.40	0.40	27.90
Westlake	2.50	6.30	2.20	0.90	0.00	0.10	4.30	2.10	1.10	0.00	1.20	1.40	22.10
West View	3.90	6.20	1.30	1.10	1.80	0.00	4.10	2.60	0.00	0.00	0.10	1.10	22.40
Woodmere	8.50	25.40	2.80	0.00	0.00	0.00	5.10	1.40	0.00	0.20	1.40	0.90	46.90
Mean	10.00	18.40	7.30	1.30	0.80	0.00	11.30	3.50	0.90	0.10	3.30	1.50	59.10
Median	5.80	8.80	NC	NC	NC	NC	6.30	NC	NC	NC	NC	NC	30.60
Townships													
Chagrin Falls	93.30	0.00	6.70	0.00	00.0	0.00	89.90	2.20	0.00	0.00	0.00	2.20	195.50
Olmsted	.90	1.70	0.60	0.00	0.10	0.00	0.00	0.70	0.00	0.10	0.10	0.00	5.70
Riveredge	0.00	0.00	0.00	0.00	0.00	0.00	0.00	0.00	0.00	0.00	0.00	0.00	0.00
Warrensville	.80	0.50	0.00	0.00	0.10	0.00	0.30	0.30	0.00	0.00	0.00	0.10	2.00

NC—Not Computed. 0—Less than $.05 or none recorded.

ship are shown by school district. Unlike the municipalities, there is no concentration of high-expenditure school districts in the core area. High expenditures are geographically concentrated in sets of contiguous communities, moving from the older wealthy community of Bratenahl through East Cleveland, Cleveland Heights, Shaker Heights, Beachwood, and the Orange School District. In the western side of the County, Lakewood and Rocky River have high per student expenditures, with the Berea School District (Brook Park) and the Cuyahoga Heights School District completing the list of the high-expenditure districts.

If school expenditures are converted into per capita terms based on estimated populations and then allocated by municipality, the per capita school operating expenditures appear higher outside the core area than within, the reverse of municipal operating expenditures. This is plainly due to the fact that when per student operating expenditures are converted into per capita terms, they appear even lower in the core area, where the ratio of students to total population is appreciably lower than in the outlying areas. This is most noticeably true in the ranking of the Cleveland, Lakewood, and East Cleveland school districts.

If *total* per capita operating expenditures (both school and municipal) are considered by municipality, then the core area ceases to be a high per capita expenditure area. Decidedly high total per capita expenditure areas do emerge, however, namely, in the wealthier communities to the east, and in the communities with a high industrial tax base. There are also areas of low total per capita expenditures, which are found in several concentrations, most notably in the area due south of Cleveland without an industrial tax base. Similarly, Map IV-4 and IV-5 show the distribution of operating expenditures per $1,000 assessed valuation. If municipal expenditures alone are considered, the highest levels are achieved in the core area. If total operating expenditures for both municipal and school purposes are considered, then the core area no longer dominates the picture as it did in 1940 or as it does for municipal expenditures alone.

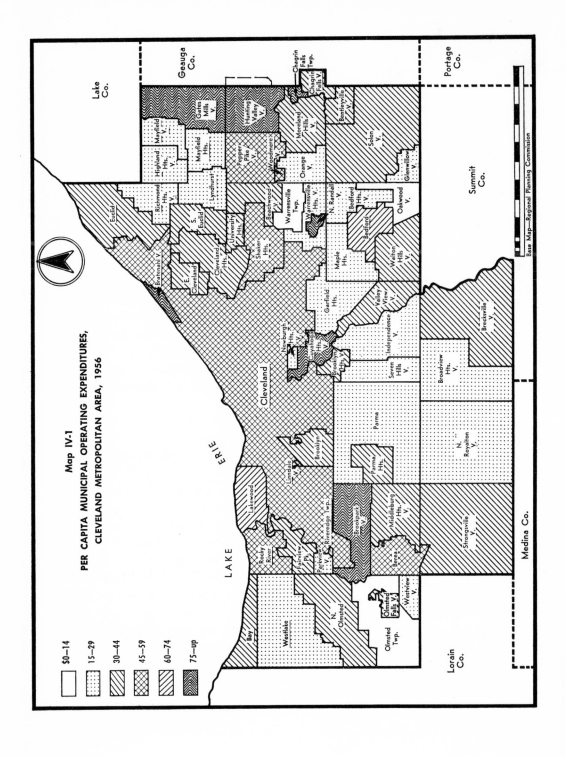

Map IV-1

PER CAPITA MUNICIPAL OPERATING EXPENDITURES,
CLEVELAND METROPOLITAN AREA, 1956

Legend:
$0–14
15–29
30–44
45–59
60–74
75–up

Base Map—Regional Planning Commission

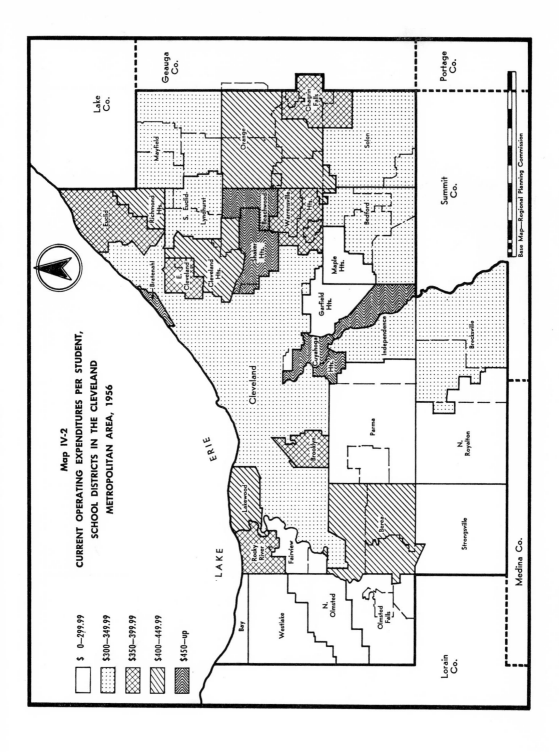

Map IV-2

CURRENT OPERATING EXPENDITURES PER STUDENT,
SCHOOL DISTRICTS IN THE CLEVELAND
METROPOLITAN AREA, 1956

$ 0—299.99

$300—349.99

$350—399.99

$400—449.99

$450—up

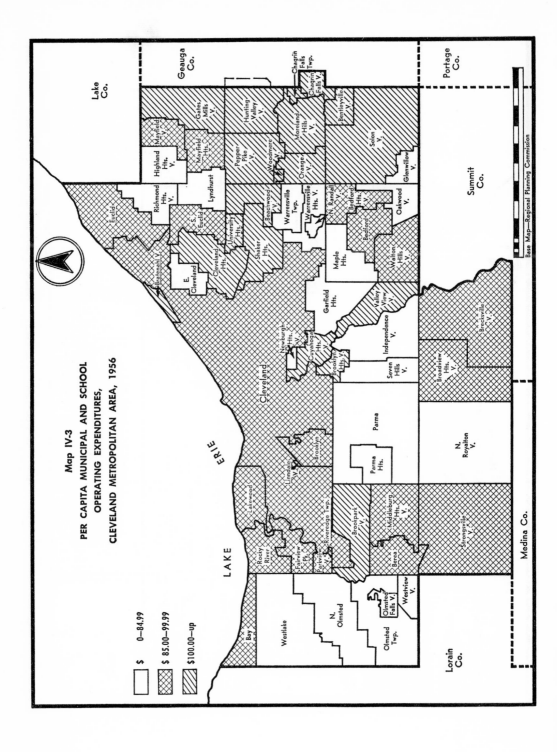

Map IV-3

PER CAPITA MUNICIPAL AND SCHOOL
OPERATING EXPENDITURES,
CLEVELAND METROPOLITAN AREA, 1956

$ 0—84.99

$ 85.00—99.99

$100.00—up

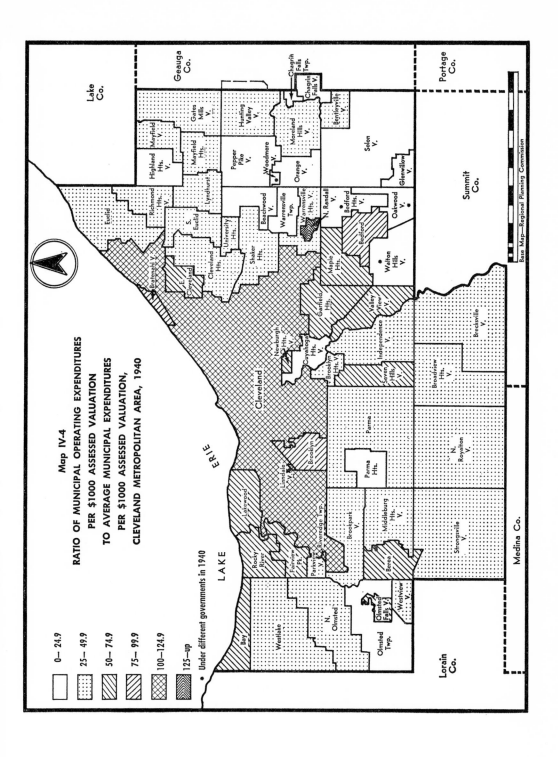

Map IV-4

RATIO OF MUNICIPAL OPERATING EXPENDITURES
PER $1000 ASSESSED VALUATION
TO AVERAGE MUNICIPAL EXPENDITURES
PER $1000 ASSESSED VALUATION,
CLEVELAND METROPOLITAN AREA, 1940

0— 24.9
25— 49.9
50— 74.9
75— 99.9
100—124.9
125—up

* Under different governments in 1940

Base Map—Regional Planning Commission

Variation in Per Capita Expenditures

How great is the variation in per capita terms or in per $1,000 assessed valuation terms among like kinds of governments, whether they be cities or villages? And how great is the variation in per student or in per $1,000 assessed valuation terms in the case of the school districts? The coefficient of variation provides a measure of the variation independent of the size of the units of measurement involved, and hence permits inter-functional and inter-jurisdictional comparisons; that is, the relative dispersions of the various classes of expenditures by governments may be compared.

$$V = \frac{\text{Standard Deviation}}{\text{Mean}} \times 100$$

In 1956, the coefficient of variation of per capita total operating expenditures was 33.5 per cent, in the case of the cities, and many times that amount in the case of the villages, 150.5 per cent. It should be noted that, in the case of city per capita expenditures, there was little effect on the coefficient of variation if Cleveland was included or excluded. The coefficient of variation for the school districts of operating expenditures per student in average daily membership resembled that of the cities' per capita expenditures.

If the above municipal data are converted into expenditures per $1,000 of assessed valuation, then the coefficients of variation change very decidedly in the case of the villages, but remain virtually unchanged in the case of the cities. In particular, the coefficient of variation for cities' per capita operating expenditures of 33.5 per cent is increased very slightly to 34.8 per cent in the case of operating expenditures per $1,000 of assessed valuation. On the other hand, the conversion in the case of villages leads to a reduction from a coefficient of variation of 150.5 per cent, for per capita total operating expenditures, to a coefficient of 48.5 per cent in the case of their per $1,000 assessed valuation measure. There is thus much more consistency on a village-to-village basis when expenditures are com-

Table IV-3—Current Operating Expenditures, Per Capita and Per $1000 Assessed Valuation, County and Municipal Governments, Cleveland Metropolitan Area, 1940, 1950, 1956

GOVERNMENTAL UNIT	EXPENDITURES PER CAPITA					EXPENDITURES PER $1000 ASSESSED VALUATION		
	(In Current Dollars)			(In 1956 Dollars)				
	1940	1950	1956	1940	1950	1940	1950	1956
Cuyahoga County	11.30	13.30	24.70	27.30	16.90	7.70	6.60	8.30
Cities								
Bay Village	20.70	24.60	36.80	50.00	31.30	9.70	12.10	13.50
Bedford	16.20	45.20	60.80	39.10	57.50	14.40	24.50	22.20
Berea	11.60	22.30	46.80	28.00	28.30	11.70	20.20	21.50
Brooklyn	22.30	16.20	40.40	53.90	20.60	5.30	5.60	8.90
Cleveland	30.80	45.50	59.30	74.40	57.80	22.30	23.60	20.80
Cleveland Heights	17.50	34.20	44.80	42.30	43.50	9.00	16.70	16.20
East Cleveland	13.20	24.80	34.90	31.90	31.50	9.70	15.20	15.00
Euclid	17.00	22.80	33.20	41.10	29.00	8.50	7.90	9.10
Fairview Park	11.90	23.40	39.70	28.80	29.70	9.20	12.90	12.90
Garfield Heights	11.10	16.10	19.10	26.80	20.50	10.50	11.40	10.30
Lakewood	17.10	35.50	68.40	41.30	45.10	12.50	21.10	29.20
Lyndhurst	17.70	23.50	25.90	42.80	29.90	8.10	12.10	11.00
Maple Heights	14.80	22.50	24.70	35.70	28.60	11.40	13.00	11.00
Mayfield Heights	10.20	15.70	29.20	24.60	20.00	8.40	9.90	12.30
North Olmsted	9.30	18.70	32.80	22.50	23.80	8.10	13.40	14.00
Parma	9.20	16.00	25.60	22.20	20.30	7.20	8.20	9.90
Rocky River	17.90	30.00	52.20	43.20	38.10	8.70	12.30	15.80
Shaker Heights	20.30	41.30	58.10	49.00	52.50	6.60	12.60	13.70
South Euclid	14.00	26.40	33.50	33.80	33.60	7.70	12.80	12.90
University Heights	14.90	25.30	35.60	36.00	32.20	7.50	10.90	11.20
Villages								
Beachwood	35.20	60.10	42.00	85.00	76.40	3.30	9.70	8.50
Bedford Heights	n	n	21.60	n	n	—	—	5.20
Bentleyville	10.30	14.50	42.70	24.90	18.40	5.60	6.50	13.20
Bratenahl	62.90	98.10	122.10	151.90	124.70	15.30	30.70	29.00
Brecksville	12.30	29.00	31.50	29.70	36.90	8.60	9.80	7.40
Broadview Heights	9.00	11.80	19.70	21.70	15.00	7.30	7.80	7.70
Brooklyn Heights	9.90	26.00	33.40	23.90	33.00	5.10	12.80	11.40
Brook Park	19.70	24.00	192.70	47.60	30.50	8.10	12.40	6.60

(Continued on next page)

Table IV-3 (Continued)

GOVERNMENTAL UNIT	EXPENDITURES PER CAPITA					EXPENDITURES PER $1000 ASSESSED VALUATION		
	(In Current Dollars)			(In 1956 Dollars)				
	1940	1950	1956	1940	1950	1940	1950	1956
Chagrin Falls	15.10	28.30	43.20	36.50	36.00	11.40	14.80	14.20
Cuyahoga Heights	99.30	447.50	527.30	239.80	568.80	1.90	5.20	4.30
Gates Mills	29.80	63.80	104.50	72.00	81.10	7.30	14.20	15.20
Glenwillow	6.40	6.20	16.80	15.50	7.90	2.90	2.00	3.80
Highland Heights	16.60	17.10	19.80	40.10	21.70	2.80	6.70	7.50
Hunting Valley	71.10	123.50	169.80	171.70	157.00	8.40	15.80	15.10
Independence	12.40	23.00	29.60	30.00	29.20	7.30	10.30	9.00
Linndale	9.90	10.30	24.10	23.90	13.10	20.60	12.80	14.10
Mayfield	14.50	28.60	29.00	35.00	36.40	6.40	14.30	11.00
Middleburg Heights	10.00	24.80	30.60	24.20	31.50	5.40	10.60	8.60
Moreland Hills	23.90	39.10	40.70	57.70	49.70	8.00	13.80	10.00
Newburgh Heights	11.40	18.20	27.00	27.50	23.10	12.90	12.90	11.10
North Randall	187.00	80.30	182.50	451.60	102.10	32.50	8.10	9.90
North Royalton	7.30	15.90	22.30	17.60	20.20	7.70	10.50	8.60
Oakwood	n	n	13.70	n	n	—	—	10.50
Olmsted Falls	13.80	22.30	30.60	33.30	28.30	10.90	14.90	12.20
Orange	24.40	21.00	22.70	58.90	26.70	14.60	10.50	7.20
Parkview	13.90	14.10	19.00	33.60	17.90	7.10	7.30	7.60
Parma Heights	7.20	18.50	31.00	17.40	23.50	3.20	9.80	13.10
Pepper Pike	22.90	42.10	55.20	55.30	53.50	3.20	7.90	8.20
Richmond Heights	17.20	18.00	16.50	41.50	22.90	6.50	7.50	7.10
Seven Hills	15.30	21.90	28.00	37.00	27.80	9.30	11.10	9.90
Solon	10.10	22.80	30.10	24.40	29.00	4.60	9.90	8.00
Strongsville	8.70	17.60	31.80	21.00	22.40	7.90	11.20	12.00
Valley View	19.80	21.80	40.00	47.80	27.70	12.70	13.40	12.80
Walton Hills	n	n	32.90	n	n	—	—	1.30
Warrensville Heights	18.60	20.10	27.90	44.90	25.60	8.80	11.70	11.40
Westlake	11.70	23.70	22.10	28.30	30.10	7.40	12.30	7.60
West View	8.40	14.20	22.40	20.30	18.00	5.10	8.20	8.90
Woodmere	n	21.20	46.90	n	27.00	—	21.50	22.10
Townships								
Chagrin Falls	258.30	184.50	195.50	623.80	235.80	50.80	1.70	1.60
Olmsted	1.70	3.20	5.70	4.10	4.10	1.60	2.70	3.50
Riveredge	n	200.00	0	n	154.20	—	6.60	0
Warrensville	2.00	1.00	2.00	4.80	1.30	9.00	.20	.20

n: Not in existence during the year in question.

pared in terms of assessed valuation rather than in terms of population.

The resulting geographical distribution of per capita expenditures reflects the fact that school operating expenditures when allocated by municipality are more important than the municipal expenditure of those municipalities. The exceptions to the rule, that is, where municipal per capita expenditures exceed per capita expenditures on education, are all small in population and wealthy in tax resources, namely the very wealthy villages and industrial enclaves. At the other extreme are the governments which have been growing very rapidly or which have a limited residental tax-base.

The municipal pattern is somewhat modified by the fact that at times the thirty-two school districts include an industrial enclave and some of its less fortunately endowed neighbors. This is the only reason why communities like Brooklyn Heights and Valley View appear so high on the spending spectrum.

Factors Affecting Operating Expenditures

What are the factors that affect municipal and school expenditures in a major metropolitan area such as Cleveland? Specifically, what are the factors that "explain" the variations in total operating expenditures? In the observed differences in operating expenditures per capita and per student? To what extent can the variations in the level of expenditures, both in total and in per capita terms, be accounted for statistically?

Many factors have been suggested as being responsible for the level of operating expenditures as well as for changes in levels, whether they be of total or of per capita expenditures (per student in average daily membership—per ADM—in the case of the schools). The factors affecting the following four distinct, but related, aspects of expenditures will be considered:

a) the level of expenditures;
b) changes in the level of expenditures over time, in this case the changes from 1950 to 1956;

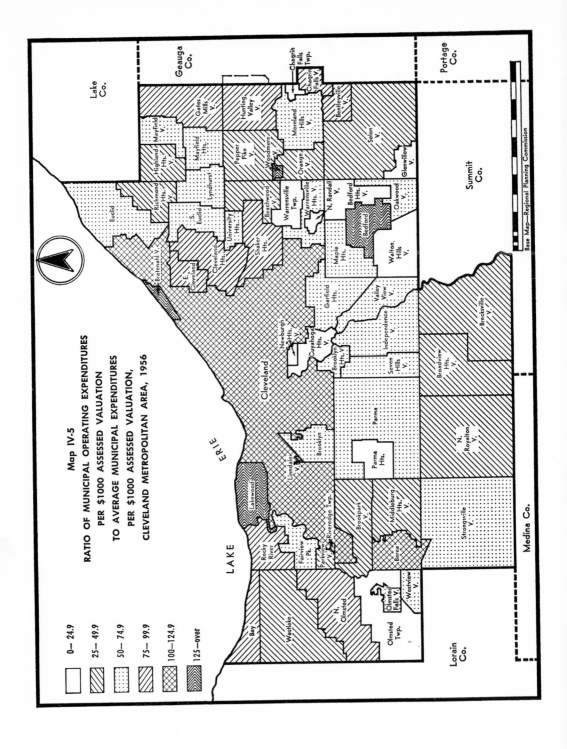

Map IV-5

RATIO OF MUNICIPAL OPERATING EXPENDITURES
PER $1000 ASSESSED VALUATION
TO AVERAGE MUNICIPAL EXPENDITURES
PER $1000 ASSESSED VALUATION,
CLEVELAND METROPOLITAN AREA, 1956

0— 24.9
25— 49.9
50— 74.9
75— 99.9
100—124.9
125—over

c) the level of per capita (or per student) expenditures;
d) changes in the level of per capita (or per student) expenditures over time, from 1950 to 1956.

The methods utilized range from simple to rather complex statistical techniques. The present analysis will be based on what appears to be the most fruitful approach, namely the use of multiple regression analysis. The aim of this approach is to provide an analysis of variations in expenditure within a single metropolitan area.

Municipal operating expenditures for 1956 are assumed to be influenced by the resident population, assessed valuation, and wealth of that year. It is assumed that the relative importance of each varies with respect to different functions as well as to the total of all operating expenditures. School operating expenditures in 1956 are assumed to be affected by the number of students in average daily membership, assessed valuation, wealth, and state aid in the form of School Foundation Programs of that year.

In the case of per capita municipal operating expenditures, a number of factors in addition to those considered in Chapter II were suggested. They included the following:

a) Population, 1956;
b) Area, 1956;
c) Density, 1956;
d) Assessed Valuation, 1956;
e) Per capita assessed valuation, 1956;
f) Per capita personal property, 1956 (a measure of industrialization and commercialization);
g) Per capita Intangible Levy, 1956;
h) 1956 population as a percentage of 1950 population;
i) Value of residential property as a percentage of total value of real property, 1956 (limited in value because of the exclusion of apartment houses of more than four units);
j) Per capita residential assessed valuation, 1956 (limited because of the exclusion of apartment houses of more than four units).

Table IV-4—Current Operating Expenditures, Per Student and Per $1000 Assessed Valuation, School Districts, Cleveland Metropolitan Area, 1940, 1950, 1956

SCHOOL DISTRICTS	EXPENDITURES PER STUDENT					EXPENDITURES PER $1000 ASSESSED VALUATION		
	(In Current Dollars)			(In 1956 Dollars)				
	1940	1950	1956	1940	1950	1940	1950	1956
Bay Village	130.29	238.90	280.50	314.70	303.60	9.75	20.30	21.50
Bedford	93.32	203.80	340.70	225.40	259.00	12.36	19.20	15.00
Berea	94.88	185.30	405.30	229.10	235.50	11.40	20.20	12.40
Brooklyn	103.91	224.00	369.20	250.90	284.70	5.13	11.70	16.90
Cleveland	116.97	242.50	331.60	282.50	308.20	11.50	13.67	14.80
Cleveland Heights	185.81	293.10	403.50	448.70	372.50	12.85	18.60	22.60
East Cleveland	145.55	254.80	375.00	351.50	336.60	13.27	18.60	28.90
Euclid	129.24	207.50	361.40	312.10	263.70	10.57	11.60	17.20
Fairview Park	72.11	183.60	290.90	174.20	233.40	9.28	14.90	18.20
Garfield Heights	116.33	231.10	282.40	280.90	293.70	16.23	20.40	22.20
Lakewood	161.47	325.10	422.00	390.00	413.20	13.77	18.50	19.60
Maple Heights	90.82	217.70	281.10	219.30	276.70	11.88	18.90	22.40
North Olmsted	85.69	183.10	263.90	206.90	232.70	12.95	22.80	20.40
Parma	94.31	207.40	282.40	227.80	263.60	10.64	12.40	19.70
Rocky River	117.30	261.00	391.00	283.30	331.70	9.62	16.00	17.90
Shaker Heights	223.54	399.80	516.30	539.90	508.10	10.24	16.60	19.90
So. Euclid-Lyndhurst	123.36	206.60	301.80	297.90	262.60	10.06	15.70	22.00
Local & Exempted								
Beachwood	717.65	464.70	676.40	1,733.10	590.60	3.04	7.10	15.50
Bratenahl	435.09	641.70	686.70	1,050.70	815.60	8.93	17.30	19.10
Brecksville	78.38	216.20	310.90	189.30	274.80	10.38	18.70	21.70
Chagrin Falls Ex.	107.58	240.00	352.70	259.80	305.00	14.32	24.40	32.60
Cuyahoga Heights	199.29	519.70	678.90	481.30	660.50	2.26	4.10	5.00
Independence	117.84	248.80	341.10	284.60	316.20	10.22	14.30	14.30
Mayfield (City)	149.61	222.50	316.40	361.30	282.80	11.36	16.90	22.20
North Royalton	84.01	183.50	292.70	202.90	233.20	16.76	21.20	23.40
Olmsted Falls	99.82	219.30	277.50	241.10	278.70	17.07	31.50	31.50
Orange	146.65	254.10	416.40	354.20	323.00	8.04	14.10	16.10
Richmond Heights	211.63	293.40	440.30	511.10	372.90	7.64	17.60	23.30
Solon	95.81	287.10	349.80	231.40	364.90	7.99	21.90	18.60
Strongsville	100.90	222.70	287.00	243.70	283.10	18.41	26.60	23.60
Warrensville Heights	106.16	217.90	355.70	256.40	277.00	5.90	14.10	20.90
Westlake Ex.	98.22	207.90	287.90	237.20	264.20	9.80	17.70	16.40

Table IV-5—Coefficients of Variation: Current Operating Expenditures Per Capita and Per $1000 Assessed Valuation, 1956

PURPOSE	Expenditures Per Capita					
	ALL CITIES			ALL VILLAGES		
	Standard Deviation	Mean	Coefficient of Variation	Standard Deviation	Mean	Coefficient of Variation
General Government	$ 1.36	$ 4.58	.298	$13.59	$10.04	1.360
Police	1.91	7.10	.269	23.56	18.39	1.280
Fire	1.97	4.92	.402	12.88	4.72	3.680
Streets & Highways	3.03	7.74	.390	12.52	11.29	1.115
All Operating	13.41	40.04	.350	89.07	59.05	1.505

PURPOSE	Expenditures Per $1000 Assessed Valuation					
	ALL CITIES			ALL VILLAGES		
	Standard Deviation	Mean	Coefficient of Variation	Standard Deviation	Mean	Coefficient of Variation
General Government	$0.27	$ 1.60	.169	$0.81	$ 2.00	.405
Police	0.62	2.60	.239	2.61	3.40	.768
Fire	0.54	1.70	.318	0.47	0.50	.940
Streets & Highways	0.80	2.80	.286	1.63	2.30	.709
All Operating	5.08	14.60	.348	5.14	10.60	.485

These variables were correlated individually with various per capita expenditures of 1956 for twenty cities and the forty-two villages and townships. As a check, 1954 data were tested for cities, excluding Cleveland (i.e., nineteen cities), and thirty-eight villages. The results of this initial analysis for twenty cities are presented in Tables IV-23 and IV-24 where the correlations between the independent variables are presented. Operating expenditures per student in average daily membership in 1956 were correlated with students in average daily membership, assessed valuation per student in average daily membership, wealth per student, and state aid per student.

The factors assumed to influence changes in the levels of municipal total operating expenditures between 1950 and 1956 were changes in population, assessed valuation, and wealth. In the case of schools, the changes in the levels of operating expenditures between 1950 and 1956 were associated with changes in number of students in average daily membership, assessed valuation, and state school foundation aid.

The factors that are assumed to influence changes in the levels of municipal per capita operating expenditures between 1950 and 1956 are the same as those assumed to influence changes in the level of total operating expenditures over the same period.

In order to ascertain whether or not the factors mentioned above are related to expenditures as well as to each other, it is necessary to determine whether variations in the dependent variable expenditure are similar to variations in the independent variables. Multiple regression techniques provide a means of comparing different groupings of governments and expenditures and independent variables.

If variations in all the sets of data moved together, the problem would be simple—the sets would be interchangeable, and any one could be used to represent the others. This, however, does not happen to be the case. By utilizing the methods of multiple regression analysis, it is possible to ascertain not only the relationships of two variables alone, but also that between any two variables while holding the affects of other variables constant, as well as between one variable and several others. The degree of relationship is indicated by the correlation coefficient "r", if two variables, and "R", if more than two variables are involved. The nature of the latter is such that a perfect positive relationship between variables would result in a correlation coefficient, "r or R" of 1.0000, and a perfect inverse relationship in an "r" of -1.0000. The coefficient of multiple correlation R is only positive. The square of the coefficient of correlation, the coefficient of determination, is the proportion of the total variance that has been explained by regression.

In order to avoid distorting effects due to special features of individual jurisdictions, the municipalities were grouped into the following categories: All Cities, Cities excluding Cleveland, All Villages, and Villages excluding Industrial Enclaves. Because their functions are limited by law, townships were excluded from this analysis. Cleveland, it must be remembered, towers in population and other aggregates over other cities; and industrial enclaves are villages whose resident population is no indication of the number of people that may actually require the facilities of the community and/or whose assessed valuation is inordinately high relative to its population.

The expenditures analysis was made with the most recent complete data available, that for 1956. The first step was to compute the simple correlation between each of the sets of data (variables) for municipalities; namely, 1) total of all municipal operating

Table IV-6—Coefficients of Correlation: Total Current Operating Expenditures and Selected Variables, 1956

CORRELATION COEFFICIENTS *	CITIES		VILLAGES	
	All (N=20)	Excluding Cleveland (N=19)	All (N=38)	Excluding Industrial Enclaves (N=34)
r_{12}	.9986	.8499	.4827	.8726
r_{13}	.9974	.7508	.8556	.8832
r_{14}	.7200	.5230	.0808	.2410
r_{23}	.9986	.9764	.1942	.9872
r_{24}	.7120	.3635	.1342	—.1720
r_{34}	.7230	.4806	—.0880	.0085

* In this and subsequent similar tables, the subscripts of the correlation coefficients indicate the variables being correlated. The variables above are:
1. Total All Operating Expenditures,
2. Population,
3. Assessed Valuation,
4. Wealth.
The first subscript indicates the dependent variable and the second and successive subscripts the independent variable or variables.

Table IV-7—Coefficients of Determination: Total Current Operating Expenditures and Selected Variables, 1956

COEFFICIENTS OF DETERMINATION	CITIES		VILLAGES	
	All (N=20)	Excluding Cleveland (N=19)	All (N=38)	Excluding Industrial Enclaves (N=34)
r^2_{12}	.9972	.7233	.2330	.7614
r^2_{13}	.9948	.5637	.7321	.7800
r^2_{14}	.5184	.2735	.0065	.0581
r^2_{23}	.9972	.7681	.0370	.8230
r^2_{24}	.5069	.1321	.0175	.0299
r^2_{34}	.5227	.2310	.0077	.0001

* See footnote to Table IV-6 for explanation of subscripts.

expenditures, the dependent variable, with 2) population, 3) assessed valuation, and 4) personal wealth (as measured by the Intangible Property Levy), the independent variables.

The purpose of the analysis, it should be recalled, is to ascertain the extent to which variations in the independent variables relate to variations in the dependent variable, in this case, the total of all municipal operating expenditures.

Table IV-8—Coefficients of Partial Correlation and Determination: Total Current Operating Expenditures and Selected Variables,* 1956

	CITIES		VILLAGES	
Coefficient of Partial Correlation	All (N=20)	Excluding Cleveland (N=19)	All (N=38)	Excluding Industrial Enclaves (N=34)
$r_{12.34}$	.6929	.6750	.6869	.7348
$r_{13.24}$	—.0013	—,0161	.9070	.0226
$r_{14.23}$	.2321	.3615	.4706	.5690
Coefficient of Partial Determination				
$r^2_{12.34}$	.4801	.4556	.4718	.5399
$r^2_{13.24}$	.0000	.0003	.8226	.0005
$r^2_{14.23}$	.0539	.1307	.2215	.3276

* See footnote to Table IV-6 for explanation of subscripts.

A glance at Table IV-7 reveals that, for All Cities, over 99 per cent of the variations in total expenditures is explained by variations either in population or in assessed valuation. For All Villages, however, variations in assessed valuation explain about 73 per cent of the variations in expenditures, and population only 23 per cent. When Cleveland is excluded from the city category, the explanatory power of the independent variables is reduced, graphically illustrating the importance of the central city in explaining variation in total expenditures. In the case of the villages, an opposite phenomenon takes place, for if the industrial enclaves are excluded, the explanatory power of the independent variables is increased.

But the use of simple correlation techniques is limited, as they do not take into account the interactions of the independent variables with each other. These interactions are indicated by the coefficients of correlation which do not include total operating

Chart IV–1
1956 CURRENT OPERATING EXPENDITURES AND POPULATION
ALL CITIES EXCLUDING CLEVELAND AND ALL VILLAGES

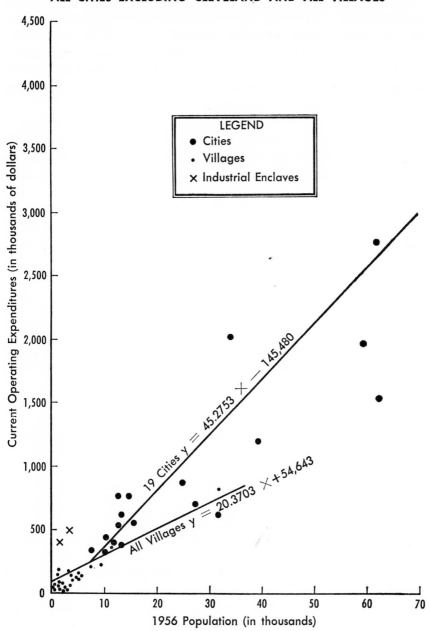

expenditures as a variable. A method known as partial correlation measures the relationship of two variables while holding the effects of other independent variables constant. The analysis of the data using the partial correlation method results in some surprises.

Assessed valuation, which loomed so large for the cities in the simple correlation ($r_{13} = .9974$), is reduced almost to the vanishing point in the partial correlation ($r_{13.24} = -.0013$).

For All Villages, a reverse indication is true; assessed valuation plays a greater role in the partial ($r_{13.24} = .9070$) than in the simple ($r_{13} = .8556$). But if the industrial enclaves are excluded, assessed valuation is of practically no importance in explaining total operating expenditures ($r_{13.24} = .0226$).

Having determined the relation of each of the independent variables to the total of all municipal operating expenditures, holding the effects of the other independent variables constant, the next step in the analysis was to compute a measure indicating the relationship between all three independent variables and the extent to which they vary with total expenditure. This measure is called the coefficient of multiple correlation.

Table IV-9—Coefficient of Multiple Correlation and Determination: Total Current Operating Expenditures and Selected Variables,* 1956

	CITIES		VILLAGES	
Coefficient	All (N=20)	Excluding Cleveland (N=19)	All (N=38)	Excluding Industrial Enclaves (N=34)
$R_{1.234}$	.9987	.8839	.9313	.9612
$R^2_{1.234}$	.9973	.7812	.8672	.9239
$R_{1.234}$ **	.9984	.8539	.9250	.9572
$R^2_{1.234}$**	.9968	.7375	.8555	.9163

* See footnote to Table IV-6 for explanation of subscripts.
** This is the coefficient of multiple correlation and determination corrected for the degrees of freedom lost in computation.

The relationship between all three independent variables and the dependent variable is always closer (i.e., the coefficient of correlation is higher) than between any one of the independent variables and the dependent variable, but sometimes it is appreciably greater as in the case of the villages above.

The results indicate that variations in population, assessed valuation, and wealth, acting together, account for the following percentages of the variations in total operating expenditures for the various groups of jurisdictions:

All Cities	99.7%
Cities excluding Cleveland	73.8%
All Villages	85.6%
Villages excluding Industrial Enclaves	91.6%

Having the results of the correlation analysis and the computational constituents thereof, it is possible to formulate an estimating equation showing the relationship of the variables with each other. For cities excluding Cleveland, for example, the multiple estimating equation is:

$$X_1 = 414{,}977 + 47.810179X_2 + .000268X_3 + .509812X_4$$
$$(.8975)^* \qquad (-.0168)^* \qquad (.2068)^*$$

where

X_1 is total municipal operating expenditure in dollars
X_2 is population
X_3 is assessed valuation
X_4 is wealth

* The figures in parentheses are Beta coefficients and are explained below.

The procedure described above was carried through for other data to be described. The relationship between the variables using the same subscripts as in Table IV-6 may be shown in mathematical formulae.

For All Cities:
$$X_1 = 57.940210X_2 - .000028X_3 + .370358X_4 - 524{,}124$$
$$(.9676) \qquad (-.0013) \qquad (.0182)$$

For All Villages:
$$X_1 = 14.913931X_2 + .004574X_3 + .459082X_4 - 7{,}224$$
$$(.3534) \qquad (.8014) \qquad (.1961)$$

For Villages excluding Industrial Enclaves:
$$X_1 = 17{,}917 + 22.243340X_2 + .000159X_3 + .323634X_4$$
$$(.7871) \qquad (.0162) \qquad (.2114)$$

Since the coefficients in the above equations are expressed in different units and differ in variability, they are not comparable. But a measure has been developed, called the Beta Coefficient (β), which expresses the coefficients in terms of the units' own variability, their standard deviation. In other words, the Beta Coefficient reveals the change (in terms of the standard deviation) in the dependent variable, when the independent variable is increased by one standard deviation, the effects of the other independent variables being constant.

Using the subscripts from Table IV-6 the Beta Coefficients for the above equations are as follows:

	Population ($\beta_{12.34}$)	Assessed Valuation ($\beta_{13.24}$)	Wealth ($\beta_{14.23}$)
All Cities	.9676	—.0013	.0182
Cities excluding Cleveland	.8975	—.0168	.2068
All Villages	.3534	.8014	.1961
Villages exc. Ind. Enclaves	.7871	.0162	.2114

The Beta Coefficient may be interpreted as stating that an increase of one standard deviation in population, and holding the effects constant because of changes in assessed valuation and wealth, the total of all municipal operating expenditures increased by .8975 of a standard deviation in the case of Cities excluding Cleveland, .3534 of a standard deviation in that of All Villages, and .7871 in that of Villages excluding Industrial Enclaves. The total of all municipal operating expenditures and population were then more closely related in the Cities than in the Villages. Or looking at it another way, within the Cities, total population is the factor most associated with expenditures, followed by wealth.

Since the square of the Beta Coefficient of each factor represents the direct contribution of that factor to the coefficient of multiple determination,[2] it is now possible to relate the correlation and regression analyses. The relationship may be expressed:

---

2. Robert Ferber, *Statistical Techniques in Market Research*, McGraw Hill Book Company (1949), p. 364.

Coefficient of Multiple Determination = Direct Contribution of the Independent Variables on the Dependent Variable + Indirect Contributions, or : $R^2_{1.234} = (\beta^2_{12.34} + \beta_{13.24} + \beta_{14.23})$ + indirect contribution.

In the case of Cities excluding Cleveland:

$$R^2_{1.234} = .7812 = (.8055 + .0003 + .0428) - .0674$$
$$R^2_{1.234} = .7812 = (.8486) - .0674.$$

The above is interpreted as meaning that the three factors account directly for 78 per cent of the variation in the total of all municipal operating expenditures, 81 per cent the direct effect of population, .03 per cent that of assessed valuation, and 4 per cent that of wealth; the total indirect effects of the interrelationship between these variables are negative and reduce the direct effects of the independent variables some 7 per cent when they are considered together.

For the total of all municipal operating expenditures, therefore, this analysis may be summarized as follows:

Table IV-10—Per Cent of Variation in Total Municipal Current Operating Expenditures Accounted for by Population, Assessed Valuation, and Wealth, 1956

GOVERNMENTAL UNIT	DIRECT CONTRIBUTION			COMBINED INDIRECT CONTRIBUTION	TOTAL
	Population	Assessed Valuation	Wealth		
All Cities	93.6	*	*	6.1	99.7
Cities excluding Cleveland	80.6	*	4.3	−6.7	78.1
All Villages	12.5	64.2	3.9	6.2	86.7
Villages excluding Industrial Enclaves	62.0	*	4.5	25.9	92.4

* Less than .05%.

It would seem that the three factors chosen have a much stronger explanatory power in the case of All Cities than in that of the other three categories. Population appears as the crucial factor in accounting for variations in total of all municipal operating expenditures, except in the case of All Villages where resident population is not a good measure of the population served, and assessed valuation is a better gauge of the demand for services.

School Operating Expenditures

As stated earlier, school operating expenditures, in the present study, are analyzed using students in average daily membership, and state school foundation aid, in addition to assessed valuation, as

Table IV-11—Regression Coefficients: Current Operating Expenditures and Selected Independent Variables, Municipalities, Cleveland Metropolitan Area, 1956

Operating Expenditures	Constant	Population	Assessed Valuation	Wealth	Coefficient of Multiple Determination
All Cities (N=20)					
General Government	4,990	3.039	.0002271	.053131	.9996
Police	—150,844	9.289	.0009906	—.0116967	.9975
Fire	—83,827	1.534	.0019681	.0889719	.9970
Streets & Highways	—2,708	5.512	.0005263	.0541662	.9986
Total	—524,124	57.941	.0000280	.3703580	.9973
Cities excluding Cleveland (N=19)					
General Government	13,125	2.890	.0001592	.0670962	.9535
Police	9,960	5.124	.0002299	.0860908	.9293
Fire	—653	3.880	.0000455	.1166790	.9524
Streets & Highways	25,803	4.854	.0003111	.0710104	.8829
Total	+414,977	47.810	.000286	.5098120	.7812
All Villages (N=38)					
General Government	2,529	2,338	.0005154	.0468263	.8101
Police	3,286	3.703	.0009666	.1937642	.8351
Fire	—4,843	—.777	.0012918	—.0113902	.8597
Streets & Highways	982	4.651	.0003385	.1581712	.7562
Total	—7,224	14.914	.0045740	.459082	.8672
Villages excluding Industrial Enclaves (N=34)					
General Government	2,933	2.350	.0049212	.0448991	.7806
Police	4,691	4.839	.0005175	.1684212	.8034
Fire	—1,772	1.103	.0004236	.0010339	.5237
Streets & Highways	2,754	3.731	.0006793	.0581332	.7934
Total	17,917	22.243	.0001590	.3236340	.9239

factors associated with the expenditures. Computations were made, including and excluding districts with less than 1,000 students in average daily membership.

Each factor when taken individually "explains" the variations in total school expenditures. However, these factors are highly interrelated with each other. While each could be used to "explain" more than 99 per cent of the variation in total expenditures, differences emerge if the several factors are isolated by the methods of partial correlation analysis. First, none of these variables individually accounts for more than 39 per cent of the variation in total school operating expenditures. Surprisingly, less than 1 per cent is accounted for by variations in assessed valuation once the effects of the number of students and State Aid are removed. And as expected, school aid, after the influence of the number of students in average daily membership and assessed valuation is removed, varies inversely with total expenditures; the more that is available locally, the smaller the amount of school aid. However, taken together, they do account for over 99.8 per cent of the variation in total school operating expenditures. The exclusion of the smaller districts with less than 1,000 students in average daily membership would not materially alter the picture. The result may only be partially understood in terms of the inclusion of the City of Cleveland in the data. The use of partial correlation only partly helps to segregate out the obvious influence of size.

Table IV-12—Contribution of Independent Variables to Coefficients of Multiple Determination: School Current Operating Expenditures and Selected Varabiles, 1956

School Districts	ADM	Assessed Valuation	School Foundation	Combined Indirect Effects	Total R²
All	.394	.009	.238	.358	.999
Excluding those with Less than 1000 ADM	.317	.009	.211	.462	.999

Factors in Individual Expenditures

In 1956, operating expenditures on individual functions varied considerably among municipal governments. As in the case of total operating expenditures, the following factors were hypothesized as explaining differences in operating expenditures of the individual functions: population, assessed valuation, and wealth as measured by the Intangible Levy. These have been tested with respect to the following function, which, as shown earlier in this chapter, make up a considerable portion of the operating expenditures of the municipalities in the Cleveland Metropolitan Area: general government, police, fire, and street and highway expenditures. With the exception of fire, the other three classes of expenditures are undertaken by every single municipality, city and village alike, in the Cleveland Metropolitan Area.

In the case of each of the operating expenditures of each of the individual functions, as in the case of the total of all operating expenditures, the three variables explain a statistically significant and important part of the variation in expenditure. Viewed on a functional basis, no obvious pattern emerges.

What is the importance of the independent variables, of population, assessed valuation, and wealth, individually and in interaction with each other? In the case of general government expenditures, the largest portion of the variation is explained by variations in population, except in the All Villages category, where the presence of the industrial enclaves is so overwhelming as to make assessed valuation rather than population the most important explanatory factor. It should be noted that, unlike the other classifications of communities, there is virtually no correlation between population and assessed valuation in the All Villages category. Although they do not explain as much of the variation in general government expenditures as do variations in population, variations in wealth of the different categories of municipalities are significantly associated with general government expenditure variations, except in the All Villages case, where the influence of the industrial enclaves is predominant.

The factors determining the variations in police operating expenditures resemble those of general government expenditures. Population is a significant factor in explaining variations in total police operating expenditure regardless of how the municipalities are grouped. Because of the intercorrelation between population and assessed valuation in the case of the All Cities and All Villages categories, variations in assessed valuation appear more important than population. Variations in the personal wealth of the community do not play a significant role in explaining variations in police expenditures.

Variations in total fire expenditures are associated with variations in population only in the case of Cities excluding Cleveland. If All Cities and All Villages are considered, then assessed valuation plays a statistically significant and more important role in explaining variations in fire expenditures. It should be noted that, if the industrial enclaves are excluded, there is no significant nor predominant factor explaining variations in expenditures on fire protection in the remaining villages, although all three taken together account for 52.4 per cent of the variation in fire expenditures. As with police, fire expenditures are explained to a greater extent by variations in assessed valuation than by variations in population. Excluding Cleveland, personal wealth is significantly associated with city expenditures on fire protection.

Variations in street and highway operating expenditures are most clearly explained by variations in population. Even in the All Villages category resident population is more important than assessed valuation. However, variations in wealth also explain a large proportion of the variation in villages. A municipality that departs by a few standard deviations from the average of its category will have operating expenditures which vary accordingly. On the high side this is especially true of Cleveland in population and assessed valuation; Shaker Heights in personal wealth; and among the villages, Cuyahoga Heights and Brook Park in assessed valuation; and Bratenahl, Gates Mills, and Hunting Valley in personal wealth.

Factors Associated With Changes in Total Expenditures 1950-56

Between 1950 and 1956 there were great changes in population, assessed valuation, and wealth in each particular municipality within the Cleveland Metropolitan Area. What were the effects of these changes on total expenditures? Using the same four groupings of municipalities as above, the changes in total operating expenditures over this period were compared to changes in population, assessed valuation, and wealth.

The simple relationships between expenditures and the several independent variables, were in no manner striking, save for the fact that changes in population were shown to be practically unrelated to changes in total expenditures. Changes in assessed valuation, on the other hand, were closely associated with changes in expenditures in all cases. Changes in wealth were most closely associated with changes in population.

If account is taken of the interrelationships between the independent variables, population, assessed valuation, and wealth, then the results of this further analysis are most unexpected. Regardless of whether Cleveland is or is not included in the analysis of cities, changes in total operating expenditures were negatively associated with changes in population, 26.2 per cent of the variation in changes in total expenditures being explained inversely by changes in population. On the other hand, abstracting from changes in population and changes in wealth, changes in assessed valuation explained over 98.0 per cent of the variation in changes in total operating expenditures. These results, if they are an accurate picture of the effects of these several independent variables, are surprising to the student of metropolitan growth.

The relationship between changes in population and changes in total operating expenditures is most interesting. As can be seen, the common assumption that municipal operating expenditures vary directly with changes in population does not hold in the case of the cities in the Cleveland Metropolitan Area. Instead, the relation has turned out to be an inverse one, for what is probably a variety of reasons. First, it must be noted that there may be priorities established as between school and municipal functions, and between operating and capital expenditures. Secondly, there may be a lag between the growth in population and the growth in total operating expenditures that may be operative for a period as short as that from 1950 to 1956. A third factor would seem to depend on the extent to which population changes are intercorrelated with changes in assessed valuation, or are in fact dependent on growth in the property tax base, i.e., the assessed valuation, in order to finance increased governmental activity. It would appear that some of the common assumptions concerning the effect of population growth on operating expenditures might well be questioned.

An alternative would be to view the inverse relationship between changes in population and changes in expenditures in terms of those governments that have experienced declines in population or which have remained comparatively static, like the city of Lakewood or Cleveland. A static population appears to be associated with increased total expenditures. It appears that the changes in the composition of the population and their increased circulation may more than offset the effects of stable or declining resident populations especially in core area municipalities. In the villages, the growth in population is positively associated with changes in operating expenditures. Both kinds of municipalities require expansion of old services or the introduction of new ones, although the services involved may differ by municipality. And the fact that a municipality has stopped growing does not mean a reduction in expenditures, but may, in fact lead to larger increases in expenditures than ever.

These conclusions are reinforced by the association between changes in assessed valuation and changes in operating expenditures which are quite strong for the cities. An increase in assessed valuation which is closely associated with an increase in total operating expenditures apparently may be reinforced by a decrease in resident population. Changes in wealth are unrelated to changes in total expenditures.

The three variables—population, assessed valuation, and wealth—explain 98.7 per cent of the variation in changes in total operating expenditures for All Cities, and a considerable, though not as large, percentage for Cities excluding Cleveland.

The data, dominated as they are by the large central city and immediately surrounding area, pose a crucial question concerning expenditures in those areas in the future. The suggestion that a decreased population accompanied by large rapid movements within fixed areas may have more powerful effects than increases in population on municipal expenditures is worthy of consideration. Major increases in population however, would almost certainly result in over-all increased operating expenditures. But the data are suggestive that other forces intimately associated with changes in assessed valuation are more likely to dominate changes in operating expenditures. Finally, it appears that some communities will improve service levels regardless of changes in population, and are perhaps even more likely to do so if there are population decreases rather than increases.

An analysis was also made of the factors influencing changes in total operating expenditures for the villages. If the industrial enclaves are excluded, then the assumed relationship between changes in population and changes in total operating expenditures emerges; over 34 per cent of the variation in changes in total operating expenditures is explained by changes in total population. However, it should be noted that changes in assessed valuation in all instances explain almost as much or more than population. In the case of All Villages, using the coefficients of net determination, population changes explain 40 per cent of the variations in changes in total operating expenditures. But changes in assessed valuation explain 86 per cent. If the industrial enclaves are excluded, then the changes in population account for about 35 per cent of the variation in changes in total operating expenditures; changes in assessed valuation explain only 2.5 per cent. However, the intercorrelation between the changes in assessed valuation and the changes in population and wealth is so strong that the combination of changes taken together explain the difference between the sum of partial correlations and the multiple correlation 91.7 per cent.

If both the wealthy villages and the industrial enclaves were excluded the result is both obvious and paradoxical. Changes in operating expenditures for the remaining villages are much more closely associated with changes in population than in any other case because the correlation between changes in assessed valuation and population is so great as to reduce the meaning of either alone to a level approximating that of changes in wealth, which has practically no explanatory powers. But the combination of changes in population, assessed valuation, and wealth does explain 78.2 per cent of the variation, where none individually explain even 6 per cent, and the direct sum of the three is less than 8 per cent.

As has been noted in the villages, it appears that the growth in population is directly associated with increased total operating expenditures. The problem appears cut and dried; increases in population are accompanied by increases in assessed valuation; in order to have the one you must have the other. Without changes in population, there are no major changes in assessed valuation. If the industrial enclaves and the wealthy villages are included, this is of course not true. But in all cases increases in population as well as increases in assessed valuation were associated with increases in total expenditures.

Changes in School Expenditures. In the case of school operating expenditures, changes in the number of students in average daily membership, assessed valuation, and school foundation aid were all closely associated with changes in total expenditures. The simple associations between changes in each of these variables explain over 90 per cent of the changes in expenditures.

But it should be pointed out that the association between these independent variables is very close. If these associations are excluded, then a different picture emerges. Changes in the number of students in average daily membership have less association with changes in total expenditures when changes in assessed valuation are not considered than when they are. If school foundation aid is abstracted from consideration, there is virtually no association between changes in number of students and changes in total expenditures.

Changes in school operating expenditures are directly associated with changes in assessed valuation. 82.5 per cent of the variation in the changes in school operating expenditures were explained by changes in assessed valuation. If changes in school foundation aid are also taken into account, an additional 10.5 per cent of the changes in expenditures is "explained." All in all, changes in the three variables explain over 99.0 per cent of the variations in the changes in school operating expenditures.

The growth in assessed valuation, which was pervasive if not uniform both in the municipalities and the school districts of the Cleveland Metropolitan Area, was associated directly with changes in school operating expenditures. The same could not be said of changes in population or in number of students in average daily membership. In and of itself, growth in student population was not directly associated with changes in total operating expenditures. This result was more striking in the case of school districts than in municipalities, particularly in cities, where population growth was significantly associated with the growth in expenditures.

The "Average Municipality"

Using the concept of an "average municipality" in each of the four categories of municipalities, an alternate approach was developed to analyze the effect of changes in population on expenditures. Explicitly the problem was to determine what would happen to expenditures if 100 persons were added to the resident population of the average municipalities in each category. It was further assumed that new residents would have the same average characteristics as those of the persons already residing there. This approach is valuable because it explicitly shows the changes in expenditures associated with the same changes in population in classes of municipalities with varying characteristics.

In the present context, the All Cities category has meaning primarily as a control on the Cities excluding Cleveland category, because, in the former case, the average municipality's population reflects to a very great extent the influence of Cleveland. The average city in the All Cities category has a population of 73,150 (standard deviation 196,637), a figure which exceeds the population of all cities in 1956 except that of Cleveland. On the other hand, the average population of the Cities excluding Cleveland is 28,260 (standard deviation 19,992). The average per capita assessed valuation is virtually the same in both communities—$2,807 in the

Table IV-13—Current Operating Expenditures and Selected Variables: Contribution of Independent Variables to Coefficients of Multiple Determination, 1956

OPERATING EXPENDITURES	DIRECT CONTRIBUTION			COMBINED INDIRECT CONTRIBUTION	$R^2_{1.234}$
	Population	Assessed Valuation	Wealth		
All Cities (N=20)	$\beta^2_{12.34}$	$\beta^2_{13.24}$	$\beta^2_{14.23}$		
General Government	.6522	.0297	.0017	.3160	.9996 **
Police	.0012	.9738	.0000	.0225	.9975 **
Fire	.0454	.6093 *	.0013	.3410	.9970 **
Streets & Highways	.5914	.0440	.0004	.3628	.9986 **
Total Current	.9362	.0000	.0003	.0608	.9973 **
Cities excluding Cleveland (N=19)					
General Government	.4685	.0139	.1179	.3532	.9535 **
Police	.5402	.0106	.0712	.3019	.9239 **
Fire	.4801	.0007	.2028	.1604	.9524 **
Streets & Highways	.4960	.0199	.0496	.3174	.8829 **
Total Current	.8055	.0003	.0428	—.0674	.7812 **
All Villages (N=38)					
General Government	.1944	.5184	.0254	.0719	.8101 **
Police	.1481	.5516	.1317	.0037	.8351 **
Fire	.0058	.8776	.0004	—.0241	.8597 **
Streets & Highways	.4548	.1316	.1707	—.0009	.7562 **
Total Current	.1249	.6422	.0385	.0616	.8672 **
Villages excluding Industrial Enclaves (N=34)					
General Government	.3176	.1149	.0395	.0386	.7806 **
Police	.4960	.0402	.1761	.1604	.8034 **
Fire	.1217	.1480		.2540	.5237 **
Streets & Highways	.3074	.0840	.0254	.3766	.7934 **
Total Current	.6195	.0003	.0447	.2594	.9239 **

** Coefficients of Multiple Determination, R^2, not corrected for degrees of freedom lost in computation.

All Cities category (standard deviation $676), and $2,805 in the Cities excluding Cleveland category (standard deviation $693).

In the case of the villages, there are no important differences between the average populations in the All Villages and the Villages excluding the Industrial Enclaves categories. The population is 3,066 (standard deviation 2,586) in the former, and 3,273 (standard deviation 2,640) in the latter category. But the per capita assessed valuations in the two village categories are not at all comparable. The average village in the All Villages category has a per capita assessed

Table IV-14—Regression Coefficients: Changes in Municipal Current Operating Expenditures and Selected Variables, Cleveland Metropolitan Area, 1950-56

Municipal Expenditures	Constant Term	Change in Population	Change in Assessed Valuation	Change in Wealth	Coefficient of Multiple Determination R²
All Cities (N=20)					
General Government	246,529	5.022	.004067	.124490	.936
Police	3,166	—2.763	.003256	.017073	.998
Fire	—2,881	—2.981	.002427	.054984	.996
Streets & Highways	13,909	1.685	.001582	.055795	.965
Total	174,062	—26.474	.015380	.122831	.987
Cities Excluding Cleveland (N=19)					
General Government	—27,149	1.374	.002413	.044065	.598
Police	18,415	—2,308	.002591	.047022	.844
Fire	18,217	0.254	.001103	.116004	.759
Streets & Highways	7,601	0.186	.002079	.048529	.489
Total	55,689	—47.327	.023670	—.256430	.578
All Villages (N=38)					
General Government	10	2.387	.000545	.002185	.554
Police	5,564	0.485	.001451	.003745	.853
Fire	n.c.	n.c.	n.c.	n.c.	n.c.
Streets & Highways	—283	4.263	.000621	.190758	.667
Total	—112	14.285	.005479	.178275	.888
Villages Excluding Industrial Enclaves (N=34)					
General Government	n.c.	n.c.	n.c.	n.c.	n.c.
Police	5,886	5.265	.000492	.019320	.766
Fire	n.c.	n.c.	n.c.	n.c.	n.c.
Streets & Highways	n.c.	n.c.	n.c.	n.c.	n.c.
Total	7,389	25.255	.0017606	.284933	.842

Exhibit: For schools the following was found:
Change in School Operating Expenditures=$110,000+.002120 (change in ADM) +.012176 (change in Assessed Valuation)+.003447 (change in School Foundation Aid).
n.c. Not computed.

valuation which is a reflection of the existence of the four industrial enclaves, $8,246 (standard deviation of $19,681.03). If the industrial enclaves are excluded, per capita assessed valuation in the average village falls to $3,472.24 (standard deviation of $1,799.56). The expenditure pattern in the average municipality in the All Villages category thus reflects the industrial enclaves, in the same manner that the average municipality in the All Cities category reflects Cleveland.

Table IV-15—Total Current Operating Expenditures of "Average" Municipalities, 1956, and the Effect of a Population Increment of 100 and Accompanying Changes in Assessed Valuation and Wealth

Municipal Expenditures	Total Expenditures of "Average" Municipality (Dollars)	Total Expenditures After Change in Independent Variables (Dollars)	Marginal Increment (Dollars)
All Cities *			
General Government	290,689	291,090	401
Police	730,185	731,385	1,200
Fire	462,289	463,053	764
Streets & Highways	525,958	526,693	735
Total Current	3,823,976	3,830,001	6,025
Cities Excluding Cleveland †			
General Government	122,060	122,439	379
Police	191,790	192,424	634
Fire	138,370	138,849	479
Streets & Highways	202,995	203,616	621
Total Current	1,856,384	1,861,427	5,043
All Villages ‡			
General Government	18,420	19,172	752
Police	33,495	35,046	1,551
Fire	11,703	12,669	966
Streets & Highways	23,919	24,986	1,067
Total Current	117,095	123,268	6,173
Villages Excluding Industrial Enclaves §			
General Government	16,793	17,296	503
Police	30,101	31,128	1,027
Fire	6,142	6,470	328
Streets & Highways	23,382	24,117	735
Total Current	100,590	103,567	2,977

* Change in Independent Variables: Population + 100, Assessed Valuation + 280751, and Wealth + 646.

† Change in Independent Variables: Population + 100, Assessed Valuation + 280520, and Wealth + 669.

‡ Change in Independent Variables: Population + 100, Assessed Valuation + 824608, and Wealth + 1980.

§ Change in Independent Variables: Population + 100, Assessed Valuation + 347224, and Wealth + 2156.

As shown in Table IV-15, if 100 persons are added to the average All Cities community, there would be an accompanying increase in operating expenditures of $6,025, or an additional municipal cost of about $60.25 per person. For the average municipality in the Cities excluding Cleveland category, the figure would be $5,043 in increased operating expenditures, or $50.43 per person.

If 100 persons were added to the average All Villages municipality, the increase in operating expenditures would be $6,173. Excluding the industrial enclaves, the comparable figure would be $2,977.

Of prime significance is the fact that in the case of the two important categories—Cities excluding Cleveland and Villages excluding Industrial Enclaves—with a greater average assessed valuation and greater wealth in the average village than in the average city, the increase in municipal expenditures would be greater in the "average city" than in the "average village."

The explanation of the differences in totals emerges when the expenditures are considered individually on a functional basis. First, if the total increase in expenditures is compared to the increase in expenditures on the enumerated functions (i.e., general government, police, fire, and streets and highways), there are differences between the categories. In the "average village" excluding the industrial enclaves, on the average 87.1 per cent of the additional expenditures would be on the four designated functions. In the "average city" excluding Cleveland, only 42.1 per cent would be so expended. Second, the absolute increase in the four designated functions is greater in the "average village" category than in the "average city" category; $2,593 as compared to $2,113. And this is true in each function, except fire, as well. The increase in city expenditures is thus on other functions such as hospitals, miscellaneous commercial activity, recreation, etc., rather than on the designated functions.

If the industrial enclaves are included in the village category, then the expenditures in total and on each function associated with the increase in population are larger than when they are excluded.

Factors Affecting Per Capita Expenditures

As has been pointed out earlier, at the heart of the study of municipal expenditure is the question which has attracted considerable interest in recent years, namely that of the factors which determine the level of per capita (or per student) expenditures.[3]

---

3. See especially Harvey E. Brazer, *City Expenditures in the United States,* Occasional Paper 66, National Bureau of Economic Research, New York, 1959, *passim.*

For purposes of analyzing per capita operating expenditures, municipalities and school districts in the Cleveland Metropolitan Area were
grouped in the same manner as they were for total operating expenditures; and of the large number of variables originally tested,
three were retained for detailed analysis of municipalities—population, per capita assessed valuation, and per capita wealth.

Before any attempt is made to analyze the degree of association
of the three factors with per capita expenditures, it is necessary to
be aware of their association with each other. As is indicated in
Table IV-16 above, only in the case of per capita wealth and per

**Table IV-16—Coefficients of Determination: Population, Per
Capita Assessed Valuation, and Per
Capita Wealth, 1956**

Governmental Unit	Population and Per Capita Assessed Valuation	Population and Per Capita Wealth	Per Capita Assessed Wealth and Per Capita Wealth
All Cities (N = 20)	0.1	0.5	24.1
Cities Excluding Cleveland (N = 19)	0.1	2.0	24.4
All Villages (N = 38)	4.1	—5.3	—6.7
Villages Excluding Industrial Enclaves (N = 34)	5.9	0.1	72.6

capita assessed valuation is the relationship very strong, and only in
the case of the Villages excluding Industrial Enclaves is the correlation significant. The result is the relative obliteration of the importance of per capita assessed valuation in the case of this latter
group.

The initial results are rather unexpected, but on second thought
explicable, since practically none of the variations in the per capita
total operating expenditures of the cities in the Cleveland Metropolitan Area is explained by the three chosen variables; whereas in
the case of the villages, almost all the variation is "explained" by
these three variables. As shown in Table IV-17, while only 18.0 per
cent of the variation in per capita operating expenditures of All
Cities is "explained," 95.22 per cent of the variation in All Villages
per capita operating expenditures is. For Cities excluding Cleveland
and Villages excluding Industrial Enclaves, the three variables
"explain" 6.8 per cent and 85.3 per cent of the variation respectively.

Table IV-17—Regression Coefficients: Per Capita Municipal Current Operating Expenditures and Selected Variables, Cleveland Metropolitan Area, 1956

City and Per Capita Operating Expenditure Category	Constant	Population	Per Capita Assessed Valuation	Per Capita Wealth	Coefficient of Multiple Determination, R^2
All Cities (N = 20)					
General Government	0.23	—.0000012	.0015623	.0068522	.6726
Police	3.28	.0000056	.0011066	.04651098	.6416
Fire	0.89	.0000030	.0011668	.0808741	.6183
Streets & Highways	4.84	—.0000009	.0009277	.0566791	.1238
Total	26.73	.0000250	.003240	.316142	.1797
Cities Excluding Cleveland (N = 19)					
General Government	0.94	—.0000188	.0014664	.0143852	.7305
Police	3.76	—.0000062	.0104097	.0515268	.4924
Fire	0.81	.0000042	.0011844	.0806028	.5918
Streets & Highways	6.69	—.0000458	.0006785	.0714981	.2029
Total	26.59	.000037	.003114	.395234	.0680
Villages (N = 38)					
General Government	7.55	—.0010599	.0005923	.0434947	.8608
Police	12.00	—.0012310	.0008883	.1438116	.7984
Fire	—0.97	.0002170	.0006278	—.0075371	.9029
Streets & Highways	7.52	—.0003871	.0002585	.1427459	.7429
Total	31.86	—.001242	.003153	.252483	.9519
Villages Excluding Industrial Enclaves (N = 34)					
General Government	4.48	—.0004717	.0009316	.0377544	.8534
Police	13.28	—.0007789	.0004087	.1817160	.7570
Fire	1.68	.0000693	—.0000730	.0070931	.0732
Streets & Highways	5.48	.0000216	.0001128	.1542630	.9414
Total	27.43	.0000793	.001435	.401911	.8526

The failure of these independent variables to "explain" variation in city per capita total operating expenditures stands in contrast with their high explanatory power in the case of the individual functions. The apparent reason for the failure of these variables to explain per capita total operating expenditure is that there is far less uniformity in the groups of public services provided by cities than by villages.

The results reflect the fact that some cities provide hospital and such miscellaneous commercial activities and that these are apparently independent of population, per capita assessed valuation, and per capita wealth. The inclusion of Cleveland gives population in the All Cities category more importance than it attains elsewhere, but it still explains only 13.2 per cent of the variation in per capita total operating expenditures. For Cities excluding Cleveland, per capita wealth explains a greater proportion of the variation in per capita total operating expenditures than any other factor considered; however, the figure of 11.9 per cent is not very great.

In the All Villages category, 95.2 per cent of the variation in per capita total operating expenditures is explained by variations in per capita assessed valuation and indirectly by the interaction of per capita assessed valuation and per capita wealth. That the latter interaction is important is brought out when the industrial enclaves are excluded. A lesser amount of variation is explained, 85.3 per cent; but per capita wealth explains 70.7 per cent of the total variation in per capita total operating expenditures, and variation in per capita assessed valuation only .7 per cent. This result emphasizes perhaps that it is the demand for government services, rather than the tax base, that determines the level of expenditure, although the required tax base must be in existence.

The use of rank orders, which is such a prominent feature of Morris Lambie's work,[4] provides a preliminary check on the meaningfulness of per capita totals. The principal check is to determine the extent to which the per capita totals reflect a general level of high expenditure or an emphasis on an individual expenditure, such as a hospital. An analysis of rank orders shows the effect of hospitals on per capita total operating expenditures. If hospital expenditures are included, Lakewood ranks first, Bedford second, and Cleveland third in per capita operating expenditures. If hospitals are excluded, then Shaker Heights rises to first, Cleveland to second, Rocky River to third, and Lakewood drops to fourteenth.

Not all per capita rank orders serve as measures of quality of

---

4. See especially *Experiments in Methods of Municipal Analysis* (Harvard Bureau for Research in Municipal Government, 1941) and *Status of the Property Tax 1945 and 1949 in 43 Cities and Towns within the Boston Metropolitan Area* (Harvard Bureau for Research in Municipal Government, 1950).

Table IV-18—Rank Orders: Expenditures Per Capita and Per $1000 Assessed Valuation by City and by Village, Cleveland Metropolitan Area, 1956

	PER CAPITA							PER $1000 ASSESSED VALUATION
	General Government	Police	Fire	Streets & Highways	Miscellaneous Commercial Activity	Total Operating	Total Operating Less Hospitals	Total Operating
Cities								
Bay Village	9	17	13	5	9	10	9	10
Bedford	4	6	20	3	1	2	6	2
Berea	8	10	7	6	2	6	4	3
Brooklyn	1	5	2	14	14	8	7	20
Cleveland	13	1	4	9	9	3	2	4
Cleveland Heights	6	8	6	8	3	7	5	5
East Cleveland	19	3	10	16	10	12	11	7
Euclid	15	12	12	13	15	14	13	19
Fairview Park	12	9	11	2	8	9	8	11
Garfield Heights	20	20	17	20	19	20	20	17
Lakewood	17	13	8	11	7	1	14	1
Lyndhurst	16	18	19	17	16	17	17	16
Maple Heights	18	15	14	19	11	18	19	15
Mayfield Heights	7	14	15	20	17	16	16	13
North Olmsted	14	16	18	7	18	15	15	8
Parma	11	19	16	12	20	19	18	18
Rocky River	5	7	5	1	6	5	3	6
Shaker Heights	2	2	1	4	5	4	1	9
South Euclid	10	11	9	15	12	13	12	12
University Heights	3	4	3	18	13	11	10	14
Villages								
Beachwood	15	16	27	13		11		24
Bedford Heights	19	34	34	20		32		35
Bentleyville	11	8	9	33		10		7
Bratenahl	7	4	3	5		5		1
Brecksville	26	19	15	17		17		31
Broadview Heights	34	30	31	34		34		27
Brooklyn Heights	8	23	20	23		14		13
Brook Park	4	5	2	6		2		34

Table IV-18 (Continued)

| | PER CAPITA | | | | | | PER $1000 ASSESSED VALUATION |
	General Government	Police	Fire	Streets & Highways	Miscellaneous Commercial Activity	Total Operating	Total Operating Less Hospitals	Total Operating
Chagrin Falls	22	14	24	12		9		5
Cuyahoga Heights	1	1	1	3		1		35
Gates Mills	5	6	16	4		6		3
Glenwillow	10	38	17	37		36		37
Highland Heights	20	35	26	21		33		30
Hunting Valley	3	3	11	1		4		4
Independence	32	20	35	9		22		20
Linndale	21	37	37	7		27		6
Mayfield	14	15	19	28		23		15
Middleburg Hts.	30	29	5	32		20		23
Moreland Hills	13	9	32	11		12		17
Newburgh Heights	16	22	30	19		26		14
North Randall	2	2	4	2		3		18
North Royalton	36	24	33	29		30		22
Oakwood	37	36	36	25		38		16
Olmsted Falls	27	27	12	15		19		10
Orange	35	13	37	22		28		32
Parkview	18	28	18	38		35		29
Parma Heights	24	25	10	24		18		8
Pepper Pike	9	10	14	8		7		25
Richmond Heights	29	26	29	36		37		33
Seven Hills	33	18	28	26		24		19
Solon	17	21	21	16		21		26
Strongsville	25	17	23	14		16		11
Valley View	6	11	7	35		13		9
Walton Hills	23	12	25	10		15		38
Warrensville Hts.	28	31	6	18		25		12
Westlake	38	32	13	30		31		28
West View	31	33	22	31		29		21
Woodmere	12	7	8	27		8		2

service, but the analysis shows that in general, after hospitals are excluded, the municipalities with high total per capita expenditures also have high ranking on the individual expenditures, as can be seen in the case of Shaker Heights, Cleveland, Rocky River, Berea and Cleveland Heights at one end of the city spectrum and Parma, Maple Heights, and Garfield Heights at the other. The only major exceptions occur when the services are provided either cheaply or at no cost by the inhabitants of the jurisdiction or by another government, a situation which is more common on the village than on the city level.

Factors Affecting Per Capita Operating Expenditures for Individual Functions

If per capita expenditures on general government, police, fire, and streets and highways are analyzed individually, using the same independent variables as above, a different picture emerges. In most cases the three variables explain a statistically significant portion of the variation in per capita expenditure of the four most important municipal functions. They are of no help, however, in explaining variations in per capita fire expenditures for the Villages excluding Industrial Enclaves. The existence of volunteer or of full-time fire departments on the village level appears unrelated to any of the independent variables individually or together under consideration. In the case of per capita expenditures on highways, all three variables again fall short, but in this case on the cities level. Neither individually nor in combination with each other do any of the three relate significantly to variations in per capita street and highway expenditures. Factors such as miles of road, conditions of the road, volume of traffic, and nature of traffic are probably much more important determinants of city per capita expenditures on streets and highways than are the variables chosen. As a result of these factors, University Heights has very low per capita street and highway expenditures, while its expenditures on other functions is very high. On the other hand, Fairview Park's expenditures on streets and highways are high while its other per capita expenditures are low.

If the relationship of the individual independent variables and the several functional classifications of per capita expenditures are analyzed, definite problems of interpretation emerge.

First, population is significantly associated with only two functional categories of expenditures—per capita general government expenditures of the Villages excluding Industrial Enclaves, and per capita police operating expenditures for All Cities. But, its relative direct weight is low as indicated by the 1.1 per cent squared Beta Coefficient in the case of police, and 6.5 per cent in the case of per capita general government expenditures. In the latter case, furthermore, as shown in Table IV-17 the per capita expenditures are *negatively* associated with variations in population. In no other case, either including or excluding Cleveland, is population significantly associated with variations in per capita operating expenditures. Of some interest is the fact that, excluding expenditures on fire, the per capita expenditures were inversely related to population size with only two exceptions, that aforementioned per capita expenditure on police in the All City category and excluding the industrial enclaves the per capita village expenditures on streets and highways.

Per capita assessed valuation is significantly associated with variations in per capita government expenditures in all groupings of governments; with per capita police expenditures in the All Cities and All Villages groups; with per capita fire expenditures, except in the aforementioned Villages excluding Industrial Enclaves category; and with per capita street and highway expenditures in the All Villages grouping.

Variations in per capita wealth are significantly associated with variations in per capita expenditures of All Villages on general government, police, and streets and highways. If the industrial enclaves are excluded, the relative importance of per capita personal wealth in explaining variations in per capita village operating expenditures in every category of expenditure increases. Finally it is assumed that in two instances the correlation between per capita assessed valuation and per capita wealth in the Villages excluding Industrial Enclaves category partially, if not totally, obliterated the relationship between per capita assessed valuation and per capita expenditures on police and streets and highways. In each of the above cases, the simple correlation coefficient between per capita assessed valuation and the per capita expenditures is significant on the 1 per cent level of significance.

If the relationships are grouped by governmental category rather than by function, then a slightly different picture emerges. The co-efficient of multiple correlation, R, between per capita operating expenditures and the several independent variables is significant in the case of All Villages. This is also true of the Villages excluding the Industrial Enclaves if per capita fire expenditures are omitted from consideration as they should be.

In the case of the cities, both including and excluding Cleveland, the three variables explain a statistically significant portion of the variation in per capita general government, police, and fire expenditures, but not of per capita streets and highways nor of per capita total operating expenditures.

Although no test has been applied, it appears from observation in only one instance, and that involving per capita fire expenditures, that a larger proportion of variation for every function is explained by the three variables in the case of the villages than in the case of the cities. In the case of All Cities and Cities excluding Cleveland, insofar as any factor stands out, it is per capita assessed valuation.

In the All Villages category both per capita assessed valuation and per capita wealth were significantly associated with per capita expenditures except in the case of fire, where only per capita assessed valuation was significant. If the industrial enclaves are excluded, per capita assessed valuation is no longer significant except in the case of per capita general government expenditures, where it remained significant although of lesser importance. The significant and important variable in the Villages excluding Industrial Enclaves was per capita wealth. However, it is felt that high correlation between per capita assessed valuation and per capita wealth is partly responsible for the reduction in the importance of per capita assessed valuation.

Operating Expenditures Per Student

As has been noted earlier, fiscally, the most important single gov-ernmental function in the Cleveland Metropolitan Area, as in

Table IV-19—Per Capita Current Operating Expenditures and Several Independent Variables: Contribution of Variables to Coefficients of Multiple Determination, Cleveland Metropolitan Area, 1956

CURRENT OPERATING EXPENDITURES	DIRECT CONTRIBUTION			COMBINED INDIRECT CONTRIBUTION	COEFFICIENT OF MULTIPLE DETERMINATION $R^2_{1.234}$
	Population $\beta^2_{12.34}$	Per Capita Assessed Valuation $\beta^2_{13.24}$	Per Capita Wealth $\beta^2_{14.23}$		
All Cities (N = 20)					
General Government	.0275	.6000	.0031	.0420	.6726
Police	.0107	.3453	.0324	.2522	.6416
Fire	.0873	.1605	.2080	.1625	.6183
Streets & Highways	.0033	.0429	.0431	.0345	.1238
Total	.1318	.0267	.0686	—.0474	.1797
Cities Excluding Cleveland (N = 19)					
General Government	.0734	.5382	.0139	.1050	.7305
Police	.0058	.1993	.1307	.1566	.4924
Fire	.0018	.1758	.2179	.1963	.5918
Streets & Highways	.0870	.0230	.0683	.0246	.2029
Total	.0033	.0277	.1194	—.0824	.0680
All Villages (N = 38)					
General Government	.0407	.7356	.0405	.0440	.8608
Police	.0183	.5506	.1473	.0822	.7984
Fire	.0019	.9187	.0014	—.0191	.9029
Streets & Highways	.0064	.1652	.6165	—.0452	.7429
Total	.0013	.4853	.0318	.4335	.9519
Villages Excluding Industrial Enclaves (N = 34)					
General Government	.0650	.1211	.2619	.4054	.8534
Police	.0218	.0028	.7499	.0155	.7570
Fire	.0184	.0095	.1212	.0759	.0732
Streets & Highways	.0000	.0006	1.5122	—.5714	.9414
Total	.0044	.0066	.7074	.1342	.8526

other areas, is that of education, a fact that is true both for operating and for capital expenditures. Even with state aid, the operating expenditures per student in average daily membership vary from $264 in North Olmsted to $687 in Bratenahl. What factors explain these variations?

Operating expenditures per student vary because of a variety of factors, including the scope and quality of the educational product.

The scope and quality are in turn the result of a variety of factors of which the major factor is the amount of money spent per student. There exist obvious exceptions to this case, but there tends to be a very high correlation unless very special circumstances exist, such as a high transportation cost or a very small school plant, between the amount spent per student and the scope and quality of education.

Initially three factors were considered as explaining the variations in expenditures, but later a fourth was added. The three initial factors were number of students in average daily membership (ADM), assessed valuation per student, and school foundation aid per student. Later, wealth, as measured by the Ohio Intangibles Levy, was added. On the basis of the simple correlations, 50.8 per cent of the variation in operating expenditures per student was accounted for by variations in per capita assessed valuation, and 40.8 per cent by variations in wealth. After data on wealth became available, and its effect as well as the effects of students in ADM, assessed valuation per ADM, and school foundation in ADM were held constant, it was discovered that per student assessed valuation accounted for 7.8 per cent of the variations in per student operating expenditure, whereas wealth per ADM explained 72.9 per cent. The coefficient of multiple determination, $R^2_{1.2345}$, was .8728.

The estimating equation for pupil operating expenditures is as follows:

$$\text{Operating per student in ADM} = \$28.76 + .0001526 \, (\text{ADM})$$
$$+ .0046514 \text{ (assessed valuation per ADM)} + 2.77$$
$$\text{(School Foundation Aid per ADM)} + .6281015 \text{ (personal}$$
$$\text{wealth per ADM)}$$

In terms of the squares of the Beta Coefficients which indicate the relative contribution of the four variables toward an explanation of per pupil expenditures, neither total ADM nor assessed valuation per ADM contributes much; however, school foundation per ADM and wealth per ADM contribute a great deal. The respective contributions of squared Beta Coefficients to the coefficient of multiple determination of .873 are as follows:

ADM	.007
Assessed Valuation	.078
School Foundation per ADM	.321
Personal Wealth per ADM	.729
Indirect Contribution	—.195

In terms of their respective variables, it is evident that differences in wealth per student, rather than differences in assessed valuation per student, is the critical variable in determining expenditures. The availability of resources per student does not guarantee high expenditures, but the high personal wealth correlated as it is with high assessed valuation per student does.

Summary and Conclusions

Operating expenditures in the Cleveland Metropolitan Area show great diversity regardless of how they are measured; in the aggregate, in per capita, or per $1000 of assessed valuation terms. The diversity exists not only because of historical and political factors, but because of readily identifiable economic characteristics of the governments involved. These characteristics include the location of the government within the metropolitan area; its nature, that is, whether it is a municipality, city, village, or township; its population; property tax base and the personal wealth contained within the geographic boundaries of the various governments.

Basic to an understanding of operating expenditures in the Cleveland Metropolitan Area is the almost complete fiscal independence of the county, municipalities, and school districts. The range and diversity of expenditures of the municipalities are influenced by the functions assumed by the County, especially welfare, but also hospitals and other functions that the County has since assumed. Of even greater importance to an understanding of the variations in local expenditures in the Cleveland Metropolitan Area is the fact that the most important local function in terms of expenditures, education, is governed by independent school districts whose boundaries are not generally coterminous with those of individual municipalities. Yet the schools are financed from the same tax base as the municipalities. If school expenditures are allocated by municipality, then the striking importance of school operating expenditures is brought out by the fact that, if they are thus allocated, school operating expenditures exceed municipal operating expenditures in every case except the industrial enclaves, the three wealthiest villages, and the cities of Cleveland and Lakewood (the last because its hospital expenditures are reported on a gross basis). Only seven out of the sixty-two cities, villages, and townships have per capita municipal operating expenditures in excess of per capita school expenditures. On the basis of a claim on the property base, only in two of the seventy-eight taxing districts, as listed by the Auditor of Cuyahoga County in 1956, were the municipal property tax rates in excess of school tax rates, these being Cleveland and Brooklyn Heights. In the latter case this was due to the fact that Brooklyn Heights was part of the Cuyahoga Heights School District with its low tax rate, rather than because of an extraordinarily high municipal rate.

How can this intra-metropolitan diversity be explained? Two alternative approaches were followed in the preceding pages, the first, in the form of spatial consideration; the second, by applying multiple regression techniques to the operating expenditures of various classes of governments.

Viewed spatially, total municipal and school expenditures were concentrated as they have been in the past in the core areas. However, this concentration of total expenditure does not warrant the assumption that expenditures per person or expenditures per $1000 of assessed valuation are necessarily greater in the core area with its higher density and preponderant share of total population than in the periphery area. This is evident if the total of municipal and school expenditures rather than municipal expenditures alone are considered, because school rather than municipal expenditures is now dominant. The highest per capita municipal expenditures were concentrated in sets of contiguous communities outside the core area, although most of this outside area had lower per capita municipal costs than the older core area. Per capita school operating expenditures were uniformly higher outside the core area, for only one school district had a lower *per capita* school operating expenditure than did the City of Cleveland. High per capita costs of education or even per student costs were not evident in the core area.

Since expenditures outside of Cleveland are dominated by education except in special cases, the overall pattern of expenditures reflects school rather than municipal expenditures, with the result that the core area is no longer distinctively high either in expenditures per person or in expenditures per $1000 assessed valuation.

Spatial considerations suggest that the characteristics of the government rather than their location determined the 1956 level of total expenditures. Population accounted for a significant portion of the variation in expenditures not only for all functions, but for most individual classes of functions as well, fire expenditures being an exception to the rule. However, there was no evidence that this was the case in per capita expenditures. In fact, in most cases per capita expenditures were negatively related to population, although the evidence can in no way be presumed to be conclusive. On the other hand, some combination of per capita assessed valuation and per capita personal wealth account for a statistically significant portion of the variations in all per capita village operating expenditures except for fire prevention. In cities, these two variables account for most of the variation in general government, police, and fire, while expenditures on streets reflect other forces, especially location, and the amount of streets and highways. In the case of the cities, exclusion of hospital and miscellaneous commercial activities expenditures would doubtless have made the results for per capita total operating expenditures more in accord with those of the individual functions. In the case of streets and highways, some measure of the use of street mileage and some measure of traffic volume would doubtless account for a considerable portion of the variation.

Per student school operating expenditures are in no way influenced by variations in total enrollment, but by the assessed valuation, wealth, and State Aid per student which account for 81.3 per cent of the variations in per student operating expenditures.

Table IV-20—Municipal Expenditures, Cleveland Metropolitan Area, 1956

(In Thousands of Dollars)

Governmental Unit	General Gov't.	Police	Fire	Other Public Safety	Public Health	Hospitals	Public Welfare	Streets & Highways	Misc. Comm. Activity	Recreation & Culture	Land Use & Development	Pension	Misc. & Unallocable	Total Current Expend.	Interest	Capital
Cuyahoga County	8,274	659	0.0	1,578	6	4,004	19,637	3,090	630	33	256	784	96	39,047	496	7,394
Cities																
Bay Village	51.5	59.2	46.2	13.2	3.9	0.0	0.0	108.2	66.7	31.6	1.8	27.6	4.8	414.7	16.5	343.3
Bedford	66.3	101.4	7.1	19.6	5.1	212.6	2.0	130.6	135.5	23.7	0.0	60.7	9.3	773.9	44.8	376.3
Berea	65.5	95.9	74.3	15.9	8.6	20.9	0.0 *	123.1	135.4	42.9	2.2	34.5	7.0	626.2	31.1	561.0
Brooklyn	68.8	66.6	58.0	2.6	3.5	0.0	0.0 *	50.1	37.0	2.4	0.3	25.3	6.2	320.8	35.5	226.7
Cleveland	3,496.0	10,958.0	6,617.9	2,369.5	1,541.1	5,671.3	1,423.7	6,640.1	8,656.1	3,152.0	231.9	3,699.8	492.7	54,950.1	5,837.7	16,652.1
Cleveland Heights	310.0	449.4	344.5	39.8	47.7	0.0	16.9	446.5	626.0	261.6	2.5	183.9	44.9	2,773.7	34.4	392.1
East Cleveland	129.0	376.5	200.2	19.2	23.8	0.0	10.2	214.2	228.5	64.0	2.1	101.1	17.4	1,386.2	11.3	264.6
Euclid	221.3	393.7	254.1	37.5	22.7	0.0	9.5	396.2	277.1	132.2	1.3	211.0	24.2	1,980.8	169.2	2,163.3
Fairview Park	52.8	94.0	64.7	6.1	5.1	0.0	0.0	136.2	93.8	31.7	0.0	31.5	8.3	524.2	22.8	34.1
Garfield Heights	91.1	129.5	110.4	14.2	10.2	0.0	2.7	129.5	82.6	0.0	0.5	42.1	11.7	624.5	33.8	216.6
Lakewood	237.6	436.8	369.3	23.9	50.3	2,176.2	33.6	464.6	512.2	110.2	0.5	218.9	18.9	4,653.0	86.6	460.7
Lyndhurst	49.6	41.0	41.6	12.6	4.1	0.0	0.0	73.2	50.0	30.4	0.0	8.2	13.3	354.0	34.7	77.0
Maple Heights	90.7	149.7	94.0	2.1	8.5	0.0	9.5	127.4	137.8	10.5	0.5	33.1	8.3	672.1	87.7	1,295.7
Mayfield Heights	51.8	66.8	35.8	6.3	3.2	0.0	0.0	73.5	33.2	4.2	0.3	18.3	11.2	304.6	25.9	137.6
North Olmsted	45.2	65.2	40.7	14.8	3.6	20.4	0.0 *	107.3	34.8	19.0	0.0	41.1	6.5	398.6	25.9	186.1
Parma	261.2	309.8	211.6	69.4	14.2	0.0	29.3	418.9	66.7	43.4	0.0	136.2	47.5	1,608.1	281.5	2,197.3

Rocky River	78.6	112.8	88.6	10.6	6.1	0.0	0.2	275.8	130.4	34.9	0.3	50.6	8.0	796.9	56.1	74.0
Shaker Heights	252.5	368.2	344.4	37.6	20.1	0.0	3.2	353.5	305.7	93.3	4.0	184.8	54.1	2,021.4	23.2	267.1
South Euclid	112.0	167.6	133.2	20.1	12.4	0.0	0.2	146.7	123.7	45.0	3.7	58.6	18.1	841.3	61.3	484.4
University Heights	83.9	129.8	109.6	12.1	6.2	0.0	0.0	80.0	73.8	4.5	1.0	43.3	7.1	543.5	6.3	123.9
Villages																
Beachwood	27.1	47.1	4.2	12.5	1.3	0.0	0.0	40.2	23.5	10.2	1.1	1.3	5.2	173.7	13.5	11.2
Bedford Heights	26.1	26.6	3.3	2.3	1.3	0.0	0.0	25.9	4.7	1.6	0.0	0.9	2.5	95.2	0.0	41.5
Bentleyville	2.5	6.4	0.7	0.1	0.1	0.0	0.0	1.0	0.0	0.0	0.0	0.0	0.1	10.9	0.0	2.3
Bratenahl	13.7	70.8	8.3	0.7	0.5	0.0	0.0	33.9	9.9	7.0	0.1	5.3	5.5	155.7	0.0	5.7
Brecksville	19.9	38.3	8.7	4.6	1.2	0.0	0.0	34.2	11.9	5.0	0.0	8.1	2.4	134.3	2.0	24.6
Broadview Heights	13.4	27.0	3.5	6.6	0.3	0.0	0.0	15.9	10.9	0.0*	0.0	0.0	4.3	81.9	2.9	10.5
Brooklyn Heights	14.0	10.3	2.1	0.8	0.3	0.0	0.0	7.5	3.0	1.7	0.2	1.1	3.1	44.1	2.2	6.0
Brook Park	46.7	113.4	95.0	11.8	6.6	60.2	0.0	57.9	51.1	9.5	0.5	50.9	9.9	513.5	46.6	773.2
Chagrin Falls	18.8	38.1	4.1	1.7	0.7	0.0	0.0	33.1	42.3	1.5	1.4	1.7	3.2	146.6	9.2	189.5
Cuyahoga Heights	62.3	92.3	137.6	8.7	7.5	0.0	0.0	27.7	11.5	0.9	0.0	58.2	7.2	413.9	15.5	17.8
Gates Mills	20.8	36.7	2.4	1.7	0.6	0.0	0.0	39.6	6.3	8.2	0.9	0.0	7.6	124.8	0.7	6.8
Glenwillow	3.1	0.6	0.6	0.3	0.1	0.0	0.0	0.6	0.0	0.0	0.0	0.0	0.0*	5.3	0.0	0.2
Highland Heights	11.3	11.0	2.1	1.9	0.3	0.0	0.0	11.4	0.3	0.4	0.1	0.0	0.5	39.3	6.9	0.5
Hunting Valley	12.7	31.3	1.1	0.1	0.4	0.0	0.0	26.7	0.0	0.7	0.1	2.2	1.3	76.6	0.0	7.5
Independence	22.2	48.8	4.0	2.9	0.0	0.0	0.0	64.1	4.6	1.9	0.2	7.0	12.2	167.9	0.3	6.4
Linndale	2.2	1.1	0.0	0.0	0.0*	0.0	0.0	5.2	0.4	0.0	0.0	0.0	0.6	9.5	0.0	3.9
Mayfield	10.8	18.9	2.6	4.0	0.3	0.0	0.0	7.7	1.8	0.0	0.1	0.0	0.6	46.8	10.2	2.2
Middleburg Heights	21.2	34.7	26.0	4.8	3.0	14.3	0.0	21.6	14.1	0.9	0.0	13.7	7.1	16.4	6.5	28.1
Moreland Hills	13.0	28.0	1.4	3.4	0.4	0.0	0.0	17.1	1.2	0.1	0.2	2.0	1.9	68.7	0.8	5.1
Newburgh Heights	22.6	28.5	3.3	0.7	0.7	0.0	0.0	24.8	10.8	0.0	0.0	4.1	2.1	97.6	0.8	4.1
North Randall	12.2	21.8	1.7	0.9	0.5	0.0	0.0*	13.6	1.9	0.0	0.0	0.0	0.7	53.3	0.0	58.4
North Royalton	17.4	46.3	4.8	7.6	0.9	0.0	0.0*	27.4	19.2	1.3	0.0	1.3	8.1	134.3	22.5	10.2
Oakwood	9.9	13.2	2.1	2.8	0.3	0.0	0.0	20.1	1.3	0.0	0.3	0.0	1.2	51.2	0.0	8.7
Olmsted Falls	7.7	12.7	4.1	0.9	0.3	3.4	0.0	14.4	6.3	2.9	0.1	0.5	0.6	53.9	0.0	4.7

(Continued on next page)

Table IV-20 (Continued)

(In Thousands of Dollars)

Governmental Unit	General Gov't.	Police	Fire	Other Public Safety	Public Health	Hospitals	Public Welfare	Streets & Highways	Misc. Comm. Activity	Recreation & Culture	Land Use & Development	Pension	Misc. & Unallocable	Total Current Expend.	Interest	Capital
Orange	4.9	20.7	0.0	0.2	0.3	0.0	0.0	9.3	0.0	0.0	0.6	0.3	0.6	36.9	0.0	4.6
Parkview	10.5	11.5	3.0	0.7	0.3	0.0	0.0	3.2	2.3	0.4	0.0	0.1	1.1	33.1	1.5	26.5
Parma Heights	59.8	84.2	31.4	14.3	1.9	0.0	0.0	63.7	47.9	4.9	0.0	21.2	29.3	358.6	49.1	335.2
Pepper Pike	22.3	34.3	3.8	1.5	0.7	0.0	0.0	24.3	22.1	0.0	0.0	7.0	1.7	117.7	4.3	123.7
Richmond Heights	13.9	24.1	3.1	1.3	0.4	0.0	0.0	6.8	2.4	0.0	0.6	1.8	1.0	55.4	17.6	173.7
Seven Hills	13.9	32.5	3.3	10.6	0.6	0.0	0.0	18.3	8.6	5.6	0.1	3.6	2.3	99.4	8.3	6.1
Solon	31.0	41.5	7.8	7.9	1.2	0.0	0.0*	41.5	8.4	0.8	3.8	8.6	1.4	153.9	0.4	28.5
Strongsville	26.6	53.8	6.9	3.8	0.9	10.2	0.0	48.3	3.3	5.1	0.0	7.2	3.6	69.7	7.6	9.2
Valley View	13.9	17.5	3.5	0.5	0.8	0.0	0.0	4.2	2.6	0.2	0.3	0.0	1.6	45.1	0.0	11.7
Walton Hills	8.0	21.5	1.6	0.6	0.0	0.0	0.0	15.2	1.9	0.0	0.0	0.0	0.1	48.9	0.0	0.0
Warrensville Heights	31.6	48.2	33.8	8.3	1.4	0.0	0.0	55.0	26.1	0.0	0.8	3.4	3.3	211.9	6.3	11.9
Westlake	24.3	61.3	21.1	8.4	1.7	0.0	0.1	41.5	20.0	10.8	0.0	12.1	13.3	214.6	35.3	65.2
West View	4.2	6.6	1.4	1.2	0.2	1.9	0.0	4.4	2.8	0.0	0.0	0.1	1.2	24.0	0.0	1.1
Woodmere	3.7	11.0	1.2	0.4	0.1	0.0	0.0	2.2	0.6	0.0	0.1	0.6	0.4	20.3	0.0	2.1
Townships																
Chagrin Falls	8.3	0.0	0.6	0.1	0.0	0.0	0.0	8.0	0.2	0.0	0.0	0.0	0.2	17.4	0.0	0.0
Olmsted	3.9	7.4	2.6	0.0	0.4	5.7	0.0	0.2	3.2	0.0	0.4	0.4	0.2	24.4	0.0	2.7
Riveredge	0.0	0.0	0.0	0.0	0.0	0.0	0.0	0.0	3.2	0.0	0.0	0.0	0.0	0.0	0.0	0.0
Warrensville	1.7	1.0	0.0	0.0	0.2	0.0	0.0	0.7	0.7	0.0	0.0	0.0	0.3	4.2	0.0	24.7
Total	14,804	16,542	9,695	4,467	1,845	12,201	21,178.	14,504	12,826	5,071.	521	982	982.0	120,846	7,744	36,318.

* Less than $100.00.

Table IV-21—School District Expenditures, Cleveland Metropolitan Area, 1956

(In Thousands of Dollars)

School Districts	Instructional	Current Operating	Interest	Capital	Total
Cities					
Bay Village	422.8	658.9	44.9	213.1	916.9
Bedford	850.1	1,332.3	96.6	707.6	2,136.5
Berea	935.8	1,572.1	152.9	2,275.7	4,000.7
Brooklyn	354.4	609.2	48.2	230.4	887.8
Cleveland	25,487.7	39,039.1	24.1	2,768.0	41,831.3
Cleveland Heights	3,064.5	4,859.7	169.4	948.6	5,977.7
East Cleveland	1,246.3	2,031.2	12.2	46.1	2,089.5
Euclid	2,476.6	3,765.7	77.3	843.2	4,686.2
Fairview Park	478.0	686.7	56.8	44.4	787.9
Garfield Heights	782.9	1,220.7	88.8	918.7	2,228.2
Lakewood	1,925.4	3,123.1	48.0	402.0	3,573.1
Maple Heights	867.1	1,364.3	93.7	312.6	1,770.6
North Olmsted	344.4	578.3	42.1	534.3	1,154.7
Parma	2,337.9	3,789.4	280.5	1,222.6	5,292.5
Rocky River	622.2	1,032.3	56.2	182.1	1,270.6
Shaker Heights	2,068.7	3,392.0	95.5	1,802.9	5,290.4
So. Euclid-Lyndhurst	1,315.5	1,999.1	180.0	762.6	2,941.7
Local & Exempted					
Beachwood	106.9	128.8	21.9	130.3	281.0
Bratenahl	63.4	103.0	0.0	5.0	108.0
Brecksville	328.2	589.1	31.6	274.7	895.4
Chagrin Falls Ex.	252.6	423.6	14.8	70.1	508.5
Cuyahoga Heights	286.0	515.3	13.3	25.4	554.0
Independence	158.1	265.7	21.5	292.9	580.1
Mayfield (City)	565.7	945.1	103.0	817.5	1,865.6
North Royalton	227.2	402.4	30.5	264.2	697.1
Olmsted Falls	244.2	425.2	14.2	24.4	463.8
Orange	256.4	618.0	57.9	694.9	1,370.8
Richmond Heights	65.5	154.1	5.2	176.5	335.8
Solon	200.3	376.4	31.8	155.0	563.2
Strongsville	190.8	333.2	30.6	260.4	624.2
Warrensville Heights	315.6	527.1	57.1	385.0	969.2
Westlake Ex.	278.4	461.8	46.3	357.3	865.4
Total	61,195.0	78,511	2,047	18,147.0	98,705

Table IV-22—Library District Expenditures, Cleveland Metropolitan Area, 1956

(In Thousands of Dollars)

Metro Code	Library District	Operating	Capital	Interest	Total Expenditures
250	Cleveland	4229	19	0	4248
251	Cleveland Heights	265	9	0	274
252	Cuyahoga County	1059	362	0	1421
253	East Cleveland	189	56	0	245
254	Euclid	154	9	0	163
255	Lakewood	267	196	0	463
256	Porter (Westlake)	11	4	0	15
257	Rocky River	32	0	0	32
258	Shaker Heights	157	3	0	160
	Total	6364	658	0	7022

Table IV-23—Simple Correlation Coefficients: Per Capita Current Operating Expenditures and Selected Independent Variables, All Cities, Cleveland Metropolitan Area, 1956

Dependent Variables	a. Population	b. Area	c. Density	d. Assessed Valuation	e. Per Capita Assessed Valuation	f. Per Capita Personal Property	g. Per Capita Intangible Property Levy (Wealth)	h. 1956 Pop. as Per Cent of 1950 Population	i. Value of Res. Prop. as Per Cent of Total Val. of Real Property	i. Per Capita Residential Assessed Valuation 1956
A. Per Capita General Government	—.164	—.179	—.301	—.144	.801	.299	.449	—.201	—.070	.503
B. Per Capita Police	.559	.463	.527	.575	.528	.272	.419	—.687	—.640	.138
C. Per Capita Fire	.267	.195	.370	.284	.629	.120	.631	—.550	—.257	.481
D. Per Capita Streets & Highways	—.697	—.058	—.308	—.058	.301	—.161	.298	—.119	.119	.387
E. Per Capita Recreation & Culture	.334	.301	.173	.345	.009	—.126	.351	—.448	—.108	.164
F. Per Capita Pensions	.250	.209	.168	.272	.571	.260	.484	—.576	—.432	.268
G. Per Capita Total Current Exp.	.340	.259	.360	.347	.332	.008	.391	—.689	—.395	.141
H. Per Capita Interest	.568	.643	—.197	.572	.196	.560	—.266	—.174	—.419	—.353
I. Per Capita Capital Outlays	—.001	.069	—.324	—.008	—.022	.430	—.372	—.273	—.098	—.325

20 Cities
Levels of Significance
5% level r ≥ .4438
1% level r ≥ .5614

Table IV-24—Simple Correlation Coefficients: Selected Independent Variables, All Cities, Cleveland Metropolitan Area, 1956

	a. Population	b. Area	c. Density	d. Assessed Valuation	e. Per Capita Assessed Valuation	f. Per Capita Personal Property	g. Per Capita Intangible Property Levy	h. 1956 Pop. as Per Cent of 1950 Population	i. Valuation of Res. Prop. as Per Cent of Total Val. of Real Prop.	j. Per Capita Residential Assessed Val. 1956
a. Population										
b. Area	.977									
c. Density	.511	.397								
d. Assessed Valuation	.999	.976	.503							
e. Per Capita Assessed Valuation	.007	—.009	—.101	.038						
f. Per Capita Personal Property	.291	.313	.031	.306	.556					
g. Per Capita Intangible Property Levy (Wealth)	—.073	—.102	.081	—.053	.491	—.272				
h. 1956 Pop. as Per Cent of 1950 Population	—.317	—.166	—.656	—.322	—.265	—.168	—.252			
i. Valuation of Residential Prop. as Per Cent of Total Val. of Real Property	—.580	—.531	—.552	—.585	—.332	—.748	—.132	.567		
j. Per Capita Residential Assessed Valuation 1956	—.345	—.348	—.263	.325	.462	—.434	.845	.070	—.529	

20 Cities
Levels of Significance
5% level r $>$ .4438
1% level r $>$ .5614

V

Capital Outlay

CAPITAL OUTLAYS IN THE CLEVELAND METROPOLI-
tan Area in 1956 were over five and a half times their 1940 level,
while current operating expenditures were slightly less than three
times as great, and interest expenditures were virtually unchanged
between these years. Taken at face value, the period appears to be
one of extraordinary growth for capital outlays. Viewed in a broader
context, however, a different picture emerges. Except for 1929 when
the capital outlays were almost equal to those of 1940, capital outlays by *all* governments in 1940 were less than those of the City of
Cleveland *alone* for every year between 1926 and 1932. And there
is good reason to believe that in real terms the capital outlays of
the Cleveland Metropolitan Area in 1927, to mention only the most
outstanding instance, exceeded those of any year from 1932 up to

and including the present. This conclusion is based on the fact that
the $27.6 millions of capital outlays of Cleveland and its overlying
governments [1] in that year were more than $65.0 millions in 1956
dollars. Therefore the real value of total capital outlays for all governments in the Cleveland Metropolitan Area probably was in excess of those recorded for any year during the 1950's, and far in
excess in per capita real terms.

A long run view of Cleveland and its overlying governments
places capital outlays in the Cleveland Metropolitan Area in an entirely different perspective from a short-run view based on the period
1940 to the present. The 1920's were characterized by exuberant
municipal growth and outlay. Emphasis during that decade was on
the construction of highways and sewage systems and, to a lesser
extent, schools.

Capital outlays had a far greater relative importance in the late
1920's and early 1930's than at any time since. From 1926 through
1931, capital outlays of Cleveland and its overlying governments
never fell below 42 per cent and once rose as high as 65 per cent of
current operating expenditures. In the latter part of the 1930's, on
the other hand, they never rose to more than 23 per cent of operating expenditures, and fell to as low as 11 per cent. Based on the
same data, the ratio from 1941 through 1945 never exceeded 8 per
cent.

Capital outlays of Cleveland and its overlying governments are
shown in Table V-1. From 1926 through 1931, outlays varied between $18.1 millions and $22.9 millions, with comparable stability
in detail, if the exceptional 27.6 millions spent in 1927 is excluded.
If 1932 is considered as a transition year, then during the period
1933-40 capital outlays varied between $5.2 and $7.7 millions providing the two peaks caused by school building programs in 1936
and 1939 are excluded. From 1932 through 1946 then, capital outlays in the whole of the Cleveland Metropolitan Area did not reach
the levels of the six-year period immediately preceding.

---

1. The overlying governments consist of the Cleveland School District, the Cleveland Library District, the proportionate share of Cuyahoga County expenditures
based on the ratio of Cleveland population to the population of Cuyahoga County,
and the Cleveland Metropolitan Park District. The ratios of Cleveland to total
Cuyahoga County population were as follows: 1920—85.5 per cent; 1930—75.1
per cent; 1940—72.2 per cent; 1950—65.8 per cent.

During the period 1926-40 current operating expenditures also varied within narrow limits: $47 to $51 millions between 1936 and 1940; $38 to $44 millions between 1926 and 1935. Increased welfare expenditures were responsible for the difference in levels of operating expenditures.

During World War II, capital outlays were radically curtailed, as would be expected. They were thus reduced to levels even lower than those of the depressed 1930's. The outlays for the City of Cleveland, the only municipal government in the Cleveland Metropolitan Area for which detailed time series data is readily available, fell to about one-third of the level of the Depression decade. The fourteen-year period, 1932-46, with its low capital outlays was responsible for a huge back-log of capital projects. From 1946 on, capital outlays had not only to keep up with rapid growth in newer areas, but with the need for updating existing facilities in older areas. The increased outlays from 1946 to the present, nevertheless, still seem moderate in total and in relationship to operating expenditures, when compared to the late 1920's.

Capital outlay comprises expenditures for contract or force account construction of buildings, roads and other improvements, and expenditures for purchase of equipment, land, and existing structures. Accordingly, this "includes amounts for additions, replacements, and major alterations to fixed works and structures," but not for maintenance and operation.[2] Using economic criteria, this means that capital expenditures by governments can be divided into two categories: new construction and expenditures on machinery and equipment. Additions to inventory, the third element in the usual description of capital outlay, is missing in government capital outlay, with the exception of those additions included in public service enterprises which are self-supporting.

As in the case of private accounting, one of the major problems in government accounting is the distinction between current operating and capital expenditures. As noted by Burkhead, a division based on life expectancy "emphasizes the difference between final product which is used up during the accounting period and final

---

2. *Compendium of City Government Finances in 1955,* U. S. Department of Commerce, Bureau of Census, p. 145.

product which produces benefits that accrue partly in the future. This criterion is admittedly arbitrary, but at least it conforms with the practice of most countries that have attempted to separate current and capital expenditures in the government sector." [3]

In practice, the principal problems involve the distinction between "major repairs and alterations that extend the life expectancy of capital assets or increase their usefulness which should be included as a capital expenditure," and "ordinary maintenance and repairs which should be treated as a current expenditure." [4] Another important problem involves certain expenditures for improvements whose life expectancy is longer (and at times considerably longer) than a year, but which are reported as current expenditures. These problems are inherent in any attempt to compare data on capital outlays. They are responsible for the difficulties in comparing the capital outlays made by different governments or by the different functions of one government.

Capital Outlays, 1940-56

During the period 1940-56, a number of individual functions dominated capital outlays in the Cleveland Metropolitan Area. Schools, highways, sewage disposal, recreation and culture, accounted for the major portion of local capital outlays; police, fire, and other general functions accounted for a smaller proportion. Capital outlays on water and mass transit, which are considered independently as public service enterprises, also increased during this period.

Capital outlays, unlike current operating expenditures, tend to move unevenly over time. They are usually concentrated and, for many governments, random over time insofar as the expenditures for any particular function are concerned. In many instances, the only predictable capital expenditures involve those which are committed or already underway. Underlying the particular movement of a partical capital outlay, however, is the question of the general level of

3. Jesse Burkhead, *Government Budgeting* (John Wiley & Sons, Inc.: 1956), Chapter 9, p. 230.
4. *Ibid.*

Table V-1—Capital Outlays of Cleveland and Overlying Governments, 1926-56

(In Thousands of Current Dollars)

Year	City	County	School	Cleveland Metropolitan Park District	TOTAL
1926	13,477	5,021	2,738	461	21,697
1927	17,826	6,401	2,886	524	27,606
1928	10,674	5,963	2,816	498	22,853
1929	9,354	4,902	3,604	241	18,101
1930	11,604	6,590	1,623	320	20,138
1931	11,475	5,731	3,608	99	20,913
1932	9,676	3,413	846	72	14,008
1933	4,428	868	364	17	5,671
1934	4,100	689	327	36	5,152
1935	4,706	303	26	196	5,231
1936	5,806	783	1,827	36	8,453
1937	5,436	340	465	59	6,230
1938	3,041	2,324	47	80	5,493
1939	5,097	2,729	3,962	n.a.	11,891
1940	5,492	1,738	389	114	7,773
1941	2,778	n.a.	n.a.	n.a.	n.a.
1942	1,684	n.a.	n.a.	n.a.	n.a.
1943	1,190	n.a.	n.a.	n.a.	n.a.
1944	1,279	n.a.	n.a.	n.a.	n.a.
1945	2,459	n.a.	n.a.	n.a.	n.a.
1946	2,641	n.a.	n.a.	n.a.	n.a.
1947	3,904	n.a.	n.a.	n.a.	n.a.
1948	5,488	n.a.	n.a.	n.a.	n.a.
1949	7,924	n.a.	n.a.	n.a.	n.a.
1950	9,417	2,648	1,371	†	13,336
......	......	......	......	......	......
1954	22,503	3,728	2,475	†	28,706
1955	17,573	6,769	4,244	†	28,586
1956	16,652	5,087	2,768	†	24,507

† Included in the county total.
n.a. Not available.
Source: 1926-1950: *Financial Statistics of Cities.*
　　　　1954-1956: Cleveland Metropolitan Services Commission Worksheets.

capital expenditures and its movement. The random nature of any particular capital expenditure should not hide the underlying upward movement of capital expenditures in virtually all sectors since World War II.

The year 1940 is the first year for which data for all governments in the Cleveland Metropolitan Area are available. Capital expenditures in that year amounted to $12.5 millions. By 1950, that figure reached $39.9 millions; by 1954, it attained the unprecedented total of $85.8 millions, from which it dropped to $69.0 millions in 1956. Preliminary information indicates that the 1957 total will be higher than that of 1956, but not as high as that of 1954.

If water, mass transit, and electric light and power are excluded from consideration, then the basic pattern is followed with some variation. Expenditures on capital outlays grew from $9.4 millions in 1940 to $27.4 millions in 1950,[5] or an increase of 191 per cent. If account is taken of changes in the government's purchasing power, however, the increase was only 53 per cent. In 1956 dollars, the change was from $22.7 millions in 1940 to $34.9 millions in 1950. Although 1956 represented a post-Korean low for capital outlays, it was considerably, 92 per cent, higher than in 1950—$55.8 millions as compared to $27.4 millions in current dollars. While in terms of 1956 dollars the increase was 58 per cent—$34.9 millions as compared to $55.1 millions. There was an increase of 485 per cent in current dollars in capital outlay for the entire 1940-56 period, but only a 142 per cent increase in constant dollars. If, in addition, account is taken of population, then the increase in per capita outlays is still sizeable, but is reduced to an 87 per cent increase per capita between 1940 and 1956, as compared to the aforementioned 485 per cent aggregate increase.

The largest part of capital outlay in 1940, 66.5 per cent, was made by the City of Cleveland, Cleveland School District, and Cleveland Library District. An additional 25.0 per cent was made by the County, so that these four jurisdictions alone accounted for 91.5 per cent of all capital outlays in the Cleveland Metropolitan Area. By 1950, the relative share of the City of Cleveland had been reduced to 42.8 per cent and the share of the County to 14.7 per cent for a combined total of 57.5 per cent. Although capital outlays were

---

5. See Table V-2.

considerably higher than those of 1940 or 1950, by 1956 Cleveland and the County accounted for only 49.3 per cent of the total. The municipalities and school districts outside of Cleveland, which accounted for 8.5 per cent of all capital outlays in 1940, were responsible for 50.7 per cent of all capital outlays in 1956. This phenomenon reflects not only the amount, but the nature of growth outside the central city. Due to rapid growth of population, commerce, and industry, capital outlay often exceeded current operating expenditures during the 1950-56 period. This was true not only of smaller jurisdictions with very small operating expenditures, but also of larger governments experiencing very rapid population increases such as Parma, Parma Heights, and of industrial enclaves such as Brook Park. Over the three-year period 1954-56, twenty-nine separate governments (seven cities, twelve villages and townships, and ten school districts) had capital outlays in excess of current operating expenditures.

While capital expenditures of all classes of governments in the Cleveland Metropolitan Area increased between 1940 and 1950 and again between 1950 and 1956, the largest absolute increase for the entire period took place in the municipalities, almost equally divided between the City of Cleveland and all other municipalities. The second largest increase occurred in the school districts; unlike municipal experience, however, here the Cleveland School District was of minor importance, the increase outside of Cleveland being far in excess of that occurring in the central city.

If account is taken of changes in both population and prices, a different picture emerges. Per capita real outlays increased 34 per cent between 1940 and 1950, as compared to the 191 per cent aggregate increase. It should be noted that per capita real outlays increased, while per capita real operating expenditures and per capita real interest expenditures decreased. From 1950 to 1956 the increase in per capita real outlays was 39 per cent as compared to a 101 per cent aggregate increase, but it was for a short period of time and hence involved higher annual rates of increase. During this latter period, per capita real operating expenditures and interest expenditures moved in the same direction as per capita real outlays.

As shown in Table V-2, there was considerable diversity in the relative amounts of growth in per capita real outlays of the several categories of governments between 1940 and 1950, but there was

Capital Outlay

Table V-2—Relative Change in Capital Outlay Expenditures of All Governments: Cleveland Metropolitan Area, Including and Excluding City of Cleveland and Cleveland Board of Education, Selected Periods. (Implicit Price Deflator, 1956=100)

YEAR	GOVERNMENTAL UNIT	AGGREGATE CHANGE (Per Cent)		PER CAPITA CHANGE (Per Cent)	
		Current Dollars	Constant Dollars	Current Dollars	Constant Dollars
1940-50	County & Metropolitan Park District	72	—10	51	—20
	Cities, Villages & Townships	142	28	112	12
	Excl. Cleveland	(760)	(354)	(518)	(224)
	Cleveland Only	(80)	(—5)	(73)	(—9)
	School Districts	907	431	779	364
	Excl. Cleveland	(2,727)	(1,389)	(1,921)	(961)
	Cleveland Only	(153)	(34)	(142)	(28)
	Library Districts	3,400	1,718	2,700	1,600
	Total	191	53	155	34
1950-56	County & Metropolitan Park District	92	51	53	32
	Cities, Villages & Townships	68	47	52	31
	Excl. Cleveland	(141)	(89)	(75)	(37)
	Cleveland Only	(61)	(27)	(60)	(25)
	School Districts	136	85	107	62
	Excl. Cleveland	(143)	(91)	(76)	(38)
	Cleveland Only	(102)	(59)	(99)	(67)
	Library Districts	70	34	50	20
	Total	101	58	60	39
1940-56	County & Metropolitan Park District	229	36	154	4
	Cities, Villages & Townships	354	88	254	47
	Excl. Cleveland	(1,972)	(758)	(979)	(345)
	Cleveland Only	(191)	(21)	(177)	(14)
	School Districts	2,272	883	1,722	655
	Excl. Cleveland	(6,766)	(2,743)	(3,461)	(1,369)
	Cleveland Only	(412)	(112)	(382)	(101)
	Library Districts	5,882	2,337	4,100	2,000
	Total	485	142	351	87

surprising uniformity between 1950 and 1956. On the other hand, between 1950 and 1956 growth in per capita outlays ranged from 20 per cent in the case of the library districts to the 67 per cent of the Cleveland School District.

Capital Outlay: Individual Governments

When viewed in terms of the individual governments comprising the Cleveland Metropolitan Area, the year 1940 stands in distinct contrast with 1950 and later years for which detailed data is available. In 1940, only the isolated government undertook capital expenditures, and they tended to be nominal, with the exceptions of those of the County, Berea, Cleveland, East Cleveland, Lakewood, and Rocky River. School district outlays were considerable only in Cleveland, and even they were quite small relative to total expenditures. By 1950, it was only the isolated municipal or school government that did not undertake capital outlays, and in many cases the outlays were considerable. Only Bentleyville, Cuyahoga Heights, Glenwillow, Newburgh Heights, and Westview, among the villages, and the Richmond Heights School District, and the Rocky River Library District did not undertake any outlays. By 1956, only one municipal government did not undertake any capital outlay, and that was Walton Hills which had just completed some major projects. Again, the Rocky River Library District had no capital expenditures. Although many other jurisdictions spent only nominal sums on capital outlays, a considerable number made major outlay efforts in 1956.

In 1940, of all the jurisdictions in the Cleveland Metropolitan Area, only Berea and East Cleveland had capital outlays greater than one third of their total expenditures. Not so by 1950, when ten municipalities, ten school districts and one library district had capital outlays equal to, or greater than, one third of their total expenditures. If a geographic pattern could be discerned in 1950, it was that there appeared to be slightly greater emphasis on municipal outlays east of Cleveland, and on school outlays south and west of Cleveland. In 1956, fourteen municipalities and twelve school districts had capital outlays exceeding one third of their total expenditures. As shown in Maps V-1 and V-2, high ratios of municipal outlays to

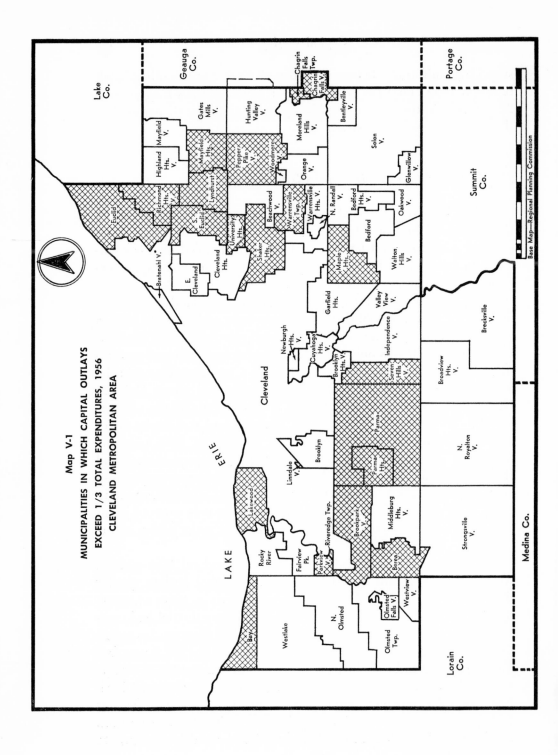

Map V-1

MUNICIPALITIES IN WHICH CAPITAL OUTLAYS
EXCEED 1/3 TOTAL EXPENDITURES, 1956
CLEVELAND METROPOLITAN AREA

Base Map—Regional Planning Commission

total expenditures tend to be concentrated in an inner ring around the City of Cleveland, while high ratios of school outlays to total school expenditures tend to be high in an outer ring.

Capital Outlays in Detail: Functional

It is possible to use exactly the same breakdown in analyzing municipal outlays as in analyzing operating expenditures. This would, however, isolate certain categories of outlays which are unimportant, and ignore other categories which are individually important but which are grouped together, as in the Miscellaneous Commercial Activity category. Using the same basic breakdown as in the case of operating expenditures, a number of modifications were, therefore, introduced to cope with these cases. A General Control category was established which grouped together outlays on general government, police, fire, and other public safety, categories which are, as a matter of fact, often grouped together elsewhere. The Miscellaneous Commercial Activity category was broken down into the following: Sewerage Systems; Rubbish and Garbage Disposal; and a residual Other Miscellaneous Commercial Activity category which includes, as its most important components, outlays on airports and the lakeport. Outlays on public health, public welfare, land use and development, and pensions are included in the Miscellaneous and Unallocable category, as are those on schools and libraries. All other categories are kept intact, including the Public Service Enterprise category, this latter having been included for purposes of comparison.

The principal municipal outlays throughout the period 1940-56 have been on streets and highways and sewerage systems. The amount and relative importance of school outlays changed considerably from the early 1940's, when they were negligible, to their primacy after 1950. For this period as a whole, school outlays show the greatest growth; from less than $.8 million in 1940 (of which more than 70 per cent was spent by the Cleveland School District), they rose to $7.7 millions in 1950, and then to $18.0 millions in 1956. Furthermore, by 1950, there was a complete reversal as school districts outside of Cleveland came to account for more than four-fifths of an increased total of outlays. The growth in school outlays was county-

Table V-3—Amount and Distribution, Capital Outlays in the Cleveland Metropolitan Area, Selected Years (All Governments)

FUNCTION	(THOUSANDS OF CURRENT DOLLARS)					DISTRIBUTION (PER CENT)				
	1940	1950	1954	1955	1956	1940	1950	1954	1955	1956
Total Municipal	8,625	19,308	38,547	39,770	36,248	92	71	64	65	67
General Control *	171	1,321	4,959	3,454	4,297	21	5	8	6	8
Hospitals	184	3,087	1,858	1,814	1,492	2	11	3	3	3
Street and Highways	3,015	5,639	12,316	17,669	12,314	32	21	21	29	21
Miscellaneous Commercial Activities:										
Sewerage	1,221	4,040	9,841	7,604	8,385	13	15	17	12	15
Rubbish & Garbage Disposal	60	1,028	376	988	1,566	1	4	1	2	3
Other Misc. Comm. Activities	3,204	1,724	5,356	3,193	4,653	34	6	9	5	9
Recreation and Culture	773	2,311	3,135	3,121	2,270	8	8	5	5	4
Other and Unallocable	47	158	705	1,936	1,271	.....	1	1	3	2
Schools	765	7,705	20,800	21,247	18,149	8	28	34	34	33
Libraries	11	386	159	710	658	.....	1	1	1	1
Total Capital Outlay	9,401	27,399	59,506	61,735	55,054	100	100	100	100	100
Exhibit: Outlays by										
Public Service Enterprise	3,090	12,480	26,314	17,382	13,964	33 †	46 †	44 †	28 †	25 †

* Includes General Government, Police, Fire, and Other Public Safety.
† Per cent of total outlays above.

wide, but mainly concentrated outside the older built-up core area of Cleveland, East Cleveland and Lakewood. In fact, fifty buildings in use by the Cleveland School District in 1956 were built prior to 1910, and another twenty-five prior to 1920.

The growth in school outlays outside the core area is natural enough, since enrollment in the three core area school districts remained virtually unchanged between 1940 and 1956. After falling about 10 per cent between 1940 and 1950, it rose by an almost equal amount between 1950 and 1956. The figures are 132,189 in 1940; 120,959 in 1950; and 130,548 in 1956. This was happening while the enrollment of the remaining districts increased from 36,007, in 1940, to 96,536, in 1956. It has been estimated that just between 1954 and 1956, 500 classrooms per year have been added in an all-out effort to keep up with the increased public school attendance resultant from the still continuing "baby boom."

Although no individual municipal outlay equaled that devoted to schools during the early 1950's, outlays on streets and highways and sewerage systems have *in toto* tended to exceed school outlays. And this does not seem a new development, but one going back many years. Individually, outlays on streets and highways have generally ranked second in importance to school outlays. The relationship between the automobile and the growth of the suburbs is too well known to require comment, except to note that it has affected all municipal governments. The actual pattern and timing of local highway programs has been modified by the state and federal road programs and by State Aid.

Capital outlays for sewer systems increased from $1.2 millions, in 1940, to $8.4 millions, in 1956, after reaching a peak of $9.8 millions, in 1954. Another shift unfolded as sewerage outlays shifted from a predominantly Cleveland function in 1940 and 1950 (85 per cent and 66 per cent respectively), to one in which the County and the other municipalities have steadily increased their share of the total to 61 per cent, so that they now dominate the picture. At this point, note should be taken of the relationship between outlays on sewerage and the outlays on water systems in the Cleveland Metropolitan Area. The latter is still predominantly a Cleveland function, the service of which is provided to municipalities with adequate sewage facilities.

General control outlays (general government, police, fire, and other public safety) are widely dispersed among municipalities and the County. They have not shown any significant shifts geographically and/or by level of government. Since 1950, total outlays for general control purposes have remained stable at between 6 per cent and 8 per cent of total capital outlay. On the other hand, outlays on other miscellaneous commercial activities (commercial activities excluding public service enterprises, sewerage and rubbish disposal expenditures), which were historically almost exclusively a function of Cleveland, have fluctuated considerably since 1940. From outlays of $3.2 millions in that year, miscellaneous commercial activities outlays declined to $1.7 millions in 1950. Then they grew to $5.4 millions in 1954, declined to $3.2 millions in 1955, and rose again in 1956, this time to $4.7 millions. This category, like the public service enterprises, is composed of the type of functions involving outlays which one might expect to be quite volatile over time—airports and the lakeport, primarily. To illustrate: more than 99 per cent of the 1940 miscellaneous commercial activity outlay was for lakeport development. In 1954, virtually the same total amount was spent for the Cleveland-Hopkins Airport construction. The same was true in 1955.

Outlays on refuse and garbage disposal have also varied during the period under consideration. The variation in dollar amounts, however, was limited. The rising importance of this category in municipalities outside Cleveland has been the outstanding development in recent years.

As the responsibility for hospitals shifted from Cleveland to the County, the amounts spent by individual governments varied considerably. A single municipality like Lakewood or Bedford could influence total hospital outlays for any given year, a situation which is far less likely with other functions.

Outlay for recreation and culture has declined relative to other functions. On the other hand, it has remained fairly constant on a per capita basis. Expenditure on this function has remained very near $2.00 per capita since 1950. As to the pattern of responsibility, this too has remained fairly stable, on an area-wide basis. It would appear that, increasingly, the major item is municipal swimming pools.

Finally, capital expenditures for libraries have been relatively stable. They have been about 1 per cent of total outlay since 1950.

If capital outlays are broken down functionally, the choice of terminal years 1950-56 or even 1940-56 tends to understate rather than overstate the growth in capital outlays, because of the peak in 1954. The relative stability of the shares devoted to each function is very impressive when viewed in terms of the data available for 1940, 1950, 1954, 1955, and 1956. This is true even though the 1940 data, for instance, is dominated by three activities: county road building, and large outlays by the City of Cleveland for its lakeport and its sewerage system.

If the period 1950-56 is taken, the stability of the percentage of capital outlays devoted to the individual functions is even more pronounced. This can be seen in Table V-2. Considering the variations in totals, the stability of the various functional categories is surprising. The expected importance of certain individual functions year after year is brought out by the figures, and is consistent with the earlier data on Cleveland and its overlying governments.

As was noted earlier, by 1950, practically every local government was undertaking some capital outlay, in contrast with 1940, when many undertook little or no capital improvements, either because they were financed by the County or because their borrowing power and tax revenues were limited. The most pervasive and the largest municipal capital outlay in 1950 was on streets and highways. Second in general importance, but not in total amount spent, were the expenditures on general control, which reflected the growth of an urbanized community outside of the central city area. These outlays were devoted to police and fire (where there was a full-time department). The importance of outlays on police is especially striking in the villages.

Although they were not undertaken by as many governments, capital outlays on sewer systems in 1950 were high; this was a concomitant of the post-war growth of the Cleveland Metropolitan Area. As would be expected, the more densely settled city areas devoted a larger proportion to this function than those more sparsely settled septic tank areas. Related to the expenditures on sewers were expenditures on water.

Capital expenditures on recreation and culture in 1950 were not undertaken by governments other than the City of Cleveland and the Metropolitan Park District, and the amounts were modest.

The picture of outlays that emerged tentatively in 1950 has been maintained since. As was noted earlier, only very unusual circumstances preclude some capital outlay by practically every city, village, and school district, as well as by the County and the Cleveland Metropolitan Park District. The generalization does not apply in the case of the townships because their fiscal powers are restricted.

If outlays are classified by function and government, the most common capital outlays have not been those responsible for the highest capital outlays. Capital outlays for general control, although they do not bulk large in the aggregate, are especially important in the village and smaller city outlay patterns. Hospital capital outlays, like hospital current operating expenditures, were restricted to a limited number of municipalities, mainly Cleveland and Lakewood, and to the County. Street and highway outlays reflect partly the availability of state monies, partly growth, and partly the need for major repairs or alterations in existing streets and highways. Street and highway outlays are important both in the aggregate and for the individual governments.

A major shift has occurred in the case of capital outlays on sewer systems and garbage disposal. Formerly, these outlays were important in the aggregate, but they were not a usual municipal expenditure. Since 1950, outlays on sewers have become about as usual as outlays on streets and highways, at least for the larger municipalities and the County.

In like manner, the number of governments undertaking recreation and culture outlays has expanded, as an increasing number of municipalities provide outdoor swimming pools and other recreational and cultural facilities. Note should finally be made of the fact that other such facilities are provided by schools and libraries, but that expenditures on these facilities are not included in the total.

Past capital outlays are the result of balancing needs against resources. In the early 1950's, the needs were great but so were the resources. During the 1930's, local capital outlays declined as resources became far more restricted. Some of the communities had indeed "overbuilt" (if that term is permissible) during the 1920's; others were able to make ends meet; but most governments found themselves foregoing needed capital improvements. During the 1940-45 war period whatever needed improvements were going on were called to a halt as the men and materials were put to more important uses. After the end of hostilities in the Pacific in late 1945, the repressed boom in capital outlays manifested itself. But the growth of the Cleveland Metropolitan Area, no matter how measured, was so rapid that local governments were unable to keep up with the demand for new capital facilities.

The principal outlays after 1945 were, in accord with expectations, modified by existing inter-governmental arrangements in the case of sewers, water, and hospitals. Outlays on schools, streets and highways, and sewer systems were almost universal, as were outlays on general control in any rapidly growing community. On the other hand, capital expenditures on mass transit, electricity, lakeports, and airports depended on other circumstances, because they were revenue-producing.

Where a government supports a hospital, most public service enterprises, or miscellaneous commercial activities, there is a situation analogous to the private enterprise sphere. From a fiscal point of view, the financing of self-supporting capital improvement is treated differently both in terms of debt and tax limitation.

The existence of separate school and library districts independent of other governments points out a basic problem in the planning of capital outlays in the Cleveland Metropolitan Area; namely, that although these outlays are undertaken by different governments, the decisions are made and are ultimately financed by the same set of taxpayers for a variety of different, yet related governments. This is of special importance where two or three governments pursue a capital outlay policy in an unco-ordinated and often contradictory manner. It should be recognized that a given capital program has effects on future operating and capital expenditures. It may lead to increased operating expenditures, or it may be an alternative to operating and maintenance expenditures.

Past capital outlays reflect two sets of considerations—engineering and economic. Engineering considerations determine the various technical possibilities; from these the community must choose what capital plant it desires. In the case of government, this is decided by the community's demand for the given facility and its fiscal resources. In some instances, definite economies of scale in the construction of capital plant can be achieved. In others, due to the nature of the demand or the resources available, there may not only be failure to achieve economies, but there may even be actual dis-economies involved. This may be so particularly in the case of certain outlays considered governmental in nature. In some cases, this may be reflected in lower costs of current operation, whereas in others it may not.

Only a facility-by-facility analysis of capital outlays could provide the possibility of an answer to the very important question of economies of scale in capital outlays. There is, however, agreement in many areas concerning the possibility and probability of such economies in many of the local government functions considered in this and other reports of the Cleveland Metropolitan Services Commission. In some instances, there are definite advantages in the construction and operation of large capital facilities, and these must be seriously considered if the entire community, the Cleveland Metropolitan Area, is to be adequately served in the future.

The Isard and Coughlin study of municipal costs and revenues provides a good beginning to a study of individual capital facilities.[6] It must be supplemented, however, by the more specific studies, such as those carried out by Cleveland METRO for sewerage, transportation, and public recreation, as well as by a more comprehensive study of the over-all school requirements.

If there are economies of scale to be found in government operations, they are likely, but not invariably, to be found in the provision of capital outlays. Although there are such economies in the area of current expenditures, they are often related to capital plant. It should be noted that the largest-sized is not necessarily the most efficient-sized capital outlay. In fact, the optimum size for a given function may be smaller than is currently the case. However, the question of small or large is relevant only to given alternative conditions of requirements and resources and must be solved accordingly.

---

6. Walter Isard and Robert Coughlin, *Municipal Costs and Revenues Resulting From Community Growth*, Federal Reserve Bank of Boston, American Institute of Planners (Wellesley, Mass.) Chandler-Davis Publishing Company, 1957.
    See also:
    George H. Esser, Jr., *Greensboro Suburban Analysis*, Institute of Government, University of North Carolina, Chapel Hill, N. C., 1956.
    Wm. L. C. Wheaton and M. J. Schussheim, *The Cost of Municipal Services in Residential Areas*, U. S. Department of Commerce, Washington, 1955.

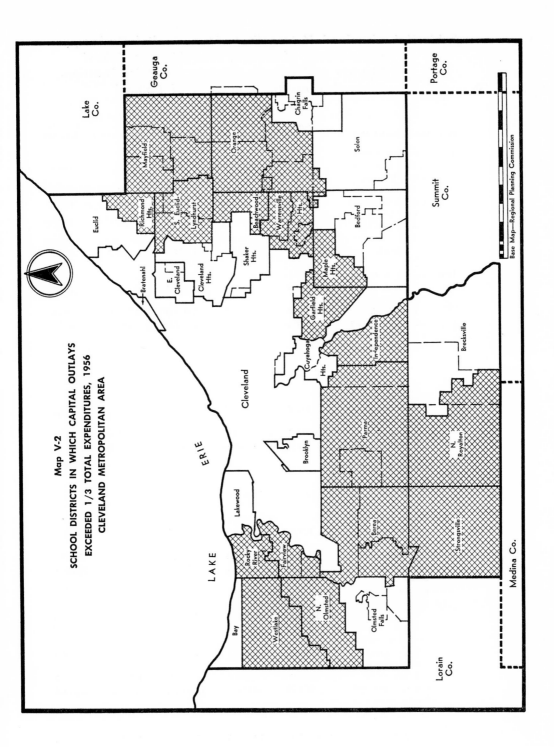

Map V-2

SCHOOL DISTRICTS IN WHICH CAPITAL OUTLAYS
EXCEEDED 1/3 TOTAL EXPENDITURES, 1956
CLEVELAND METROPOLITAN AREA

Base Map—Regional Planning Commission

Geauga Co.

Portage Co.

Lake Co.

Summit Co.

Mayfield

Orange

Chagrin Falls

Solon

Euclid

Richmond Hts.

S. Euclid

Lyndhurst

Beachwood

Warrensville Hts.

Bedford

Bratenahl

E. Cleveland

Cleveland Hts.

Shaker Hts.

Maple Hts.

Garfield Hts.

Cuyahoga Hts.

Independence

Brecksville

Cleveland

ERIE

Parma

N. Royalton

Brooklyn

Lakewood

Berea

Strongsville

LAKE

Rocky River

Fairview

Bay

Westlake

N. Olmsted

Olmsted Falls

Medina Co.

Lorain Co.

Table V-4—Cleveland Metropolitan Area, Capital Outlay Expenditures of County, Municipalities, School Districts and Library Districts, by Major Function, Selected Years (In Thousands of Dollars)

Year	Governmental Unit	General Control	Streets & Highways	Sewerage	Rubbish & Garbage Disposal	Recreation & Culture
1940	County & Metro. Park District	8.7	2,125.9	60.3		152.4
	Cities, Villages & Townships	162.0	889.2	1,161.0	60.0	570.1
	City of Cleveland	(113.7)	(752.6)	(1,042.2)	(60.0)	(437.8)
	School Districts					
	Library Districts					
	TOTAL	170.7	3,015.1	1,221.3	60.0	772.5
1950	County & Metro. Park District	167.9	1,865.2	139.1		221.3
	Cities, Villages & Townships	1,152.9	3,774.0	3,901.0	1,028.1	2,090.0
	City of Cleveland	(628.8)	(2,783.7)	(2,647.8)	(286.2)	(1,905.2)
	School Districts					
	Library Districts					
	TOTAL	1,320.8	5,639.2	4,040.1	1,028.1	2,311.3
1954	County & Metro. Park District	616.4	3,672.4	429.9		305.2
	Cities, Villages & Townships	4,342.5	8,643.8	9,411.5	376.2	2,829.4
	City of Cleveland	(2,009.3)	(4,578.4)	(6,396.1)	(231.4)	(2,092.8)
	School Districts					
	Library Districts					
	TOTAL	4,958.9	12,316.2	9,841.4	376.2	3,134.6
1955	County & Metro. Park District	877.9	7,399.5	852.7		380.8
	Cities, Villages & Townships	2,576.4	10,269.2	6,751.1	987.6	2,740.2
	City of Cleveland	(1,000.9)	(5,137.4)	(3,145.1)	(276.7)	(1,957.7)
	School Districts					
	Library Districts					
	TOTAL	3,454.3	17,668.7	7,603.8	987.6	3,121.0
1956	County & Metro. Park District	1,920.3	3,225.8	1,507.9		327.6
	Cities, Villages & Townships	2,376.9	9,087.8	6,877.4	1,565.5	1,942.2
	City of Cleveland	(874.0)	(4,890.5)	(2,639.4)	(353.3)	(1,313.4)
	School Districts					
	Library Districts					
	TOTAL	4,297.2	12,313.6	8,385.3	1,565.5	2,269.8

Other Misc. Comm. Activities	Hospitals	Schools	Libraries	Other & Unallocable	Total	Public Service Enterprises
					2,347.3	
3,204.4	183.7			47.1	6,277.5	3,090.3
(3,204.3)	(57.4)			(46.1)	(5,714.1)	(3,079.2)
		764.9			764.9	
			11.4		11.4	
3,204.4	183.7	764.9	11.4	47.1	9,401.1	3,090.3
3.1	1,609.8			23.2	4,029.6	
1,720.7	1,476.9			134.4	15,278.0	12,479.7
(1,719.1)	(323.2)			(22.8)	(10.316.8)	(11,861.1)
		7,704.8			7,704.8	
			386.2		386.2	
1,723.8	3,086.7	7,704.8	386.2	157.6	27,398.6	12,479.7
	588.6			56.3	5,668.8	
5,356.0	1,269.5			649.0	32,877.9	26,313.7
(6,355.7)	(1,201.1)			(637.9)	(22,502.7)	(23,777.9)
		20,800.1			20,800.1	
			159.3		159.3	
5,356.0	1,858.1	20,800.1	159.3	705.3	59,506.1	26,313.7
	740.8			32.4	10,284.1	
3,193.3	1,073.3			1,903.6	29,494.7	17,381.7
(3,193.1)	(982.4)			(1,879.8)	(17,573.1)	(15,235.5)
		21,246.5			21,246.5	
			709.7		709.7	
3,193.3	1,814.1	21,246.5	709.7	1,936.0	61,735.0	17,381.7
3.9	740.9			32.4	7,758.8	
4,649.3	751.2			1,238.7	28,489.0	13,963.7
(4,645.8)	(724.9)			(1,210.8)	(16,652.1)	(11,512.1)
		18,148.5			18,148.5	
			657.6		657.6	
4,653.2	1,492.1	18,148.5	657.6	1,271.1	55,053.9	13,963.7

VI

Revenues

T HE CURRENT AND PROSPECTIVE REVENUE PROBLEM of local governments is important and challenging, but we can take some solace in the fact that it is not new. The perennial problem was stated very well half a century ago in answer to the question: what are the most pressing needs and important problems in the government of American cities?

"To make a little money go a long way. No city in the United States, so far as I know, has the means to do all that is required of it. The rich ones and the poor ones are alike in this respect." [1]

---

1. Mayor McClellan of New York City, quoted by C. C. Williamson, *The Finances of Cleveland,* page 11 (1907).

The fiscal and revenue problems of metropolitan areas are more than the problems of city or county finances. To the traditional local problems is added another dimension—that of a single economic and social unit divided between many different local governments.[2]

A family in a metropolitan area will often live in one community, go to work in a second, and patronize a shopping center in a third municipality. What tax system would be equitable and conform to the economic effects of this situation? How can many separate and independent local governments and political constituencies face up to the area-wide problems?

The decisions as to taxes and other revenues are made at least quasi-independently for each of the local governments in the metropolitan area. Each local decision, however, has important repercussions for the policies and decisions of other local governments throughout the metropolitan area. Each decision to raise property tax rates, to utilize a new revenue source, or to borrow, together with the accompanying change in expenditure and service, affects the relationship of the local municipality or school district to other governments in the area. The influence is greater the larger the change, and the more important the local government in size and prestige, and the effects are more potent on the adjacent governments.

Each citizen and public official sees the problem of his local municipality and school district. Even in the richer taxing districts, certain wants and desires are not met. Every jurisdiction has its own revenue problems. But in closely knit metropolitan Cleveland, the revenue choices of the various local jurisdictions have repercussions on the other local governments and on home owners, tenants, and businesses throughout the area. Inability or unwillingness of a local jurisdiction to support certain services satisfactorily affect not only its own citizens but also all the citizens of the entire area. Highways, health, storm and sanitary sewers, education, welfare, and public safety standards and services affect the entire metropolitan area. Location of a large industrial plant or shopping center in one local

2. S. Leland, "An Ideal Theoretical Plan of Finance for a Metropolitan Area" in Tax Institute Symposium, *Financing Metropolitan Government* (Princeton, 1955), pp. 233, 239.

taxing district may ease the district's revenue problems, but aggravate the problem of other communities in the metropolitan area due to low-priced housing developments, additional traffic, and more school children resulting from the new installation.

Metropolitan areas generally have adequate economic capacity to support the financial needs of local government. The revenue problems are due largely to 1) limited powers granted by the state as to tax sources, tax rates, and borrowing powers to raise the funds within the capacity of the local economy; 2) fragmentation of the economic unit of the metropolitan areas in many local governments so that a) an overall capacity adequate to meet needs is poorly distributed between different jurisdictions and different functions, and b) competition, rather than co-operation, for tax base and revenue occurs between the different units.

Metropolitan Cleveland is a high-income, wealthy area in a prosperous state. The income and wealth of the Cleveland Metropolitan Area reflects the area's strong and diversified economic base, resulting from its position as a major commercial and manufacturing center. The people have the economic and financial capacity to support practically any level of local government services they choose.

The people of Ohio in 1956 received personal income of $19.8 billion, or $2,184 per capita against the national average of $1,961 per capita. In Cuyahoga County alone, personal income was about $4.1 billion, or $2,650 per capita. Personal income in the Cleveland area thus is about $500 per capita above the Ohio average and about $700 per person above the national average. Put another way, the population of Cuyahoga County includes 92 out of every 10,000 people in the United States while personal incomes in Cuyahoga County account for $125 out of every $10,000 of personal income in the United States.

What is true of the whole is not true of each of the parts. The imbalance of tax-paying capacity between different jurisdictions and the lack of any relation between revenue capacity and revenue need create a critical problem in every metropolitan area. The varying revenue capacities, shown in Tables II-8, II-9, VI-7, and VI-8 for the fifty-eight different municipalities and thirty-two school districts in the Cleveland area, exemplify this imbalance. The range of tax-paying capacity in terms of assessed property valuation per capita is almost 100 times as great in Cuyahoga Heights as in Oakwood. The range within the Cleveland Metropolitan Area dwarfs the range of difference between the richest and poorest county in Ohio; Cuyahoga County, the wealthiest county in Ohio, has only 3 times the assessed valuation per person of Vinton County, the poorest. If measured by personal income, the contrast within the metropolitan area is also great, as shown in Table VI-7. These wide inequalities pose a problem to all the people of the metropolitan area.

In discussing revenues for financing metropolitan governments, we will first summarize the present revenue situation and its historical development, including comparisons with other metropolitan areas and central cities in Ohio and other states. Next will come a description of the legal framework for Ohio local government revenues. The changing significance of various local governments and of state-local fiscal relations will be discussed. The capacity of the entire county and of individual jurisdictions to raise revenues locally will be examined. In view of the revenue capacity, the local taxing effort will then be considered. The revenue sources currently in use and possible new revenue sources will be analyzed and evaluated. Then the present revenue system will be tested and evaluated as to its performance in meeting the probable demands for additional revenue in the future.

Staff recommendations for improvement of the present revenue system and for additional revenues, as needed, are included in this chapter and Chapter IX. A projection of revenue for 1965 is included in Chapter VIII, along with a projection of 1965 expenditures. Revenues for 1965 are projected both for a stable price level and for inflation continuing at the 1950-56 rate.

THE PRESENT REVENUE PICTURE

General revenues of Cleveland Metropolitan Area local governments from all sources—local, state, and federal—total $250 million in 1956. An additional $51 million was obtained by long-term borrowing. Table VIII-2 presents the data in income statement form. (Funds received from operation of transit, water, and electric utilities, from investment transactions, from short-term borrowing and from employee payments into pension funds are not included.) These receipts from revenues and borrowing, amounting to $301 million, were used to pay $205 million of current operating expenses, $55 million of capital outlays, and $37 million for debt service ($7 million of interest charges and $30 million to retire long-term debt). The remaining $4 million went to increase cash balances. The net change in long-term debt was a $21 million increase. If the public enterprises—water, mass transit, and municipal electric—are included, just over $50 million is added to both revenue and expenditure.

A profit and loss statement of the type used in business would show for local governments, excluding public service enterprises, 1956 current revenue of $244 million and current expenses of $242 million, leaving a profit from current operations of $2 million. Expenses do not include any 1956 expenditures for capital improvements, but an estimate is made for depreciation on existing capital assets by including the 1956 expenditures for retirement of long term debt. Debt retirement is not the exact equivalent of depreciation, but no exact measure or even direct estimate of depreciation of governmental capital assets is available. Long term debt may be created only to finance new capital assets, not to meet current deficits. On any given capital improvement, all the accompanying debt is retired faster than the asset wears out. Also a minor part of total capital outlays is financed from current revenue. Debt retirement, from this viewpoint, thus tends to overstate annual depreciation. On the other hand, many capital assets—such as schools, water mains, and highways—outlast by years the debt which financed them originally, so that debt retirement in any year does not measure the current use received from much governmental plant and equipment. Thus debt retirement is included as a crude, but probably the best available, measure for depreciation of the durable physical assets of local government.

The 1956 capital outlays of $55 million were financed by borrowing $51 million and utilizing $6 million from earmarked taxes. The remainder together with the operating surplus increased cash balances by about $4 million.

The more than $300 million revenue local governments in Cuyahoga County received from all sources in 1956 compares with

$102 million in 1940 and almost $200 million in 1950, as indicated in Table VI-1. Total revenues thus increased almost $100 million in the decade of the 1940's and slightly more than $100 million in the period 1950-56. Data for 1958 indicate total revenue of approximately $340 million, and for 1959 an estimated total of about $380 million.

Revenues for all types of governments increased sharply between 1940 and 1956. Excluding municipal transit, water, and electric functions, the revenues of both the County and the cities increased to about two and a half times their 1940 level. School revenues more than tripled while library revenues almost tripled. Village and township revenue, not shown separately in Table VI-1, jumped to more than five times their 1940 levels. The major shift apparent in Table VI-2 and Chart VI-1 is the increasing importance of schools—from 31.1 to 35.7 per cent of total revenue excluding utilities—and a decline in the share of the cities. If an adjustment of about $6 million revenue is made to allow for the post-1956 change of City Hospital, Blossom Hill, and Boys' Farm from Cleveland to county operation, the cities' adjusted share of revenues would be down further to about 39 per cent and the county's share up to 20 per cent. The surprising increase in the share of revenues to villages from 1.3 to 2.9 per cent indicates the urbanized nature of almost the entire county and the pressure for revenues to provide urban-type services.

Major changes have taken place in the relative use of different revenue sources, as shown in Chart VI-1. The County now relies on the state and federal governments for almost half its revenue, compared with about a quarter in 1940. The cities and the schools, on the other hand, now depend more on local revenue sources than in 1940. The schools have increased heavily their reliance on the property tax—from 69.6 per cent in 1940 to 76.8 per cent in 1956.

Revenues Adjusted for Price Level and Population Changes

The large and almost continuous rise in prices in recent years makes invalid any comparison of revenues between different years,

Table VI-1—Revenues, by Source and by Type of Government, Cleveland Metropolitan Area, 1940, 1950, 1956 (In Thousands of Dollars)

Revenue by Source	1940					
	County & Metro. Park	Cities, Villages & Townships	Schools	Libraries *	Total	County & Metro. Park
Locally Collected						
General Property	10,101	23,064	19,674	45	52,885	11,785
Intangible Property	...	112	...	2,274	2,386	...
Licenses & Other Taxes	137	1,131	...	...	1,269	156
Total Local Taxes	10,239	24,308	19,674	2,319	56,539	11,941
Fees & Misc. Charges	1,112	3,930	290	...	5,333	2,066
Special Assessments	815	2,013	...	...	2,828	1,406
Interest	46	546	13	...	604	500
Other Local Sources	166	2,047	519	112	2,844	627
Total Non-Tax Sources	2,139	8,536	822	112	11,609	4,598
TOTAL LOCAL SOURCES	12,378	32,843	20,496	2,431	68,148	16,539
State Aid						
Local Government Fund	1,705	2,040	...	...	3,745	2,705
School Foundation	...	...	6,143	...	6,143	...
Gas Tax & Motor Veh. Lic.	1,918	2,623	...	...	4,541	2,899
Other State Aid	291	5,551	243	...	6,085	2,820
Total State Aid	3,914	10,214	6,386	...	20,514	8,424
Federal Aid	976	33	1,391	...	2,400	1,084
TOTAL INTERGOVERNMENT	4,890	10,247	7,777	...	22,914	9,508
TOTAL LOCAL AND INTERGOVERNMENT	17,268	43,090	28,273	2,431	91,062	26,046
Public Service Enterprises	...	10,791	...	...	10,791	...
TOTAL ALL REVENUES	17,268	58,881	28,273	2,431	101,853	26,046

* Revenue data for libraries for 1940 were not available for East Cleveland and Euclid.

Note: Cities and villages are classified throughout the table according to their status in 1956. For example the data for Fairview Park, which became a city following the 1950 Census, are included with the city data for all 3 years given.

| | 1950 | | | | 1956 | | | |
Cities, Villages & Townships	Schools	Libraries	Total	County & Metro. Park	Cities, Villages & Townships	Schools	Libraries	Total
39,367	34,852	75	86,078	15,751	51,379	68,554	108	141,792
3,612	...	4,470	8,082	...	958	...	6,437	7,395
2,610	...	...	2,766	321	3,860	...	...	4,180
45,589	34,852	4,545	96,927	16,071	62,197	68,554	6,544	153,367
9,676	841	...	12,583	3,182	14,990	1,498	...	19,670
4,395	...	...	5,800	383	6,068	...	...	6,451
1,121	90	...	1,711	700	2,738	236	...	3,674
1,893	1,778	168	4,467	2,307	3,525	4,182	434	10,447
17,085	2,710	168	24,561	6,572	27,320	5,916	434	40,242
62,674	37,562	4,713	121,488	22,644	89,517	74,469	6,979	193,608
3,684	...	...	6,388	3,467	8,355	...	...	11,823
...	8,930	...	8,930	...	...	13,850	...	13,850
4,832	...	...	7,731	4,661	8,048	...	...	12,710
5,282	517	...	8,619	9,355	2,484	711	...	12,550
13,798	9,446	...	31,688	17,484	18,888	14,561	...	50,933
360	44	...	1,487	3,147	1,769	176	...	5,093
14,157	9,490	...	33,155	20,631	20,657	14,738	...	56,025
76,831	47,052	4,713	154,643	43,274	110,174	89,206	6,979	249,634
43,448	...	...	43,448	...	53,788	...	...	53,788
120,280	47,052	4,713	198,091	43,274	163,961	89,206	6,979	303,421

Table VI-2—Per Cent of Revenues by Source, and by Type of Government, Cleveland Metropolitan Area, 1940, 1950, 1956

Revenue by Source	1940						1950						1956					
	County & Metro. Park	Cities	Villages & Townships	Schools	Libraries	TOTAL	County & Metro. Park	Cities	Villages & Townships	Schools	Libraries	TOTAL	County & Metro. Park	Cities	Villages & Townships	Schools	Libraries	TOTAL
Locally Collected																		
General Property	19.1	42.8	0.8	37.2	0.1	100	13.7	44.6	1.2	40.5	0.1	100	11.1	38.5	2.0	48.3	0.1	100
Intangible Property	...	1.1	3.6	...	95.3	100	...	40.0	4.7	...	55.3	100	...	11.1	1.9	...	87.0	100
Licenses & Other Taxes	10.8	77.4	11.8	...	...	100	5.6	86.8	7.5	...	...	100	7.7	77.2	15.2	...	...	100
Total Local Taxes	18.1	41.8	1.2	34.8	4.1	100	12.3	45.4	1.6	36.0	4.7	100	10.5	38.2	2.3	44.7	4.3	100
Fees & Misc. Charges	20.9	73.0	0.7	5.4	...	100	16.4	75.8	1.1	6.7	...	100	16.2	74.3	1.9	7.6	...	100
Special Assessments	28.8	61.6	9.7	...	...	100	24.2	66.9	8.9	...	...	100	5.9	73.0	21.0	...	...	100
Interest	7.6	88.1	2.2	2.1	...	100	29.2	61.3	4.2	5.3	...	100	19.1	73.4	1.1	6.4	...	100
Other Local Sources	5.8	68.8	3.2	18.3	4.0	100	14.0	36.7	5.7	39.8	3.8	100	22.1	26.5	7.2	40.0	4.2	100
Total Non-Tax Sources	18.4	70.0	3.6	7.1	1.0	100	18.7	65.6	4.0	11.0	0.7	100	16.3	61.6	6.3	14.7	1.1	100
TOTAL LOCAL SOURCES	18.2	46.7	1.6	30.1	3.6	100	13.6	49.5	2.1	30.9	3.9	100	11.7	43.1	3.1	38.5	3.6	100
State Aid																		
Local Government Fund	45.5	53.0	1.3	...	...	100	42.3	55.6	2.1	...	...	100	29.3	68.1	2.6	...	...	100
School Foundation	...	...	...	100.0	...	100	...	...	...	100.0	...	100	...	...	...	100.0	...	100
Gas Tax & Motor Veh. Lic.	42.2	55.5	2.2	...	...	100	37.5	59.1	3.4	...	...	100	36.7	58.3	5.0	...	...	100
Other State Aid	4.8	89.9	1.3	4.0	...	100	32.7	60.3	1.0	6.0	...	100	74.5	18.7	1.1	5.7	...	100
Total State Aid	19.1	48.6	1.2	31.1	...	100	26.6	42.0	1.5	29.8	...	100	34.3	35.0	2.1	28.6	...	100

Federal Aid	40.7	1.4	...	58.0	...	100	72.9	24.2	...	3.0	...	100	61.8	34.6	0.1	3.5	...	100
TOTAL INTERGOVERNMENT	21.3	43.7	1.0	33.9	...	100	28.7	41.2	1.5	28.6	...	100	36.8	34.9	1.9	26.3	...	100
TOTAL LOCAL AND INTERGOVERNMENT	19.0	45.9	1.4	31.1	2.7	100	16.9	47.7	2.0	30.4	3.0	100	17.3	41.3	2.9	35.7	2.8	100
Public Service Enterprises	...	99.8	0.2	...	...	100	...	99.9	0.1	...	...	100	...	99.9	0.1	...	...	100
TOTAL ALL REVENUES	17.0	51.6	1.3	27.8	2.4	100	13.2	59.2	1.6	23.8	2.4	100	14.3	51.7	2.4	29.4	2.3	100

Note: Due to rounding totals may not add to 100.0%.

Chart VI—1
REVENUE BY SOURCE AND TYPE OF GOVERNMENT, CLEVELAND METROPOLITAN AREA, 1940, 1950 and 1956

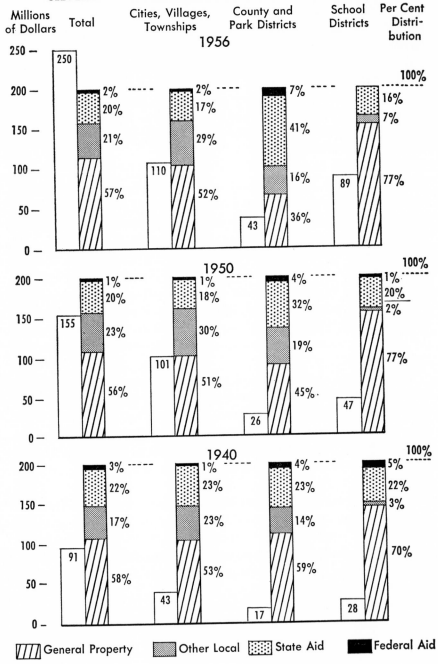

unless the dollar amounts are converted into dollars of constant buying power. In this chapter the consumer price index is used to deflate local government revenues because this index is best for measuring the buying power given up by taxpayers and the most important state and local taxes in Ohio are paid directly or indirectly by the consumer.

The adjustment to dollars of constant purchasing power has been made in Table VI-3. It indicates a rise in revenues in constant dollars of only 41 per cent between 1940 and 1956, not the 174 per cent increase shown in current dollars.

Changes in the value of the dollar entirely canceled out the revenue increase between 1940 and 1950, so that citizens actually sacrificed slightly less real buying power through taxes and government charges in 1950 than they did in 1940. Data for the property tax revenues for individual years during the 1940's indicate a very sharp drop in revenue in constant dollars to about 1946, as a sharp rise in the price level occurred along with a very small increase in property tax payments. The tax duplicate was almost constant and property tax rates increased little during this period. Expenditures also declined with virtual elimination of unemployment, the wartime shortage of employees, and restrictions on capital improvements.

Beginning about 1947, local revenues began to increase due to business and residential construction, which increased the tax duplicate, shown in Table VI-19, and to higher rates resulting from demands to catch up on public service and public construction after the neglect of the depression and war years. But by 1950, the postwar rise had not overcome the great reduction in real revenues up to 1946.

Revenues from local sources increased about 4 per cent between 1940 and 1950, but were more than offset by a decline in intergovernmental revenues. In constant dollars, non-property taxes, licenses, fees and charges, and interest were the only sources to show substantial increases. Property taxes declined more than 5 per cent during the 1940's.

Between 1950 and 1956, revenues in current dollars rose more rapidly and the prices increased at a smaller rate than in the 1940's,

Table VI-3—Revenues in Constant Dollars, Aggregate and Per Capita, All Local Governments, Cleveland Metropolitan Area, 1940, 1950, 1956

REVENUE BY SOURCE	Aggregate					Per Capita				
	IN THOUSANDS OF 1956 DOLLARS			CHANGE IN PERCENTAGE TERMS		IN 1956 DOLLARS			CHANGE IN PERCENTAGE TERMS	
	1940	1950	1956	1940-1950	1950-1956	1940	1950	1956	1940-1950	1950-1956
Locally Collected										
General Property	102,687	97,268	141,792	−5.28	45.77	84.37	70.00	89.71	−17.03	28.16
Intangible Property	4,633	9,133	7,395	97.13	−19.03	3.81	6.58	4.68	72.70	−28.88
Licenses & Other Taxes	2,464	3,126	4,180	26.13	33.72	2.02	2.25	2.64	11.39	17.33
Total Local Taxes	109,782	109,528	153,367	−.23	40.03	90.19	78.83	97.03	−12.60	23.09
Fees & Misc. Charges	10,355	14,219	19,670	37.32	38.34	8.50	10.24	12.45	20.47	21.58
Special Assessments	5,491	6,554	6,451	19.36	−1.57	4.50	4.71	4.08	4.67	−13.38
Interest	1,172	1,940	3,674	65.53	89.38	.96	1.40	2.32	45.83	65.71
Other Local Sources	5,522	5,041	10,447	−8.71	107.24	4.54	3.63	6.61	−20.04	82.09
Total Non-Tax Sources	22,541	27,754	40,242	23.13	45.00	18.52	19.98	25.46	7.88	27.43
TOTAL LOCAL SOURCES	132,323	137,281	193,608	3.75	41.03	108.72	98.80	122.49	−9.12	23.98
State Aid										
Local Government Fund	7,272	7,218	11,823	−.74	63.80	5.98	5.20	7.48	−13.04	43.85
School Foundation	11,928	10,091	13,850	−15.40	37.25	9.81	7.27	8.76	−25.89	20.50
Other State Aid	20,634	18,476	25,260	−10.46	36.72	16.95	13.30	15.98	−21.53	20.15
Total State Aid	39,832	35,785	50,933	−10.16	42.33	32.72	25.75	32.22	−21.30	25.13
Federal Aid	4,660	1,680	5,093	−63.95	203.15	3.83	1.21	3.22	−68.41	166.12
TOTAL INTERGOVERNMENT	44,492	37,465	56,025	−15.79	49.54	36.54	26.96	35.45	−26.22	31.49
TOTAL ALL REVENUES	176,815	174,747	249,634	−1.17	42.85	145.26	125.76	157.94	−13.42	25.59
Consumer Price Index (1956 = 100)	51.5	88.5	100.0	+71.8	+13.0	1,217,250	1,389,532	1,580,553	+14.2	+13.1
Total All Revenues (In curr. dollars)	91,062	154,643	249,634	+69.8	+61.4	74.81	111.29	157.94	+48.8	+41.9

so that revenues went up 43 per cent in real terms. Except for intangible property taxes and special assessments which both declined in constant dollars, all sources generated increases of at least a third. Revenue from the most productive general property tax rose 46 per cent, and State Aid, the second largest source, rose by 42 per cent.

Comparability of revenues between different years depends on population changes as well as price level changes. Population in the Cleveland Metropolitan Area increased 14 per cent between 1940 and 1950 and another 13 per cent by 1956.

Per capita revenues in current dollars, not shown in a table, more than doubled from $74.81 in 1940 to $157.94 in 1956 with the greater part of this increase occurring after 1950. But the increase was only about 112 per cent in per capita terms against 174 per cent increase in aggregate terms.

An even better measure of the burden of government revenues or costs is the amount per capita in constant dollars, presented in Table VI-3. On this basis, total revenues per capita actually declined 13.4 per cent, from $145.26 per capita in 1940 to $125.76 in 1950. The decline was due largely to a $14.37 drop in the real value of property tax receipts and an almost $10 drop in intergovernmental revenues, with only minor increases in other sources.

The 61 per cent increase in total revenues in current dollars between 1950 and 1956 was reduced to a 25.6 per cent increase in total revenues per capita in constant dollars. This raised the per capita revenue figure to $157.94, well above 1950, though only $12.68 above 1940. Again the property tax change dominated with an almost $20 per capita increase, supported by a more than $6 per capita gain in State Aid. Revenues from the property tax increased due to the larger tax base, reflecting both a real increase from new construction, equipment, and inventories and higher assessed valuations of existing properties. The average property tax rate applicable to assessed values in the Cleveland area in 1956 was only slightly higher than in 1950.

Historical Comparison

A longer-range view of local revenues is provided by a quick review of the property tax base and levy and its distribution between Cleveland and the suburbs since 1910. In 1910, the 637,000 people in Cuyahoga County paid local taxes of about $13 million to support their local governments. The property tax, levied at an average rate of 34.1 mills per dollar on $316 million of taxable value yielded $11 million to provide the major revenue to operate the County, municipalities, townships, and school districts. The property taxes were about $17 per capita, as indicated in Table VI-4.

Ninety per cent of the people in Cuyahoga County in 1910 lived in the City of Cleveland. The city accounted for 90 per cent of the county tax duplicate, as indicated in Chart VI-2. A property tax rate of 34.8 mills per dollar raised $9.6 million in Cleveland.

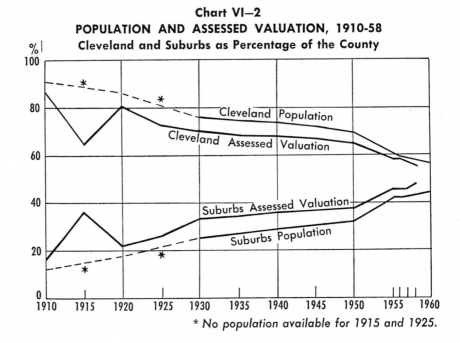

Chart VI—2

POPULATION AND ASSESSED VALUATION, 1910-58

Cleveland and Suburbs as Percentage of the County

* No population available for 1915 and 1925.

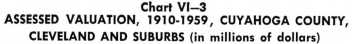

Chart VI—3
ASSESSED VALUATION, 1910-1959, CUYAHOGA COUNTY,
CLEVELAND AND SUBURBS (in millions of dollars)

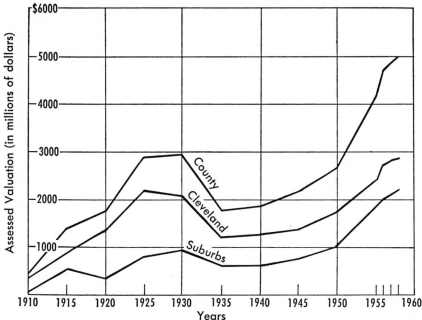

In 1956, the 1,580,000 people in Cuyahoga County paid $514 million of local taxes. The property tax, levied at an average rate of 30.68 mills per dollar on $4,641 million of taxable value, yielded $142 million and thus still provided the major source of local revenue. The property taxes averaged $90 per capita throughout the county.

By 1956, only about 59 per cent of the people of the county lived in the central city. Cleveland's tax duplicate was now 57 per cent of the county total. The City's 33.6 mill tax rate raised $87,471 million to support the County, City and School District.

The property tax in 1959 is expected to yield about $188 million in Cuyahoga County, about $114 per capita.

If these data are adjusted for changes in the price level and expressed in constant 1956 dollars, the 1910 figure becomes $54.60 compared to $90 per capita in 1956. The estimated 1959 amount would deflate to a comparable $108.

Table VI-4—Property Tax, Assessed Valuations and Tax Levies in Current Dollars and 1956 Constant Dollars, Cleveland Metropolitan Area, Selected Years, 1910-59

Tax Year	Aggregate				Per Capita			
	ASSESSED VALUATION (In millions)		CURRENT TAX LEVY (In thousands)		ASSESSED VALUATION		CURRENT TAX LEVY	
	Current Dollars	Constant Dollars*	Current Dollars	Constant Dollars*	Current Dollars	Constant Dollars*	Current Dollars	Constant Dollars*
1910	298.6	880.9	10,787.7	31,823.7	468	1,382	16.92	49.93
1920	1,743.1	2,361.9	29,444.3	39,897.0	1,847	2,503	31.21	42.29
1930	2,968.8	4,836.2	74,468.0	121,308.4	2,471	4,025	61.98	100.97
1940	1,799.1	3,493.9	53,389.2	103,681.8	1,478	2,870	43.86	85.18
1950	2,717.6	3,070.9	83,757.0	94,645.4	1,956	2,210	60.28	68.11
1955	4,214.6	4,277.8	131,462.0	133,433.9	2,807	2,849	87.56	88.87
1956	4,640.7	4,640.7	142,423.0	142,423.0	2,936	2,936	90.11	90.11
1957	4,845.9	4,684.8	160,240.0	154,911.7	3,046	2,946	100.32	97.02
1958	5,113.0	4,810.9	178,684.0	168,126.0	3,187	3,000	111.39	104.81
1959	5,223.0†	4,904.2†	188,000.0†	176,500.0†	3,206†	3,010†	115.41†	108.35†

* Adjusted with 1956 = 100, using the consumer price index. 1959 adjustment based on March 1959 price index. Population for non-census years from Cleveland Real Property Inventory estimates for October of the year of collection.

† Estimated.

Note: The tax year 1956 refers generally to the taxes which are paid during 1956. A single uniform rate of tax in each local taxing district applies to real estate and public utility property as of January 1, 1955, and to tangible personal property (other than inventories) with a taxable status as of January 1, 1956. Tax paid on inventories during 1956 is based on the average of monthly inventory values held during 1955. Taxes are due on the tangible personal property of express, telegraph, and telephone companies valued as of December 31, 1955. The applicable tax rate is determined by the local governing body or, if necessary, by referendum. Legally the first half of the 1955 payment on real estate and public utility property is due on December 20, 1955, and the second half payment by June 20, 1956. In practice the legal date is met only rarely and practically all payments occur during 1956.

The share of all the revenues going to the central city for Cleveland's municipal government, schools, and libraries, declined from 60 per cent in 1940 to 48 per cent in 1956. The largest increases were in the proportions of revenues going to the suburban school districts and municipalities.[3]

COMPARISONS WITH OTHER METROPOLITAN AREAS

Comparisons between metropolitan areas disclose some major differences in revenue and expenditures per capita and in relative emphasis on different revenue sources and expenditures. The reader, however, should remember that such comparisons are difficult and of limited validity for several reasons. Data are not readily available for *all* local governments in different metropolitan areas. In Ohio, for example, financial summaries for cities and counties are printed by the Auditor of State, but similar information was not available for 1956 and earlier years for the many villages and townships in the metropolitan areas. Financial data for school districts are published in a different form on a school-year basis by the School of Education of Ohio State University. Comparisons of the Cleveland area with metropolitan areas in other states are further complicated by differences in the division of responsibilities between state and local governments, in organizational structures of county, municipalities, and school districts, and in methods of accounting and reporting.

Data from the State of Ohio and the Bureau of the Census, however, do provide the basis for some useful comparisons and interpretation. Data for Ohio local governments are published in State reports as received from local governments, without adjustments for different reporting methods or corrections of errors. For example, an error in revenue of $2 million reported by one moderate-sized city in 1950 was published without correction in the *Comparative Statistics: Cities of Ohio, 1950*.

---

3. Cf.: *A Fiscal Profile*, p. 12.

Comparison of Ohio Metropolitan Areas

The Cleveland area differs from other metropolitan areas in Ohio on four counts. 1) Cuyahoga County is more urbanized than any other county in the state, with over 97 per cent of the people living in urban areas in 1956 by Census definition. Of the 1957 total real and personal property subject to tax, 99.8 per cent is in municipalities in Cuyahoga County, again a higher percentage than any other Ohio county. One financial reflection of urbanization is the high proportion of local government revenues collected and expenditures made by the cities and city school districts. City school districts accounted for more than 99 per cent of all school revenues and expenditures. 2) Cuyahoga County has more taxable property and income per capita than other metropolitan areas. The 1956 assessed valuation per capita of $3,066 in Cuyahoga County is very high compared to other areas in the state.[4] Hamilton County was close behind with $3,018 but all other counties were below $2,800 per capita. The state-wide average is $2,574. Vinton County apparently was low in the state at $1,477 per capita. The 1956 per capita average income of $2,650 in the Cleveland area compares with $2,280 in the Cincinnati area (Hamilton County) and $2,465 in the Columbus area (Franklin County), the next largest metropolitan areas in Ohio. The average income in Ohio was $2,150 per person in Vinton County, the poorest county in Ohio.

3) Average revenue per capita is higher for local governments in Cuyahoga County than in most other metropolitan areas in Ohio. A summary of 1954 financial data for the counties, cities, villages

---

4. Assessed valuations for Cuyahoga County vary for the same year depending on whether the actual or estimated tangible personal property valuations are used. The 1955-56 difference amounted to $40,356,000. Comparisons between counties are based on actual valuation ($3,066 per capita for 1956 for Cuyahoga County). Table VI-19 presents the differences by years since 1936 and explains the basis of the differences. In other chapters of this study, assessed valuations based on estimated tangible personal property are used as this figure is available when budget and expenditure plans are made.

Inter-county comparisons of assessed valuations are not precise, due to different assessment ratios in different Ohio counties. All Ohio counties were equalized in 1952, however, and Cuyahoga County, in 1956, was about at the state-wide assessment ratio, as indicated below in Table VI-14.

and townships composing the eighteen metropolitan counties in Ohio, compared with Metropolitan Cleveland is presented in Table VI-5. Revenues per capita of cities and villages in the Cleveland Metropolitan Area were sharply above the average for comparable governments in all metropolitan areas in Ohio. Cuyahoga County revenues per capita were slightly above the average for all eighteen metropolitan counties.

4) The fourth characteristic of Cuyahoga County local governments is the heavy emphasis on the property tax as a source of revenue, also shown in Table VI-5. Both in per capita and in

Table VI-5—Revenues of Local Governments in Cleveland Metropolitan Area; Cuyahoga County Compared to Those in the 18 Metropolitan Counties in Ohio, 1954

Revenue by Source	CITIES		VILLAGES		COUNTIES	
	In Cuyahoga County	In Eighteen Counties	In Cuyahoga County	In Eighteen Counties	In Cuyahoga County	All Eighteen
	Per Capita (In Dollars)					
Locally Collected						
General Property Tax	34.31	22.12	24.83	11.57	8.83	6.94
Special Assessments	2.78	2.20	5.89	2.62	.01	.42
Income Tax	. . .	6.00	. . .	. . .	. . .	. . .
Fees & Misc. Charges	7.95	6.90 ⎫	13.20	6.83	2.88	3.18
Other Local Revenues	5.75	5.23 ⎭				
Total	50.79	42.45	43.91	21.02	11.71	10.54
Non-Locally Collected						
Local Government Fund	5.06	3.73	2.92	1.97	2.08	1.95
Other State Aid	5.73	7.29	6.84	4.45	7.33	7.30
Federal Aid	.18	.12	. . .	. . .	1.52	1.54
Total	10.97	11.14	9.76	6.42	10.93	10.79

(Continued on next page)

Table VI-5 (Continued)

	CITIES		VILLAGES		COUNTIES	
Revenue by Source	In Cuyahoga County	In Eighteen Counties	In Cuyahoga County	In Eighteen Counties	In Cuyahoga County	All Eighteen
	Per Capita (In Dollars)					
Total Local and Intergov't	61.76	53.59	53.67	27.44	22.64	21.33
Public Service Enterprises	37.41	23.53	.60	9.31	...	...
GRAND TOTAL	99.18	77.12	54.27	36.75	...	...
	Percentages					
Locally Collected						
General Property Tax	55.55	41.28	46.26	42.17	39.00	32.54
Special Assessments	4.50	4.10	10.97	9.56	...	1.96
Income Tax	...	11.19	...	...	...	...
Fees & Misc. Charges	12.88	12.87	...	...	...	...
Other Local Revenues	9.30	9.77	24.59	...	12.72	14.91
Total	82.24	79.21	81.81	76.60	51.72	49.41
Non-Locally Collected						
Local Government Fund	8.19	6.97	5.44	7.19	9.19	9.12
Other State Aid	9.28	13.59	12.74	16.21	32.38	34.23
Federal Aid	0.29	0.23	...	...	6.71	7.24
Total	17.76	20.79	18.18	23.40	48.28	50.59
	100.00	100.00	100.00	100.00	100.00	100.00

Source: Division of Research and Statistics, Ohio Department of Taxation.
Note: Data for townships are omitted here. The townships in all 18 counties raised $9.47 per capita, against $8.38 per capita in Cuyahoga County.

percentage terms, the cities, villages, and county in the Cleveland area rely more heavily on the property tax than do other Ohio metropolitan cities. The difference is especially pronounced in the case of cities, due in large measure to the use of municipal income taxes in most Ohio metropolitan areas, but not in the Cleveland area.

Per capita revenues from transit, water, and electricity operations were above average for cities and below average for villages in Cuyahoga County, reflecting service to a wide area by the city of Cleveland water system and by bus and rapid transit provided largely by a few cities.

Comparison of Large Central Cities

A comparison of local governments serving Cleveland and the forty other cities in the United States with 1950 populations over 250,000 is possible from Bureau of the Census studies.[5] This study permits comparison between the total revenue per capita of all local governments serving the forty-one largest cities. A further comparison is possible for the five Ohio cities with 1950 populations over a quarter of a million, as the data are shown separately for each type of local government—city, county, school district, and special district. The obvious limitations of these data are that they cover only the central city of the metropolitan area and apply only to 1953.

In terms of amount and sources of revenues, the local governments serving the City of Cleveland seem to be about the average of the major city areas throughout the nation. Cleveland's revenues per capita, as shown in Table VI-6a, place her as the median city or just below the median on all general revenues (Cleveland's $135.87, the median, $138.31 or $2.44 higher), total local taxes, intergovernmental revenue, and charges for service and miscellaneous. Cleveland was above average in the per capita revenue from property taxes; her $82.93 about $7.50 above the median for all forty-one cities. Boston, Jersey City, Newark, Los Angeles, San Francisco, Milwaukee, Detroit and Minneapolis were highest, ranging between $90 and $132 per capita. Grouped closely with Cleveland between $80 and $87 per capita were New York, Chicago, Cincinnati, Indianapolis, Denver, Portland, Atlanta, and Long Beach. Smaller property tax revenues were collected by governments of the other large cities, including Philadelphia, Baltimore, St. Louis, and Pittsburgh.

Comparisons with revenue data for all the local governments

------

5. *Local Government Finances in City Areas in 1953*, State and Local Government Special Studies No. 39 (Washington, D. C., 1955).

Table VI-6(a)—Per Capita Revenues and Expenditures of Local Governments Serving All Cities with Populations over 600,000 in the United States, 1953

	Median 41 largest cities	Cleveland	New York	Chicago	Los Angeles	Phila-delphia	Detroit	Boston	San Francisco	Pitts-burgh	Washington DC	Baltimore	Milwaukee
General Revenue * Total	138.28	135.84	203.25	126.66	208.91	126.43	167.83	211.67	180.71	111.78	175.05	140.84	191.05
Distribution of Revenue by Source													
Taxes, Total	86.88	85.41	133.92	95.10	114.68	92.38	98.97	135.85	100.63	86.88	139.91	76.79	106.74
Property	75.44	82.93	83.05	80.42	100.41	54.07	97.06	131.75	90.17	74.85	62.88	66.48	99.82
Other	11.65	2.48	50.87	14.70	14.26	38.31	1.91	4.10	10.46	12.04	76.02	10.31	6.92
Intergovernmental Revenue	29.17	29.17	42.08	21.35	68.84	10.84	46.00	53.77	56.56	10.79	22.02	47.45	59.12
Charges and Misc. Revenue	22.85	21.27	27.25	10.19	25.38	23.21	22.85	22.05	23.51	14.09	14.11	16.60	25.17
Distribution of Revenue by Type of Government													
General Revenue, City		71.31	198.38	56.91	61.57	86.48	86.84	199.61	127.63	49.72	170.27	135.43	90.85
General Revenue, County		21.74		17.49	73.58		28.23			22.72			57.12
General Revenue, School Districts		38.34		35.01	67.59	35.30	52.08		42.83	33.66			35.89
General Revenue, Special Districts		4.45	4.87	17.25	6.17	4.65	.68	12.06	10.25	5.68	4.78	5.41	7.19
General Expenditures † Total	146.00	146.76	186.24	135.40	221.13	135.68	159.85	213.95	189.33	124.81	169.87	156.26	184.05
Selected Expenditures													
Education	43.60	42.11	44.93	36.33	71.58	37.49	50.86	35.43	57.08	33.59	40.28	43.06	37.92
Public Welfare	8.83	8.83	23.98	5.59	36.13	3.22	5.50	39.36	28.43	2.33	10.82	13.38	19.18
Highways	14.36	14.31	14.50	19.64	13.12	8.16	14.36	10.57	10.60	10.89	11.41	15.30	24.77
Health and Hospitals	9.94	13.41	22.65	8.52	13.33	7.47	17.80	21.99	11.85	4.53	29.14	8.18	18.78
City Population (in thousands), 1950		915	7892	3621	1970	2072	1850	801	775	677	802	950	637
Population of Standard Metropolitan Area (in thousands), 1950		1466	12920	5495	4368	3671	3016	2876	2241	2213	1464	1337	957
City as Percentage Standard Metropolitan Area, 1950		62.4	61.1	65.9	45.1	56.4	61.3	27.9	34.6	30.6	54.8	71.0	66.6

* General Revenues exclude utility and employee retirement or other insurance trust revenue.
† General Expenditures exclude expenditures on utilities and employees retirement or other insurance trust expenditures.

Notes: Median data are for the 41 largest cities in the United States, that is for all cities with populations over 250,000. Cities are listed in order of size of their 1950 population. Per Capita figures are based on 1950 population and 1953 expenditures and revenues. City share of county revenues are based on the ratio of its population to the total county population.

Source; Bureau of the Census, Local Government Finances in City Areas in 1953.

Table VI-6(b)—Per Capita Revenues and Expenditures of Local Governments Serving All Cities in Ohio with Populations over 250,000, 1953

	Cleveland	Cincinnati	Columbus	Toledo	Akron
General Revenue * Total	135.84	165.19	99.79	139.21	128.75
Distribution of Revenue by Source					
Taxes, Total	85.41	91.76	54.85	81.22	71.04
Property	82.93	86.56	39.87	51.05	69.03
Other	2.48	5.20	14.99	30.17	2.01
Intergovernmental Revenue	29.17	32.28	30.74	29.10	33.54
Charges and Miscellaneous Revenue	21.27	41.17	14.19	28.92	24.18
Distribution of Revenue by Type of Government					
General Revenue, City	71.31	89.55	45.77	69.80	63.61
General Revenue, County	21.74	28.72	22.31	25.95	19.13
General Revenue, School Districts	38.34	40.79	30.27	40.53	42.00
General Revenue, Special Districts	4.45	6.13	1.44	2.93	4.01
General Expenditures † Total	146.76	180.49	107.75	146.00	128.21
Selected Expenditures					
Education	42.11	62.45	44.92	49.16	63.62
Public Welfare	8.83	13.10	5.44	8.30	9.23
Highways	14.31	20.67	10.96	21.93	15.97
Health and Hospitals	13.41	15.50	4.49	7.60	3.19
City Population (in thousands) 1950	915	504	376	304	275
Population of Standard Metropolitan Area, 1950	1466	904	503	396	410
City as Percentage Standard Metropolitan Area, 1950	62.4	55.7	74.7	76.8	67.0

* General Revenues exclude utility and employee retirement or other insurance trust revenue.
† General Expenditures exclude expenditures on utilities and employee retirement or other insurance trust expenditures.
See also Note to Table VI-6(a).

serving the five Ohio cities with populations in excess of a quarter of a million, reveal the Cincinnati area clearly highest with $165.19 per capita, Toledo second with $139.21 followed closely by Cleveland at $135.87 and Akron with $128.75, with Columbus much lower at $99.79.

For the central city governments only, Cincinnati's revenue was about $18 per capita above Cleveland's, accounted for by higher city charges (partly for the municipal university) and miscellaneous revenues. Toledo and Columbus, in their city governments, relied more on municipal income taxes in 1953, in comparison with Cleveland. (Cincinnati did not begin its municipal income tax until 1954.) The water, transit and electric utilities are not included in these comparisons.

Preliminary reports on local government finance from the 1957 Census of Governments and from 1956 and 1957 Ohio financial reports support the following generalizations:

1. Cleveland is about average for large central cities throughout the country, and is second to Cincinnati of the five largest cities in Ohio in revenues per capita.

2. County governments are less important in proportion of local revenues and of revenues per capita in Ohio metropolitan areas than in rural areas.

3. Municipal governments receive the largest amount of revenue of all local governments in Cuyahoga County, although schools receive the largest amount throughout the state. This reflects the fact that municipal revenues and expenditures vary more between metropolitan areas and the rest of the state than do school revenues and expenditures.

4. School revenues are rising rapidly throughout the country, the state, and the Cleveland area. The rise has been greater on a per capita than on a per pupil basis, as the school enrollment is rising at a faster rate than the total population.

5. For all types of local government, the property tax provides greater support to Cuyahoga County jurisdictions than for comparable governments elsewhere in Ohio and in the United States. This heavy emphasis is due both to the greater per capita property values in Cuyahoga County, and to deliberate local choice. The higher valuation both facilitates a large yield from this tax and reduces the claim of local governments for state aid, especially for school districts where state funds are distributed to an increasing extent on an equalization basis.

LEGAL AND INSTITUTIONAL

The property tax is the only local tax generally available to counties, school districts, and townships in Ohio. Generally, cities and villages may use any taxes which are not being used by the State. In practice, municipalities in Ohio use the property tax, the income tax, and admissions taxes. The types and forms of revenue are prescribed by the Ohio Constitution, state statutes, and judicial decisions.

The powers and functions of local governments, other than schools, vary depending on the type of government. As a local area shifts from township to municipal status, it acquires more powers and responsibilities, including access to new revenue sources, to higher debt limits, and the right to a home-rule charter. Partly the powers and responsibilities acquired by a new municipal corporation represent those formerly exercised by the county and the state. The decision of an area to incorporate is voluntary; an area may remain a township as long as a majority of its voters wish.

Probably the three most important legal factors influencing the revenue sources subject to local control are: 1) the rate limitation on property taxes, adopted in its present form as a Constitutional amendment in 1933, which prohibits tax rates above 10 mills without approval by the voters; 2) the "home rule" Constitutional provisions which allow cities and villages (1912 amendment) and counties (1933 and 1957 amendments) to adopt charters to determine the form and powers of their local governments; 3) the preemption doctrine, dating from Ohio Supreme Court decisions of 1919 and 1925, holding that the State use of any tax sources denied the use of that source to local governments, unless the legislature explicitly allowed concurrent use by local governments.

Revenue Sources

The Ohio Constitution both provides for tax sources for State and local purposes and places restrictions on the use of certain taxes. "Article XII—Finance and Taxation" is the key part of the Ohio Constitution dealing with state and local taxes. Its several sections may be summarized as follows: no poll tax; property taxes may not be levied in excess of 10 mills on true value, except by at least a majority vote of the taxing district or by charter of the municipal corporation; real estate shall be taxed uniformly according to value; classification of personal property was permitted by a Constitutional amendment effective in 1931; revenues from motor vehicle licenses and gasoline taxes shall be dedicated to highway use; the State of Ohio shall not go more than $100,000 in debt, except by Constitutional amendment; income and inheritance taxes may be used, at uniform or graduated rates, with specified limited exemptions permitted; at least half of any state income and inheritance taxes must be returned to the local government(s) of origin; excise and franchise taxes may be adopted; severance taxes are authorized on coal, oil, and other minerals; no excise tax shall be levied on food for off-premises consumption.

"Article XIII—Corporations" also has two sections dealing with taxation. Section 4 of this article states that the property of corporations "shall forever be subject to taxation, the same as the property of individuals." Section 6 authorizes the General Assembly to "provide for the organization of cities and incorporated villages, by general laws; and restrict their power of taxation, assessment, borrowing money, contracting debts and loaning their credit, so as to prevent the abuse of such power."

"Article XVIII—Municipal Corporations" prescribes the powers and limitations of powers of cities and villages. Section 3 states: "Municipalities shall have authority to exercise all powers of local self-government and to adopt and enforce within their limits . . . regulations, as are not in conflict with general laws." Section 13 prescribes: "Laws may be passed to limit the power of municipalities to levy taxes and to incur debts . . . , may require reports . . . , and may provide for the examination of the vouchers, books, and accounts of all municipal authorities . . ." Under these sections, the courts have ruled that municipalities may not levy a tax where the State of Ohio is levying the same or a similar tax.[6] This is the "preemption doctrine, i.e., that any state tax by implication pre-empts the right to that tax source, and use of this tax is therefore denied to local governments." The Attorney General has ruled that the

---

6. *State ex rel. Zielonka, City Solicitor* vs. *Carrel, Auditor,* 99 Ohio St. 220, 124 N.E. 134 (1919; *Cincinnati* vs. *American Tel & Tel Co.,* 112 Ohio St. 493, 147 N.E. 806 (1925); *Firestone et al.* vs. *City of Cambridge,* 113 Ohio St. 57, 148 N.E. 470 (1925). For recent discussion, see Ohio Legislative Service Commission—*Local Government Financing Problems in Ohio* (Columbus, 1959), pp. 33-36.

Ohio Constitution does not expressly prohibit the levy of excise taxes simultaneously on the same subject by state and local taxing units and that the General Assembly can remove the implied prohibition by legislation (1949 O.A.G. 483). But more about this later.

The legislature has authorized all local governments to use the general property tax. The State uses the property tax now only to service the debt incurred to pay bonuses to Ohio veterans of both World Wars and the Korean conflict. The debt and taxes to pay these bonuses were authorized as Constitutional amendments by state-wide referendums. The levy of any tax, other than the general property tax, by the State of Ohio thus denies that source to the counties, cities, villages, townships, school districts and special districts. As of 1959, a list of the *major* State taxes and charges would include:

sales tax [7]	motor vehicle licenses [7]
use tax	drivers' licenses [7]
excise tax on:	highway use
cigarettes	corporate franchise
beer and wine	intangible personal property [7,8]
gasoline [7]	
public utility [7]	liquor gallonage tax
horseracing tax [7]	liquor store profits
inheritance tax [7]	liquor permits [7]

None of these taxes can be imposed now by local governments without a Constitutional amendment, express permission of the General Assembly, *or* a new opinion of the Ohio Supreme Court limiting or removing the current pre-emption doctrine.

Legislative provisions plus the Constitution and court decisions have further limited the tax sources available to counties and school districts. The *only* local tax source available *to school districts* is the general property tax (on land and improvements, public utility property, and tangible personal property). School districts also collect fees and charges for activities such as the school lunch

---

7. Portion of the receipts are shared with or distributed to local governments.
8. Rates set by Ohio statute; local collection and distribution.

program, admissions to athletic contests, adult education courses, rentals, and sales of property.

The general property tax is also the major local revenue source for Ohio cities and villages and is levied by every municipality in Ohio. The municipal income tax, used by thirty-one cities and six villages as of January 1, 1959, is the second most productive local revenue source. No municipality in Cuyahoga County has adopted an income tax. The admissions tax is also used by sixty-three of 144 cities and many villages in Ohio including thirteen cities in metropolitan Cleveland. Special assessments for capital improvements and less frequently for current services as street lighting and garbage collection are used by cities and villages. Local licenses and permits, fines and court costs, fees, charges, and minor sales also provide substantial revenues to practically every municipality. Many municipalities and some counties derive large revenues from the operation of transit systems, water and sewer systems, hospitals, cemeteries, recreation facilities, electric power systems, airports, lakeports, and other commercial-type enterprises. Any other tax sources, except those prohibited by the Constitution or pre-empted by the State, are also available to municipalities.

Library districts may levy property taxes through their school districts and collect fees and charges. Their major source of revenue, however, is the state-imposed by county-collected tax on intangibles, against which the public libraries have first claim on the amount collected within the county.[9]

All local jurisdictions may earn interest on their deposit balances and on their holdings of federal, state, and local government debt obligations.

In addition to the general property tax, counties and townships rely on special assessments, fees and charges for services rendered such as recording deeds, certain licenses and permits, and court costs.

If Cuyahoga County adopts a county charter, the charter could provide for the organization of the County as a municipal corpora-

---

9. See *Public Libraries in Cuyahoga County* (Cleveland Metropolitan Services Commission, 1959), Ch. 5.

tion. The pertinent part of Article X, Section 3 of the Constitution reads as follows:

"Any such charter may provide for the concurrent or exclusive exercise by the county, in all or in part of its area, of all or any designated powers vested by the Constitution or laws of Ohio in municipalities; it may provide for the organization of the county as a municipal corporation, and in any case it may provide for the succession by the county to the rights, properties, and obligations of municipalities and townships therein incident to the municipal power so vested in the County, and for the division of the county into districts for purpose of administration or of taxation or of both."

A tentative interpretation of this section suggests: 1) that a charter could grant the power to use a county income tax only if all the municipalities in the county ceded their right to adopt a municipal income tax; 2) that an amendment to the Ohio Constitution is necessary to permit a county charter provision providing a higher property tax rate than the county is now permitted under the 10-mill limit.

Tax Rates

Local governments set their tax rates within the framework set by Ohio law. All property tax rates above 10 mills must be approved by the voters in the taxing jurisdiction, by a vote ranging from a simple majority up to 60 per cent, depending on the type of local government, the purpose and duration of the tax, and whether the vote is at a general or special election. As the lowest 1958-59 tax rate in Cuyahoga County is 16.9 mills and as a check of tax rates in the County back to 1941 indicates no overall tax rate as low as 10 mills, this discussion will focus on property tax levies voted by the taxpayers. The purpose and effects of the 10-mill limitation are discussed in detail in METRO's *Financial Management* report.[10]

Charter cities and villages may provide in their charters for municipal property tax rates above the rates otherwise allowed to

---

10. See also Ohio Legislative Service Commission, *Local Government Financing*, Ch. II.

them under the 10-mill limit, by a vote of the municipal taxing body and without a vote of the people. In Cuyahoga County, seventeen of the twenty-two cities and five of the thirty-six villages as of mid-1958 operated under home rule charters. The charter provisions of all the charter cities, adopted by majority vote, provide tax rates higher than would be permitted within the 10-mill limit, if operating under general Ohio law for municipal corporations. The voters in charter municipalities may also vote tax levies by only a majority vote, not the higher percentage required under State law. The tax rates set by charter may continue indefinitely unless limited by the charter. This subject is discussed further in the section on property taxes later in this chapter.

TAXABLE CAPACITY IN THE CLEVELAND METROPOLITAN AREA

The taxable capacity of any country or community depends on both objective and subjective factors. Tax capacity is a term to denote an area's ability and willingness to pay taxes and other charges to support governmental activities. The concept of tax capacity is important, but even the best measure of tax capacity for a particular government or metropolitan area is imprecise, somewhat crude, and probably controversial.

The *economic* capacity of an area or political jurisdiction to finance government services depends on the objective factors such as the income and wealth of the people and businesses in the area. It also depends on the competitive position of the local businesses in the regional and wider markets and the impact of local taxes on this competitive position. The economic capacity of an area would be measured by objective factors, such as personal and corporate income, taxable property, sales, value added, inheritances, and other possible bases for taxation and charges.

Tax capacity is based on economic capacity modified to recognize the revenue sources legally available to local governments and the subjective factors. These include the political support for the government, the popularity of the various governmental programs relative to their cost, the customary level of taxes and other governmental charges—both historically and compared with other nearby jurisdictions, and the attitude of the people, businessmen, and community leaders toward government services and tax rates. The type of community—such as urban or rural; primarily residential or industrial or combination of industrial, commercial, and residential; stable or rapidly growing; rich or poor; many or few children —influences the government services needed and indirectly the willingness of the citizens to pay the costs.

In a federal system, such as that in the United States, the relationships between federal, state, and local governments is important in an analysis of the tax capacity of any level of government. The level of revenues collected and the use made of particular taxes by one government substantially affect the amount and sources of revenues available to other overlapping taxing jurisdictions. In this century, the big change in the division of government revenues in the United States has been the increasing importance of the federal government. Since the end of World War II, however, the revenues of state and local governments have increased at a more rapid rate than those of the federal government.[11]

Practically everyone in the United States is subjected to taxes levied by three levels of government—federal, state, and local. If the taxes collected by one government are high and increasing, it is generally more difficult for other governments to collect additional revenues. Political resistance is greater to higher local taxes, for example, if federal tax rates are high or have just been increased. Also, a rising level of activity by one level of government means, at least in the short run if the economy is relatively fully employed, that fewer resources are available both for other governmental activities and for the private sector of the economy. The net burden of most state and local taxes, however, is reduced for many individuals and all businesses who itemize and deduct their state and local tax payments in computing their income to federal income tax.

In most metropolitan areas, the large numbers of local taxing districts are at least partially in competition for revenues not only with the federal and state governments, but also with each other. Overlapping local tax jurisdictions compete for the same tax capacity, especially in areas where a single source (such as the property

---

11. See Tables III-2 and III-3.

tax) provides most of the local revenue to local governments. Taxpayers are probably more concerned with the amount of the tax
and the tax rate than with the most desirable allocation among the
overlapping jurisdictions.

The number of overlapping tax jurisdictions in metropolitan
areas varies depending on the organization of local government
responsibilities and powers within the state and on the number,
coverage, and powers of special districts. In the central cities of
New York, Baltimore, St. Louis, Boston, San Francisco, New Orleans,
and Denver, only one local taxing jurisdiction covers both the
schools and the municipality, with the county either consolidated
with the city or non-existent. Washington, D. C., also has a unitary
taxing authority. The remaining thirty-three major cities all have two
or more overlapping local taxing districts. Chicago, Minneapolis,
Cincinnati, Oakland, San Diego, Toledo, and Long Beach are high
with five local taxing units overlying the central city.[12] Almost all
the major cities have other governmental bodies, such as housing
authorities and port authorities, with revenues from sources other
than taxes. Everyone living in Cuyahoga County, for example, is
subject to taxation by the federal, state, and four local governments
—County, municipal, school district, and Cleveland Metropolitan
Park District. The library district serving this area also has taxing
power through the school district, although only the Euclid and
Lakewood libraries, through their school districts, were levying
taxes in 1956.

Neighboring taxing districts are in competition, each usually
striving to expand its economic and tax bases on a per capita basis,
to improve local government services, and to keep tax rates relatively low. Through the same newspapers, tax notices, and political
campaigns, people in different communities in the same metropolitan
area are in a better position to compare their tax situation with
their neighbors, than people outside metropolitan areas. The many
local communities offer certain advantages of choice to residents of
the metropolitan area. They have the opportunity to include in their

---

12. U. S. Dept. of Commerce Bureau of the Census, 1957. *Census of Governments*, Vol. I, No. 2, *Local Government in Standard Metropolitan Areas*, Table 3
(Washington, 1957).

choice of a residence or business location the local governments which offer the level of service and related costs (taxes) which most nearly match their needs and pocketbook. If one prefers the best schools for one's children, a few communities in the metropolitan area stand out, usually with higher school taxes to purchase the better service. If he prefers low taxes and is indifferent to the type and quality of government service, other jurisdictions in the metropolitan area will suit him better.

Thus, competition for revenues is sharp both between overlying jurisdictions which rely on the same tax source and between neighboring communities in the same metropolitan area to supply good service at low cost, according to the tastes of their taxpayers and local government officials.

Tax capacity depends also on the taxes used and administration of these taxes. A poor tax badly administered would approach capacity at a relatively small revenue yield. It is inconceivable, for example, to imagine the present total revenues of federal, state and local governments being collected from the property tax alone. Taxes which are equitable and convenient, and which have minimum adverse economic effects, have a large potential capacity. If revenue needs are large, even the best tax might be exploited beyond its capacity. Tax capacity tends to be increased by a variety of taxes, tapping different bases without excessively high average or maximum rates. The capacity of any tax and of the entire tax system depends also on the administration of the tax and on the taxpayers' confidence in the justice and efficiency of the tax and its administration.

The tax system of the United States now has a productive yield not dreamed of twenty years ago. World War II necessitated drastic increases in federal revenues. Economic growth and inflation expanded the tax base. Development especially of the income tax at the federal level and of sales and income taxes by the states added to the capacity.

The maximum tax levies which are politically possible depend in part on custom, competition, and change over time. The political limit on the yield from the property tax, still the basic local revenue source, varies between metropolitan and other areas, between states, and between localities with different access to other large revenue sources—such as a local income tax—as well as with the economic base, the local leadership, and the level and scope of services expected by the local voters.

Historical Changes in the Tax Base

The potential tax base changes with the amount and form of economic activity in the area served by a government. The major tax bases in any society are stocks of property and other wealth, the periodic flow of income and production, and commercial transactions, including foreign trade. A century ago, the federal government obtained its revenues mostly from the tariff; Ohio used the general property tax as the major source of both state and local revenues. In a largely agricultural economy, land, buildings, farm animals, and inventories and equipment of agriculture and business were the best and almost the only measure of wealth and income.

Today, following great population growth, industrialization, and urbanization, many other measures of taxable capacity, such as annual income of individuals and corporations, sales of all or selected commodities, and inheritances, have come to the fore. With the great needs for revenue for defense, education, welfare, highways, aids to agriculture and veterans, and other government activities, these relatively new revenue sources have been highly developed, beginning with World War I. The federal government now depends primarily on the personal and corporate income taxes and selected excises, while the State of Ohio relies on the general sales tax, tobacco taxes, liquor taxes and profits, and taxes and fees on highway users for most of its revenues.

Local governments throughout the country still rely on the property tax for about half of all their revenues and for about 70 per cent of revenues from their own sources, i.e., excluding intergovernmental payments. With the development of Cleveland and its suburbs into a major manufacturing and commercial center, several good tax bases in addition to the property tax are available.

Distribution of Taxable Capacity Within the Metropolitan Area

With most metropolitan areas blanketing scores of local governments of all sorts—cities, villages, townships, school districts, and special districts—one of the most serious fiscal problems is the wide range of taxable capacity between different local jurisdictions.

For local governments in the Cleveland vicinity, classification of municipalities in terms of their economic base is valuable.[13] It reveals the source of the taxable capacity and a major reason for the wide differences between communities. Another use of the classification is to indicate the type and level of expenditures required to serve communities with different needs for service. An over-all summary of most of the major measures of tax capacity— assessed value per capita, disposable income per capita, intangibles tax collected per capita, and inheritance tax collected per capita— is presented in Table VI-7(a). Assessed valuation per capita under the property tax is most important as a measure of tax capacity. This most productive of the present revenue sources collected 56.8 per cent of all revenues and 73.2 per cent of revenue from local sources in 1956 and will probably remain the mainstay of the local revenue system for decades to come. Income per capita or per family is an excellent measure of ability to pay and approximates the base which would be available if a municipal (or metropolitan) personal income tax were adopted. The intangibles and inheritance taxes collected reflects primarily the situs of financial wealth.

Most significant from Table VI-7(a) and Map VI-1 is the wide range in tax-paying capacity between the various municipalities. With assessment on a county basis in Ohio, the average assessed valuation per person for the entire county is about $3,000. But the richest municipality, Cuyahoga Heights, is about forty times the average while the poorest, Oakwood, is only two-fifths the average. (Assessed

---

13. See Chapter II *supra*. Also see Julius Margolis, "The Variation of Property Tax Rates Within a Metropolitan Area," *National Tax Journal*, Vol. IX, pp. 326, 327-28 (1956).

Table VI-7(a)—Measures of Taxable Capacity, Cleveland Metropolitan Area, by Municipality, 1956

Governmental Unit	Income		Investments		Property Tax (Assessed Valuation Per Capita)		Aggregate Assessed Valuation		Average Residential Valuation 1956
	Median Family Income, 1949 (Dollars)	Average Disposable Income, 1956 (Dollars per Family)	Intangible Tax Collected, 1956 (Dollars per Capita)	Inheritance Tax Collected, 1956 (Dollars per Capita)	1956 (Dollars)	Ratio 1956/1950 (Per Cent)	1956 (In Thousands of Dollars)	Ratio 1956/1950 (Per Cent)	Dollars per Capita
Cuyahoga County (average or total)	3,901	7,735	4.51	1.10	3,066	150.7	4,845,189	171.5	1,216
Cities									
Bay Village	5,390	n.a.	4.87	1.38	2,730	134.7	30,769	219.6	2,469
Bedford	3,717	7,215	1.28	0.27	2,795	149.1	35,553	208.4	1,463
Berea	4,110	8,637	1.70	0.52	2,198	196.6	29,380	218.0	1,487
Brooklyn	4,054	n.a.	0.94	0.19	4,635	155.7	40,892	217.4	1,484
Cleveland	3,531	6,966	2.22	0.60	2,964	152.2	2,744,398	154.0	769 *
Cleveland Heights	5,646	11,801	15.73	5.36	2,772	135.2	171,411	141.4	2,136 *
East Cleveland	4,261	7,947	3.35	0.61	2,399	146.9	95,180	145.6	988 *
Euclid	4,537	8,355	1.48	0.45	3,901	133.4	232,687	192.2	1,332 *
Fairview Park	4,756	n.a.	3.90	0.23	3,107	171.0	41,045	242.6	2,016
Garfield Heights	4,288	7,940	0.37	0.19	1,889	132.9	61,853	200.9	1,365
Lakewood	4,705	9,616	6.88	2.49	2,350	138.2	159,833	138.0	1,353 *
Lyndhurst	4,925	n.a.	9.02	0.18	2,357	122.1	32,222	226.8	2,100
Maple Heights	4,285	7,333	0.35	0.06	2,298	132.8	62,556	231.9	1,413
Mayfield Heights	4,278	n.a.	1.24	0.16	2,420	150.5	25,261	270.5	1,821
North Olmsted	4,305	n.a.	0.99	0.24	2,353	167.6	28,593	308.3	1,847
Parma	4,499	8,127	0.63	0.13	2,533	121.7	158,556	263.6	1,600

Rocky River	5,973	11,932	12.27	3.46	3,318	135.8	50,621	184.3	2,536
Shaker Heights	8,109	16,215	51.42	6.73	4,266	129.4	148,321	159.4	3,110 *
South Euclid	5,243	9,665	3.20	0.38	2,593	125.5	65,222	204.6	1,919 *
University Heights	7,151	15,170	7.43	0.96	3,179	135.9	48,557	179.4	2,748
Villages									
Beachwood	7,600	n.a.	19.19	0.76	4,988	80.2	20,614	308.9	4,536
Bedford Heights	n.a.	n.a.	0.97	0.05	4,155	...	18,346	...	778
Bentleyville	4,250	n.a.	3.89	0.00	3,243	147.6	827	247.6	2,935
Bratenahl	4,250	n.a.	101.66	89.02	4,203	131.5	5,359	135.2	3,767
Brecksville	4,725	n.a.	6.29	2.15	4,312	146.2	18,410	234.3	3,943
Broadview Heights	4,054	n.a.	0.21	0.14	2,542	170.3	10,590	311.2	2,259
Brooklyn Heights	4,318	n.a.	1.08	0.02	3,036	147.0	4,005	208.3	1,521
Brook Park	3,365	n.a.	0.71	1.09	29,427	1,311.9	78,423	1,282.9	1,930
Chagrin Falls	3,513	n.a.	27.36	0.20	3,054	161.2	10,367	177.3	1,708
Cuyahoga Heights	3,357	n.a.	12.57	4.97	125,925	145.5	98,851	160.0	1,750
Gates Mills	6,300	n.a.	173.12	4.98	6,845	151.9	8,173	171.8	6,808
Glenwillow	3,083	n.a.	0.47	0.00	4,425	141.5	1,394	173.4	2,018
Highland Heights	4,375	n.a.	0.92	0.00	2,659	103.9	5,263	269.8	2,404
Hunting Valley	6,500	n.a.	350.88	59.27	11,259	143.5	5,078	150.5	10,956
Independence	4,048	n.a.	2.31	0.22	3,449	150.4	19,549	274.5	2,297
Linndale	n.a.	n.a.	0.08	0.10	1,688	222.4	665	219.5	1,695
Mayfield	5,500	n.a.	3.33	0.52	2,569	126.3	4,152	253.6	2,350
Middleburg Heights	4,317	n.a.	1.20	0.04	3,666	147.8	19,358	339.4	2,246
Moreland Hills	6,300	n.a.	5.57	0.30	4,063	142.7	6,859	231.6	3,589
Newburgh Heights	3,464	n.a.	0.25	0.11	2,487	175.4	9,004	172.2	1,118
North Randall	4,125	n.a.	5.29	0.00	19,736	193.7	5,763	317.7	3,043
North Royalton	3,960	n.a.	0.64	0.10	2,623	173.7	15,765	265.1	2,179
Oakwood	n.a.	n.a.	0.26	0.22	1,308	...	4,895	...	1,068
Olmsted Falls	4,469	n.a.	3.35	2.30	2,518	167.6	4,430	259.4	1,933

(Continued on next page)

Table VI-7(a) (Continued)

Governmental Unit	Income		Investments		Property Tax (Assessed Valuation Per Capita)		Aggregate Assessed Valuation		Average Residential Valuation 1956
	Median Family Income, 1949 (Dollars)	Average Disposable Income, 1956 (Dollars per Family)	Intangible Tax Collected, 1956 (Dollars per Capita)	Inheritance Tax Collected, 1956 (Dollars per Capita)	1956 (Dollars)	Ratio 1956/1950 (Per Cent)	1956 (in Thousands of Dollars)	Ratio 1956/1950 (Per Cent)	Dollars per Capita
Orange	n.a.	n.a.	0.96	0.68	3,142	158.0	5,119	286.9	2,833
Parkview	4,350	n.a.	1.16	0.20	2,516	130.6	4,376	343.5	2,364
Parma Heights	4,278	n.a.	0.92	0.10	2,389	126.1	25,592	373.4	2,075
Pepper Pike	8,000	n.a.	15.75	1.25	6,721	125.9	14,336	307.2	5,828
Richmond Heights	4,812	n.a.	2.27	0.13	2,392	88.8	7,809	325.4	2,161
Seven Hills	4,375	n.a.	0.75	0.03	2,829	141.3	10,068	372.6	2,636
Solon	4,135	n.a.	2.76	1.41	3,925	170.8	20,063	339.8	2,574
Strongsville	3,692	n.a.	1.12	0.34	2,730	172.6	14,583	263.1	1,546
Valley View	4,062	n.a.	0.44	0.13	2,289	204.2	3,707	230.5	1,240
Walton Hills	n.a.	n.a.	0.73	0.19	25,909	...	38,552	...	2,426
Warrensville Heights	4,444	n.a.	1.09	0.69	2,502	143.5	18,969	263.6	1,806
Westlake	4,189	n.a.	2.45	0.56	2,936	150.5	28,507	297.5	2,312
West View	3,750	n.a.	0.22	0.14	2,434	141.0	2,604	241.3	1,349
Woodmere	3,500	n.a.	0.05	0.00	2,150	218.1	931	225.4	4,781
Townships									
Chagrin Falls	8,500	n.a.	7.13	0.00	5,225	137.5	465	222.5	4,833
Olmsted	3,438	n.a.	0.37	0.45	1,661	140.8	7,104	234.9	970
Riveredge	n.a.	n.a.	n.a.	0.00	630	...	58	32.2	n.a.
Warrensville	5,000	n.a.	0.07	0.10	621	178.4	1,300	198.8	n.a.

* Multiple dwelling units not included in totals.
n.a. not available.

Table VI-7(b)—Cleveland Metropolitan Area

Distribution of Tax Duplicate by Percentage of Each Class of Property, 1956-57

	Residential	Commercial	Industrial	Public Utility	Tangible Personal	Total
Cuyahoga County (average or total)	39.7	19.7	8.4	7.6	24.6	100
Cities						
Bay Village	90.4	1.9	0.4	5.5	1.8	100
Bedford	52.4	11.9	9.0	9.2	17.5	100
Berea	67.6	13.7	0.9	7.8	0.0	100
Brooklyn	28.8	7.0	16.8	9.4	38.0	100
Cleveland	25.9	26.0	9.7	9.0	29.3	100
Cleveland Heights	76.8	15.1	0.1	5.0	2.7	100
East Cleveland	41.3	29.9	7.0	8.5	13.3	100
Euclid	34.1	8.5	16.0	4.2	37.2	100
Fairview Park	64.9	20.7	0.0	4.0	10.4	100
Garfield Heights	72.3	8.0	3.7	6.0	10.0	100
Lakewood	57.6	23.6	2.8	6.0	10.0	100
Lyndhurst	89.1	5.8	0.0	3.5	1.6	100
Maple Heights	61.5	9.7	4.3	7.5	17.0	100
Mayfield Heights	75.3	12.2	0.0	5.7	6.8	100
North Olmsted	78.5	5.5	1.6	7.8	4.8	100
Parma	63.2	8.3	5.5	4.3	18.7	100
Rocky River	76.4	13.1	0.8	6.3	3.4	100
Shaker Heights	72.9	18.7	0.0	5.6	2.8	100
South Euclid	77.0	11.8	0.1	5.7	5.4	100
University Heights	86.4	7.8	0.0	2.9	2.9	100
Villages						
Beachwood	91.0	2.9	0.0	4.4	1.7	100
Bedford Heights	18.7	7.2	19.1	6.6	48.3	100
Bentleyville	90.4	0.0	0.0	9.4	0.2	100
Bratenahl	89.6	4.6	0.0	4.5	1.3	100
Brecksville	68.1	7.3	9.9	8.5	6.2	100
Broadview Heights	84.0	8.3	0.0	6.2	1.5	100
Brooklyn Heights	50.1	26.6	1.1	6.2	12.5	100
Brook Park	6.6	2.1	24.1	3.7	62.7	100
Chagrin Falls	55.9	18.0	2.7	4.8	18.3	100
Cuyahoga Heights	1.3	0.6	28.1	5.1	64.9	100
Gates Mills	92.0	1.4	0.0	4.1	1.2	100
Glenwillow	45.6	2.7	8.4	25.8	17.5	100

(Continued on next page)

Table VI-7(b) (Continued)

Distribution of Tax Duplicate by Percentage of Each Class of Property, 1956-57

	Residential	Commercial	Industrial	Public Utility	Tangible Personal	Total
Highland Heights	88.1	3.7	0.0	6.7	1.5	100
Hunting Valley	97.3	0.0	0.0	1.5	0.5	100
Independence	63.8	7.4	1.6	13.8	13.4	100
Linndale	52.0	22.3	0.0	13.8	11.9	100
Mayfield	91.5	3.5	0.0	3.7	1.3	100
Middleburg Heights	61.3	15.1	0.3	9.2	12.4	100
Moreland Hills	88.3	5.5	0.0	4.5	0.9	100
Newburgh Heights	44.9	6.5	22.5	8.8	17.3	100
North Randall	15.4	55.4	3.1	9.2	16.9	100
North Royalton	83.0	6.4	0.0	5.5	3.0	100
Oakwood	81.7	9.4	0.8	6.3	1.8	100
Olmsted Falls	76.3	7.0	0.0	11.6	4.9	100
Orange	89.7	6.8	0.0	3.1	0.4	100
Parkview	93.4	2.7	0.0	3.5	0.4	100
Parma Heights	86.9	4.3	0.0	6.4	2.3	100
Pepper Pike	87.0	9.0	0.0	3.6	0.4	100
Richmond Heights	90.4	4.5	0.0	3.1	1.9	100
Seven Hills	91.6	2.1	0.0	3.7	1.9	100
Solon	65.6	7.6	5.5	7.5	11.5	100
Strongsville	56.6	12.3	0.4	8.1	8.4	100
Valley View	37.7	10.2	1.8	16.6	15.1	100
Walton Hills	9.4	0.9	22.8	6.4	60.5	100
Warrensville Heights	72.2	12.4	0.1	6.0	8.9	100
Westlake	79.0	7.4	0.5	7.7	4.1	100
West View	55.5	23.1	0.0	9.8	4.6	100
Woodmere	82.6	3.0	0.0	12.5	1.9	100
Townships						
Chagrin Falls	92.5	0.0	0.0	5.6	1.9	100
Olmsted	58.4	11.9	0.0	13.3	4.0	100
Riveredge	0.0	51.8	0.0	24.1	24.1	100
Warrensville	67.9	14.1	0.0	16.4	1.6	100

Sources: 1. 1950 Census.
         2. *Sales Management* "Survey of Buying Power" (May, 1957).
         3. Based on tax and valuation data of Ohio Department of Taxation and County Auditor, Cuyahoga County and population estimates for October 1956 by Cleveland Real Property Inventory. 1956 per capita valuations are 1956-57 actual tax duplicate divided by 1956 population estimate.

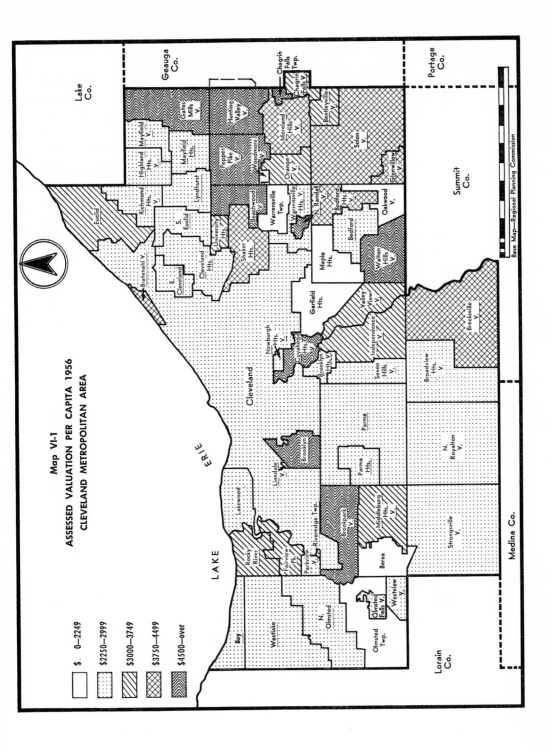

Map VI-1
ASSESSED VALUATION PER CAPITA 1956
CLEVELAND METROPOLITAN AREA

$ 0—2249
$2250—2999
$3000—3749
$3750—4499
$4500—over

Base Map—Regional Planning Commission

valuations were estimated at about 40 per cent of market value for 1956.) Among cities, the highest, Brooklyn, has an assessed valuation per capita of about 2.4 times that of the lowest, Garfield Heights. The differences are greatest among villages, where the valuation of large industries or expensive homes in the richer villages is divided among relatively few people or where there are only lower priced homes with no industry or shopping center to pull up the average. The distribution of the property tax duplicate between residential, commercial, and industrial real estate, public utility property, and tangible personal property (business inventories, machinery, and equipment) mirrors the economic characteristics of each municipality.

The variation in disposable income per family for 1956 is from $6,966 in Cleveland to $16,215 in Shaker Heights, among the fourteen cities for which recent estimates are available. Information on median family incomes for all municipalities from the 1950 Census, also shown in Table VI-7(a), indicated that the high community (Shaker Heights) was 2.4 times the lowest (Cuyahoga Heights).[14]

The intangibles (local situs only) and inheritance taxes are minor revenue sources for the total area but very important for some jurisdictions, as shown in Table VI-7(a). The intangibles tax listed here is levied at a rate of 5 per cent on investments which are productive (those which pay interest or dividends during the year) or 0.2 of 1 per cent on non-productive investments. Capitalizing the tax yield at 5 per cent indicates 1956 investment income ranging from a high of $7,000 per person in Hunting Valley to $1 per person in Woodmere. For the inheritance tax, only the half remaining with the local municipality is reported. Revenues from this source vary widely for any community from year to year. Hunting Valley, a wealthy village, had inheritance tax receipts which varied from $9,918, in 1954, to $166,831, the following year. The range for 1956 local collection is from $.06 per person in Maple Heights to $59.27 per person in Hunting Valley.

Imbalance shows up in each of the measures of capacity,

---

14. This use of the median narrows the range as it does not weigh the higher incomes as an average would.

Revenues **197**

although some communities which are low by one standard may be high by another. South Euclid, for example, is below average in terms of assessed valuation but comparatively high in terms of disposable income. Cuyahoga Heights is unique in the great amount of assessed valuation per person, but is below average in income per capita. Other communities are uniformly high, such as Shaker Heights and Hunting Valley. Some communities are low in taxable capacity, by every measure. These communities, including Garfield Heights and Maple Heights among the cities, and Newburgh Heights, Oakwood, and Woodmere among the villages, are generally the problem communities for service levels and tax capacity. Greatest weight, based on the present local tax system, must be given to assessed property valuation, as this accounts for almost three quarters of all revenues raised locally.

Taxable Capacity—Property Tax

Municipalities: Taxable capacity, measured in terms of assessed valuation per capita, or per pupil, varies widely between different municipalities and school districts. The disproportionate division of population and assessed valuation creates problems especially for those jurisdictions in which the valuation is substantially below the average. From an examination of the assessed valuations, the rate of growth, the amount of assessed valuation, and other variables, the only clear conclusion is that no single course of development promises a generally high tax base—in assessed valuation per capita terms.

Three major groups of communities have property tax bases which are more than $700 above the average on a per capita basis,[15] the five industrial enclaves, four balanced municipalities, and eight dormitory suburbs. Each industrial village has large valuations of industrial properties or of race tracks (North Randall), spread over small populations. The residential valuation in each of these communities is less than 20 per cent of the total assessed valuation.

---

15. $700 is approximately one standard deviation from the average not including the industrial enclaves.

Cuyahoga Heights can be expected to maintain its very high per capita valuations indefinitely, as it has little land available for residential growth. North Randall and Walton Hills should expect some dilution of their industrial valuation as their expected future population growth reduces somewhat their per capita valuations to perhaps three to four times the present County average. Brook Park leaped ahead between 1950 and 1956 with a thirteen-fold increase in assessed valuations per person, the highest rate of increase in the area. This community is likely to lose its present high per capita valuation, as its industrial growth came first and its population growth is just beginning. An increase from 2,665 people, in 1956, to 15,600, in 1970, is expected; this five-fold rise in population will probably cut sharply the per capita valuation and place Brook Park perhaps at twice the area average instead of its present lofty ten times the average valuation.

The other group of communities with very high valuations are the residential villages with expensive homes. In 1956, Hunting Valley had 129 residences with the highest average assessment of about $38,300 per home. With the sales price usually two and a half to three times the assessed valuation, the market value of the average home would probably be over $90,000 in Hunting Valley, and over $30,000 in Beachwood. Some of these villages are attempting to maintain their high valuation per person by zoning and by minimum acreage per house, limiting their population growth. Beachwood, on the other hand, with the most rapid population growth in the county between 1950 and 1956, grew to almost four times its 1950 population, but its assessed valuation rose only to three times its 1950 level. This absolute decline in per capita valuation between 1950 and 1956 for Beachwood suggests what is likely to happen as (or if) the other wealthy residential villages provide ground for new housing developments.

Bedford Heights, with the lowest suburban residential valuation per capita as shown in Table VI-7, is lifted well above average by business property—largely industrial real estate and tangible personal property—which accounts for four-fifths of its tax base. The other villages with per capita valuations more than $700 above the 1956 average are Brecksville, Moreland Hills, and Solon. All three had population increases of 60 to 100 per cent, with the new homes of above average value. The population surge in these areas is expected to continue. Solon, with substantial industrial and commercial growth within the past few years, is favorably situated with space and road and rail facilities to become a balanced suburban city over the next decade.

Brooklyn, Shaker Heights, and Euclid are the only cities with property tax capacities above $3,800 per capita. Brooklyn and Euclid are balanced cities with more than half their assessed valuation on business.[16] Shaker Heights has a valuable shopping center but no industry and is largely a residential community with homes and apartments of high value.

The suburbs with high per capita assessed valuations are able to finance municipal and school services of a relatively high quality. The problem here, if any, is whether they are doing their share in terms of their taxpaying capacity to support local government functions in the metropolitan area of which they are a vital part.

Problems of tax capacity for the County and municipalities arise from several reasons:

1) There are municipalities which are too small to have a tax base adequate to support the usual municipal services. The villages of Bentleyville, Glenwillow, Linndale, and Woodmere and the townships other than Olmsted, with assessed valuations below $2 million, all face a revenue crisis for this reason, if they attempt to provide urban service.

2) There are municipalities which have been relatively poor in terms of property tax base continually, or as a result of a slow rise in tax base relative to population growth and increases in the price level. Garfield Heights, Linndale, and Oakwood represent the first classification, while Lyndhurst and Richmond Heights illustrate the municipalities with declining tax base per capita in real terms.

3) A shift in legal status from village to city creates new responsibilities, such as maintenance of highways, with an auto-

---

16. The assessed valuation on business is derived from the percentages of residential valuation to total assessed valuation and the division of assessed valuation between residential, commercial, industrial, and tangible personal property (Table VI-7(a)).

matic, sharp increase in costs perhaps averaging $100,000 annually for each new city but no automatic increase in revenue. About eleven Cleveland-area villages, including Broadview Heights and North Royalton, are expected to show over 5,000 population in the 1960 Census and acquire these additional costly responsibilities.

4) A shift of functions to the County or other area-wide government will create problems unless appropriate revenues are made available. Any transfer of functions to the County must rely on the property tax and cannot escape the 10-mill tax rate limitation even by a county charter without a constitutional amendment. Cuyahoga County, for example, spent about $25.8 million in 1958 to perform functions mandated by the State, but the County's share of the 10-mill limit provided only $7.2 million.[17] Additional funds to finance services which the State requires the County to perform had to come from voted levies.

School Districts

Changes in valuation per pupil result from both the change in assessed valuation and the change in enrollment. Despite the 72 per cent increase in total assessed valuation between 1950 and 1956 the average valuation per pupil rose only 24 per cent to $21,430 in 1956 (Table VI-8). This reflects the increase in school enrollment from 164,000 in 1950, to 226,000 in 1956. Every school district in the county had increases in assessed valuation, although the increases in Lakewood and Bratenahl were due almost entirely to the increase from revaluation. All thirty-two school districts also had increases in the school enrollment, from an 11 per cent increase in East Cleveland to a 242 per cent rise in Parma.

Public school enrollment is not a fixed percentage of population, but varies widely depending on the type of community. Generally,

17. Ohio Legislative Service Commission, *Local Government Financing Problems in Ohio*, p. 12.

the older communities with a stable or slowly rising population have the smaller percentages of children in public schools, while the rapidly growing dormitory suburbs attract more young families with a higher proportion of school-age children. Public school enrollment also varies inversely with enrollment in private and parochial schools, depending largely on the religious composition of the population and on the capacity and convenience of the parochial schools. The ratio of public school pupils to total population ranged from a high of 30.9 per cent in the Orange School District to a low of 10.9 per cent in Lakewood School District, as shown in Table VI-8.

Only Cuyahoga Heights and Berea enjoy assessed valuations sharply above the 1956 average of $21,430 valuation per pupil. Both of these districts depend on large industrial valuations, reflected in the percentage of tangible personal property in Table VI-8, to achieve the high per pupil figures. Generally taxable property is divided more equally on a per pupil basis among school districts than on a per capita basis among municipalities. With fewer school districts than municipalities, this narrower range follows from the fact that the school districts are usually larger and more diverse in their economic base. For example, the Cuyahoga Heights School District includes two villages of average valuations per person, along with the top municipality for valuation per person. And the ratio of pupils to total population is 23.5 per cent in this school district, against the County average of 14.3 per cent.

Again the more serious problems occur with the school districts at the lower end of the range of taxable valuation per pupil. Eleven school districts, with enrollments totaling 43,909 pupils in 1956, had valuations of less than $15,000 per pupil. All these districts were growing rapidly, with enrollment in each increasing at least 70 per cent between 1950 and 1956.

The problem school districts divide into two categories: 1) Districts such as Bratenahl which are too small in population to offer a full program including high school. This is not primarily a financial problem, at least as long as other districts will accept pupils on a tuition basis.

2) School districts which are poor in terms of assessed valuation

Table VI-8—Measures of Taxable Capacity, Cleveland Metropolitan Area, by School District, 1956

SCHOOL DISTRICTS	AVERAGE DAILY MEMBERSHIP		
	1956	Ratio 1956/1950	Ratio: ADM to Pop., 1956
Cities			
Bay Village †	2,349	197.6	20.8
Bedford	3,911	157.3	22.2
Berea	3,879	146.7	17.9
Brooklyn	1,650	171.9	20.8
Cleveland	117,730	118.5	12.9
Cleveland Heights	12,044	129.6	16.0
East Cleveland	5,417	111.0	12.5
Euclid	10,421	155.7	17.5
Fairview Park	2,361	164.6	16.5
Garfield Heights †	4,322	183.6	13.9
Lakewood	7,401	113.9	10.9
Maple Heights †	4,853	208.3	17.8
North Olmsted †	2,191	191.5	18.0
Parma †	13,418	336.9	17.3
Rocky River	2,640	155.9	16.6
Shaker Heights	6,570	148.8	14.4
So. Euclid-Lyndhurst	6,625	213.2	18.9
Local & Exempted			
Beachwood	750 *	416.7 *	16.3
Bratenahl	179 *	140.0 *	14.0
Brecksville †	1,895	208.9	25.0
Chagrin Falls Ex.†	1,201	168.4	22.1
Cuyahoga Heights	759	146.8	23.5
Independence	779	193.8	13.7
Mayfield (City) †	2,987	224.7	19.6
North Royalton †	1,375	175.4	20.0
Olmsted Falls †	1,532	186.8	22.0
Orange	1,484	177.5	30.9
Richmond Heights	350	282.3	12.1
Solon	1,076	213.5	20.4
Strongsville †	1,161	177.0	21.7
Warrensville Heights	1,482	242.0	13.5
Westlake Ex.	1,604	198.0	16.5
County Ave./Total	226,084	138.8	14.3

* Tuition pupils enrolled in other districts attributed to Beachwood and Bratenahl, actual figures 1956, METRO staff estimates for 1950. These were only districts without high schools in 1956, and thus had a high proportion of tuition pupils.

† School districts qualifying for additional aid under the Ohio Foundation Program in 1956-57, determined roughly by assessed valuation below $17,000 per pupil.

ASSESSED VALUATION			ASSESSED VALUATION PER ADM	
1956 (In Thousands of Dollars)	Ratio 1956/1950 (Per Cent)	Tangible Personal Prop. (Per Cent)	1956 (Dollars)	Ratio 1956/1950 (Per Cent)
30,769	219.6	1.7	13,099	111.2
90,169	334.9	37.5	23,055	212.8
127,860	500.4	42.5	32,962	341.0
40,892	217.4	38.0	24,783	126.5
2,737,100	153.9	29.4	23,249	129.9
214,928	146.7	2.9	17,845	113.2
107,525	148.7	11.9	19,850	134.1
232,687	192.2	37.2	22,329	123.4
38,161	212.0	3.3	16,163	131.0
56,050	208.7	10.8	12,929	113.7
159,833	138.0	10.1	21,596	121.2
62,556	231.9	16.9	12,890	111.3
28,593	308.3	4.8	13,050	161.0
196,216	279.4	15.6	14,623	82.9
57,881	209.3	8.2	21,925	134.3
171,091	160.9	3.1	26,041	108.1
91,362	222.3	4.1	13,791	104.3
20,614	308.9	1.7	27,485	74.1
5,359	135.2	1.3	29,939	96.7
27,406	261.7	4.6	14,462	125.3
13,030	184.7	14.7	10,849	109.6
106,563	163.2	61.2	140,399	111.2
19,549	274.5	13.4	25,095	141.7
42,849	242.3	4.6	14,345	107.8
17,358	257.7	3.0	12,624	146.9
13,496	235.6	4.6	8,809	126.1
38,779	249.2	12.6	26,131	140.4
6,585	316.4	2.0	18,814	112.1
20,885	319.7	12.2	19,410	149.7
14,583	263.1	8.4	12,561	148.7
25,953	269.7	10.3	17,512	111.7
28,507	297.5	4.1	17,772	150.3
4,845,189	171.5	24.4	21,430	124.2

per pupil relative to other districts in the metropolitan area. Three distinct groups of relatively poor districts appear: a) Some districts have been relatively poor and continue so, such as Chagrin Falls and Olmsted Falls, with valuations per pupil about half the County average. Several districts, such as Bay Village, Garfield Heights, Maple Heights, Mayfield, and South Euclid-Lyndhurst, with low valuations per pupil, had a growth in valuation per pupil between 1950 and 1956 which was below the county average, smaller than the increase in the price level, and less than the increase in valuation due to reappraisals. Without the 1952 and 1955 reappraisals of property, the per pupil valuation would have declined. In other words, the real value of taxable property supporting each pupil was less in 1956 than in 1950.

b) Several poorer districts, in which the trend of assessed valuation rising more rapidly than enrollments is favorable, are represented by North Olmsted, Strongsville, and Westlake.

c) Districts, formerly with average valuations which are becoming relatively poor in valuation per pupil as enrollments rise more rapidly than the tax base—Parma is the prime example. The Parma School District faces one of the most critical problems. It has the fastest rate of growth in the county, from under 4,000 pupils in 1950 to 13,418 in 1956 and an estimated 17,500 in September, 1958. Although total valuation in the school district has risen sharply, the enrollment has ballooned so rapidly that there has been an absolute decline in valuation per pupil. Parma has fallen from a school district with above average valuation per pupil in 1950 to substantially below average in 1956. Preliminary data for 1958 indicate that the tax capacity per pupil has deteriorated further to about $12,300 per pupil. With prices rising 27 per cent between 1950 and 1956, the assessed valuations per pupil overstate the local ability to bear the increased operating and capital costs of this school system with an exploding total enrollment. And the end is not in sight; the superintendent of the Parma schools forecasts a drastic further increase in enrollments to an estimated 30,000 pupils in 1965. This is clearly a case of a need for revenue rapidly outgrowing the local financial capacity.

Fortunately the State School Foundation program serves an equalization function by more generous support for the poorer school districts. The possibility of an intra-county equalization program is discussed below.[18]

Considering a jurisdiction's capacity to support *both* its municipal government and the overlying school district, the assessed valuation per capita and per pupil must be considered together. The level of the average valuations indicates whether a problem already exists. Generally low valuations for both municipal and school functions suggest real weakness in local revenue capacity. Of course, revenue capacity must be considered in relation to needs; with the same revenue capacity, needs may vary for a variety of factors, such as different rates of growth, valuable property which requires expensive police and fire protection, location on major traffic arteries which require policing and maintenance, and the level and stability of employment. The trend of per person or per pupil valuations along with the present level of average valuations in the jurisdiction suggests the likelihood of financial problems in the future.

A few political subdivisions, as shown in Table VI-9, are wealthy in terms of property tax assessments for both municipality and school district. Shaker Heights, of the cities, and Cuyahoga Heights and Hunting Valley, of the villages, exemplify this group.

Several areas are in relatively poor municipalities and school districts. Garfield Heights and Maple Heights of the cities and North Royalton and Olmsted Falls, of the villages, are presently in this class. The trend in Parma, the second largest city in the metropolitan area, is toward this group.

Numerous communities are relatively rich in valuation in their school district but poor in assessed value in the municipal boundaries, or vice versa. Berea, Brecksville, Brooklyn Heights, Gates Mills, and Woodmere are some of the communities with this schizophrenic financial position.

For future revenue capacity of the property tax, Parma, the largest suburban city, is approaching a serious situation rapidly; East Cleveland, Lakewood, and Lyndhurst are declining more slowly in financial capacity.

In summary, taxable capacity under the property tax is very

18. See below, pp. 360-1, and also *Public Education in Greater Cleveland,* ch. 3 (Cleveland Metropolitan Services Commission, 1959).

Table VI-9—Tax Rates, Cleveland Metropolitan Area, 1950, 1956, 1959; and Relative Property Tax Capacity, 1956**

GOVERNMENTAL UNIT	1949-50			1955-56			1958-59			Ratio of Municipal Per Capita Assessed Value to Mean Per Capita Countywide Assessed Value	Ratio of S.D. Assessed Value Per Pupil Countywide Assessed Value
	Municipal	School	Total*	Municipal	School	Total†	Municipal	School	Total*		
County Weighted Average (mills)	13.7	12.5	30.8	12.3	14.8	30.7	12.6	17.9	36.0	100.0%	100.0%
Cities											
Bay Village	8.8	22.3H	35.3H	11.5	21.9	37.0H	11.2	24.3	41.0	89.0	61.1
Bedford	10.3	15.6	30.6‡	9.4	16.5	29.5	8.8	21.9	36.2	91.2	107.6
Berea	13.1	16.3	33.6	12.8	16.6	33.0	11.8	22.3	39.6	71.7	153.8
Brooklyn	12.5	14.1	30.8	10.9	15.6	30.1	10.8	16.8	33.1L	151.2	115.6
Cleveland	17.5H	11.0L	23.7	15.6H	11.9L	31.1	16.4H	14.4L	36.3	96.7	108.5
Cleveland Heights	7.8	16.7	28.7	9.0	20.4	33.0	9.4	28.9H	43.8H	90.4	83.3
East Cleveland	7.9	15.7	27.8	7.3	16.3	27.2L	8.9	18.7	33.1L	78.2	92.6
Euclid	7.5	12.5	24.8†	8.3	20.2	31.6†	10.0	24.3	39.8	127.2	104.2
Fairview Park	12.5	14.6	31.3	11.7	18.3	33.6	9.4	20.0	34.9	101.3	75.4
Garfield Heights	9.7	17.0	30.9	7.0	20.5	31.1	8.8	24.6	38.9	61.6	60.5
Lakewood	10.5	17.3	32.0	10.9	16.7	31.6†	12.7	19.9	38.1	76.6	100.8
Lyndhurst	8.4	16.6	29.2	8.4	22.9	34.9	8.4	27.4	41.3	76.9	64.4
Maple Heights	10.3	15.0	29.5	10.1	23.2H	36.9	11.5	23.9	40.9	74.9	60.1
Mayfield Heights	10.2	15.0	29.4	7.5	19.8	30.9	9.5	24.6	39.6	78.9	66.9
North Olmsted	9.1	14.8	28.1	11.1	19.9	34.6	11.1	22.6	39.2	76.7	60.9
Parma	10.0	13.5	27.7	5.7L	19.2	28.5	7.4L	25.3	38.2	82.6	68.2
Rocky River	7.0L	16.5	27.7	10.2	20.5	34.3	12.4	22.0	39.9	108.2	102.3
Shaker Heights	9.3	14.2	27.7	8.0	20.2	31.8	8.3	25.6	39.4	139.1	121.5
South Euclid	10.2	16.6	31.0	9.2	22.9	35.7	10.1	27.4	43.0	84.6	64.4
University Heights	9.3	16.7	30.2	8.1	20.4	32.1	9.1	28.9H	43.5	103.7	83.3
Villages											
Beachwood	11.8	8.7	24.7	6.1	16.0	25.7	4.2	28.3	38.0	162.7	128.3
Bedford Heights §	...	...	...	4.0	16.5	24.1	7.2	21.9	34.6	135.5	107.6
Bentleyville	3.4	16.9	24.5	3.4	20.1	27.1	6.4	33.5H	45.4	105.8	50.6
Bratenahl	4.0	18.5	26.7	4.0	20.5	28.1	4.0	20.6	30.1	137.1	139.7
Brecksville	3.8	17.3	25.3	3.9	19.5	27.0	4.0	36.4	35.9	140.6	67.5
Broadview Heights	3.1	17.3	24.6	3.4	19.5	26.5	3.6	26.4	35.5	82.9	67.5/58.9
Brooklyn Heights	10.0	4.7L	18.9	10.1H	5.6L	19.3	11.7H	6.6L	23.8	99.0	655.1
Brook Park	5.7	16.3	26.2	5.2	16.6	25.4	7.3	22.3	35.1‡	959.8	153.8
Chagrin Falls	8.0	16.9	29.1	9.7	20.1	33.8†	9.8	33.5H	49.6‡H	99.6	50.6
Cuyahoga Heights	5.7	4.7L	14.6L	5.1	5.6L	14.3L	4.8	6.6L	16.9L	4,107.0	655.1
Gates Mills	10.7	15.0	29.9	7.7	19.8	31.1	9.4	24.6	39.5	223.2	66.9
Glenwillow	1.0L	21.5H	26.7	3.0	18.9	25.5	3.6	26.0	35.1	144.3	90.6
Highland Heights	2.8	15.0	22.0	3.4	19.8	26.8	4.2	24.6	34.3	86.7	66.9

Hunting Valley	4.6	14.6	24.0 ‡	5.3	17.7	26.6	5.3	23.0	33.8	367.2	121.9
Independence	4.4	13.3	21.9	7.3	15.9	26.8	3.9	17.6	27.0	112.5	117.1
Linndale	2.8	11.0	18.0	3.4	11.9	18.9	3.8	14.4	23.7	55.1	108.5
Mayfield	7.5	15.0	26.7	7.4	19.8	30.8	7.4	24.6	37.5	83.8	66.9
Middleburg Heights	12.7H	16.3	33.2H	6.2	16.6	26.4	6.0	22.3	33.8	119.6	153.8
Moreland Hills	7.4	16.9	28.5	6.8	20.1	30.5	6.5	33.5H	45.5	132.5	50.6/121.0
Newburgh Heights	4.9	11.0	20.1	4.9	11.9	20.4	4.8	14.4	24.7	81.1	108.5
North Randall	2.0	14.6	20.9 ‡	1.3	26.7H	31.7 ‡	1.2L	29.9	36.8 ‡	643.7	81.7
North Royalton	3.6	16.4	24.2	4.9	24.0	32.5	5.0	25.1	35.6	85.5	58.9
Oakwood §	...	...	...	2.8	16.5	22.9	3.8	21.9	31.2	42.7	107.6
Olmsted Falls	9.0	17.9	31.1	7.0	22.4	33.0	7.2	28.6	41.3	82.1	41.1
Orange	3.2	14.6	22.0	3.5	17.7	24.8	3.7	23.0	32.2	102.5	121.9
Parkview	3.9	14.6	22.7	5.8	18.3	27.7	5.8	20.0	31.3	82.1	75.4
Parma Heights	9.4	13.5	27.1	8.5	19.2	31.3	8.5	25.3	39.3	77.9	68.2
Pepper Pike	9.6	14.6	28.4	4.7	17.7	26.0	4.5	23.0	33.0	219.2	121.9
Richmond Heights	2.8	15.0	22.0	6.0	20.3	29.9	4.2	22.7	32.4	78.0	87.8
Seven Hills	3.3	13.5	21.0	6.3	19.2	29.1	6.1	25.3	36.9	92.3	68.2
Solon	7.2	21.5H	32.9	4.0	18.9	26.5	4.4	26.0	35.9	128.0	90.6
Strongsville	7.9	15.8	27.9	6.8	20.0	30.4	6.8	26.0	38.3	89.0	58.6
Valley View	5.8	4.7L	14.7	5.9	5.6L	15.1	6.4	6.6L	18.5	107.3	655.1
Walton Hills §	...	...	...	1.2L	16.5	21.3	2.0	21.9	29.4	845.0	107.6
Warrensville Heights	8.6	14.6	27.5 ‡	6.1	26.7H	36.5H ‡	6.2	29.9	41.8 ‡	81.6	81.7
Westlake	2.7	14.7	21.6	6.2	20.9	30.7	9.5	22.8	37.8	95.8	82.9
West View	3.8	17.9	25.9	4.0	22.4	30.0	4.0	28.6	38.1	79.4	41.1
Woodmere	5.2	14.6	24.0	4.8	17.7	26.1	5.3	23.0	33.8	70.1	121.9
(Bedford) (Twp.) §	(2.0)	(15.6)	(21.8)								
Townships											
Chagrin Falls	...	16.9	21.1	0.4	20.1	24.1	0.4	33.5	39.4	170.4	50.6
Olmsted	2.8	17.9	24.9	3.2	22.4	29.2	3.4	28.6	37.5	54.2	41.1
Riveredge	5.4	16.3	25.9	...	16.6	20.2	4.4	22.3	32.2	20.5	153.8
Warrensville	0.1	14.6	18.9	0.1	26.7	30.4	0.1	29.9	35.5	20.3	81.7

* All totals include following levies in addition to municipal and school rates:

	County	State
1949-50	5.0 mills	0.5 mills
1955-56	3.4 mills	0.2 mills
1949-50	4.2 mills	None

† Euclid total includes fraction of a mill for Euclid Library District in 1950 and 1956 and Lakewood total for Lakewood Library in 1956.
‡ Municipal rate includes small amounts, never in excess of 0.6 mill for overlying township.
§ Bedford Township was replaced in 1951 by villages of Bedford Heights, Oakwood, and Walton Hills. Bedford (City) had also been part of the Township.
** Ratio of relative property tax capacity calculated for each municipality as to its assessed valuation per capita to county average and for each school district as assessed valuation per pupil to county average.
Note: School district figure is for school district which covers all or major part of municipality. Two municipalities are split about in half in different school districts. For Broadview Heights, figure for Brecksville School District is given first, then for North Royalton, S. D. For Moreland Hills, Chagrin Falls figure is first, followed by Moreland Hills.
H—High for the year
L—Low for the year

unevenly distributed among the political jurisdictions which compose the entire Cleveland community. With the property tax the backbone of the local revenue system, this raises several crucial questions:

1) Should steps be taken to equalize taxable capacity within the metropolitan area? If so, how? By a metropolitan area tax, shared perhaps on a per pupil or per capita basis? By the development of new revenue sources?

2) Or do the people want consciously to let some municipalities and school districts make great local efforts to provide minimum levels of services—for health, streets, education, sanitation and other functions of area-wide concern—while other jurisdictions—perhaps where factories or higher-income groups are concentrated—provide above-average service with little taxing effort?

Recommendations bearing on these problems are included in Chapters VIII and IX. Various possible revenue sources are described and evaluated in the latter part of this chapter.

Tax Effort

Tax effort must be considered with tax capacity to analyze the revenue potential and the revenue produced by each taxing jurisdiction and by the metropolitan area as a unit.

Tax effort is an important factor to be considered in deciding whether a local jurisdiction (or area) merits additional help from the state government or metropolitan area. Formulas for the distribution of intergovernmental aids often require a substantial local effort to qualify for federal and state grants. The extension of additional powers to use additional revenue sources or to adopt higher rates usually requires a showing that available sources are being heavily utilized.

In a metropolitan area, changes in government organization, shifting of responsibilities, or redistribution of financial resources are not intended to assist communities which are making a below-average effort. One important justification for such changes would be to assist those jurisdictions which are unable, despite an average or above-average tax effort, to support local government services of a scope and quality which are acceptable to the metropolitan area.

The level of tex effort in a community or area is partially a reflection of the variety and quality of local government services. Comparison of the tax effort between different communities tends to reveal wide diversities between the communities and the services performed. Generally, the wider differences in tax effort occur between the higher-rate urban and the lower-rate rural communities. As the rural areas become urbanized, the development of new housing subdivisions and shopping areas calls forth additional government services. Typically, the needs for revenue grow more rapidly than the tax base and the tax rates rise relatively faster than in the entire area. As the new urban areas are developed, their tax rates tend to increase and cluster around the metropolitan area average. As the entire area is urbanized, the tax efforts are more uniform.

For the Cleveland area, the tax rates of both cities and villages increased and became more uniform between 1940 and 1959. Table VI-10 shows the increase in the average property tax rates, and the cluster around the average is evidenced by the declining coefficients of dispersion.

Table VI-10—Property Tax Rates in Cleveland Metropolitan Area, Level and Dispersion, 1940, 1950, 1956, 1959

CITIES

Tax Collection Year	Arithmetic Mean * (Mills)	Standard Deviation (Mills)	Coefficient of Variation (Per Cent)
1940	21.5	2.3	10.7
1950	26.6	2.6	9.7
1956	32.5	1.9	5.8
1959	39.1	2.2	5.6

VILLAGES

1940	17.6	4.6	25.9
1950	21.3	4.6	21.5
1956	26.9	3.6	13.2
1959	33.9	4.7	14.0

* Means computed with equal weight for each jurisdiction, without weighting for amount of revenue collected. Figures given are total rates for county, municipal, school, and state purposes combined.

Note: The classification of cities and villages for all the years is based on the municipal status in 1956.

The tax effort varies widely between jurisdictions and changes in level and by purpose over time. The best single way to weigh the property tax effort is to relate tax rate to tax capacity. With the school districts distinct from municipal government, relative tax capacity for 1956 and tax rates by the purpose are shown in Table VI-9.

The narrower range of tax rates indicates less diversity between communities in Cuyahoga County now than in 1940. When the municipal and school tax rates are analyzed separately, the school rates have been more uniform in each year than the municipal tax rates.

The more uniform effort throughout the metropolitan area is evidenced by the change in the relative ranking of the City of Cleveland. In 1940, the total tax rate paid by taxpayers in Cleveland was highest in the county. By 1950, four jurisdictions had gone ahead of Cleveland and, in 1959, Cleveland's combined tax rate ranked thirty-second from the top of the fifty-eight municipalities in the county.

The change in the relative size of the tax rates of the county, municipalities, and school districts has been sharp. The school districts show a steady growth in their average tax rates from 1940 to 1959, both absolutely (from 10.9 mills, in 1940, to 17.9 mills, in 1959) and relative to the County and municipalities. This reflects the rising school expenditures, the lack of alternative local revenue sources to the property tax, and the public support for school levies.

The central city dominates the weighted average tax rate, as it collects more than half the total revenues in the county. Because the tax base has been growing more rapidly outside the central city and the suburbs have been raising their tax rates faster than Cleveland, the share of the central city for municipal and school purposes combined has declined from about 70 per cent of the county property tax revenue in 1940, to just over 50 per cent, in 1956.

The property tax rate for municipal government in the City of Cleveland has been the highest municipal rate in the county in every year right up to the present. The school rate in the central city, however, has been among the lowest in the area, with only the industrial enclave of Cuyahoga Heights being lower in recent years.

A quantitative measure of over-all local effort is probably impossible. Such a measure ideally would vary directly with the level of local tax rates and the utilization of available local revenue sources. The ideal measure would take into account the taxable capacity of a jurisdiction, on the ground that an identical tax rate in both a rich community and a poor one would represent a greater effort and a greater sacrifice in the poorer taxing district.

The Cleveland area on the whole would be rated as making an average effort among comparable metropolitan areas. The local effort has concentrated on the property tax; an above-average effort has been made with this tax. Relatively little effort, however, has been made with other taxes due in part to local choice. Tax rates in Cuyahoga County are distinctly higher than in the adjacent counties, although Akron, the largest nearby city, has a tax rate about equal to Cleveland's.

Tax effort seems to follow a neighborhood pattern. The suburbs to the east and southeast of the central city have generally had the highest service levels in the metropolitan area, especially for schools. These jurisdictions are characterized generally as high-income residential communities with average or above-average efforts on the property tax. Shaker Heights, with high property valuations per capita and an above-average effort, seems to set the goal which neighboring jurisdictions aim to match. See Map VI-2.

The main point of interest in the detail of the revenues for each municipality and each school district (shown in Tables VI-11 and 12) is the variety of emphasis in different jurisdictions.[19] Cities with hospitals, such as Lakewood, show large collections from fees and charges. A few municipalities rely heavily on traffic fines; Bratenahl is the best example.

For school districts, the effect of equalization in the State Aid program is shown. The district with the lowest assessed valuation per pupil, Olmsted Falls, received almost 30 per cent of its revenue from the State while the richest district received only about 6 per cent in State Aid.

---

19. These tables are also revealing if interpreted on a per capita (per pupil) revenues by source, as shown in detail in *A Fiscal Profile*.

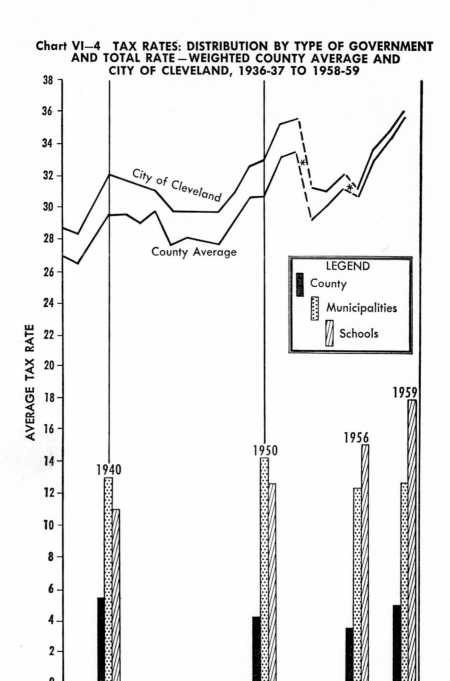

Chart VI–4 TAX RATES: DISTRIBUTION BY TYPE OF GOVERNMENT
AND TOTAL RATE—WEIGHTED COUNTY AVERAGE AND
CITY OF CLEVELAND, 1936-37 TO 1958-59

LEGEND
County
Municipalities
Schools

City of Cleveland

County Average

Year of Collection

AVERAGE TAX RATE

* Reassessments effective with 1953 and 1956 collections which
require automatic revision of voted tax rates above ten mills.

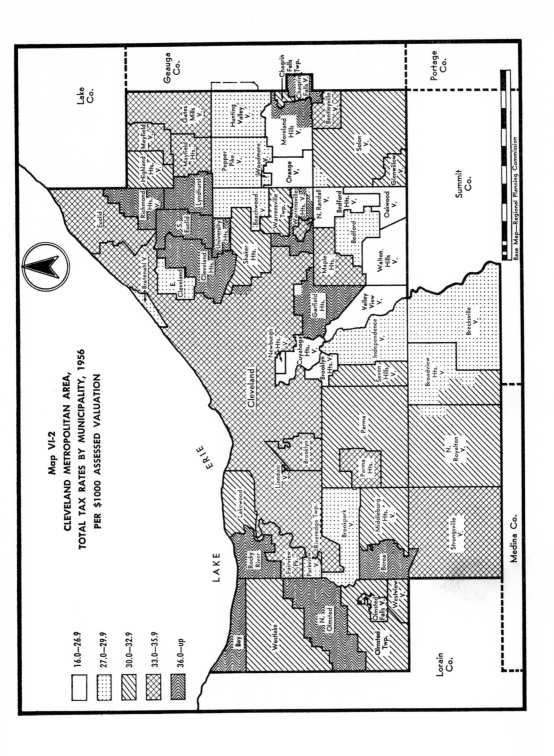

Map VI-2
CLEVELAND METROPOLITAN AREA,
TOTAL TAX RATES BY MUNICIPALITY, 1956
PER $1000 ASSESSED VALUATION

16.0—26.9
27.0—29.9
30.0—32.9
33.0—35.9
36.0—up

Table VI-11—County and Municipal Revenues, Cleveland Metropolitan Area–1956 (In Thousands of Dollars)

| Governmental Unit | Locally Collected Revenue | | | | | | | | | State Aid | | | Federal Aid | Total Revenues (Local & Intergovernmental) | Public Service Enterprises | Total Revenues Excluding P.S.E. |
| | LOCAL TAXES | | | | LOCAL NON-TAX SOURCES | | | | TOTAL | Local Govt. Fund | Other State Aid | Total | | | | |
	General Property	Intangible Property	Licenses & Other Taxes	Total	Fees and Misc. Charges	Special Assessment	Interest	Other Local Sources								
Cuyahoga County	14,778.2	0.0	320.7	15,098.9	3,120.5	383.1	700.0	2,189.4	21,491.9	3,421.8	14,016.3	17,438.1	3,147.2	42,077.2	0.0	42,077.2
Cleve. Metro. Park	972.5			972.5	61.4			117.7	4,152.0	45.6		45.6		1,197.2		1,197.2
	15,750.7			16,071.4	3,181.9			2,307.1	22,643.9	3,467.4		17,483.7		43,274.4		43,274.4
Cities																
Bay Village	323.9	4.2	26.0	354.1	35.8	89.5	14.6	12.8	506.8	33.7	56.2	89.9	0.0	596.7	0.0	596.7
Bedford	383.8	1.8	20.8	406.4	477.6	29.2	1.6	27.0	942.0	32.5	105.7	138.2	0.0	1,219.2	139.0	1,080.2
Berea	334.6	2.3	35.8	372.7	128.1	122.0	21.4	39.9	684.1	50.3	89.8	140.1	0.0	964.4	140.2	824.2
Brooklyn	374.5	0.4	32.0	406.9	.2	40.8	3.6	21.9	473.4	34.6	39.8	74.4	0.0	547.8	0.0	547.8
Cleveland	41,562.6	276.9	1,664.3	43,503.8	10,822.6	1,115.3	2,396.6	1,746.2	59,584.5	5,797.1	6,812.8	12,609.9	1,764.2	123,591.0	49,632.4	73,968.6
Cleveland Heights	1,564.6	117.9	376.3	2,058.8	372.2	217.1	21.3	65.7	2,735.1	276.5	321.5	598.0	0.0	3,924.3	591.2	3,333.1
East Cleveland	658.1	14.4	54.1	726.6	143.1	0.0	45.2	221.3	1,136.2	248.2	201.9	450.1	0.0	1,836.3	250.0	1,586.3
Euclid	1,667.2	10.6	100.2	1,778.0	27.0	852.5	15.2	92.4	2,765.1	184.3	311.5	495.8	0.0	3,669.8	408.9	3,260.9
Fairview Park	448.8	25.0	15.8	489.6	18.5	163.5	4.6	21.6	697.8	49.7	98.5	148.2	0.0	846.0	0.0	846.0
Garfield Heights	406.8	1.6	48.2	456.6	4.7	196.9	2.6	62.0	722.8	163.4	152.5	315.9	0.0	1,038.7	0.0	1,038.7
Lakewood	1,739.2	54.9	191.3	1,985.4	2,386.0	1.4	18.8	134.0	4,525.6	334.1	417.5	751.6	0.0	5,662.2	385.0	5,277.2
Lyndhurst	246.3	12.4	38.6	297.3	41.8	171.3	14.5	38.3	563.2	44.8	59.2	104.0	0.0	667.2	0.0	667.2
Maple Heights	525.1	46.2	28.2	599.5	53.2	50.7	4.2	23.1	730.7	214.8	132.1	346.9	0.0	1,353.9	276.3	1,077.6
Mayfield Heights	184.7	0.6	17.8	203.1	1.8	150.8	3.0	16.3	375.0	38.2	57.4	95.6	0.0	470.6	0.0	470.6
North Olmsted	283.3	1.6	16.6	301.5	6.2	74.9	2.4	31.3	416.3	45.2	72.0	117.2	0.0	880.5	347.0	533.5
Parma	1,133.2	8.2	163.5	1,304.9	6.0	495.1	60.2	103.1	1,969.3	167.6	323.3	490.9	0.0	2,460.2	0.0	2,460.2
Rocky River	468.3	22.2	72.4	562.9	7.9	199.5	8.4	20.4	799.1	58.0	92.1	150.1	0.0	951.2	2.0	949.2
Shaker Heights	1,314.9	199.1	273.3	1,787.3	31.9	288.8	34.7	59.3	2,202.0	183.3	192.4	375.7	0.0	4,119.8	1,542.1	2,577.7
South Euclid	607.7	8.0	21.7	637.4	48.3	315.1	14.6	19.8	1,035.2	63.4	132.0	195.4	0.0	1,230.6	0.0	1,230.6
University Heights	378.9	13.0	28.1	420.0	10.4	135.8	9.6	15.2	591.0	28.2	91.5	119.7	0.0	710.7	0.0	710.7
CITY TOTAL	54,606.5	823.1	3,225.0	58,652.8	14,623.3	4,710.2	2,697.1	2,771.6	83,455.2	8,047.9	9,759.7	17,807.6	1,764.2	156,602.1	53,715.0	103,037.0
Villages																
Beachwood	147.8	4.4	20.4	172.6	29.3	175.0	0.0	30.9	407.8	5.2	18.9	24.1	0.0	431.9	0.0	431.9
Bedford Heights	70.6	0.0 *	5.6	76.2	3.3	0.0	.1	17.9	97.5	3.7	23.3	27.0	0.0	124.5	0.0	124.5
Bentleyville	2.7	0.9	0.3	3.9	0.0*	0.0	0.0	9.5	13.4	1.0	1.1	2.1	0.0	15.5	0.0	15.5
Bratenahl	21.0	18.0	113.9	152.9	.2	0.0	2.1	38.8	194.0	2.1	6.0	8.1	0.0	202.1	0.0	202.1
Brecksville	73.1	4.2	18.7	96.1	9.3	23.3	.9	49.7	179.2	10.1	25.1	35.2	0.0	214.4	0.0	214.4
Broadview Heights	40.4	0.1	11.9	52.4	4.9	88.5	0.0	26.0	171.8	2.7	18.0	20.7	0.0	192.5	0.0	192.5
Brooklyn Heights	37.2	0.8	1.8	39.8	1.1	1.4	.1	7.6	50.0	6.8	7.3	14.1	0.0	64.1	0.0	64.1
Brook Park	331.3	0.1	77.9	409.3	23.9	293.9	15.0	19.4	761.5	10.5	17.4	27.9	4.8	794.2	0.0	794.2

	1	2	3	4	5	6	7	8	9	10	11	12	13	14	15	16
Chagrin Falls	105.3	10.0	2.4	117.7	43.4	2.1	.4	6.4	170.0	13.6	30.5	44.1	0.0	270.9	56.8	214.1
Cuyahoga Heights	489.5	0.8	6.8	497.7	7.3	0.0	.4	5.1	509.9	0.0	33.5	33.5	0.0	543.4	0.0	543.4
Gates Mills	71.2	22.8	7.4	101.4	6.8	0.0	0.0	11.0	119.2	5.8	12.2	18.0	0.0	148.5	11.3	137.2
Glenwillow	4.5	0.0	0.3	4.8	0.0	0.0	0.0	.1	4.9	2.2	.5	2.7	0.0	7.6	0.0	7.6
Highland Heights	13.7	0.1	4.5	18.3	.2	29.1	2.7	7.1	57.4	3.7	10.6	14.3	0.0	72.2	.5	71.7
Hunting Valley	28.0	57.9	27.3	113.2	5.0	1.8	9.7	10.6	140.3	2.2	3.6	5.8	0.0	146.1	0.0	146.1
Independence	69.3	2.0	16.5	87.8	136.8	76.5	.2	37.7	339.0	7.9	34.5	42.4	0.0	381.4	0.0	381.4
Linndale	1.2	0.0	0.1	1.3	0.0	0.0	0.0	3.3	4.6	2.5	2.3	4.8	0.0	9.4	0.0	9.4
Mayfield	27.0	0.2	3.9	31.1	.6	37.3	0.0	23.0	92.0	4.2	8.5	12.7	0.0	104.7	0.0	104.7
Middleburg Heights	90.4	0.6	23.1	114.1	15.6	35.5	1.8	16.6	183.6	22.5	25.0	47.5	0.0	231.1	0.0	231.1
Moreland Hills	46.6	0.9	10.3	57.8	.1	0.0	0.0	7.9	65.9	10.5	9.8	20.3	0.0	86.2	0.0	86.2
Newburgh Heights	50.8	0.1	1.5	52.4	2.9	0.0	0.0*	33.3	88.6	16.8	21.5	38.3	0.0	126.9	0.0	126.9
North Randall	5.7	0.0	44.3	50.0	4.4	0.0	0.0	20.1	74.5	.3	10.4	10.7	0.0	85.2	0.0	85.2
North Royalton	69.4	0.0	12.1	81.5	7.7	31.8	0.0	9.3	130.3	15.7	39.3	55.0	0.0	185.3	0.0	185.3
Oakwood	13.9	0.0*	2.4	16.3	.2	0.0	0.0	8.8	25.3	5.6	16.1	21.7	0.0	47.0	0.0	47.0
Olmsted Falls	29.2	0.4	5.9	35.5	2.4	11.7	0.0	7.2	56.8	4.2	19.3	23.5	0.0	81.1	.8	80.3
Orange	19.1	0.1	9.9	29.1	1.7	0.0	0.0*	8.5	39.3	1.6	8.7	10.3	0.0	49.6	0.0	49.6
Parkview	22.5	0.1	4.3	26.9	.4	3.6	0.0*	7.7	38.6	7.3	6.2	13.5	0.0	52.1	0.0	52.1
Parma Heights	198.6	1.4	44.7	244.7	3.9	224.6	2.3	71.1	546.6	27.8	47.6	75.4	0.0	622.0	0.0	622.0
Pepper Pike	98.1	5.1	19.5	122.7	1.4	63.9	.4	11.5	199.9	11.9	9.7	21.6	0.0	222.1	.6	221.5
Richmond Heights	35.6	0.4	11.4	47.4	.1	29.9	.9	33.2	111.5	6.3	13.7	20.0	0.0	131.5	0.0	131.5
Seven Hills	56.2	0.3	13.7	70.2	.2	31.8	0.0	24.5	126.7	4.2	19.1	23.3	0.0	150.0	0.0	150.0
Solon	75.6	0.7	24.7	101.0	5.3	49.9	1.1	14.1	171.4	18.7	35.2	53.9	0.0	225.3	0.0	225.3
Strongsville	105.2	0.6	12.0	117.8	16.3	1.5	.4	59.5	195.8	8.4	42.8	51.2	0.0	247.0	0.0	247.0
Valley View	19.8	0.1	3.4	23.3	.6	0.0	0.0*	19.3	43.2	4.0	8.3	12.3	0.0	55.5	0.0	55.5
Walton Hills	41.9	0.1	2.4	44.4	.9	35.7	0.0*	38.9	119.9	5.2	9.2	14.4	1.9	136.2	1.9	134.3
Warrensville Heights	89.4	1.4	39.4	130.2	10.4	21.1	.7	18.2	180.6	18.9	78.0	96.9	.7	278.2	.7	277.5
Westlake	141.9	2.1	24.8	168.8	4.8	82.0	1.4	20.3	277.3	20.9	56.7	77.6	0.0	354.9	0.0	354.9
West View	7.0	0.0	0.8	7.8	3.2	1.3	0.0	6.6	18.9	2.3	4.9	7.2	0.0	26.1	0.0	26.1
Woodmere	4.6	0.0	1.1	5.7	0.0	0.0*	0.0	11.3	17.0	3.7	1.5	5.2	0.0	22.2	0.0	22.2
VILLAGE TOTAL	2,755.3	136.7	631.4	3,524.1	354.6	1,353.5	40.6	752.6	6,024.2	301.0	736.3	1,037.3	4.8	7,138.9	72.6	7,066.3
Townships																
Chagrin Falls	3.6	0.0	.2	3.8	4.3	0.0	0.0	.2	8.3	.3	8.4	8.7	0.0	17.0	0.0	17.0
Olmsted	11.7	0.0	2.7	14.4	5.9	4.1	.3	.1	24.8	3.7	8.9	12.6	0.0	37.4	0.0	37.4
Riveredge	0.0	0.0	0.0	0.0	0.0	0.0	0.0	0.0	0.0	0.0	10.9	10.9	0.0	10.9	0.0	10.9
Warrensville	2.3	0.0	.4	2.7	1.4	0.0	0.0	0.0	4.1	2.3	8.3	10.6	0.0	14.7	0.0	14.7
TOWNSHIP TOTAL	17.6	0.0	3.3	20.9	11.6	4.1	.3	.3	37.2	6.3	36.5	42.8	0.0	80.0	0.0	80.0
GRAND TOTAL	73,130.1	958.0	4,180.4	78,269.2	18,171.4	6,450.9	3,438.0	5,831.6	112,160.3	11,822.6	24,548.8	36,376.2	4,916.2	207,095.4	53,787.6	153,457.7

* Less than $100.00

Analysis of Alternative Revenue Sources

This chapter now turns to an analysis of the strengths and weaknesses of the property tax and other taxes which could provide large revenues for local governments in the metropolitan area. The emphasis is on major taxes which the local governments might utilize, not on aid from the State and federal governments. Local governments in Cuyahoga County now raise more than $200 million from local sources—taxes, charges, interest, etc. By 1965, additional revenues estimated at $200 million a year above the 1956 level from all sources [20] will be needed. How is it possible to raise these moneys? What are the advantages and disadvantages of different taxes and service charges? How does the problem vary if the objective is to insure that existing local governments have adequate financial resources, compared with financing a metropolitan area government to perform certain functions? The following discussion attempts to analyze and evaluate possible major local taxes on property, income, sales, value-added, motor vehicles, and others.

THE GENERAL PROPERTY TAX

The general property tax continues to be the mainstay of local revenue systems for local governments in Ohio and throughout the country, producing 14.8 billion in the United States in 1959, about half of all local government revenue and 88 per cent of all local tax revenue.[21] This tax has been declining in importance in the total revenue system due to expansion of federal and state budgets financed from other taxes. Local governments also are making increasing use of other revenue sources.

In view of the criticism of the property tax and the heavy dependence on this tax by local governments in the Cleveland area, this section will summarize the property tax as used in Ohio and analyze its advantages and disadvantages.

---

20. See Chapter VIII, pp. 310-319.
21. U. S. Bureau of the Census, *Summary of Governmental Finances in 1959*, p. 14 (Washington, 1960).

The crucial question is whether the property tax should be *the major* source for large *additional* revenues needed to support local governments during the 1960's. How do the advantages and disadvantages of the property tax compare with those of the income, sales, and value-added taxes? If, under present assessments, property tax rates averaging 36 mills per dollars are preferable to other taxes, would this still be true if the average rate were 50 mills? 60 mills?

Historical

The general property tax has been the bulwark of local government revenue in the Cleveland area since the Ohio General Assembly passed legislation incorporating the Village of Cleveland on December 23, 1814. The incorporating act authorized the trustees "to levy an annual tax on all lots and other property."

At the first valuation of taxable property in Cuyahoga County made in 1825, total assessed valuation was $876,782. Land accounted for most of the taxable property being valued at an average of $3.33 per acre. By 1956 taxable value had grown to $4,845.6 million, with only about one-seventh in land, although the average assessed value of land was now about $2,300 per acre. Table VI-4 presents growth since 1910.

Property Tax Base, by Type of Property

The total general property tax duplicate for 1956-57 was $4,845.9 million, as shown in Table VI-19. Real estate accounted for 68 per cent of the total duplicate, with a valuation of $3,295.4 million. Real estate is assessed at about 40 per cent of market value, but with substantial variations between classes of real property. The almost 400,000 parcels of land accounted for about a fifth of this value. At the time of the 1955 reappraisal, there were 314,302 major building structures, of which 289,631 were residences with an average assessment of about $6,400 and 24,671 were commercial buildings and industrial plants. In terms of use, residential property accounted for 58 per cent of the value of real estate in the county, commercial

Table VI-12—School District Revenues, Cleveland Metropolitan Area, 1956 (Thousands of Dollars)

SCHOOL DISTRICTS	LOCAL					STATE AID		FEDERAL AID	TOTAL ALL SOURCES
	General Property	Fees & Charges	Interest	Other Local Sources	Total	School Found. Program	Other State Grants		
Cities									
Bay Village	617.2	6.3	2.5	38.4	644.4	162.9	0.0	0.0	827.3
Bedford	1,442.0	8.7	0.2	80.5	1,531.4	289.2	25.6	0.0	1,846.2
Berea	1,617.9	20.5	17.8	452.6	2,108.8	217.1	0.1	60.4	2,386.4
Brooklyn	678.7	0.5	0.4	52.7	732.3	100.9	55.3	0.0	888.5
Cleveland	31,624.9	451.7	73.2	1,358.7	33,508.5	6,995.0	507.9	0.0	41,011.4
Cleveland Heights	4,330.0	236.1	25.0	135.9	4,727.0	711.9	23.7	0.0	5,462.6
East Cleveland	1,667.6	45.8	3.4	100.9	1,817.7	349.9	19.3	0.0	2,186.9
Euclid	4,143.6	154.4	3.6	222.0	4,523.6	595.5	18.4	12.3	5,149.8
Fairview Park	645.4	8.1	0.0	38.2	691.7	130.4	1.5	0.0	823.6
Garfield Heights	1,069.9	11.1	33.9	27.8	1,142.7	289.1	10.3	8.0	1,450.1
Lakewood	2,737.0	94.6	4.8	169.1	3,005.5	439.5	0.3	0.0	3,445.3
Maple Heights	1,245.5	15.2	2.5	165.2	1,428.4	329.8	1.9	18.4	1,778.5
North Olmsted	493.1	1.4	6.2	53.0	553.7	166.6	0.2	7.8	728.3
Parma	3,425.4	20.3	3.5	343.8	3,793.0	863.6	9.6	11.2	4,677.4
Rocky River	1,108.3	5.1	2.4	123.6	1,239.4	143.6	1.3	0.0	1,384.3
Shaker Heights	3,610.7	263.4	18.9	137.5	4,030.5	369.6	10.3	0.0	4,410.4
So. Euclid-Lyndhurst	1,988.9	50.6	2.1	105.8	2,147.4	391.7	0.2	0.0	2,539.3
City Total	62,446.6	1,393.8	200.4	3,605.7	67,646.0	12,546.3	685.9	118.1	80,966.3

Local & Exempted

Beachwood	347.1	1.2	1.0	13.3	362.6	39.7	0.0 *	0.0	402.3
Bratenahl	107.0	0.0	0.0	0.0	107.0	0.1	0.0	0.0	107.1
Brecksville	478.9	6.1	0.4	72.5	557.9	129.8	5.8	0.0	693.5
Chagrin Falls Ex.	344.1	10.7	0.0	31.3	386.1	103.1	0.0	0.9	490.1
Cuyahoga Heights	511.1	1.2	0.5	27.8	540.6	33.5	0.0 *	0.0	574.1
Independence	270.0	3.3	0.0	15.5	288.8	38.3	2.9	0.0	330.0
Mayfield (City)	841.2	5.5	8.9	82.7	938.3	206.7	0.1	13.6	1,158.7
North Royalton	321.8	1.6	9.1	81.5	414.0	128.4	0.3	8.2	550.9
Olmsted Falls	311.7	8.1	1.3	33.9	355.0	153.3	0.4	17.5	526.2
Orange	687.3	38.3	0.5	59.3	785.4	82.8	0.3	0.0	868.5
Richmond Heights	100.3	0.5	0.0	10.4	111.2	65.5	0.0 *	0.0	176.7
Solon	371.2	4.5	0.3	32.1	408.1	54.6	1.5	0.4	464.6
Strongsville	270.7	3.0	7.5	36.3	317.5	101.6	10.9	17.6	447.6
Warrensville Heights	623.5	16.1	0.5	30.5	670.6	78.9	0.3	0.0	749.8
Westlake Ex.	521.3	4.3	5.4	48.7	579.7	87.4	2.9	0.0	670.0
Local Total	6,107.2	104.4	35.4	575.8	6,822.8	1,303.7	25.4	58.2	8,210.1
TOTAL	68,553.8	1,498.2	235.8	4,181.5	74,468.8	13,850.0	711.3	176.3	89,206.4

* Less than $10

for 29 per cent, and industrial for 12 per cent. Commercial
property, unfortunately for purposes of analysis, includes large
apartments as well as retail, wholesale, and service establishments.
More than 10 per cent of the families in East Cleveland, Shaker
Heights, Lakewood, Cleveland Heights, Cleveland and Euclid live
in large apartments, so that the "residential" classification under-
states substantially the total assessed value of residential properties
in these jurisdictions.

Public utility property accounts for 7.6 per cent of the assessed
valuation in the County. This public utility valuation of $369 million
includes both real estate and tangible personal property, divided
about 30 per cent real estate and 70 per cent tangible personal
property.

Tangible personal property amounted to $1,181 million, almost
one-fourth of the tax duplicate. This taxable value is the statutory
percentage of the book value of the equipment and inventories of
firms in commerce, industry, agriculture, and other businesses
during 1956.

Cuyahoga County has over one-fifth of the total valuation in
Ohio, as shown in Table VI-13.

The Cleveland area is above the state average in assessed valuation per capita and real estate per capita, and tangible personal
property per capita, and in proportion of commercial and industrial
property. The County reflects the state proportions on residential
property and tangible personal property. The Cleveland area is
below the Ohio average on public utility and agricultural property,
both in proportion and in dollars per capita.[22] Cuyahoga County has
the highest percentage of commercial property and the lowest of
agricultural property of any county in Ohio. The national figures
are added for interest, but due to varying bases for taxation and
varying assessment ratios, comparison would have very limited
validity.

The tax base for the 1956-57 tax year consisted of the real estate

---

22. The proportion of public utility to total valuation is low because two large
generating plants serving the Cleveland area are located across the Cuyahoga
boundary in Lake and Lorain Counties, suggesting that the metropolitan tax base has
already spread beyond the major County. Also Cleveland operates a municipal electric plant which is not included on the tax duplicate.

Table VI-13—Assessed Value Subject to Property Tax,
Total and by Type of Property, Cuyahoga
County, State of Ohio, and United States, 1956

Assessed Value	Cuyahoga County	State of Ohio	United States
Aggregate (Billions of Dollars)	4.8	23.7	272.4
Per Capita (Dollars)	3,066	2,601	1,620
Distribution by Type of Property (Per Cent)			
Real Estate			
Residential	39.7	36.4	40.3
Commercial	19.7	12.4	12.3
Industrial	8.4	6.6	8.1
Agricultural	0.2	7.4	10.3
Subtotal	68.0	62.8	74.4
Public Utility	7.6	12.6	7.3
Tangible Personal	24.4	24.5	17.4
TOTAL	100.0	100.0	100.0*

* About 4.3% not shown separately applicable to vacant lots or not allocable between classifications.

Note: Assessment ratios differ between classes of property and between different assessing jurisdictions. The County and Ohio data are reasonably comparable. No claim is made for comparability between the Ohio and national data and any national per capita figure would be misleading.

with a tax lien date of January 1, 1956, tangible personal property, except inventories of merchants and manufacturers, listed as of December 31, 1956, and the inventories of merchants and manufacturers at their monthly average during 1956. The taxes are due in two installments during 1957. The tax duplicate, tax rates, and tax per capita in the ninety-four municipalities, townships, and school districts in Cuyahoga County were presented in preceding sections of this chapter.

The State prescribes the tax base for the property tax. Until 1931, the Ohio Constitution provided that all property be taxed at a uniform rate, except exempt property and personal property not exceeding $100 in value for each individual. Under constitutional amendments effective in 1931, authority was granted the Ohio legislature "to determine the subjects and methods of taxation or exemptions therefrom" subject to the restriction that "land and improvements thereon shall be taxed by uniform rule according to value." Legislation adopted under these amendments classified personal property separately from real property. Intangible personal property—mostly stocks, bonds, mortgages, and bank deposits— is taxed at rates set by state law, with the distribution discussed later. Tangible personal property is defined to exclude from tax personal effects, household goods, and autos for non-business use.

The base for the local general property tax consists now of land and improvements and tangible personal property. The locally determined tax rates apply to all property subject to the general property tax in a local jurisdiction.

Tangible Personal Property

Tangible personal property consists of inventories, equipment, and machinery used in business or agriculture. Its taxable value is generally 70 per cent of book value, less depreciation if applicable. However, only 50 per cent of book value is taxable for agricultural products on farms; manufacturing inventories; machinery and equipment used in manufacturing, mining, quarrying, agriculture, laundries and dry cleaning establishments, towel and linen supply, radio and television broadcasting; domestic animals used in agriculture; and rural electric companies (except their motor vehicles). Taxable at 100 per cent of depreciated book value is electrical generating and distributing equipment, not for the owner's use.[23] The list of exemptions from the general 70 per cent valuation reflects 1) the rural strength in the legislature, 2) the desire for a favorable tax position to attract manufacturing plants, 3) possibly a wish to help certain depressed industries, and 4) the political strength of certain industries.

The Ohio laws are vague on the boundary line between realty and tangible personalty. Several decisions of the Ohio Supreme Court over the past fifteen years have broadened the scope of tangible personal property. Many properties, such as steam boiler plants, oil storage tanks, and blast furnaces of steel mills, which are accessory to business carried on upon the premises and which, if the industry were removed, would be of no benefit to the land, are

23. Section 5711.22, Revised Code of Ohio.

classified as *personal property* and not as real estate.[24] The expanding concept of tangible personal property accounts in part for its very rapid rate of growth since 1940, shown in Table VI-19.

The present rule of the Ohio Department of Taxation follows:

"For the purpose of classifying property for taxation, items of property devoted primarily to the general use of the land or buildings thereon are to be considered as real property and all other items of property including their foundations and all things accessory thereto which are devoted primarily to the business conducted on the premises are to be considered as personal property." [25]

Under this rule, all scales, concrete welding booths, underground tanks for storage of gasoline and other fuels, pneumatic tube systems, brick kilns, and florists' refrigerated cold rooms are among the items classified as personal property.[26]

The present definition of tangible personal property is broader and that of real property narrower than is true in most states.[27] On the other hand, Ohio does tax tangible personal property used in business and agriculture. New York and Delaware exempt all personal property.[28]

To minimize their taxes taxpayers seek classification of property such as structures and equipment as tangible personalty. For such properties, the taxable value set at the statutory percentage of initial cost is probably higher in the first year than if classified as real estate and assessed at the prevailing ratio of 35 to 50 per cent of cost. However, as time passes, book value declines each year by the amount of the annual depreciation. The Ohio Department of Taxation prescribes annual rates of depreciation for various classes of property, but no depreciation on properties still in use is allowed after net value reaches 20 per cent of original costs.[29] This means

24. *Zangerle vs. Standard Oil Co.*, 144 OS 506, 60 NE (2d) 52 (1945); *Zangerle vs. Republic Steel Corp.*, 144 OS 529, 60 NE (2d) 170 (1945).

25. Rule No. 19-26, December 24, 1953.

26. Department of Taxation of Ohio, Bulletin No. 70 (June 9, 1954); Bulletin No. 74 (September 3, 1954).

27. Interview with Paul Ballou, Chief Assessor, Cuyahoga County Auditor's Office, April, 1958.

28. H. M. Groves, *Financing Government* (5th edition), p. 48 (New York, 1958).

29. Department of Taxation, *Ohio Personal Property Tax Manual* (1956 edition) pp. 366-368. The Department requires straight-line depreciation of this property.

that, if the statutory percentage is 50 per cent, taxable value would be 10 per cent of original cost for any remaining years of use. If the same item of property were classified as real estate, a change of assessed value would not occur each year but only when a general reappraisal is made, every six years if the county reappraises as required by state law. When real estate is reappraised, consideration is given to reproduction cost less depreciation, sales price of similar properties, and capitalized earning power. Inflation and other factors may cause the value to be increased at time of reappraisal. Reappraisals do not apply to tangible personal property.

Generally, the longer the life of the asset, the faster the State-authorized depreciation rate, and the higher the initial assessment-cost ratio, the more favorable is the tangible personal classification to the taxpayer. An example will indicate the advantages of the tangible personalty classification for depreciable property which is valued for taxation at fifty per cent of net book value. Assume a piece of property with a prescribed depreciation rate of 5 per cent a year and an actual life of thirty years. Chart VI-5 indicates the per-

Chart VI—5
EXAMPLE COMPARING VALUES SUBJECT TO TAXATION
FOR PROPERTY AS REAL ESTATE
OR TANGIBLE PERSONAL

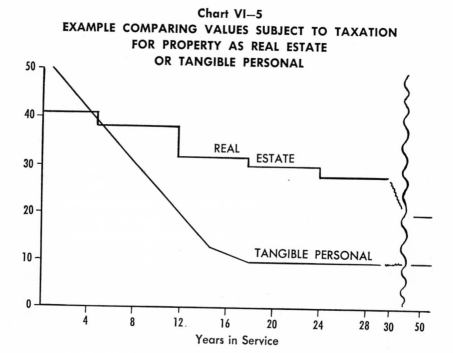

Years in Service

centage of original cost which is on the tax duplicate each year, contrasting the effect of a tangible personal versus a real property classification. Several assumptions must be stated: (1) real property is assessed initially at 42 per cent of cost; (2) only physical depreciation affects real property and this factor (and only this factor) is recognized every six years when the property is reappraised; (3) the item is depreciated under the real estate classification as a structure of average construction.

The present situation in Ohio is thus conducive to uncertainty and litigation. A clear boundary set by the legislature or, if legal, delegation of this power to the Department of Taxation, would remove the cause of expensive litigation, uncertainty, and possible inequities between different classes of taxable property and different taxpayers.

Exempt Property

Ohio allows few exemptions of property compared with many states. Personal property such as the taxpayer's own clothing, furniture, appliances and private automobiles are exempt. Property owned by federal, state, and local governments and used for public purposes is not taxable.[30] Also exempt is property used for hospital, education, religious, and a few other non-profit purposes. Ohio does not have homestead exemptions, veterans' exemptions, or exemptions or tax moratoriums to encourage industry to locate in the state.[31]

Exempt real estate in Cuyahoga County for the 1957-58 tax year was $526.9 million, or 10.3 per cent of total taxable valuation. This compares with $298.2 million, or 11.0 per cent of taxable property in 1949-50. The ratio for the City of Cleveland is less than 1 per cent higher than for the County and the trend is the same. Government-

---

30. The Cleveland Transit System won a case in the Supreme Court leading exemption about $17.2 million assessed value of its property from the tax duplicate in Cuyahoga County. *City of Cleveland v. Board of Tax Appeals*, 167 Ohio St., 263 (February 5, 1958).

31. Homestead and veterans' exemptions grant a flat reduction in assessment to all homeowners or veterans. Some states will not tax new industry for a stated period of years, or will offer a tax rate or assessment below that of other taxpayers. See Groves *op. cit.*, pp. 88-93.

owned property accounted for about three-fifths of the exempt property, and privately owned property of religious and charitable organizations for most of the rest.

Tax exempt real estate in Cuyahoga County in 1957-58 was distributed as follows:

Government Ownership	Assessed Valuation (Thousands of Dollars)	Per Cent of Exempt Property
U.S.A.	28,357	5.4
State of Ohio	3,714	.7
County	12,736	2.4
Municipalities	124,633	23.7
School Boards	128,997	24.4
Other (Metro. Park, Housing Auth., Ohio Turnpike)	20,942	3.9
Sub-Total	319,379	60.5

Private Ownership		
Higher Education	32,340	6.1
Worship	90,602	17.2
Charitable	70,917	13.5
Other (House for Poor Children, graveyards, monuments)	13,758	2.7
	526,896	100.0

The exemption of privately-owned motor vehicles from the property tax is questionable. The value of motor vehicles is a good measure of ability to pay, and much better than a flat-rate auto license or gasoline tax. Higher taxes on vehicles are also justified on the benefit principle; present license and gas taxes pay only about half of the local costs of streets and highways. Any revenues from such a tax would be earmarked for streets and highways, based on the Constitutional requirement to earmark these revenues. The revenue potential here is large. A crude estimate for 1956 might value the 636,000 motor vehicles at an average of $1,000 apiece, or $600 million in round numbers. Even if assessed at 50 per cent the tax base would increase $300 million—which at the 1956 average tax rate would have yielded about $10 million of local revenues.

Property Tax Administration

The County is the administrative unit for the real property tax. The County Auditor assesses all real estate in the county, except public utility property, which is the responsibility of the State. Even here, the State often requests the County Auditor to act as its agent in assessing the real property of public utilities.

County assessment of real property minimizes the problem of equalization of assessments of similar properties. The Cleveland metropolitan financial problem would be aggravated if each municipality and township assessed the properties within its boundaries. Many of the northeastern and north-central states have an assessor in each township, village, and city.

For the tangible personal property tax, the returns of inter-county corporations and of larger taxpayers go to the State and other returns to the County. The intangible property tax is also partly administered by the State and partly by the County, depending on size of income or assets and the classification of the owner. A fuller discussion of property tax administration appears in METRO's report, *Problems of Financial Administration*.

RELATION OF ASSESSED VALUE TO TRUE VALUE

Of great importance to any study of tax capacity and tax burden is the assessment ratio, i.e., the ratio of assessed value to true value, determined by representative sales or appraisal. Assessed values in Cuyahoga County and elsewhere are much lower than market value. All property in Cuyahoga County is on the tax duplicate at about $5.1 billion for 1958 although its market value is estimated at $15 billion.[32] Some of the difference reflects the value of exempt

---

32. John J. Carney, Cuyahoga County Auditor, quoted in *Cleveland News*, p. 1 (August 29, 1958).

property, but the dominant reason for the large excess of market value over assessed value is that the average property in Cuyahoga County, especially real estate, is assessed at about two-fifths of its market value.

True value is difficult to measure. It takes into account all factors affecting present and future value. Market price of the property in a representative open market sale, reproduction cost new less depreciation, and the capitalized value of current and future income from the property would all be considered, when applicable.

In making comparisons of tax rates between one jurisdiction for different periods and between different cities for the same year, the assessment ratios must be considered along with the legal tax rates to obtain the effective tax rates, the only valid basis for comparison.

The level of assessments is of crucial importance for several reasons:

1) Equalization of assessments between properties which differ in age, value, use, location, and construction materials and methods, is necessary for equity between individual taxpayers.

2) Equalization between jurisdictions in the same county is necessary for justice in taxes which apply to more than one municipality, such as county and school district levies on assessed value.

3) Equalization between counties, each a separate assessing district, is necessary because the formulas for the distribution of the local government fund and the school foundation moneys by the State of Ohio include the local assessed valuations.

4) The Ohio constitutional tax and statutory debt limits are based on the assessed values of property subject to the general property tax; different assessment ratios would substantially modify the real effects of these limitations. A low assessment ratio may have serious adverse effects: neglect of needed services, inadequate plant and equipment, lack of financial responsibility by elected officials, use of inferior revenue sources, reliance on State Aid, use of revenue bonds and other devices to escape the debt limit, etc.

5) The real burden of the property tax depends more on the real or market value of the property than on its assessed valuation.

The most recent reappraisal of all real estate in the county became effective with the January 1, 1955 valuation. This reappraisal is estimated to have given assessments equal to 50 per cent of the value of comparable sales over the 1946-52 period. Expressed differently, the 1955 assessments were equal to about 42 per cent of the reconstruction costs as of January, 1955.

Historically the assessment ratios have been as follows:

1927-29	65-70% (Time of adoption of 10 mill rate limitation)
1939-40	65-70%
1946-48	40%
1955	42%
1958	40%

The wide variation in assessment ratios in Ohio and in Cuyahoga County during this century reflect the legal definition of the tax base, the effect of depression, prosperity, and inflation on values, lags in assessments, and economic growth.

The assessed value of real estate in Cuyahoga County reached its peak pre-depression valuation in 1927. From the high in that year of $2,196 million, it declined 36.9 per cent to the 1935 low. Not until 1952 did Cuyahoga County regain its 1927 level of valuation of real property.

A number of reappraisals on a horizontal basis have been made since 1925, both up and down, as follows: [33]

1926—10% decrease on land in entire county

1928—15% decrease on land in Cleveland

1931—approximately 10% decrease from reappraisal throughout county (prescribed by State Law)

1932—15% decrease on land, 10% decrease on buildings in Cleveland and Greater Cleveland
and 20% decrease on land, 15% decrease on buildings in balance of county

1933—20% decrease on land, 15% decrease on buildings in entire county

1952—25% increase on all real estate in county, ordered by Board of Tax Appeals.

---

33. Board of Tax Appeals, State of Ohio, Journal Entry, December 1, 1952 (order directing 25% increase in assessed valuation of Cuyahoga County real estate).

There were revaluations on a selective basis in other years, the most recent being the 1955 reappraisal in which real estate assessments were increased on an average of 10.13 per cent throughout the county. The direction and percentage of change varied widely between municipalities, with Berea's real estate assessment increasing 20.40 per cent and Oakwood's 75.5 per cent, while Euclid real estate had a decrease averaging 6.42 per cent. Generally the older residential districts were increased in value, as the appraisal firms in 1955 used a slower and apparently more realistic depreciation schedule on buildings than had been used by the former auditor.[34]

In mid-1958, close observers seem to believe that present assessments are *generally* fair and equitable on residential and industrial properties in Cuyahoga County. There is more controversy over the assessment of commercial properties.[35] See Table VI-14.

Table VI-14—Assessment Ratios, Cuyahoga County and Selected States, for Classes of Property, 1956

| | Class of Property | | | | | |
Jurisdiction	NON-FARM RESIDENTIAL	SINGLE FAM. NON-FARM	ACREAGE & FARM	VACANT LOTS	COMMERCIAL	INDUSTRIAL
Cuyahoga County	36.0	n.a.	n.a.	n.a.	55.0	43.0
Ohio	36.8	35.6	24.6	25.2	43.0	42.9
Pennsylvania	32.9	31.3	18.8	26.0	39.5	32.9
New York	47.2	37.1	34.9	50.4	78.7	79.0
New Jersey	25.4	23.6	12.3	22.9	40.3	36.1
Michigan	30.6	29.9	19.7	27.6	33.7	n.a.
Illinois	40.9	41.6	42.2	36.7	44.5	n.a.
Indiana	23.3	22.9	18.4	16.4	21.6	n.a.
Wisconsin	45.1	45.4	43.5	32.3	53.4	n.a.

Note: n.a.—not available.
Sources: Census: *Assessed Values and Sales Prices of Transferred Real Property 1957* Census of Governments Advance Release No. 7 (1958) for All the States. Data relate to measurable sales for a 6 month period 1956. The sampling variability reported by Census for Ohio was ± 0.2% for nonfarm residential, ± 12.6% for commercial, and ± 2.9% for industrial properties. The estimates for Cuyahoga County are made by METRO's staff, based on discussions with interested parties in government, in research organizations in Cleveland, and data on 1956 assessment ratios by counties or cities. Of the approximately 40,000 parcels of real estate in Cuyahoga County which were sold in 1958, METRO studied a random sample of 125 residential parcels. The mean of the assessment ratios for the 125 properties was 35.8 per cent, with a standard deviation of 11.4.

34. Louis B. Mitchell, *County Auditor's Office, 1951 to 1958*, Exhibit III.
35. *Cleveland News*, July 30, 1958, reported requests for revisions of assessments on 62 downtown commercial properties which were on the tax duplicate at $98 million.

Assessment at a fraction of true value is the prevailing practice everywhere in the United States. The 1957 U. S. Census documented the wide variations in assessment ratios for different states and different types of property. Ohio is somewhat above average in assessment ratios for all states and about average among its neighboring states.

The effective rate of tax is the nominal tax rate multiplied by the assessment ratio. A thirty mill rate on property which is assessed at 40 per cent of true value is an effective tax rate of twelve mills (30 mills × 40%). Table VI-15 shows, for selected years 1940-58, the assessment ratios applied to the assessed value of real estate in Cuyahoga County to obtain 1) an estimate of market value of tax-

Table VI-15—Nominal and Effective Rates of Tax on Real Estate, Cuyahoga County, Selected Years, 1940-58

	1940	1950	1956	1958
General Property Tax Levied on Real Estate * (In Millions of Dollars)	42.0	57.2	100.1	118.3 *(est.)*
Assessed Value (In Millions of Dollars)	1,417.9	1,855.2	3,230.4	3,436.4
Average Tax Rate on Assessed Value (Mills)	29.67	30.83	30.99	34.5 *(est.)*
Aessessment Ratio (Per Cent)	67 †	38 ‡	42.8 §	40
Market Value ** (In Millions of Dollars)	2,116	4,882	7,548	8,591
Effective Tax Rate on Market Value †† (Mills)	19.9	11.7	13.3	13.8
Ratio Assessed Valuation to Replacement Cost ‡‡ (Per Cent)	74.2	41.4	42.8	40.8

* General property tax (line 1) assumes current payment of all taxes. It does not allow for delinquencies on current tax payments or for collection of delinquencies or penalties on earlier years' levies.

† Louis Mitchell, Deputy County Auditor, estimated 65-70% for 1939-40.

‡ Ratio derived from study of 68,178 sales in Cuyahoga County 1946-48. See Board of Tax Appeals, State of Ohio, Journal Entry December 1, 1952 ". . . order and directive to the Cuyahoga County Auditor . . ." p. 14.

§ Based on January, 1955 ratio of 42.8% upon completion of county-wide reappraisal.

** Market value is calculated by dividing assessed value by assessment ratio.

†† Effective tax rate is obtained by multiplying average tax rate by assessment ratio. Also equal to tax levy divided by market value.

‡‡ See Table VI-16 for construction costs indices for Cleveland area. This line is based on the 1955 relationship of 42.8% and is calculated both directions in time from 1955.

able real estate, and 2) an estimate of average effective tax rates for these years in Cuyahoga County. The calculations indicate that the effective tax rate on realty declined from 19.9 mills in 1940, to 11.7 mills in 1950, and rose to 13.3 mills by 1956, and an estimated 13.8 mills in 1958. These rates are well below the nominal or published tax rates. Public utility and tangible property are not included. Tangible personal property seems to have a taxable value averaging slightly above half its book value.

Low assessments in relation to current market prices and con-

Table VI-16—Building Cost Index * for the "Cleveland, Ohio Area" † (U.S. Average Prices, 1926-29=100)

YEAR	RESIDENCES		APTS., HOTELS & OFFICE BLDGS.		COMMERCIAL AND FACTORY BLDGS.		AVERAGE
	Frame	Brick	Brick Concrete	Brick Steel	Steel	Brick Steel	
1926-29 (Average)	107.2	113.4	111.3	108.3	103.0	110.5	109.32
1938	105.8	109.8	115.5	112.8	113.0	118.1	111.96
1939	106.2	109.6	115.3	112.8	112.9	117.7	111.90
1940	107.8	111.1	116.1	113.5	112.3	117.9	112.85
1941	118.3	120.5	122.6	120.2	116.9	124.1	120.85 ‡
1942	123.2	125.8	127.6	124.8	119.9	128.0	125.60 ‡
1943	128.6	130.0	130.3	128.1	122.0	130.3	129.08
1944	143.6	143.6	193.4	138.9	131.2	140.6	140.96
1945	154.9	154.7	148.3	147.3	136.9	148.7	150.49
1946	169.2	169.4	160.2	159.9	146.4	161.0	163.91
1947	205.7	203.9	185.6	185.9	168.9	187.3	193.85
1948	229.8	228.2	209.4	208.7	190.5	210.9	217.69
1949	224.8	225.7	216.0	213.0	198.5	217.2	219.07
1950	237.9	237.8	227.8	224.1	207.2	228.4	230.66
1951	255.0	255.8	243.8	240.8	221.5	244.5	247.42
1952	262.7	264.3	255.5	250.4	232.2	257.2	257.34
1953	267.7	271.1	266.5	260.1	244.6	269.5	266.43
1954	264.8	270.3	271.9	263.2	251.6	276.1	268.60
1955	273.9	280.2	281.8	272.6	263.5	287.7	278.77
1956	286.7	294.4	296.3	286.1	277.9	303.0	293.05
1957	293.9	305.0	311.0	298.5	294.6	320.2	305.57
1958	294.2	306.5	316.0	301.8	307.7	327.0	309.03
1959 Mar.	300.9	312.6	322.1	307.4	308.5	333.9	315.31

* Data omitted on some types of construction. Labor, materials, profits and overhead included.
† E. H. Boeckh & Associates.
‡ 1941-42 Average 123.23.

struction costs are justified both by taxpayers and government officials on the grounds that today's prices are unreasonably high.
Compared with past prices, this is certainly true. But to expect that
costs or prices of real estate will revert to a drastically lower level
is clearly unrealistic. Government costs which must be met are at
today's prices.

Tax assessments based on 1941 costs are out-of-date and perhaps
inequitable between owners of older versus newer buildings. Building styles, methods, and materials change. It is awkward and unrealistic to value a building completed in 1959 on a schedule based on
1941 construction costs. Cuyahoga County is now the only county
in Ohio to appraise property on a 1941-42 construction cost basis. In
about seventy-five counties, the present assessments are based on
50 per cent of 1950 construction costs. The State issued instructions
in 1954 to assess on the basis of January, 1950 costs. Unfortunately
field work on the reappraisal in Cuyahoga County was then far
advanced at 100 per cent of 1941-42 costs, and therefore was
completed on this basis.

The Board of Tax Appeals ordered a reappraisal, December 7,
1957, of all real property in Ohio. Land was to be valued at current
value as of the date of assessment. Buildings and other improvements were to be valued as of January 1, 1956. The taxable valuation
of tangible personal property was not affected by this ruling, and
remained at various statutory percentages of book value.[36]

If the taxable valuation of real property is set at a higher percentage of true value than at present, the result would be an increased tax burden on real estate and a reduced burden on tangible
personal property. If the revenue to be raised from the property tax
is unchanged, a larger tax duplicate would mean a lower tax rate.
The lower rate applied to the constant taxable value of personal

---

36. John J. Carney, Auditor of Cuyahoga County, brought suit against the State
Board of Tax Appeals, on the grounds that the setting of a percentage of true value
as "taxable value" was an unconstitutional delegation of legislative power to an
administrative board. The Franklin County Court of Common Pleas ruled in favor
of Carney on March 29, 1958. The Board of Tax Appeals appealed this decision to
the Ohio Supreme Court, where the case is now pending as Supreme Court Case No.
35943 which is to be heard on May 13, 1959. *John J. Carney as Auditor of Cuyahoga County and a citizen and taxpayer of Cuyahoga County* vs. *Board of Tax
Appeals, Department of Taxation, State of Ohio.*

property would provide these taxpayers with a smaller tax bill, both in dollars and in proportion of total taxes. Table VI-17 illustrates the effect of a changed percentage of taxable value to true value. If the taxable value of real estate were increased to 50 per cent from the present estimated 40 per cent of true value, the tax base would increase due to the 25 per cent increase in the real estate portion. The average tax rate would decline by 14.4 per cent. The owners of real property would face tax payments $8.3 million or 7 per cent

Table VI-17—Probable Effect of Revaluation of Real Estate on Tax Burden on Owners of Different Types of Property

ASSESSED VALUATION (In Millions of Dollars)

1957-58 Tax Valuations	Real Estate	Public Utility	Tangible Personal Property	Total Taxable Value	Ratio: Taxable Value/ True Value
Actual Values	3,436.4	383.9	1,293	5,113	40 (est.)
Adjusted Values	4,295.5	383.9	1,293	5,972	50
Per Cent Difference	+ 25	0.0	0.0	+ 16.8	...

TAX LEVIES (In Millions of Dollars)

1958 Taxes	Real Estate	Public Utility	Tangible Personal Property	Total Tax	Tax Rate (mills)
Actual Levies	118.3	13.2	45.5	176.0	34.42 (est.)
Adjusted	126.2	11.3	38.1	176.0	29.47
Increase or Decrease	+ 8.3	— 1.9	— 6.4	0.0	— 4.95
Per Cent of Change	+ 7.0	— 14.4	— 14.4	0.0	— 14.4

higher. Owners of other property would enjoy a 14.4 per cent decline in their tax payments.[37] Further, *if* the reassessment were selective and each class of real estate were assessed at 50 per cent of true value, residential real estate would bear the largest increase, industrial property a smaller increase, and the average commercial property would receive a reduction *if* our estimates in Table VI-14 are accurate.

Any revaluation of one type of taxable property should be combined with consideration of the valuation of all types of property

---

37. The 1952 increase in real estate assessed values did shift the tax burden, raising it about 9.6% on real estate and lowering it about 12% on other property. Mitchell, *op. cit.*, Exhibit VI.

subject to the general property tax. Shifting the relative burden of the tax would be changing public policy and would best be done only deliberately and publicly after full consideration and discussion of the problems and issues involved. The taxable value of *new* tangible personal property adjusts automatically to current price levels as new inventories and equipment are acquired. "Last-in First-out" valuation, however, would insulate book value of inventories from current prices.

Incidence of the Property Tax

Who pays the property tax? Does it fall on the property owner or is he able to shift it in the form of a higher rent or price for the goods or services he offers for sale?

Let us consider separately taxes on land, on improvements, and on personal property. Taxes on land rest on the owner. A tax on land values does not alter either the demand or supply, and thus cannot be shifted.[38] This is especially true of urban land where value depends on location and not fertility. A buyer of land may offer a lower price if the land is subject to taxes higher than alternative investments, including land in other lower-tax jurisdictions. In this case, the tax is capitalized on the person who owns the land at the time the tax is levied or increased.[39] The value of benefits to landowners financed by the property tax, however, must be weighed against the tax to analyze the net effect on land values.

Improvements must be considered from several viewpoints. 1) A periodic tax on owner-occupied residential property cannot be shifted. 2) Taxes on rented residential properties are an important cost of production and are passed on to the tenant in the form of higher rent in the long run. If owners do not earn a normal profit above costs including property taxes, the supply of rental units will decrease and rents will rise. In the short run, the ability of the land-

---

38. R. A. Musgrave and others, "Distribution of Tax Payments by Income Groups: A Case Study for 1948," *National Tax Journal,* Vol. IV (March, 1951), pp. 1, 22. W. J. Shultz & C. L. Harriss, *American Public Finance* (6th edition), p. 179 (N. Y., 1954).

39. For a discussion of "capitalization of a tax" see METRO's *Problems in Financial Administration,* Ch. 3; Shultz & Harriss, *op. cit.,* pp. 181-82.

lord to pass on property taxes and other costs depends on the relative strength of demand and supply. In an economic recession or in a geographic area with an overabundance of houses and apartments for rent, the owner may not be able to cover all costs including property taxes. 3) Taxes on improvements and on tangible personal property used in business are a general cost of doing business. Property tax costs as well as other costs are normally covered by the price charged the consumer. Thus property taxes on buildings used by manufacturing, wholesale, retail, and service industries are assumed to be passed forward to the consumer in the form of higher prices.[40]

If business cannot cover all costs including property taxes, new investments in reproducible taxed property will not be made, the supply will decline and the price will rise. In the short run again, a decline in demand relative to supply may mean the owner will bear the incidence of the tax for a period depending on the durability of the taxed property, on the degree of specialization of the property—such as a movie theater—on the elasticity on demands for the property, and on variations in effective tax burdens between competitive jurisdictions.

Generally the property taxes on buildings, equipment, inventories, and other taxable assets of retail and service businesses in Cleveland area are passed on in the form of higher prices to their consumers in proportion to their expenditures. Retail and service businesses must locate in the Cleveland area to serve their customers. Their only choice on location is to weigh different locations within the metropolitan area. Only unfavorably high differentials in costs, including the property tax, cannot be passed to the consumers in a competitive industry.

Manufacturing businesses have a wider choice of locations than a retail firm, as they usually serve a regional or national market. Important considerations in plant location are markets for their products, raw materials, transportation, labor force, utility services, as well as local taxes and other factors. Most of these considerations can be expressed in dollar terms and the total costs of various possible locations compared. Here the various jurisdictions in Cuyahoga

40. Musgrave, *op. cit.*, pp. 36-37.

County are in competition not only with each other but also with other areas in Ohio and neighboring states. Local property taxes usually are not ranked among the most important factors in deciding on plant locations. Local property taxes are easily calculated, however, and being definite and sometimes emotionally-tinged, the tax consideration may be important, especially for businesses with a large amount of taxable property.

A particular location is at a disadvantage in attracting manufacturing industry if the total array of costs, including taxes, in that location is greater than total costs in other locations. Higher taxes in one area do not automatically disqualify it. The unfavorably higher taxes may be offset by differentially lower costs for labor, materials, transportation, utilities, and other factors. Or a higher quality or broader scope of local government services may cancel out the higher taxes.

Locational decisions are influenced by tax administration and assessment procedures, the attitude toward business as a taxpayer (the golden goose to be plucked—*or* nourished), and the certainty, stability, and trend of taxes as well as the level of taxes.

A recent study compared the cost of state and local taxes to manufacturing industry for a possible location in 185 municipalities in ten eastern and midwestern states, including Ohio.[41] In all ten states, the land and buildings of industrial corporations were taxed. New York, Delaware, and Pennsylvania exempt tangible personal property. In Maryland, local option prevails on whether to tax tangible personal property. Other local taxes as well as all state taxes were included in the calculations.

The comparisons were made for three representative corporations: "A" with a relatively low level of inventories, large investment in fixed assets and relatively large net income; "B" with approximately equal investments in fixed assets and inventory and relatively low net income on sales and net worth; and "C" with inventories larger than fixed assets and net income high on sales and net worth.

---

41. Pennsylvania Economy League, Inc., Western Division, *The Relative Tax Cost to* Manufacturing Industry: *A New Comparison of Pennsylvania with Several Other* States (1957 Revision, Pittsburgh, 1957). The 10 states studied were Ohio, New York, New Jersey, Delaware, Maryland, West Virginia, Pennsylvania, Michigan, Indiana, and Illinois.

The average Ohio location studied gave either the lowest or second lowest state and local tax bill of the ten states studied for all three corporations. The five Cuyahoga County locations included in the study—Cleveland, Bay Village, Bedford, Parma, and Solon—enjoyed favorable competitive positions, except Cleveland and Bay Village for Corporation "B," as shown in Table VI-18. Local taxes in the forty-five Ohio locations were about average for all localities studied but the state taxes were substantially below the average, giving a total which was low relative to taxes for locations in other states.

Evaluation of Property Tax

The strength of the property tax is that it does yield half or more of all revenues to local governments throughout the country. The tax is well developed; its effects are built into present property values; property owners are accustomed to it; it is the most important source of local revenue available; it is the only major source now left almost exclusively to local governments.

The property tax is regarded as a poor measure of taxpaying ability. Income and total wealth are better measures of ability to pay than ownership of property. The assessed valuation of property may be poorly correlated with income from, or use of, property. Valuable properties tend to be more under-assessed relative to true value or market value than are properties of average or low value.

A good tax, according to one criterion, should be based either on ability to pay or benefits received. The property tax in part is a benefit tax paying for numerous local government services which benefit the property and the users of the property: police and fire protection, the local courts, roads and streets, refuse collection and disposal, public health, sanitary and storm sewers, and others. The property tax payment for these services is probably a real bargain for most property owners and tenants, in the sense that local government provides these services at lower cost and probably in the only way they could be provided for at all. Assessed valuation, however, is but an erratic measure of benefits received.

Although some services are closely related to property, a large

Table VI-18—Competitive Position of Selected Municipalities in Terms of State and Local Taxes on Manufacturing Plants, 1957

Government State County & Municipality	CORPORATION "A" (In Thousands of Dollars)				CORPORATION "B" (In Thousands of Dollars)				CORPORATION "C" (In Thousands of Dollars)			
	Local	State	State & Local	Rank*	Local	State	State & Local	Rank*	Local	State	State & Local	Rank*
Ohio												
Cuyahoga												
Cleveland	105.9	18.7	124.5	118	101.3	20.3	121.5	67	103.8	18.2	122.0	117
Bay Village	116.6	18.7	135.3	111	111.9	20.3	132.1	41	114.2	18.2	132.3	101
Bedford	94.8	18.7	113.5	139	90.4	20.3	110.6	131	93.1	18.2	111.3	133
Parma	96.9	18.7	115.6	133	92.4	20.3	112.7	126	95.1	18.2	113.3	129
Solon	101.1	18.7	119.8	124	96.6	20.3	116.8	108	99.2	18.2	117.3	123
Ohio												
Hamilton												
Cincinnati	113.5	18.7	132.2	113	105.0	20.3	125.2	52	110.6	18.2	128.8	106
Franklin												
Columbus	89.7	18.7	108.3	150	81.4	20.3	101.7	156	87.6	18.2	105.8	146
Summit												
Akron	106.2	18.7	124.9	117	101.7	20.3	121.9	64	104.2	18.2	122.3	116
New York												
Erie												
Buffalo	80.1	111.4	191.5	28	30.6	86.9	117.5	100	37.8	104.5	142.3	87
Pennsylvania												
Allegheny												
Pittsburgh	56.1	131.2	187.3	32	19.3	106.0	125.3	51	24.8	128.1	152.9	33
Michigan												
Wayne												
Detroit	209.8	84.1	293.8	3	223.0	88.3	311.3	3	215.5	85.5	301.0	3
Illinois												
Cook												
Chicago	123.6	12.4	135.9	110	116.2	14.0	130.2	43	114.5	12.3	126.8	110
Maryland												
Baltimore	156.3	121.8	278.1	5	163.9	100.8	264.7	7	158.7	116.4	275.1	5

* The lowest rank indicates the largest tax and 185 the lowest total state and local tax bill.
Note: Detail may not add to total due to rounding.
Source: Pennsylvania Economy League, Inc., Western Division—Op. Cit.

part of property tax revenues provide more personal services, such as education, health, and welfare, which benefits are not closely related to the property tax duplicate.

The property tax is discriminatory between different types of investments. It is a particular burden on improvements to real estate. It tends to discourage residential construction and investment in homes and apartments. Local property taxes absorb one-eighth to one-sixth of the rent on the average rental dwelling unit. In the Cleveland area, the average house is assessed at about $6,000, with a market value of about $18,000. An average tax in the county of about thirty-six mills would require a $270 tax payment. This annual tax would be over an eighth of the reasonable annual rent of $2,000 a year. Choice of property taxes as the major revenue source is probably a major deterrent to residential construction.

If an Ohio resident invests $10,000 in different assets, his tax bill will be substantially different.

	Taxable Value ✕ Rate	Annual Tax
$10,000 in real estate	$ 3,600 ✕ 36 mills	$130
$10,000 in bank deposits	$10,000 ✕ 0.2 mills	$ 20
$10,000 in stocks and bonds yielding $500 income	$ 500 ✕ 5%	$ 25

The higher tax on real property would be partially justified by services received benefiting the property.

The property tax is regressive, i.e., it takes a higher percentage of income from the lower income groups than from the higher income groups. Expenditures for housing absorbs a smaller proportion of income as the average family moves up the income scale. The property tax is regressive both for owner-occupied and rental housing. Property taxes on business properties—real, tangible, and intangible—are also regressive. The incidence of taxes on land is generally on the owners but the incidence of taxes on other business property (like excise taxes) is on the consumers, in proportion to their expenditures.

Administration of the property tax seems to have achieved a relatively high level of development in Cuyahoga County. Even so, the continuing problems of administration are many and difficult:

discovery, assessment, and equalization—both intra-county and inter-county.

The property tax base does not respond automatically to price level changes, as revealed by the inflation of the past eighteen years. Between 1939-40 and 1951-52, the consumer price level increased 90 per cent while the per capita assessed valuation rose only 45 per cent. (Calculations from data in Tables.) Only by revaluations upward in 1952 and 1955, averaging 36.5 per cent, was the per capita valuation kept even with the rise in the price level. This reflects a substantial time lag between price level increases and changes in valuation. Assessed value per capita in 1958-59 is 116 per cent above the 1939-40 level, compared with an increase of 107 per cent in the consumer price index, a negligible increase.

If inflation continues, the market value of real property and the government's need for revenue will increase steadily, while assessed values of existing properties are revalued only periodically (every six years if Ohio law is followed). More frequent adjustments to reflect rising prices would be a desirable change if inflation continues, especially with the tax limit and the debt limit of local governments in Ohio tied to the district's assessed valuation. This could be done annually from real estate price indices or from sales-assessment ratio studies.

Despite these shortcomings, both theoretical and practical, the property tax is a large revenue producer and undoubtedly will remain the major revenue source under control of local governments during the decades to come.

Local Income Tax [42]

A local income tax in a metropolitan area could be used to bolster the revenues of existing governments, to reduce imbalance

---

42. The best references on local and municipal income taxes are Robert A. Sigafoos, *The Municipal Income Tax; Its History and Problems* (Chicago, 1955); C. Lowell Harriss, "New York City Personal Income Taxation" in New York State-New York City Fiscal Relations Committee, *A Report to the Governor of the State of New York and the Mayor of the City of New York*, pp. 109-120 (New York, 1956). For Ohio municipal income taxes, see Ohio Legislative Service Commission, *Selected Metropolitan Area Problems*, pp. 7-19 (Columbus, 1959).

Table VI-19—General Property Tax: Duplicate and Levy, Cuyahoga County, 1937-59

Tax Year	ACTUAL GENERAL PROPERTY Total (Millions of Dollars)	Real Estate (Millions of Dollars)	Public Utilities (Millions of Dollars)	TAX DUPLICATE Tangible Personal Property (Thousands of Dollars)	Total Estimated General Property (Millions of Dollars)	Difference: Actual — Estimated (millions)	Ratio: Actual/Estimated	TAX LEVY Total General Property (Thousands of Dollars)	Real Estate (Thousands of Dollars)	Public Utilities (Thousands of Dollars)	Tangible Personal Property (Thousands of Dollars)
1937	1,747.9	1,386.9	193.6	167,429	n.a.	n.a.	n.a.	47,216	37,382	5,219	4,615
1938	1,784.0	1,388.1	193.9	201,945	n.a.	n.a.	n.a.	47,654	37,015	5,172	5,467
1939	1,797.3	1,413.8	192.0	191,562	n.a.	n.a.	n.a.	50,388	39,546	5,372	5,470
1940	1,799.7	1,417.9	190.4	190,762	1,799.9	—.8	100.0	53,382	41,976	5,637	5,769
1941	1,829.7	1,433.6	192.8	203,357	1,817.1	12.6	100.7	54,364	42,194	5,672	6,498
1942	1,924.0	1,462.9	195.4	265,676	1,861.6	62.3	103.3	56,395	42,696	5,701	7,998
1943	2,004.2	1,488.7	199.5	315,928	1,953.9	50.3	102.6	57,986	42,958	5,758	9,290
1944	2,034.9	1,502.8	192.2	339,856	2,011.0	23.9	101.2	56,652	41,862	5,354	9,436
1945	2,070.9	1,527.9	193.7	349,305	2,061.5	9.4	100.5	58,105	42,868	5,434	9,803
1946	2,055.9	1,512.0	202.8	341,070	2,064.1	—8.2	99.6	57,530	42,201	5,662	9,667
1947	2,293.2	1,679.8	250.8	407,634	2,226.7 *	66.6	103.0	63,958	46,800	5,737	11,421
1948	2,445.3	1,716.4	214.4	514,493	2,338.5	106.9	104.6	71,778	50,338	6,292	15,148
1949	2,599.6	1,782.8	228.3	588,481	2,525.6	74.0	102.9	79,813	54,776	7,013	18,124
1950	2,717.6	1,855.2	246.2	616,246	2,689.8	27.8	101.0	83,757	57,239	7,592	18,926
1951	2,825.9	1,925.1	256.9	643,887	2,798.2	27.6	101.0	93,275	63,454	8,465	21,356
1952	3,162.4	2,039.8	270.2	852,375	2,953.9	208.5	107.1	105,686	68,228	9,041	28,417
1953	3,945.1	2,683.7	289.6	971,908	3,825.6 *	119.5	103.1	115,381	78,721	8,495	28,265
1954	4,098.8	2,779.1	332.6	987,046	4,083.6	15.1	100.4	123,110	84,113	10,068	28,929
1955	4,214.6	2,856.9	349.7	1,007,957	4,193.7	20.9	100.5	131,462	89,797	10,997	30,668
1956	4,640.7	3,230.4	362.0	1,048,313	4,600.3 *	40.4	100.9	142,423	100,117	11,223	31,083
1957	4,845.9	3,295.4	369.1	1,181,373	4,712.8	133.1	102.8	160,240	110,017	12,319	37,904
1958	5,113.3	3,436.4	383.9	1,293,000 (est.)	5,001.7	111.9	102.2	178,684	135,555 ‡ (partly est.)		43,129
1959	5,223.2	3,554.3	384.1	1,284,881 (est.)	5,157.4	n.a.	n.a.	192,759	146,559 ‡ (est.)		46,200 (est.)

n.a.—not available.

Source: Office of County Auditor, Cuyahoga County, Facts and Figures, Public Information Bulletin No. 102 (1958) Table 1.

* Reappraisals effective in these years. 1957-58 and 1958-59 partially estimated by Metro Staff.

† Estimated duplicate consists of actual real estate and public utility valuation for current tax year plus estimated tangible personal property valuation—for which prior year's actual amount is used.

Difference between actual and estimated is entirely in tangible personal property and is the amount of growth from one year to the next.

‡ These intercolumnar figures represent non-differentiated totals of tax levy on real estate and public utilities.

Table VI-20—Population, Per Capita Real Estate Tax Duplicate, Per Capita Real Estate Tax Levy, Adjusted Tax Rate, Cuyahoga County, 1937-1959

Tax Year	Population	Real Estate Tax Duplicate (Dollars Per Capita)	Real Estate Tax Levy (Dollars Per Capita)	Adjusted Tax Rate *
1937	1,212,900	1,143	30,82	27.01
1938	1,214,500	1,142	30.47	26.71
1939	1,216,100	1,162	32.52	28.03
1940	1,216,700	1,165	34.50	29.67
1941	1,217,500	1,178	34.66	29.71
1942	1,217,100	1,202	35.08	29.31
1943	1,230,100	1,210	34.92	29.83
1944	1,223,100	1,219	33.95	27.83
1945	1,266,800	1,206	33.84	28.05
1946	1,316,900	1,148	32.05	27.98
1947	1,339,500	1,254	33.44	27.88
1948	1,359,000	1,263	37.04	29.35
1949	1,379,300	1,293	39.71	30.74
1950	1,389,500	1,335	41.19	30.82
1951	1,439,100	1,338	44.09	33.00
1952	1,470,800	1,387	46.39	33.41
1953	1,503,000	1,786	52.38	29.27
1954	1,527,700	1,832	55.06	30.03
1955	1,551,400	1,842	57.88	31.19
1956	1,580,500	2,044	63.34	30.69
1957	1,609,900	2,047	68.34	33.06
1958	1,604,000	2,142	n.a.	34.50
1959	1,629,200	2,182	n.a.	36.00

n.a.—not available
* Rate based on $1,000 of assessed valuation.
Source: Office of County Auditor, op cit., Table 7, 1957-58 and 1958-59 estimated by Metro staff.

between local governments, or to support a metropolitan government with an area-wide responsibility for functions not performed now by the present county government. If several political subdivisions in a metropolitan area adopt income tax ordinances, centralized administration would be more efficient and economical. The income tax would work better over a broad area than in a single municipality, particularly a small one. Administration would be more efficient and relatively less expensive. The City of Cleveland or Cuyahoga County, for example, could administer an income tax on a contract basis for all the participating municipalities. Avoidance of the tax by migration would be minimized by coverage on a county or metropolitan area basis.

Philadelphia and Washington, D.C. initiated municipal income taxes in 1939. Adoption of local income taxes has been slow except in Ohio and Pennsylvania—neither state has an individual income tax.[43] In Pennsylvania as of August, 1958, 732 local income taxes have been levied including 505 school districts.

The municipal income tax is the fastest growing major source of local revenue in Ohio, producing $52.9 million of revenue, in 1957, against $17 million, in 1951. (See Table VI-21). Toledo, in 1946, was the first Ohio city to adopt an income tax, followed by four other large Ohio cities in 1948-49. Adoption of the income tax has snowballed since 1952, with thirty-one cities and six villages in Ohio using the tax in December, 1958.

The income tax is used most heavily by the federal government, which obtains approximately 80 per cent of its conventional budget receipts (about $56.8 billion in 1957) from the taxes on individual and corporate income. Thirty-three states tax individual income and thirty-five states tax corporate income.[44] Ohio does not have an income tax on either individuals or corporations, which makes it less burdensome for local governments to utilize this tax, and recent tax decisions at the state level are likely to increase use of local income taxes in Ohio. Governor DiSalle, in his budget message to the legislature on March 3, 1959, proposed substantial increases in state taxes but specifically ruled out a state income tax on the ground that this would hamper municipalities which now depend on this tax. The legislature accepted this recommendation.

The percentage of local taxes of all Ohio municipalities obtained from income tax rose from about one-tenth, in 1950, to almost one-fifth, by 1957, as indicated in Table VI-21. However, this average fails to reveal the importance of the income tax to the cities using it. In 1956, the income tax produced between 32 per cent and 59 per cent of local tax revenues for Cincinnati, Columbus, Toledo, and Dayton, as indicated in Table VI-22.

---

43. Tax Foundation, *Facts and Figures on Government Finance, 1958-59,* pp. 218-19 (New York, 1958).

44. The Tax Foundation—*op. cit.,* pp. 168-169.

Table VI-21—Income Taxes Compared with Property and All Local Taxes as Revenue Source for Ohio Municipalities

Year	No. of Municipal Income Taxes	Municipal Property Tax	Income Tax *	Ratio: Income Tax to All Municipal Taxes
		(In Thousands of Dollars)		(Per Cent)
1951	5	94,679.6	17,350.1	10.7
1954	15	113,316.4	27,726.4	13.8
1955	15	117,569.7	34,102.6	15.8
1956	19	126,989.0	44,383.1	18.5
1957	25	149,549.3	52,935.2	19.4

* Income tax rates varied between ½ of 1% and 1%, except for Middleton where the rate is ¼ of 1%.

Sources: Auditor of State, *Comparative Statistics, Cities of Ohio*, Selected years, 1951-57 inclusive (Columbus, Ohio). Municipal income tax not shown separately before 1951.

Ohio cities levying the income tax generally have substantially lower property tax rates than other cities. If the revenue from the income tax is converted into the number of mills on the property tax needed to raise the equivalent funds, the adjusted total millage for all jurisdictions and for municipal purposes only is equal to, or higher than, the comparable actual property tax rates for cities in the Cleveland area. (See Table VI-22.) The income tax, in 1956, produced a yield equivalent to 7.61 mills in Columbus and up to 11.33 mills in Toledo, a substantial shift of burden from the property tax to the income tax. Columbus and Toledo, as a result, had significantly lower municipal property tax rates than Cleveland. Cincinnati and Dayton, with property tax rates about equal to Cleveland's, used the income tax in addition and provided the equivalent of more millage for both school and municipal purposes.

Prior to 1957, municipal income taxes were subject only to constitutional restrictions (described earlier in Chapter VI). The General Assembly passed a Uniform Municipal Income Tax Law in 1957.[45] This law provides:

1) Tax must be levied at a uniform rate. Any rate in excess of 1 per cent must be approved by 50 per cent of the voters in a general election or 60 per cent in a special election.

---

45. Chapter 718, Revised Code of Ohio.

Table VI-22—Income and Property Tax Rates and Tax Rate Equivalents of Income Taxes, Selected Ohio Municipalities, 1956

Tax Rates and Equivalents	Type of Government	Cleveland	Cincinnati	Columbus	Dayton	Toledo	Akron
Income Tax Rate (Per Cent)	Municipalities	0.00	1	1	1	0.5	0.00
Property Tax Rate (In Mills)	County	3.40	4.26	3.90	5.19	3.00	3.23
	School Districts	11.90	13.94	14.34	13.90	19.00	20.00
	Municipalities	15.60	10.94	4.56	3.45	10.00	10.30
	Total *	31.10	29.34	23.00	22.74	32.20	33.73
Millage Equivalent of Income Tax	Municipalities	0.00	8.76	7.61	11.33	7.80	0.00
Adjusted Total Millage	Municipalities	31.10	38.10	30.61	34.07	40.00	33.73
Percentage of Taxes from Income Taxes	Municipalities	0.00	32	42	59	34	0.00
Income and Property Tax, Millage Equivalent	Municipalities	15.60	19.70	12.17	14.78	17.80	10.30

* Total millage includes 0.2 mills levied by State.
Source: Property tax rates from Ohio Department of Taxation, *Annual Report 1956.* (Columbus, 1957).

2) Levies in excess of 1 per cent must be proposed and used only for a specified purpose.
3) No municipality may exempt income of persons over eighteen years of age or the net profit of a business or profession.
4) Military pay and allowances and income of religious, educational, and other charitable organizations from tax-exempt activities or property may not be taxed.
5) Alternative methods are established for determining the taxable income of businesses and professions conducted partly within and partly outside municipal boundaries.

The state action substantially limits local discretion, in effect prohibiting individual exemptions and progressive rates, although it conformed generally to local taxes already in existence.

The State leaves to local determination the problem of the taxpayer who lives in one municipality and works in another, when both municipalities levy an income tax. In every case, the municipality of employment now collects the tax, but double taxation is avoided by either a tax credit or reciprocity. The most frequent practice is for the municipality of residence to allow a credit against its tax to the full amount of the tax paid in municipality of employment. Reciprocity is effective only between Toledo and its income tax suburbs.

The Ohio municipal income taxes are not payroll taxes as in some states. Professional and business, including corporate, incomes are included, and all income is taxed at a flat rate.

The base for local income tax varies from the federal tax in several ways, according to the model income tax ordinance recommended by the Ohio Municipal League.[46] It applies the same rate to personal and corporate net income. Due to the state tax on intangibles and the "pre-emption doctrine," interest and dividend income and royalties cannot be taxed locally. Ohio tax rate is already 5 per cent on income from these sources. Capital gains and losses also are excluded from the local tax base. No personal exemptions to adjust for number of dependents are allowed. Neither standard deductions nor itemized deductions are allowed. Sick pay, deductible to a stated amount on the federal form, would be taxable in Ohio. Withholding applies in most Ohio municipalities with the income tax. Although interest and dividends are exempt now from Ohio municipal income taxes, the combined state and local tax system would be even more regressive if the present state 5 per cent tax were removed to allow some municipalities to apply an income tax of 1 per cent or less to this income.

Income is regarded as the best single measure of ability to pay. It is not a base for any state or local tax in the Cleveland area. All

---

46. See Ohio Municipal League's Income Tax Committee and Subcommittee—
Model income tax ordinance and income tax forms.

taxes are ultimately paid either out of income or capital (wealth). The income tax varies with income, and, under a pay-as-you-go payment system, is collected at the time of receipt of income. This flexibility contrasts with the fixed cost of the property tax on individuals with little, declining, or no income due to retirement, unemployment and illness or on businesses with little or no net income.

Under present Ohio law, only municipal corporations have the right to levy income taxes. A county can by charter become a municipal corporation and gain the right to use an income tax.[47]

The Ohio legislature could extend the power to use the income tax to school districts. In some ways, the schools have more reason to use the income tax than do the municipalities. School needs are growing more rapidly; education is more a personal service than many municipal services and thus has less reason to depend on the property tax than do municipal services. On the other hand, widespread municipal use of the income tax would reduce one pressure on the property tax and indirectly make it more available to the schools, and many municipalities have already staked out their claim on the income tax.

Adoption of income taxes by individual municipalities throughout the county would benefit most the industrial and commercial municipalities, and least the dormitory cities and villages. With priority to the municipality of income situs, the income tax appeals most to the core city.

An income tax would allow the municipality of employment to levy a tax on those who use its services without any direct payment. This would especially help the central city, which still is the major source of employment but a declining location for residence and retail sales. The population in the central city, in Cleveland as well as in other metropolitan areas, is increasingly composed of lower-income groups—the in-migrants and the minority groups. The higher income groups earn their incomes in the central city and then take

---

47. Legal uncertainty exists as to whether a charter county could levy an income tax on top of income taxes levied by cities and villages within the county. The most likely interpretation is that a county charter providing for a county income tax would preclude its use by any city or village in the county.

their earnings to homes and shopping centers in the suburbs.[48] The
central cities therefore do not find reciprocity with the suburbs ad-
vantageous, with the principle of priority to the jurisdiction of income situs already established. Reciprocity between the central city
and the suburbs would result to the advantage of the dormitory
suburbs only if required by state legislation.[49]

Individual communities with low capacity from the property tax
usually would be below average under the income tax also, as indicated in Table VI-7. Garfield Heights and Maple Heights, for example, are low by both measures. Exceptions are Cuyahoga Heights,
with high assessed value but low income per capita, and Cleveland
Heights, with low assessed values but high income per person.

A metropolitan or county-wide income tax would have many
advantages over separate income taxes for each community. The
major advantage is that the tax would be levied and collected by
the economic unit in which the individual or family lived, worked,
and shopped—without the artificial political boundaries which now
often separate the tax source from the location of the expenditure.
Administration, including interchange of information with the In-
ternal Revenue Service, would be facilitated. The opportunity to
avoid the tax by migrating to a non-income-tax location would be
minimized. The problem of double taxation by both municipality of
employment and municipality of residence would be eliminated.
Administration and enforcement costs would probably amount to
about 3 per cent of the taxes collected.[50] There would also be compliance costs for the taxpayers and their employers, although there
are some compliance costs for all taxes. The broader area would

---

48. A report for the New York Metropolitan Regional Study indicated that the
ratio of income spent in New York City to income earned in the City declined from
.93 in 1939 to .79 in 1956. "Flight of Wages to Suburbs Poses a City Income Tax,"
New York Times (July 14, 1958), pp. 1, 17. Similar changes occurred in the Cleveland area, measured by population, employment, and the retail sales. See above,
Chapter II.

49. Ohio Legislative Service Commission, *op. cit.*, p. 16.

50. Letters received from city officials in charge of municipal income taxes listed
the following costs of administration relative to collections in 1957: Cincinnati 1.9%,
Columbus 2.5% (1958); Dayton 4.4% and Toledo "under 5%." The larger Cleveland
population and tax base should help to keep costs in the middle or lower part of
this range.

minimize the problem of businesses allocating income between tax-ing jurisdictions. Tax withholding would apply to those on regular wages and salaries. Declaration of estimated income and payment of estimated tax would be expected of other taxpayers. The absence of a state income tax in Ohio makes a local income tax more appropriate than in most states.

Local income taxes in Ohio compared to federal personal income taxes are more stable in yield, slightly regressive, and less keyed to ability to pay. The more stable yield follows from proportional rates, no exemptions, and few or no deductions. The tax base for the per-sonal income tax thus varies approximately equally with income, and not by a multiple of the income variation. Proportional rates with federal deductibility for taxpayers who itemize their deductions on their federal tax returns makes the tax slightly regressive. A propor-tional income tax, however, is less regressive than either the property or sales tax. This feature, i.e., its being less regressive, makes a local tax on all income rank higher in terms of ability to pay than a tax on property, payroll, or sales. Ability to pay is measured by income directly, without the refinement of adjustment allowed in the federal tax for size of family and large medical bills. A tax on personal income rests on the taxpayer and is not shifted.

A tax on business net income is harder to analyze. The incidence may fall in varying proportions on the owners, the customers, the employees, and the suppliers, but is thought to be largely on the owners and the consumers in the usual case.[51] The greater the amount of competition, the weaker the demand for the product of service, the smaller the area covered by the tax, and the stronger the bargaining position of labor and suppliers, the more likely is the tax to be borne by the owners.

A rough estimate of the yield from a 1 per cent tax on individual and business net income in Cuyahoga County in 1956 would be $42 million. Available data indicate that total personal income in Cuya-hoga County in 1956 was about $4.1 billion. About 10 per cent of this would be interest, dividends, and other income not subject to tax. Income of military personnel and minors would also be excluded. Deducting these would leave about $3.7 billion of personal income

---

51. Musgrave and others, *op. cit.*, pp. 14-20.

subject to tax. In addition, corporate profits attributable to business done in the Cleveland area would be taxable. The experience of other cities indicates a 1 per cent tax rate in Cleveland would produce income tax collections equal to about 1.1 per cent of the total personal income. This ratio of collections to personal income of residents is higher where there is much industry and many employees who live in suburban communities and lower in the residential suburban communities where the tax is claimed by the jurisdiction of employment and where business profits are small. A county-wide tax including central city and suburbs would probably yield about 1 per cent of personal income, i.e., the exempt personal income would be about offset by business profits.

Retail Sales Tax

Taxes applied on purchases are other revenue sources. Sales taxes generally apply to all transactions at a certain level—retail, wholesale, or manufacture—except transactions which are specifically exempt.[52] Excise taxes, on the other hand, apply to enumerated products and services. In 1957, the sales tax family (sales, gross receipts, excise, and customs duties) produced $20.6 billion in the United States, following the individual and corporate income taxes in the amount of revenue yield. The federal government collected $11.1 billion, the states $8.4 billion, and local governments (mostly cities) $1.0 billion.[53] Sales and excise taxes collected by the State of Ohio were $517.2 million in the 1956-57 fiscal year.[54] Further discussion of excise taxes will be postponed to later sections.

Three patterns exist for local revenues from sales taxes.[55] First, the state can impose a state-wide tax and allocate a certain proportion or a fixed dollar amount to local governments. Ohio follows this

52. In Ohio, for example, the retail sales tax does not apply to services, food for consumption off the retailers' premises, transactions up to 30 cents, items for use in manufacturing and agriculture, and other specified items such as newspapers and magazines.

53. U. S. Bureau of the Census, *Summary of Governmental Finances in 1957*, Table 2 (Washington, 1958).

54. Ohio Department of Taxation—*Annual Report: 1957*, Table I (Columbus, 1958).

55. Due, John F.—*Sales Taxation* (University of Illinois Press, 1957), especially Chapter XV. See also C. V. Oster—*State Retail Sales Taxation* (Columbus, 1957).

approach in distributing some sales tax receipts to local governments. A stated sum is appropriated to the Local Government Fund, and also the School Foundation Program receives whatever is required to meet the State's commitment. The advantage here is a state-wide tax with state administration and little incentive to migrate in residence, shopping or plant location to avoid the tax. It is possible to distribute the tax uniformly perhaps on the basis of population or selectively to equalize financial capacity and service levels, a characteristic of the current Ohio School Foundation program. A tendency to ignore local autonomy is one disadvantage. A variation of this shortcoming is the danger of treating unlike local jurisdictions as if their needs were alike.

A second method allows each local government to levy its own tax, defining the tax base and setting the tax rate. This method has worked in cities which are very large or relatively isolated from major competitive trading centers and located in states without sales taxes. New York City and Denver are examples. Separate local taxes on top of state sales tax and with other cities nearby, in California before 1956, tended to cause chaos and inefficiency, with multiple tax returns for retailers, and to promote widespread evasion, uneven enforcement, and competition among taxing jurisdictions. The local sales tax seems to be satisfactory in New Orleans, which is relatively isolated from other major trading centers but is in a sales tax state. This is somewhat comparable to Cleveland or Cuyahoga County putting its own local sales tax on top of the Ohio state tax.

A third method is a combination of local with state sales taxes. This method is widely used now in Illinois and California. Illinois, in 1955, authorized municipalities to levy a sales tax at a rate up to ½ per cent on top of the state 2½ per cent rate.[56] Within two years, almost all Illinois cities had adopted the ½ per cent rate and were receiving about $50 million from this source (Chicago, almost half). The base of the local tax must correspond to the state tax base. Sales are taxed at the location of the store, regardless of where the buyer lives. The state administers the tax and retains 6 per cent as its collection charge. The retailer shows the local taxes on his return

---

56. Due, *op. cit.*, pp. 324-325. Illinois raised its state sales rate to 3% in July, 1959.

to the state. One disadvantage is an incentive for stores to locate outside city boundaries.

California, since 1956, has allowed counties to enact a 1 per cent sales tax, identical in base with the state 3 per cent tax.[57] The county contracts with the state for collection for which the state charges 1.7 per cent of the receipts. City taxes up to 1 per cent are credits against the county tax. A uniform rate exists throughout the county, reducing tax effect on shopping locations. Resistance to annexation to a city with a tax is reduced. Problems exist on allocating tax revenues from certain specialized activities such as contracting. Dormitory communities without shopping centers receive very little revenue. The collections go all to the county and municipalities, not to the schools. Pressure and bargaining are heavy in a county where some cities want a local sales tax and others do not. In California, practically all the major cities and counties had come under the state system except San Francisco and San Mateo County. San Francisco has its own 1 per cent city sales tax.

State administration minimizes problems of compliance and costs of collection. Enforcement is uniformly strict. There is still competition between retailers in neighboring tax and non-tax counties.

A retail sales tax has a relatively large revenue potential with a low tax rate. Its effects on location of economic activity is minor, except near the boundary between tax and non-tax areas. Policing of compliance is easy in the case of automobiles but more of a problem for other articles. A use tax is difficult to enforce. Collection costs for a local tax combined with an identical state tax would be very low. The yield from a sales tax is relatively stable, an important factor for local government. The tax yield, under an ad valorem tax, increases during a period of inflation, a favorable factor as inflation also pushes up government costs.

Sales taxes are considered inequitable, being highly regressive on the lower income groups. Exemption of food for home consumption, which averages almost 30 per cent of all consumer expenditures and a declining percentage the higher the consumer's income bracket, moderates the regressivity of the tax substantially.[58]

---

57. Ibid., pp. 320-323.
58. Donald C. Miller, "Sales Tax Progressivity Attributable to a Food Exemption," *National Tax Journal*, Vol. IV (June, 1951) pp. 148-159.

A second layer of sales tax, with a local tax imposed on the existing 3 per cent Ohio sales tax, is a disadvantage in that it increases the rate on a tax which is already at the top rate for nearby states. Local sales tax rates, if adopted, in the foreseeable future probably would not exceed 1 per cent. Higher rates would introduce competitive disadvantages and magnify inequities. Even a bad tax at low rates does not have economic and equity effects which are too serious. By current standards a 4 per cent rate would be high.[59] However, the administrative and compliance problems and costs are less than would be required for a new tax, assuming state administration on a cost basis using the state base.

A county- or metropolitan-wide tax would avoid competition between different taxing districts over rates and inequities between retailers in different jurisdictions. If the tax were devoted to financing either existing county functions or functions newly assumed by a metropolitan-area government, with reductions in the county property tax rate if possible, there would be no dispute over distribution of the proceeds.

Collections in Cuyahoga County of the Ohio 3 per cent retail sales tax have risen from $36.3 million in 1953 to $45.0 million in 1957, a gain of 25 per cent in four years. A 1 per cent local county-wide tax with identical coverage with the state tax and imposed on top of the state tax would have yielded $15 million in 1957. Changes by the state legislature in 1959 to expand the sales tax base by lowering exemptions to $.30 per purchase and extending coverage, sharply increased the revenue potential of a 1 per cent county tax, perhaps by one half.

A sales tax by one or a few municipalities is unlikely, due to the mobility of consumers and the large number of easily accessible shopping centers. For Cleveland alone a city sales tax would be quite inadvisable as it would probably accelerate the trend to shift buying from downtown to the suburban shopping centers.[60]

Total retail sales in Cuyahoga County in 1954 were $1,882 mil-

59. As of September 1, 1958, only in California and 10 cities in Alabama did total state and local sales tax equal 4%. (Tax increases in 1959 may produce 4% rates in several other states.) Source: Commerce Clearing House.

60. The ratio of retail sales in Cleveland to those in Cuyahoga County (including Cleveland) declined from 83.0% in 1940 to 80.5% in 1947 to 73.3% in 1954, and an estimated 69.5% in 1957. (See Table VI-21.)

lion, 30 per cent above 1948. Receipts of service industries totaled an additional $340 million. The distribution of sales between municipalities over the 1939-57 period is indicated by Table VI-23.

A sales tax distributed back to the municipality of retailer's location would ease the financial burden in areas with much retail business but not in purely residential jurisdictions. Distribution on a per capita basis (or per pupil basis, if to schools) would face the metropolitan problem more squarely and equitably. Communities with stores and shopping centers already enjoy the advantage of this property on the tax duplicate.

In summary, a local retail sales tax superimposed on the new state base would at 1 per cent rate produce about $22 million annually now and about $30 million by 1965. Authorization to use this tax would require state legislation. Administrative and compliance costs would be low. A local rate above 1 per cent is undesirable due to the regressive nature of the tax and to the effect the tax would have on location of retailing activity. The revenue capacity of the tax thus is limited. A 1 per cent local rate should be weighed carefully against a 0.5 per cent income tax rate or an additional four mills on the general property tax, which would produce equivalent amounts of revenue.

Value-Added Tax

The value-added tax is a business tax measured by the net addition to value made by each business. To avoid duplication or pyramiding of the tax, a business deducts the cost of materials from its gross income to get its receipts subject to tax. This is a tax on gross margin, i.e., revenue less cost of goods purchased. The tax applies to manufacturing, wholesale, retail, service and public utility industries. The rate of tax can be uniform for all or can vary by type of industry. Unlike the sales tax, which applies directly only to retail sales of most tangible goods in Ohio, the value-added tax would apply to all sales, regardless of the location of the buyer.

"The base of (the value-added tax) tends to be larger in the manufacturing area than in the retail area because capital and labor enjoy approximately the same return in all areas of economic activity

Table VI-23—Retail Sales by Municipality, Cleveland Metropolitan Area (In Thousands of Dollars)

JURISDICTION	YEAR			1957 Sales Figures	Percentage of Annual County Total
	1939	1948	1954		
Cuyahoga County	$506,426	$1,463,542	$1,861,700	$2,336,400	100.0
Cities					
Bay Village		327	4,500		
Bedford	3,244	12,256	20,600	29,100	1.2
Berea	2,810	9,263	18,100	27,700	1.2
Brooklyn		2,563	1,800		
Cleveland	420,426	1,178,241	1,364,200	1,624,600	69.5
Cleveland Heights	16,360	45,202	54,100	70,400	3.0
East Cleveland	10,213	31,865	36,500	42,900	1.8
Euclid	3,803	20,141	46,700	71,900	3.1
Fairview Park	496	4,463	24,470	46,900	2.0
Garfield Heights	2,216	7,792	11,000	13,800	0.6
Lakewood	21,825	53,675	73,700	95,600	4.1
Lyndhurst		1,144	3,000		
Maple Heights	1,121	4,585	15,800	27,100	1.2
Mayfield Heights	369	912	11,100		
North Olmsted	657	2,656	4,700		
Parma	2,869	9,779	27,500	45,000	1.9
Rocky River	2,981	10,666	14,300	18,100	0.8
Shaker Heights	5,237	22,716	40,500	55,500	2.4
South Euclid	1,788	16,578	22,500	39,000	1.7
University Heights		6,395	8,700	11,000	0.4
Villages					
Brecksville		1,390	3,300		
Broadview Heights		309			
Brook Park		1,010	1,703		
Chagrin Falls	2,563	7,906	12,400	16,100	0.7
Independence		1,124	3,400		
Middleburg Heights		1,250			
Newburgh Heights	516	1,013	700		
North Royalton		669	2,200		
Parma Heights		806	2,000		
Solon		1,390	2,100		
Strongsville		3,254	3,600		
Warrensville Heights		2,768	3,000		
Westlake		2,168	3,600		
Remainder of County	6,932	7,266	20,160		

Sources: U. S. Department of Commerce, Bureau of Census, U. S. Census of Business, Vol. III, Retail Trade-Area Statistics; 1939, 1948, 1954. (Vol. II, part 2). 1957 Data from "Survey of Buying Power," *Sales Management* (May, 1958).

and a greater portion of the selling price of manufactured goods consists of labor and utilized capital." [61]

The justification for the application of the tax to manufacturing is the contribution made by local government services to the value added by production. The benefits are received by all businesses, not just the profitable ones, thus justifying a value-added tax rather than an income tax. A value-added tax provides a much broader base than an income tax and thus produces an equivalent revenue at a lower tax rate than would be required with an income tax.

This tax takes its bite at the point where economic value is created and before it is divided among the factors of production. In this way, the tax is neutral between different types of economic activity and between wages, rent, and profit. The division of the gross margin after tax is left to competitive bargaining between land, labor, and capital. A property tax, a payroll tax, or a corporation income tax, on the other hand, would impinge primarily on particular recipients of income.

The value-added tax avoids duplication of the tax on ingredients and materials as they move along in the production process. In contrast, a turnover tax would tax the same raw material several times, for example as wheat is sold successively by the farmer, miller, baker, and retailer. The deduction for materials purchased makes the value-added tax neutral between firms performing several stages of production themselves and separate firms which each perform a separate step as a product moves to market.

Two versions of value-added taxes are used in the United States. The State of Michigan has had this tax since 1953. The present rates of tax are .65 per cent of adjusted receipts (a modified version of value added) of all businesses other than public utilities and .15 per cent for utilities. This tax yielded $64.3 million during the 1957 fiscal year, about 5 per cent of total state and local taxes in Michigan. Almost half of the total amount was from manufacturing industries.[62]

The other version is the gross receipts business license tax, with

---

61. *Summary Digest of Michigan Tax Study Staff Reports,* "The Business Activities Tax," p. 2 (Citizens Research Council of Michigan, Detroit, June 30, 1958). See also, *Michigan Tax Study Staff Papers 1958,* Ch. 7 (Lansing, 1958).

62. *Ibid.,* pp. 1-2.

the tax rate varying between different types of business according to the gross profit margin usual in business. Many Virginia cities use this tax. The rate schedule is based on retail trade with rates for different lines of business as percentages of the retail trade.[63]

The Regional Fiscal Survey in the Northern Virginia study recommended that the existing systems be replaced by a uniform tax on value added. The then-existing systems of rates varying with average gross margins of different lines of business failed to achieve fair treatment.[64]

A value-added tax in metropolitan Cleveland at a uniform low rate of say 0.5 per cent on a base of at about $4 billion would have produced $20 million or more in 1956. More than half of these receipts would have come from manufacturing. Value added by manufacturing in the Cleveland Standard Metropolitan Area was $2.9 billion in 1956, about a 90 per cent increase over 1947.[65]

A value-added tax would be a direct alternative to local taxes on business income, payroll, and sales and an indirect alternative to higher property taxes on real and tangible property used in business. Apparently, Ohio municipalities could adopt this tax now with no clash with the Constitution or statutes and without conflict with the pre-emption doctrine.

The incidence of this tax would depend on the relative bargaining strength of the buyers, the owners, the employees, and the suppliers. A low rate of tax would have little adverse effect on area firms competing in regional and national markets, perhaps less than income taxes or higher property taxes with the same revenue yield.

---

63. Some rates of tax per $100 of receipts in Arlington, Virginia, were $0.18 on retail merchants, $0.65 on professional occupations, $0.36 on personal service occupation, $0.18 on contractors, and $0.13 on wholesalers and manufacturers. The level of rates and the relation between rates for different occupations varied substantially, even between adjacent cities. This tax yielded between about 3 and 10% of all local revenues in these Virginia cities in 1953-54. Northern Virginia Regional Planning and Economic Development Commission, *Northern Virginia Fiscal Survey*, Ch. 7 (Alexandria, Va., 1957).

64. A sample of over 600 businesses in Alexandria and Arlington indicated sharp inequities between taxpayers in the same line of business as well as between taxpayers in different industries. Businessmen regarded the existing license system as unfair. *Ibid.*, pp. 83-86.

65. U. S. Department of Commerce, Bureau of the Census, *Annual Survey of Manufacturers;* 1956, pp. 66-67.

Excise Taxes

Many municipalities in Ohio use the admissions tax, which was vacated by the State in 1947. Other products and services which are popular as bases for excise taxes are pre-empted by the Ohio sales and excise taxes and by the state monopoly of liquor store sales. Possible bases for new local excise taxes would be 1) receipts of municipally owned utilities, including water, sewer, and the Cleveland municipal electric utility, and 2) motor vehicles.

Fifteen cities in Cuyahoga County reported collection of $464,714 from admissions taxes in 1956. This sum represented 0.3 per cent of revenues from local sources in that year. The tax is generally a 3 per cent rate on admissions with exemption for non-profit performances and activities.

Excise taxes on municipally owned utilities—water, sewer, and electric—provide a means to get revenues for the general fund of the municipalities. Any profits on the municipal operation of utilities in Ohio is segregated in the utility funds and is not available to finance general government functions. Such taxes could be levied either by the local municipalities or on a county-wide basis. The City of Cleveland operates the water and sewer services which serve most of the metropolitan area, but Cleveland would receive only the tax levied on utility users in the city limits.

A tax on the sales by the Cleveland municipal electric utility might be supported on the grounds that its competitors have to pay a state 3 per cent public utility excise tax, from which municipally owned utilities are exempt. A 3 per cent excise tax would have yielded Cleveland almost $240,000 in 1957, on receipts of $7.9 million.

The revenue from water utilities was about $16 million and sewerage charges about $2.3 million in 1956. A 3 per cent tax on these bills would have provided about $550,000 of revenue to local governments in the county.

A tax on municipal transit operations is not suggested for consideration because of the precarious financial position of these operations and because of the elastic demand for their service, i.e., the ready availability of a substitute—private motor vehicles—and diminished use of public transit facilities would further increase the demands and therefore public expenditures for roads and parking.

Taxes on utilities would yield a sizeable, steady stream of revenue. The tax base would be broad and would affect all residents in the county. Utility taxes would be regressive, as utility bills are a larger part of the expenditures of low income families than of those in higher income brackets. Taxes on business use of utility service would tend to be passed on to consumers of the products. Increased rates for water and sewerage have been necessary recently to cover the costs of expanding, modernizing, and improving the existing systems. A further charge now might be undesirable and especially inequitable for the lower-income users.

Thus on grounds of equity and possibly the competitive cost position of present and future manufacturers locating in the area, excise taxes on water and sewer utilities should be considered carefully and probably given a low ranking relative to other revenue sources.

Excise taxes on motor vehicles. Streets and highways are costing local governments about twice the amount of earmarked revenues distributed by the State from the motor vehicles licenses and gasoline tax.[66] The cost of maintenance will rise with more highways and freeways and with higher standards on the better new roads. The problem is especially severe for cities which have full responsibility for the maintenance of state highways and county roads within their boundaries.

As an alternative to putting motor vehicles in the property tax laws, several steps might be taken to bring revenues from street and highway users up to the size of the expenditures for this function. Any of these steps would necessitate action by the State. 1) The State could increase the distribution to the municipalities out of existing taxes for streets and highways. This is not likely with the State in need of more funds for both highway and general fund pur-

---

66. See Tables VI-24 and 25, for the revenues and expenditures for streets and highways.

poses. 2) The State might increase the gas tax and/or motor vehicle license fee and distribute all or a large part of the additional revenue to the local governments with responsibilities for roads. 3) The State might grant local governments the right to levy an additional license fee, up to a maximum of perhaps $10 on private cars and $25 on other vehicles. 4) The State might include motor vehicles under the property tax, as discussed earlier under property taxes. Administration of a property tax would be easy with co-operation between the Ohio Department of Motor Vehicles and the County Auditor and Treasurer; no State motor vehicle license could be issued without a tax receipt on the vehicle from the county.

A moderate local tax on motor vehicles, say $10 on private cars and $20 on commercial vehicles, would yield about $7.0 million in the county, based on 1956 registrations in the Cleveland area. This yield compares with the $14.1 million excess of street and highway expenditures over earmarked receipts in 1956. This tax could be either a local tax or an addition to the existing State license fee, distributed to the local government.[67]

Additional taxes on motor vehicles would be justified on the benefit or ability principles. The present highway-user taxes are inadequate to pay the costs of construction and maintenance of existing and new streets and highways. Highway users are now being subsidized from property taxes and other general fund revenues. Motorists and truckers have an Ohio constitutional amendment earmarking all highway-user taxes for highways. It might be argued that since owners of motor vehicles do not contribute as such to the general fund, they should not expect general revenues to go for highways. This approaches the cost equals benefit principle.

As expenditures on autos are approximately a constant proportion of income at all income levels,[68] additional flat rate taxes on autos would be regressive. Licenses or property taxes based on value of the auto would vary more closely with ability to pay.

------

67. In 1956, 372 cities in the United States including 135 over 10,000 population imposed motor vehicle license taxes. Several different bases were used for the tax, the more common ones being flat amount per vehicle weight, horsepower, and value. *Municipal Nonproperty Taxes*, pp. 27-28.

68. Musgrave and others, *op. cit.*, p. 11.

Option to use vehicle taxes locally would increase local autonomy. There would seem to be little or no adverse equity and economic effects.

State-Local Fiscal Relations in Ohio

States assign government functions and allocate revenue sources to local governments. In addition, for a variety of reasons—statewide interest in a particular activity, the superior revenue sources available to the state, incentives for minimum local standards, or the wish to equalize varying revenue capacities—the state government provides grants to local governments. This section examines briefly inter-governmental payments, especially state-local, in Ohio and the Cleveland Metropolitan Area.

Local governments in Ohio received on the average one third of all their revenues from the state and federal governments. The average local government in the Cleveland area received only 22.4 per cent of all revenue from intergovernmental payments, as shown in Table VI-24. Only cities in Cuyahoga County receive aid in proportion to State Aid going to different classes of Ohio local governments. The schools in the Cleveland area receive only about half the

Table VI-24—Intergovernmental Revenues as Per Cent of Total Revenues, Local Governments in Ohio and in Cuyahoga County, 1956

	OHIO		CUYAHOGA COUNTY	
GOVERNMENTAL UNITS	Total Revenues (In millions of Dollars)	Per Cent from State and Federal Govts.	Total Revenues (In millions of Dollars)	Per Cent from State and Federal Govts.
All Local Governments	1,209.1	33.6	249.6	22.4
County	252.0	52.3	43.3	47.7
Cities	356.1	18.6	103.0	19.0
Villages	28.1	29.8⎫	7.1 *	15.2 *
Townships	43.3	45.5⎭		
School Districts	529.6	34.2	89.2	16.5

* Detail not available.
Note: Library revenues not shown separately in Cuyahoga County. Libraries received no state aid.
Source: Ohio Department of Taxation, "Ohio State and Local Government Revenues", RE-1, 7-58.

proportion of State Aid received throughout the State. The ratios differ greatly for villages and townships but the amounts of money spent by these governments in the Cleveland area is low. Higher levels of service and greater tax capacity account for the smaller fraction of intergovernmental aid for Cleveland area governments. The Ohio school program includes a strong equalization factor for which most of the larger Cleveland area school districts do not qualify.

Another comparison examines the proportion of state tax collected and State Aid distributed in the Cleveland area. Only rough estimates of the place of collection of many of the taxes is possible, and these figures therefore should be recognized as rough estimates and used with caution. An estimated 18.4 per cent of all state taxes are paid in Cuyahoga County but the local governments receive back only about 14 per cent of all intergovernmental payments, shown in Table VI-25. It has not been possible to separate federal payments, but they are too small to affect the result.

The conclusion of this section is that state aids are not a solution to the revenue problem of the Cleveland Metropolitan Area. As the highest income area in Ohio, state taxes to finance more liberal State Aid programs would probably collect more revenues in the Cleveland area than they would return. The only way that metropolitan Cleveland would gain would be to revise the distribution formulas for State Aid to eliminate the equalization factor and emphasize wealth and property as the basis for distribution. For obvious reasons, such a change would probably be neither politically possible nor economically desirable.

Financing of Streets and Highways

Streets and highways in Ohio are financed in a large part by direct charges on highway users. The State of Ohio in fiscal year 1956 collected about $220 million from highway taxes and license fees, excluding tolls on the Ohio Turnpike. The State shares these taxes with the counties, municipalities, and townships, distributing approximately $103 millions to local governments in 1956. The State

Table VI-25—State Taxes Paid in Cuyahoga County and State Aid Received by Local Governments in Cuyahoga County, State Fiscal Year 1955-56
(In Thousands of Dollars)

State Tax Paid	State Collections	Collections in Cuyahoga County	Per Cent collected in Cuyahoga County
Retail sales and use tax	230,709.7	48,108.4	20.9
State situs intangible tax	23,973.9	6,508.2	27.1 †
Public utility excise	30,395.4	6,383.0	21.0 ‡
Cigarette excise	24,704.7	5,188.0	21.0 ‡
Beer, wine, malt beverage	23,343.4	6,069.3	26.0 ‡
Foreign insurance companies	22,184.5	4,658.7	21.0 ‡
Liquor gallonage & store profits	38,597.3	10,034.3	26.0 ‡
Corporation franchise	21,825.2	4,583.3	21.0 ‡
Horse racing	6,428.3	3,072.1	48.0 †
Motor vehicle fuel taxes	144,857.1	22,500.0	15.5
Motor vehicle license fees	50,003.1	7,200.0	14.0
Highway use tax	11,808.4	810.0	10.0 §
Other highway taxes, fees, etc.	22,152.8	3,322.9	15.0 ‡
Liquor permits	7,459.2	1,647.6	22.0 †
Inheritance tax (state share)	4,901.4	1,738.2	35.0 †
Property tax (World War II bonus)	4,358.7	920.1	21.0 †
Total	667,703.1	122,743.1	18.4

State Aid Received	Ohio	Cuyahoga County	County/State (Per Cent)
Counties, Municipalities, Townships			
Local Government Fund	43,572.7	11,822.6	27.1
Gas Tax & Motor Veh. Licenses	110,720.7	12,709.8	11.5
Other Federal & State Aid	71,631.8	16,755.2	23.4
Sub-Total	225,925.2	41,387.6	18.3
School Districts	163,196.1 *	14,737.6	9.2
TOTAL	389,021.3	56,025.1	14.1

* Average of federal and state distributions in 1955-56 and 1956-57 fiscal years for schools. Other figures are actual 1956 calendar year data.
 † Actual.
 ‡ Estimate.
 § Per cent of payments by Ohio trucks.
 Sources: State collections and distributions, Ohio Dept. of Taxation, *Annual Report-1957* and other releases.
 Notes: State-levied but locally collected taxes, such as local-situs intangibles and local half of inheritance tax not included. State charges for universities, parks, etc. not included.

received in addition $20 million of federal highway funds in 1957, and larger amounts in later years. Article 12, Section 5a of the Ohio Constitution prohibits the diversion of highway revenues to any other use.

Table VI-26—Distribution of Ohio Highway User Taxes, 1956

	RETAINED BY STATE	DISTRIBUTED AS STATE AID			
		Total	County	Munici-palities	Townships
Motor Vehicle Fuel Tax * 5c/gal.					
Distribution (Per Cent)	65	35	13 †	15 ‡	7 §
Dollar Amount (In Thousands of Dollars)					
State Total	138,926	47,557	17,600	20,352	9,605
Cuyahoga County	...	5,158	210	4,916	33
Motor Vehicle License Tax					
Distribution (Per Cent)	0	100	61 **	34 ††	5 ‡‡
Dollar Amount (In Thousands of Dollars)					
State Total	...	53,827	37,608	15,368	852
Cuyahoga County	...	7,551	4,451	3,100	1

* The effect of the additional tax of 2c a gallon, enacted in 1959, is not included.
† Distributed equally among the 88 counties.
‡ Distributed in proportion to vehicles registered in one municipality to vehicles registered in all municipalities.
§ Distributed equally among the townships. An additional 2c a gallon tax was added in 1959. Its distribution is not included here.
** Of the total distributed, 47 percent goes to counties in proportion to the number of vehicles registered, 9 percent on the basis of road mileage, and 5 percent equally among the 88 counties.
†† This amount is distributed according to municipality of residence or place of business. If not in municipality, this is added to amount going into the county.
‡‡ Divided among townships on basis of road mileage.

The State retains 65 per cent of the gas tax revenue, as indicated in Table VI-26. The remainder for local governments is distributed quite differently between counties and townships, on the one hand, and cities and villages, on the other. Each county in Ohio receives the same amount of gasoline tax money annually, regardless of area, miles of county roads, motor vehicles registered, or population. The same is true for each township. In Cuyahoga County, for example, Riveredge Township with ninety-two people and 0.52 square miles receives the same dollar amount as Olmsted Township with 4,278 population and 10.63 square miles of area. The distribution to cities and villages is in proportion to vehicle registration. On this basis the municipalities in Cuyahoga County received $4.9 millon, almost one quarter of the amount distributed to all municipalities in Ohio.

All revenues derived from motor vehicle license fees, after deduction of expenses for the state Bureau of Motor Vehicles, Highway Patrol, and Highway Safety Department, are distributed to local governments, as shown in Table VI-26.

Cuyahoga County and other populous areas fare very well under this tax as 81 per cent is distributed to the local governments on the basis of the place of registration of the vehicles. Under this formula, Cuyahoga County and its municipalities and townships shared about $7,555,000 in 1956, about one-seventh of the license fees distributed by the State.

EFFECT OF CHANGE IN STATUS FROM VILLAGE TO CITY

The finances of most growing municipalities suffer a severe jolt when the village becomes a city, due to the present allocation of responsibility for road maintenance and the present distribution of state highway aid funds.

In Ohio, the State Highway Department maintains and resurfaces state highways outside of cities. The County has responsibility to maintain and resurface county roads in villages and townships. When a village attains a population of 5,000 in a census year, it automatically becomes a city under Ohio law. The State and County, however, are not responsible for maintenance and improvement of highways and roads within cities. The shift to city status thus requires the new city to finance activities which previously have been covered by the state and county governments.

But no allocation of additional state revenue accompanies this shift of responsibilities. Villages share in the distribution of state gas tax and motor vehicle license fees under the same formula that applies to cities.

A spectacular example of the effect of this shift of responsibility will occur when the Village of Independence officially becomes a city following the 1960 Federal Census. Independence, in 1958, already had an estimated population of 6,334. As a city, it will become

responsible for maintenance and repaving of 6.2 miles of state highways and 16 miles of county roads, beginning in 1961. The State and
the County are expected to share half the burden of these costs for
three years, to ease the transition to city status. The service director
of Independence estimates that capital expenditures of $100,000 for
vehicles, equipment, garages, hoists, and tools will be necessary to
handle the additional work. The annual operating costs of the transition period 1961-63 are estimated at about $80,000 a year, $55,000
for direct labor and materials and the remainder for office help, engineering, insurance, and other overhead. Beginning with 1964, the
annual operating expense at present price levels would be more than
$130,000 above 1956 expenditures. Independence spent $67,445
($64,132 for operating expense) on streets and highways in 1956.
Total village expenditures for all purposes other than debt retirement were $270,000.

Westlake did shift from village to city status in 1957. The City
Clerk estimates that the *added* annual cost to Westlake as a city for
streets and highways in 1958 is $40,000, over the cost for this func-
tion as a village. Total operating expenditures for streets and highways in 1956 by Westlake were $40,536. The capital outlay in 1956
was unusually high at $60,996. Westlake had to assume responsibility
for fourteen miles of state highways and several miles of county
roads, in addition to its thirty-seven miles of city streets and alleys.
The additional $40,000 in 1958 went for salaries, materials such as
salt, cinders, and paint, and new equipment. The State, according to
the City Clerk, discontinued all maintenance, but the County helped
by some snow plowing, cutting weeds, and other maintenance in
1958.

The Village of Independence is only one example of the
thirteen present villages in Cuyahoga County which are expected
to shift to city status as a result of the 1960 Census. In the following
year, a sharp reduction in county responsibility and a proportion-
ately sharp increase for the new cities will occur with no corresponding change in the allocation of state funds.

The present formulae for distribution of state motor vehicle
license and gas tax funds do not differentiate between villages and
cities, although their responsibilities and costs differ substantially.

Also the distribution of funds to the county and the state highway department do not change as the new cities assume responsibility for more roads.

The State Highway Department is also relieved of responsibility for maintenance when a village becomes a city. This change, especially after a census year, is probably significant enough to justify a reallocation of highway funds between the state and the local governments. The result of the 1950 Census, for example, shifted twenty-five Ohio municipalities from villages to cities and returned one city to village status.

This non-parallel allocation of responsibilities and funds indicates that state statutes should be changed so that the responsibility and the funds for streets and highways should go together to the same governmental jurisdiction.

State Aid for streets and highways over the period covered by this study, 1940-56, has covered 47 to 50 per cent of total local expenditures for this purpose. (See Table VI-27.) Expenditures include both operating expenses and capital outlays for streets, roads, highways, bridges, street lighting, street cleaning, sidewalks, and traffic lights. The townships usually meet about all of highway expenses from State Aid. The other jurisdictions utilize general revenues about equal in amount to the State Aid they receive to finance their highway expenditures. Some street and highway capital outlays are financed by special assessments and by borrowing.

Summary

In conclusion, revenue problems of local governments in the Cleveland Metropolitan Area result from the fact that the economic boundaries and the local government boundaries do not coincide. The economic metropolis includes many separate governmental units. The governmental jurisdictions on the economic boundaries are usually partially in, and partially outside of, the metropolitan economy, with the changes occurring rapidly as the metropolitan area expands. Some of the more difficult problems arise in the split jurisdictions and the jurisdictions in transition.

Table VI-27—Financing of Streets and Highways in Cleveland Metropolitan Area: Comparison of State Aid and Local Expenditures by Type of Jurisdiction, 1940, 1950, 1956

Year and Jurisdiction	State Aid (In Thousands of Dollars)	Local Expenditure (In Thousands of Dollars)	State Aid/ Local Expenditures (Per Cent)
1940			
County	1,918.1	3,789.7	50.6
Cities	2,521.9	5,489.9	45.9
Villages	93.5	169.1	55.3
Townships	7.7	6.1	126.2
Total	4,541.2	9,454.8	48.0
1950			
County	2,898.9	3,864.8	75.0
Cities	4,566.8	11,215.6	40.7
Villages	243.7	433.8	56.2
Townships	21.6	4.0	530.0
Total	7,731.0	15,518.2	49.8
1956			
County	4,661.1	6,279.2	74.2
Cities	7,412.5	19,074.3	38.9
Villages	602.3	1,386.4	43.4
Townships	33.9	34.6	98.0
Total	13,709.7	26,774.5	47.5

Many of the financial problems of the metropolitan area would disappear if a single local government had jurisdiction over the metropolitan area. Instead, 108 local governments operate in Cuyahoga County. Every person and business in metropolitan Cleveland is under five local governments—the county, the metropolitan park district, municipality or township, school district, and library district.

Providing more funds, choice of revenue sources in view of equity, economic, and administrative effects, and equalization to help the jurisdictions with the smallest tax capacity relative to their needs for current operations and capital outlay are the problems facing Greater Cleveland. A summary of the revenue findings is presented in Chapter VIII.

COMPARED TO 1940, THE 1956 DEBT POSITION OF the governments that comprised the Cleveland Metropolitan Area grew more favorable relative to their resources. This was not only true in the aggregate, but was also true for most individual jurisdictions. Thus, while there were fourteen municipalities which had net over-all debts in excess of 16 per cent of their assessed valuation in 1940, there were none in 1956; and the median net overall debt for cities fell from 16 per cent in 1940 to 8 per cent in 1956.

In the ring immediately surrounding the older core area where the high debt was concentrated in 1940, there was, by 1956, a general reduction of debt relative to resources. In some fourteen out of seventy-eight taxing districts in the Cleveland Metropolitan Area, the ratio of debt to assessed valuation increased, but the maximum of 15.4 per cent was below the median for all cities in 1940 and considerably below the 48.4 per cent maximum in 1940.

As shown in Map VII-1 the net overall debt divides the Cleveland Metropolitan Area into two distinct geographic groups; that within the core area and that outside the core area. Not a single municipality in the core area had a net overall debt in excess of 5.4 per cent (the minimum city net overall debt in 1940). Every municipality outside the core area had a net overall debt in excess of that same 5.4 per cent figure with the exception of municipalities that are included in school districts with considerable industry, and the village of Orange, which was just on the borderline with a debt of 5.1 per cent. In every other case, the net overall debt of every municipality outside the core area exceeded that of every municipality within the core.

The higher level of debt outside the core area is due primarily, if not exclusively, to the higher ratio of school debt to assessed valuation outside the core area than within the core area. As shown in Map VII-4, all other school districts, with the exceptions of the highly industrialized Cuyahoga Heights and Euclid School Districts and the Independence School Districts, had school debts in excess of 4 per cent of their assessed valuations.

The distribution of net municipal debt (i.e., debt for municipal purposes only) shows no such clear cut geographic pattern as does the school debt. As shown in Map VII-3, the extremes of high and low municipal debt are outside the core area, although the core area does contain a number of municipalities with a low net debt. The high debt areas are centered around the rapidly growing Parma area, and the Richmond Height, Highland Heights, Lyndhurst area. Bedford, with a municipal debt in excess of 5 per cent of its assessed valuation, also appears high.

The importance of debt for the metropolitan area as a whole and for the individual jurisdictions follows from the fact that local governments must rely on long-term borrowing for major sources of funds. And, as was indicated in Chapter III, 16.61 per cent of the funds spent by governments in the Cleveland Metropolitan Area in 1956 came from such borrowing. It will be the major purpose of this chapter to focus upon debt incurred by local governments as a result of long-term borrowing.

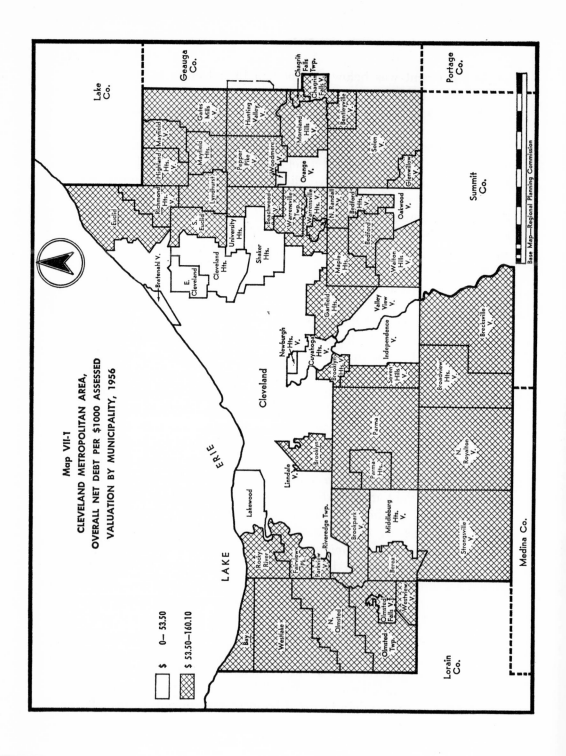

Map VII-1
CLEVELAND METROPOLITAN AREA,
OVERALL NET DEBT PER $1000 ASSESSED
VALUATION BY MUNICIPALITY, 1956

$ 0— 53.50

$ 53.50—160.10

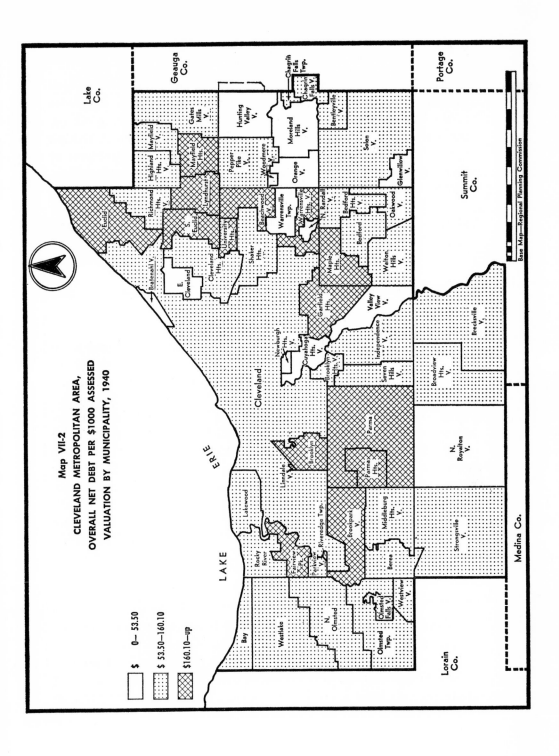

Map VII-2

CLEVELAND METROPOLITAN AREA,
OVERALL NET DEBT PER $1000 ASSESSED
VALUATION BY MUNICIPALITY, 1940

$ 0— 53.50

$ 53.50—160.10

$160.10—up

The initial portion will deal with the general problems of borrowing, the various justifications for resorting to this particular method of financing, the various ways in which borrowing occurs, and the legal limitations upon local debt in Ohio. The discussion applies primarily to local government borrowing. The problems of short-term borrowing, which tend generally to be different in nature, will be excluded insofar as it is possible to do so.

In the second portion of the chapter, debt within the Cleveland Metropolitan Area will be considered both historically and currently, as will also the cost of servicing the debt.

Principles and Methods of Borrowing by Local Governments

Many justifications have been presented, some valid and some invalid, for using borrowing as a source of funds for a local government. The most commonly accepted idea is that long term borrowing should be used in conjunction with capital expenditures, although all capital expenditures need not be financed through borrowing. This provides the means by which the cost of a particular governmental expenditure can be related to the benefit from that expenditure. Long term borrowing has also been justified during emergencies or where substantial savings may be achieved by refunding operations. In each of these cases the particular debt obligation, i.e., the kind of bond, depends on the nature of the borrowing opportunities and the legally authorized and economically feasible alternatives.

THE THEORY OF BENEFIT RECEIVED

Certain types of outlays give rise to benefits for an identifiable group of persons or properties; for example, results from the construction of a sewerage system or the laying of sidewalks. Here it is generally felt that the most equitable method of financing such long term projects is by special levies against the property owners who directly benefit from the expenditure, but to collect such a levy in a single lump sum may impose an unduly harsh burden upon these taxpayers. Consequently, the municipality may borrow for the purpose. Such bonds are called special assessment bonds and the repayment of debt and interest by the benefited taxpayer can take place over time and in a series of less burdensome payments.[1]

Even where the benefits from some capital expenditures may not be assignable to any specific taxpayer or property but accrue to all taxpayers and property within a community, as is the case in the construction of public schools, a city hall, a police or fire station, or the construction of a major highway, borrowing may be justified. For just as in the case where only some of the taxpayers benefit, it may be felt that the cost of such outlays is too high to be paid in a single lump sum and so borrowing is used to spread the cost over time.

An additional justification for borrowing for expenditures of general benefit is that the benefit is usually spread over long periods of time. Therefore, the most equitable method of financing such projects is to spread the burden of cost to both present and future taxpayers. However, the cost of such projects must be met at the time of construction, so the use of borrowing, with present and future taxpayers repaying the debt over time, makes it possible to meet the immediate cost of construction and also apportion the cost to both present and future taxpayers. This type of borrowing entails the use of general obligation bonds.[2]

Another broad justification for local borrowing under the benefit theory is that borrowing is a means by which self-supporting public enterprises can be constructed or acquired. These include not only the Public Service Enterprises (transit systems, water works, public electric light and power facilities), but also such Miscellaneous Commercial Activities as lakeport and airport facilities and such recreational facilities as swimming pools, auditoriums, etc. The distinctive feature of such public enterprises is that their services are generally

---

1. Special assessment bonds in Ohio are serviced by the special levy against certain properties but still are an obligation of the borrowing governments. That is, they are backed by the full faith and credit of the governments.

2. General obligation bonds are an obligation of the entire community and are normally serviced from taxes paid by all the taxpayers within the taxing jurisdiction.

provided in exchange for "user charges." That is, those who use such facilities pay directly for their use.

However, the initial cost of constructing such projects must be met immediately, and so borrowing is a means by which such projects can be initially financed. Bonds for such purposes are usually revenue bonds, and the interest and principal are met out of user charges collected as the debt matures. The bonds usually do not represent a lien upon taxpayers in general but rather are an obligation only of the specific enterprise.

EMERGENCY

An exception to the principle that borrowing should be related to capital outlays occurs during emergencies, when borrowing is sometimes necessary to meet extraordinary expense resulting from fire, flood, or other major disasters. This is particularly true when the alternative—meeting these expenses out of current revenue—would result in the serious curtailment of normal government services. Borrowing for this purpose may be either long term or short term (less than one year), and usually is a general obligation of the borrowing government.

REFUNDING

The final major argument for borrowing is for purposes of refunding, or borrowing to meet the principal payments on existing debt. Refunding may be justified in two instances. The first is when it is necessary to avoid defaulting on existing debt. When the source usually used to meet debt payment is delinquent, it may be that the only way to prevent defaulting is to borrow additional funds. This, however, is usually very costly because high interest rates are generally demanded in the case of refunding. The second occasion for refunding is of an entirely different nature. If a municipality has previously borrowed at high rates of interest, and its obligations are "callable," i.e., they can be redeemed prior to maturity, it may be possible to achieve substantial savings by borrowing at currently low rates of interest and redeeming the existing debt on which a higher rate is being paid.

SHORT TERM BORROWING

There are various other reasons why local governments borrow, but they pertain to borrowing for shorter periods of time, usually less than one year, and have been excluded from general consideration. Such borrowing is used to finance expenditures which must be made prior to the time that normal revenues are received, or it is used because funds must be obtained for a project which is to be financed ultimately by long term bonded indebtedness, but for which, for a variety of reasons, the long term borrowing is delayed.

UNDESIRABLE LONG TERM BORROWING

As has been shown there are perfectly valid reasons for long term borrowing by local governments, but there are also circumstances in which such borrowing should not be used as a source of funds. The pre-eminent situation for which there is no justification is that in which local governments borrow to meet current expenditures, the exception to this being the unusual emergency circumstances noted above. Borrowing for current expenditures is inherently wasteful in that it means additional costs with no related additional benefit. Furthermore, the incurrence of debt for this purpose almost inevitably leads to financial difficulty. If a local government is unable to meet the costs of current expenditures from current tax revenues or other available current sources, the solution is to curtail current expenditures or find new revenue sources. To suppose that future revenues will be sufficient to meet future current needs and service debt incurred for past current expenditures is to court fiscal disaster.

A second instance when increasing long term debt is not justified is when the level of existing debt is already too high relative to available resources. The incurrence of additional debt would mean that taxpayers would be faced with a serious curtailment of municipal services or, alternatively, an unacceptable additional tax burden to service the debt.

A third circumstance under which the use of borrowing may be both undesirable and unnecessary also exists in the case of some larger local governments, where capital requirements follow a regular pattern of substantial magnitude. When this is the case it is possible to achieve the advantages of borrowing as a method of relating cost to benefit, without incurring the cost of borrowing, the interest costs. This is done through the use of a pay-as-you-go system of financing capital outlays. Every year a certain portion of tax revenues is allocated for capital expenditures or is placed in a "capital fund," and capital outlays are made from this fund. Through the use of capital budgeting, the cost to taxpayers is spread over time, but because no actual borrowing takes place there is no interest to be paid. It should be stressed that such a system, while highly desirable, is feasible only when capital outlays follow a regular pattern and is desirable only when the yearly levy for capital purposes is maintained at a rate sufficiently high to insure that the desired level of expenditures is being sustained. Furthermore, the virtues of a pay-as-you-go system should never be controlling when its preservation necessitates the avoidance of needed expenditures.

There are other circumstances which make borrowing undesirable, but they are generally technical in nature. For instance, at a particular time the market for municipal securities (i.e., securities of all local governments are considered as municipals) may be overcrowded with potential long term borrowers so that the interest rates demanded are at a very high level. In such a situation, it may be possible and desirable for a local government to defer its long-term borrowing by borrowing for a short term or deferring its expenditures until the market situation improves. This, of course, assumes that the market will improve and not become even worse by the time that the long term borrowing can no longer be postponed. A similar technical reason for deferring the issuance of bonds may be that a government's current credit rating is low and there is reason to believe that it will improve in the near future. This may be the case if a marked increase in the tax base is anticipated in the immediate future, as, for example, when the construction of a large industrial plant is anticipated.

Statutory Limitations on Borrowing
by Local Governments in Ohio

Borrowing by local governments is regulated by state law.[3] This section will be devoted to a brief sumary of the legal restrictions governing borrowing in Ohio. The following four aspects will be considered: the limits on the amount of borrowing, the limitations on the types of bonds which can be used, the limits on the maturity of bonds, and finally an evaluation of the legal restrictions, particularly the statutory debt limit.

LIMITS ON THE QUANTITY OF DEBT

Under the Uniform Bond Law, that part of the debt of counties, municipalities, school districts and townships which is directly limited is defined as the statutory debt. There is no absolute limit, however, upon the gross indebtedness of any of these governments. Debt for purposes of legal limitations is broadly defined as gross debt outstanding at par value less the amount held in sinking funds or other bond retirement funds and less bonds or notes issued in anticipation of collection of special assessments or current revenues and public utility mortgage or revenue bonds. In addition there are specific exemptions which apply to each class of government. The net debt limitation for each class of government is always expressed as a percentage of assessed valuation on the tax duplicate at the time bonds are issued. A summary of the Ohio statutory limitations is presented in Table VII-1.

There is an indirect limitation upon debt which applies to all classes of governments as the result of the constitutional ten mill

---

3. In Ohio, the bulk of the legal restrictions upon the borrowing of local governments are included in the "Uniform Bond Law" which is Chapter 133 of the Revised Code. Additional direct limitations exist in Article XVIII, Sections 3 and 12 of the Constitution and indirect limitations in Article XII, Section 2. The Uniform Bond Law was enacted April 21, 1927, and governs the issuance of bonds for county, cities, villages, townships, and school districts. Prior to this time different provisions of the law governed the issuance of securities by each of these subdivisions.

An excellent summarization of the Ohio laws can be found in *State of Ohio, Creating Municipal Debt*, Hayden, Miller and Co., Cleveland, Ohio, 1953.

Table VII-1—Ohio Statutory Limitations on Net Debt, 1956

Government	Limits on Quantity *	Limits on Type of Bonds
COUNTY		
General Obligation and	3% of 1st $100 million of assessed valuation plus 1½% of any excess	Straight serials, may be callable, may be registered, and may not be sold at less than par plus accrued interest.
Special Assessment	1% of 1st $100 Million plus ½% of excess unvoted	
CITY & VILLAGE		
General Obligation and	5% of assessed valuation	[Same as above]
Special Assessment	1% unvoted	
TOWNSHIP	2% of assessed valuation None unvoted	[Same as above]
SCHOOL DISTRICT		
General Obligation	9% of assessed valuation .1% unvoted, and over 4% only with approval of board of taxation	[Same as above]
COUNTY		
Revenue	No limit	Serial annuity, may be deferable 5 years, may be callable
CITY & VILLAGE		
Utility Mortgage and Revenue	No limit	No restrictions

* The many minor exceptions to these general limitations are not included. Most of them are available in Hayden, Miller and Co., op cit.

limitation. The total unvoted tax levy of all overlapping jurisdictions cannot exceed one per cent of the value of taxable property to service unvoted bonds and for all other purposes. Hence, it is possible that bonds which might otherwise be unvoted would require voters' approval due to the fact that the cost of servicing the debt plus other expenditures required a levy in excess of ten mills per dollar.

LIMITS ON MATURITY

There is a limit of forty years on county revenue bonds, but no limit on the maturity of municipal utility revenue bonds.

In the case of general obligations, an elaborate schedule of maturity limits is included in Section 133.20 of the Uniform Bond Law. Some of the more important limitations are as follows:

Permanent Rapid Transit Construction	50 years
Waterworks	40 years
Real Estate Acquisition	30 years
Fireproof Buildings, Sewage Disposal Works, Expressway and Freeway Construction	25 years
Nonfireproof Buildings	15 years
Sidewalks, Streets, and Highway Construction	10 years
Motor Vehicles	5 years
Notes in Anticipation of Special Assessments	1 year

STATUTORY DEBT LIMITS

The purpose of a limitation on the size of the debt of a community is to prevent borrowing to the extent that its tax resources become overburdened. If this happens, refunding and even defaulting can result. In addition to the ethical problems, either or both of these occurrences result in severe impairment of the community's credit, and tend to make future borrowing very costly.

If a debt limit is to be effective, it must limit all the borrowing which is backed by the full faith and credit of a community. Therefore, the limit must apply to all general obligation bonds and special assessment bonds which are ultimately an obligation of the entire tax base. Even though special assessment bonds are initially serviced by special assessment, they are generally full faith and credit obligation so that if taxpayers default on the special assessment payments, the government is obligated to meet the debt service. For this reason, net debt is defined as gross debt less self-supporting revenue bonds (which are not an obligation of the community at large) and sinking funds. Sinking funds are deducted because they represent funds which are available to service debt at no cost to the taxpayer or the community. This concept differs from the Ohio statutory concept so it is here called "net debt."

The statutory debt concept does not include special assessment bonds, and in the case of municipalities, does not include general obligation bonds when the funds are used for expressways or freeways. This serious flaw in the statutory concept is sufficent to make it an ineffective limit on municipal borrowing. This is true not only in theory, but also in practice.

A comparison of the net and statutory net debt figures given in Table VII-7 reveals the extent to which the legal limit has been ineffective in limiting debt.

The Pattern of Debt: Introduction

Associated with the various definitions of the debt concept, are various measures which can be employed in an examination of the pattern of outstanding debt and the distribution of the cost or burden of meeting the financial requirements imposed by its existence. The selection of specific measures of indebtedness is dictated by both the use for which the data are intended and also its availability.

Gross or total debt figures are available but are useful only as an indication of the general magnitude of indebtedness. This is due to the fact that the gross measure includes debt of all types, general obligation, special assessment, and revenue bonds. As is indicated above, revenue bonds may not be truly an obligation of the borrowing government, and hence they differ significantly from general obligations and special assessment bonds. In a gross debt figure this fact is disregarded and hence comparison of jurisdictions at any given time or over time is not meaningful if gross debt is the basis for comparison. In addition to the fact that it prevents comparability, the gross measure neglects the existence of sinking funds which represent debt already repaid, so that failure to take this into account in a gross debt measure results in an overstatement of the actual debt obligation of a community.

Net debt is a much better measure of a government's indebtedness, excluding, as it does, those revenue bonds which are not an obligation of the borrowing government, and taking into account, as it does, the existence of sinking funds. Therefore, it is a superior measure of the debt which must be serviced by the taxpayers of a community. Like other aggregate measures, however, net debt as such is not suitable for comparing different governments, or even the same government in different years.

Perhaps debt as related to the income or wealth of those who must meet the cost of debt service would be the most satisfactory measure of relative debt in that ultimately the cost of debt must be met from some combination of the flow of income, the store of wealth, or the command over economic resources of those who collectively incur indebtedness. Though theoretically superior, such a measure has limits due to a lack of income and wealth data for most jurisdictions. Therefore, two alternative measures of debt are utilized. The first is debt (gross or net) per capita. The primary advantage of this measure is that it permits comparison over time in that population represents a common denominator. However, it has limitations, primarily because it neglects the fact that financial ability varies over time, and between governments at a given time independently of population. To take extreme cases, a debt of $10 per capita in 1956 is not as significant as a debt of $10 per capita in 1940, nor would a debt of $10 per capita in the United States be comparable to the same debt per capita in India.

In many ways for Ohio local governments, debt per $1000 of assessed valuation is a better measure than per capita debt. This measure does not completely eliminate the problem of comparison over time, because relation of assessed value to true or market value of property may vary over time especially if they are many years apart. However, within a given year assessed valuation can be the basis for comparison between communities, especially when there is area-wide assessment as in Cuyahoga County.[4] There are further reasons for selecting debt per $1000 assessed valuation as the basis for comparison. Assessed value does reflect a community's ability to meet the costs resulting from the existence of debt. Furthermore, debt service is initially distributed on the basis of assessed valuation, and debt as related to assessed valuation is the most commonly employed measurement of debt, as viewed by both potential lenders and potential borrowers, to the extent that the level of existing debt exerts an influence over the decision to borrow, tax or forego the expenditure.

---

4. See pp. 227-235.

Debt in the Cleveland Metropolitan Area

The picture which emerges below contains at the outset some indication of the local government debt in the Cleveland Metropolitan Area for the years 1940, 1950, and 1956. The first section contains an analysis of changes in the amount and composition of the gross and net local indebtedness within the county. It should be realized that where comparisons are made they refer to the county in its entirety or to broad classes of governments and may have little relation to the behavior of any specific jurisdiction. This is followed by an examination of the debt within the area as it is distributed among jurisdictions. The distribution of the costs of servicing existing debt, the interest rates being paid on existing debt, and its maturity pattern are then considered. Finally, the credit ratings of the local governments within the Cleveland Metropolitan Area are considered.

Table VII-2—Debt in Cleveland Metropolitan Area, 1940, 1950, 1956

	1940	1950	1956
Gross Debt	$230,905,000	$206,063,000	$398,442,000
Less Revenue Bonds	25,650,000	50,718,000	117,261,000
Less Sinking Funds	11,814,000	19,883,000	30,607,000
Net Debt	193,441,000	135,462,000	250,574,000
Gross Debt Per Capita	$189.69	$148.30	$252.09
Net Debt Per Capita	158.92	97.49	158.54
Gross Debt per $1000 Valuation	$127.07	$ 73.64	$ 84.76
Net Debt per $1000 Valuation	106.45	48.41	53.30

DEBT IN 1956

At the end of 1956, the gross debt of all governments in Cuyahoga County was $398.5 millions. Of this amount, $147.9 millions either was incurred through the issuance of revenue bonds or similar obligations not backed by the full faith and credit of the borrowing government or was debt which was offset by the existence of sinking funds. The net indebtedness of all the governments of the county was $250.6 millions. Slightly under six-tenths (57.8 per cent) of this debt represented borrowing of the cities and villages within the county, slightly over three-tenths (31.2 per cent) was attributable to the borrowing of school districts, about one-tenth (11.1 per cent) to the borrowing of Cuyahoga County. This net debt of over $250 million represented on the average a per capita debt of $158.54 to the citizens of the county or on the average a debt of $53.30 per $1000.00 of assessed valuation, which is equivalent to 4.33 per cent of the total assessed value of the county. The net debt had fallen from $193.4 millions, in 1940, to a figure of $135.5 millions, in 1950, from which it rose to $250.6 millions, in 1956. The aggregate burden thus fell between 1940 and 1950 and rose between 1950 and 1956, regardless of the measure used. The movements reflected the fact that the retirement of debt incurred in the twenties and early thirties, far exceeded the new debt of the 1940's, while during the 1950's little long term debt was retired and much was incurred because of the vast capital program of the 1950's.

This level of net debt per capita and net debt per $1000 of assessed valuation can be roughly compared with that of the other large metropolitan cities and counties within Ohio. See Table VII-3.

Table VII-3—Net Debt, All Local Governments, Per Capita and Per $1000 Assessed Valuation, Selected Ohio Metropolitan Counties, 1956

Metropolitan Area	County	Net Debt Per $1000 Assessed Valuation (Dollars)	Net Debt Per Capita (Dollars)
Columbus	Franklin	67.00	155.00
Dayton	Montgomery	67.00	157.00
Cincinnati	Hamilton	63.00	187.00
Cleveland	Cuyahoga	53.30	158.54
Akron	Summit	52.00	123.00
Youngstown	Mahoning	50.00	120.00
Canton	Stark	35.00	92.00
Toledo	Lucas	27.00	71.00

Source: Ohio Municipal Advisory Council.

As is indicated above, in 1956, municipalities accounted for nearly 60 per cent of the net debt within the Cleveland Metropolitan Area, school districts 30 per cent, and the County 10 per cent. On a per capita basis this represented a net debt of over $90 per capita for municipalities, nearly $50 for school districts, and $17 for the County. However, significant differences exist among municipalities and among school districts.

The per capita net debt of the City of Cleveland was over $105, while for other cities it was only $69, and for the villages it was $90. The $50 per capita net debt average figure for all school districts was even less meaningful, for it was the result of a debt-free Cleveland School District, while city school districts excluding Cleveland had net debt of over $105 per capita, and local and exempted districts had a per capita net debt of over $193, making this sub-class easily the most heavily in debt.

In 1956, the net debt per $1000 of assessed valuation was nearly $31 for municipalities, nearly $17 for school districts, and nearly $6 for the County. The net debt relative to assessed valuation for school districts followed the same pattern as net debt relative to population. On the other hand, while Cleveland still had the highest municipal net debt relative to population and assessed valuation, the net debt per $1000 of assessed valuation for cities excluding Cleveland of $24.86 was greater than the $19.91 for villages, even though their per capita order was reversed—$89.82 for the villages and $68.83 for cities excluding Cleveland. The lesser burden on property is a reflection of the fact that assessed valuation per capita was greater in the villages than in the cities excluding Cleveland.

CHANGES IN DEBT BY CLASSES OF GOVERNMENT, 1940-56

Between 1940 and 1950, debt of most classes of government followed the general pattern of debt shown in Table VII-2 as debt decreased in the aggregate and in per capita and per $1000 of assessed valuation. However, there were some notable exceptions to the general pattern. In spite of a marked decline in aggregate school debt of the Cleveland School District, net debt for school districts as a class increased, with the most rapid rise occurring in the local and exempted districts, as the need for new school plants resulting from the wartime population boom outside the core area began to be felt. This rise is also indicated in the per capita net debt for all school districts and the debt per $1000 of assessed valuation for local and exempted districts, but not in the city school districts because their assessed valuation had grown more rapidly than their debt-financed capital outlays between 1940 and 1950.

Between 1950 and 1956, total debt and per capita debt for every class and sub-class of government, with the exception of the Cleveland School District, increased. However, when net debt relative to assessed valuation is considered, a much more complicated pattern emerges.

Debt per $1000 of assessed valuation fell for the County, cities excluding Cleveland, villages and the Cleveland School District. It rose for the City of Cleveland (and consequently all municipalities as a class), city school districts excluding Cleveland, local school districts and, in spite of the decline in the Cleveland School District, for all school districts as a class. This latter is primarily a reflection of the fact that net debt per $1000 of assessed valuation in the Cleveland School District was only $.95 in 1950, and a reduction to nothing in 1956 had practically no effect on the school debt per $1000 of assessed valuation.

The most significant trend in the debt pattern for the Cleveland Metropolitan Area from 1950 to 1956 was the growth of school debt other than Cleveland School District. Because there was a rapid expansion in population and assessed valuation, these increases are best viewed in relation to these measures. Per capita net debt for city school districts excluding Cleveland nearly doubled from 1950 to 1956, while for local school districts, the 1956 level was nearly two and one-half times greater than the 1950 level. The increase is not so large when measured in relation to assessed valuation, which grew more rapidly than population between 1950 and 1956, but the increase in the city school districts was 20 per cent and in the local and exempted districts, over 115 per cent. The decline in Cleveland is not as anomalous as might as first appear in view of the fact that since the mid-1930's the Cleveland Board of Education has followed a well-publicized practice of financing its capital outlay entirely from a current tax levy.

There was also growth in municipal debt, between 1940 and 1956, but it was substantially slower than the growth of population and assessed valuation. Consequently, net debt per capita and debt per $1000 of assessed valuation fell with the single exception of debt per capita of the City of Cleveland. The opposite movements of school and municipal debt are clearly indicated by the fact that in 1940 school debt outside Cleveland was $28.47 per $1000 of assessed valuation as opposed to municipal net debt of $63.57, and, by 1956, the school net debt had risen to $37.76 while municipal debt outside Cleveland fell to $23.53 per $1000 of assessed valuation. This marked fall in municipal debt per $1000 of assessed valuation was, of course, nearly sufficient to cause the area-wide net debt per $1000 of assessed valuation to fall from $106.45 to $53.30.

Two other trends are noteworthy. The first is contraction of county debt not only in relation to population and assessed valuation over the period 1940 to 1956 but in absolute terms as well. The second is the significant fact that the decline in village net debt relative to assessed valuation was very slight from 1950 to 1956, so that in the case of this class, the rise of school debt was not being offset by any substantial decline in municipal debt.

OVERALL DEBT

The total amount of debt attributable to each $1,000 of assessed valuation is designated as, "overall debt." All debt within Cuyahoga County which must be serviced from property tax revenues appears as an obligation of either the County, city or village, or school district. In addition while borrowing may take place for library districts or sewer and water districts, such debt is an obligation of one of the three overlapping governments mentioned above. The overall debt for each municipality includes the debt of that municipality, the share of county debt assigned to the municipality on the basis of its share of the total assessed valuation of the county and the share of the debt of the school district in which the municipality is located, apportioned on the basis of assessed valuation of the school district within the municipality relative to the total assessed valuation of the school district.

Problems in apportioning arise from the fact that the school and municipal boundaries do not coincide due to the nature of the geographic boundaries of school districts. There are instances in which a single municipality lies within more than one school district. However, in only two cases, Broadview Heights and Moreland Hills, is there a substantial portion of the municipality in more than a single school district. In these two cases, no attempt has been made to segregate these small areas within various municipalities where the overall debt differs from that of the major portion of the community with the exception of the two villages mentioned.

To enhance comparison between municipalities, overall debt is considered primarily in terms of net debt per $1000 of assessed valuation and, for purposes of comparison, the statutory net debt for 1956 is also presented. It should be noted that there may be minor errors in the net debt figures for certain municipalities due to the fact that available data do not clearly indicate that portion of sinking funds which may be applicable to special assessment obligations or revenue bonds. Hence, in arriving at net debt figures from gross debt amounts, there may be a small amount of double counting resulting in an understatement of the statutory net debt.

OVERALL NET DEBT—1956

In 1956, the median net debt for municipalities in the county was $78.40 per $1000 of assessed valuation. The median net debt for villages was slightly lower and the median for cities slightly higher than the median for both classes combined. The range for villages was from $5.90 to $154.30, while the range for cities was narrower, from $18.50 to $120.80 per $1000 of assessed valuation. Specifically, one-third of the municipalities had an overall net debt of under $60.00 per $1000 of assessed valuation or under 6 per cent, and two-thirds were under $90.00 or 9 per cent. Six municipalities had overall debts in excess of $120 per $1000 of assessed valuation in 1956.

Table VII-4—Gross and Net Debt in the Cleveland Metropolitan Area, 1940, 1950, 1956

GOVERNMENTAL UNIT	1940			1950			1956		
	Gross Debt (Millions of Dollars)	Net Debt (Millions of Dollars)	Net Debt (Percentage Distribution)	Gross Debt (Millions of Dollars)	Net Debt (Millions of Dollars)	Net Debt (Percentage Distribution)	Gross Debt (Millions of Dollars)	Net Debt (Millions of Dollars)	Net Debt (Percentage Distribution)
County	45.5	45.5	28.2	25.0	21.3	15.8	28.0	27.7	11.1
Municipalities	158.4	122.6	63.4	149.3	84.5	62.4	288.0	144.8	57.8
Cleveland	116.5	84.5	43.7	115.0	56.8	41.9	228.9	97.3	38.8
Cities except Cleveland	36.1	32.9	17.0	29.1	23.8	16.9	48.3	39.0	14.7
Villages	5.7	5.2	2.7	4.4	7.0	3.6	11.7	10.0	4.2
School Districts	27.0	25.4	13.1	31.7	29.6	21.8	80.6	78.1	31.2
Cleveland City School District	8.5	8.1	4.2	2.1	1.7	1.2		0.0	0.0
City School District Except Cleveland	16.3	15.1	7.8	24.9	23.5	17.3	60.9	59.6	23.8
Local School District	2.2	2.2	1.1	4.6	4.5	3.3	19.0	18.5	7.4
Total	230.9	193.4	100.0	206.0	135.5	100.0	398.4	250.6	100.0

Table VII-5—Net Debt Per Capita and Per $1000 Assessed Valuation, Cleveland Metropolitan Area, 1940, 1950, 1956

Governmental Unit	1940		1950		1956	
	Per Capita	Per $1000 Assessed Valuation	Per Capita	Per $1000 Assessed Valuation	Per Capita	Per $1000 Assessed Valuation
County	38.69	25.05	15.36	7.63	17.52	5.89
Municipalities	104.38	67.49	60.84	30.21	91.61	30.80
Cleveland	96.22	69.79	62.08	32.15	105.05	36.84
Cities except Cleveland	111.01	66.64	58.80	28.83	68.83	24.86
Villages	122.76	49.21	56.49	20.82	89.82	19.91
School Districts	20.83	13.96	21.30	10.57	49.40	16.61
Cleveland	9.94	6.66	18.34	0.95	0.00	0.00
City S. D. except Cleveland	44.27	29.67	55.57	27.36	105.65	35.61
Local S. D.	33.20	22.25	79.00	24.96	193.85	47.85
Total	158.92	106.45	97.49	48.41	158.54	53.30

Net Debt (Dollars)

NET DEBT WITHIN CLASSES OF GOVERNMENTS—1956

The variations in the level of net school debt among the various school districts was in 1956 much greater than the variation in the level of net debt among municipalities. School debt varied from $0.00 to $93.20 per $1000 of assessed valuation, while municipal debt ranged from $0.00 to $66.80. Nearly one-third of all the villages had no net debt, while only two school districts out of thirty-two could claim this distinction. No cities were completely debt free, while all four of the townships by statute fell into this classification.

Nearly 90 per cent of the municipalities in the Cleveland Metropolitan Area had a net debt below $50.00 per $1000 of assessed valuation, while only slightly over 50 per cent of the school districts had net debt below this level. More obviously, the median net debt level for municipalities was $10.70 per $1000 of assessed valuation, while the median for school districts was $48.85.

Table VII-6—Overall Debt Per $1000 Assessed Valuation, Cleveland Metropolitan Area, 1940, 1950, 1956; and Statutory Net Debt, 1956

GOVERNMENTAL UNIT	1940			1950			1956			STATUTORY NET DEBT
	Municipal	School	Overall *	Municipal	School	Overall *	Municipal	School	Overall *	
Cuyahoga County			25.40			7.60			5.90	5.60
Cities										
Bay Village	71.90	14.70	112.00	32.40	56.30	96.30	21.20	52.60	79.70	58.20
Bedford	114.80	48.20	187.40	18.20	72.20	98.00	63.60	44.50	114.00	70.90
Berea	35.30	28.00	88.70	29.50	23.00	60.10	40.50	40.10	86.50	62.30
Brooklyn	245.20	27.10	297.70	39.20	42.90	89.70	31.20	46.70	83.80	70.70
Cleveland	69.80	6.70	101.90	32.20	.90	40.70	36.80	0.00	42.70	42.40
Cleveland Heights	7.70	33.80	66.90	14.10	14.10	35.80	10.20	36.70	52.80	51.60
East Cleveland	12.60	15.50	53.50	4.40	15.70	27.70	6.20	5.70	17.80	17.50
Euclid	147.20	25.30	197.90	37.70	37.20	82.50	41.20	12.00	59.10	37.90
Fairview Park	292.90	55.50	373.80	58.80	39.20	105.60	10.60	56.40	72.90	62.20
Garfield Heights	133.10	43.00	201.50	49.10	26.70	83.40	14.50	55.40	75.80	71.00
Lakewood	14.90	19.60	59.90	34.00	14.80	56.40	2.10	13.30	21.30	20.80
Lyndhurst	284.80	29.20	339.40	67.40	66.60	141.60	20.20	61.80	87.90	67.40
Maple Heights	322.80	64.40	412.60	71.80	76.90	156.30	64.60	50.30	120.80	67.20
Mayfield Heights	188.80	38.80	253.00	38.50	56.60	102.70	30.80	81.60	118.30	94.70
North Olmsted	35.30	72.10	132.80	24.10	35.50	67.20	30.40	66.70	103.00	79.00
Parma	169.70	61.00	256.10	29.10	12.30	49.00	54.00	54.30	114.20	70.50
Rocky River	48.50	24.80	98.70	.70	55.80	64.10	39.20	48.90	94.00	71.50
Shaker Heights	45.40	27.80	98.60	15.80	8.30	31.70	4.00	29.50	39.40	38.20
South Euclid	316.90	29.20	371.50	62.10	66.60	136.30	23.00	61.80	90.70	76.00
University Heights	129.40	33.80	188.60	17.30	14.10	39.00	3.70	36.70	46.30	44.90

Villages

Village									
Beachwood	435.70	22.40	483.50	162.20	...	169.80	12.10	67.20	85.20	72.80
Bedford Heights	††	48.20	73.60	††	72.20	79.80	11.10	44.50	61.50	53.00
Bentleyville	...	46.40	71.80	...	11.60	19.20	...	93.20	99.10	98.80
Bratenahl	...	12.10	37.50	...	3.60	11.20	...	...	5.90	5.60
Brecksville	.80	51.80	78.00	12.90	8.40	28.90	9.60	50.00	65.50	59.30
Broadview Heights	32.40	51.80†	109.60†	0.00	8.40†	16.00†	14.60	50.00†	70.50†	55.60†
		10.90‡	68.70‡		70.90‡	78.50‡		76.10‡	96.60‡	81.70‡
Brooklyn Heights	107.50	14.20	147.10	46.50	7.50	61.60	4.80	15.60	26.30	26.00
Brook Park	147.70	28.00	201.10	7.50	23.00	38.10	32.10	40.10	78.10	60.50
Chagrin Falls	15.60	46.40	87.40	27.30	11.60	46.50	21.50	93.20	120.60	119.50
Cuyahoga Heights	1.00	14.20	40.60	12.40	7.50	27.50	6.70	4.80	17.40	16.10
Gates Mills	35.50	38.80	99.70	8.60	56.60	72.80	.70	81.60	88.20	87.90
Glenwillow	...	0.00	25.40	...	41.50	49.10	...	41.30	47.20	46.90
Highland Heights	...	38.80	64.20	7.70	56.60	71.90	66.80	81.60	154.30	105.30
Hunting Valley	...	21.40	46.80	...	24.50	32.10	1.50	47.10	54.50	52.70
Independence	18.20	37.70	81.30	4.90	27.10	39.60	5.90	38.60	50.40	44.20
Linndale	...	6.70	32.10	...	.90	8.50	...	0.00	5.90	5.60
Mayfield	25.40	38.80	89.60	...	56.60	64.20	46.60	81.60	134.10	102.50
Middleburg Heights	156.80	28.00	210.20	18.90	23.00	49.50	3.90	40.10	49.90	45.70
Moreland Hills	.10	21.40 §	46.90 §	0.00	24.50 §	32.10 §	.30	47.10 §	53.20 §	52.90 §
		46.40 **	71.90 **		11.60 **	19.20 **		93.20 **	99.40 **	98.10 **
Newburgh Heights	0.00	6.70	32.10	7.10	.90	15.60	.30	0.00	6.20	5.90
North Randall	...	11.20	36.60	...	66.20	73.80	...	72.90	78.80	78.50
North Royalton	5.80	10.90	42.10	28.00	70.90	106.50	66.00	76.10	148.00	82.00
Oakwood	††	48.20	73.60	††	72.20	79.80	...	44.50	50.40	50.10
Olmsted Falls	59.50	29.60	114.50	...	28.80	36.40	0.00	86.30	92.20	91.90
Orange	1.10	21.40	47.90	...	24.50	32.10	...	47.10	53.00	52.70
Parkview	17.70	55.50	98.60	...	39.20	46.80	10.30	56.40	72.60	71.20
Parma Heights	237.70	61.00	324.10	53.40	12.30	73.30	52.40	54.30	112.60	70.90

(Continued on next page)

Table VII-6 (Continued)

GOVERNMENTAL UNIT	1940			1950			1956			STATUTORY NET DEBT
	Municipal	School	Overall *	Municipal	School	Overall *	Municipal	School	Overall *	
Pepper Pike	158.10	21.40	204.90	67.40	24.50	99.50	9.30	47.10	62.30	54.20
Richmond Heights	...	41.50	66.90	131.10	13.10	151.80	64.80	48.80	119.50	75.30
Seven Hills	18.90	61.00	105.30	27.80	12.30	47.70	17.60	54.30	77.80	59.90
Solon	112.90	0.00	138.30	17.50	41.50	66.60	21.40	41.30	68.60	50.60
Strongsville	14.60	17.30	57.30	9.00	59.90	76.50	41.90	78.80	126.60	88.10
Valley View	...	14.20	39.60	2.40	7.50	17.50	...	4.80	10.70	10.40
Walton Hills	††	48.20	73.60	††	72.20	79.80	9.10	44.50	59.50	52.70
Warrensville Hts.	137.20	11.20	173.80	...	66.20	73.80	15.40	72.90	94.20	83.30
Westlake	35.70	32.00	93.10	18.90	34.40	60.90	30.90	52.20	89.00	64.50
West View	16.00	29.60	71.00	...	28.80	56.40	...	86.30	92.20	91.90
Woodmere	...	0.00	0.00	...	24.50	32.10	...	47.10	53.00	52.70
Townships										
Chagrin Falls	...	46.40	71.80	...	11.60	19.20	...	93.20	99.10	96.80
Olmsted	...	29.60	55.00	...	28.80	36.40	...	86.30	92.20	91.90
Riveredge	...	28.00	53.40	...	23.00	30.60	...	40.10	46.00	45.70
Warrensville	...	11.20	36.60	...	66.20	73.80	...	72.90	78.80	78.50

* Includes share of County Debt.
† Portion of Broadview Heights in Brecksville School District.
‡ Portion of Broadview Heights in North Royalton School District.
§ Portion of Moreland Hills in Orange School District.
** Portion of Morelands Hills in Chagrin Falls School District.
†† Not in existence.

Table VII-7—Distribution of Municipal Overall Net Debt and Net Statutory Debt, by Classes of Municipality, 1940, 1950, 1956 (In Dollars Per $1000 Assessed Valuation)

GOVERNMENTAL UNIT	1940		1950		1956	
	Overall Net Debt	Net Statutory Debt	Overall Net Debt	Net Statutory Debt	Overall Net Debt	Net Statutory Debt
AVERAGE						
Cities	160.10	55.00	68.85	45.00	81.75	55.00
Villages & Townships	70.25	45.00	47.25	35.00	77.99	50.00
All Municipalities	89.15	48.90	58.25	40.75	78.40	61.35
RANGE						
Cities	53.50-412.60	30.20-114.20	31.70-156.30	18.70- 88.10	18.50-120.80	17.50- 94.70
Villages & Townships	25.40-483.50	14.40- 78.80	8.50-169.80	6.40- 79.30	5.90-154.30	5.60-119.50
All Municipalities	25.40-483.50	14.40-114.20	8.50-169.80	6.40- 88.10	5.90-154.30	5.60-119.50

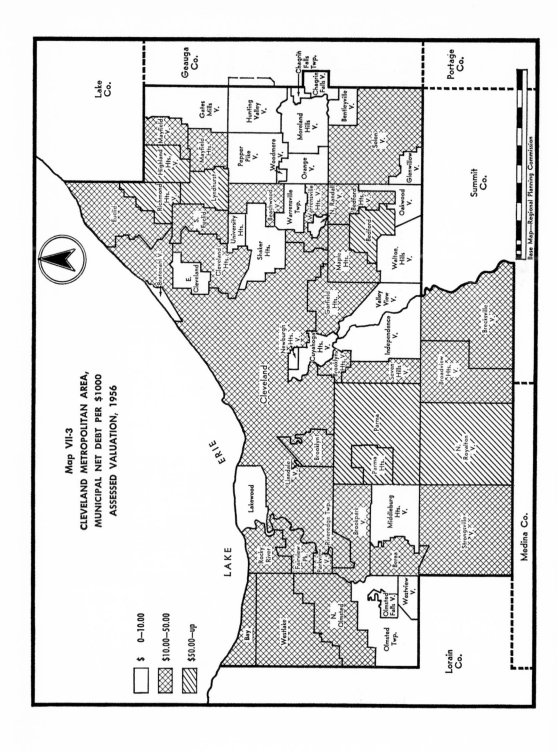

Map VII-3

CLEVELAND METROPOLITAN AREA,
MUNICIPAL NET DEBT PER $1000
ASSESSED VALUATION, 1956

$ 0—10.00

$10.00—50.00

$50.00—up

Base Map—Regional Planning Commission

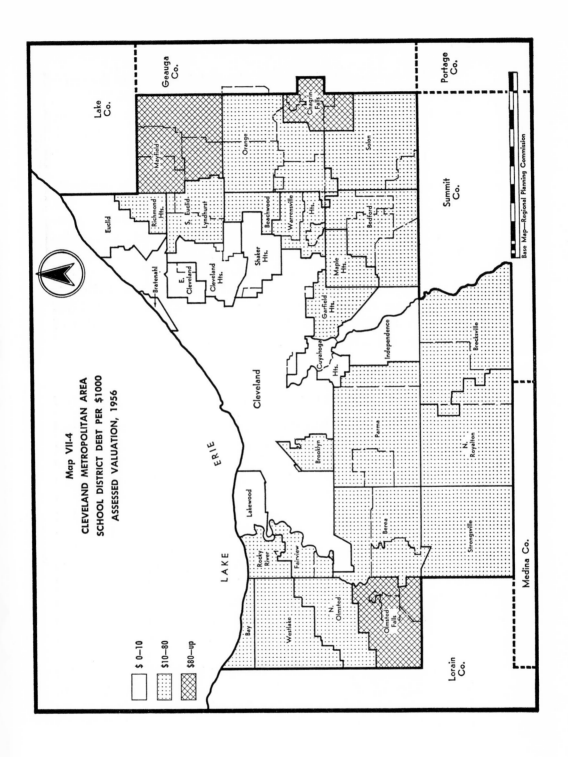

Map VII-4
CLEVELAND METROPOLITAN AREA
SCHOOL DISTRICT DEBT PER $1000
ASSESSED VALUATION, 1956

$ 0–10
$10–80
$80–up

Base Map—Regional Planning Commission

Within the municipal category, the fact is that while the range of variation in net debt for cities and for villages is about the same, cities generally have higher debt. This is indicated by comparing the median city debt of $25.60, with the median village debt, which is $6.30; even if villages without debt are excluded the village median rises only to $14.60.

Among school districts, the median level of net debt per $1000 of assessed valuation varied slightly between city and local and exempted school districts. The median for city school districts was $46.70 and $52.20 for the local and exempted districts, so that for all school districts, the median is $48.85. However, the maximum net school debt for city school districts was $66.70 per $1000 of assessed valuation, while for local and exempted school districts the maximum was $93.20. There were six local and exempted districts with net debt per $1000 of assessed valuation above that of the highest city school district.

SIGNIFICANT CHANGES IN THE PATTERN OF OVERALL DEBT—1940-56

Between 1940 and 1956, the changes in overall debt which stand out most clearly are the general contraction that occurred between 1940 and 1950 and expansion between 1950 and 1956. These changes have been accompanied by more significant changes. While the median net overall debt for all municipalities declined from $89.15 per $1000 of assessed valuation in 1940 to $58.25 in 1950, it rose from 1950 to 1956 and was at $78.40 by the end of 1956. The overall debt of villages also declined from 1940 to 1950 and then rose from 1950 to 1956, but the level in 1956 was above the 1940 level. The 1956 level for cities fell and then rose, but the 1956 level was slightly greater than one-half the 1940 level. Finally, these ratios are even more striking because of the decline in the assessment ratio from 65 to 70 per cent of true value, in 1939-40, to 42 per cent in 1955.

The similar yet more striking movement has been the contraction in the range of divergencies between various municipalities. In 1940, one-quarter of the municipalities had overall net debts in excess of $170 per $1000 of assessed valuation. In both 1950 and

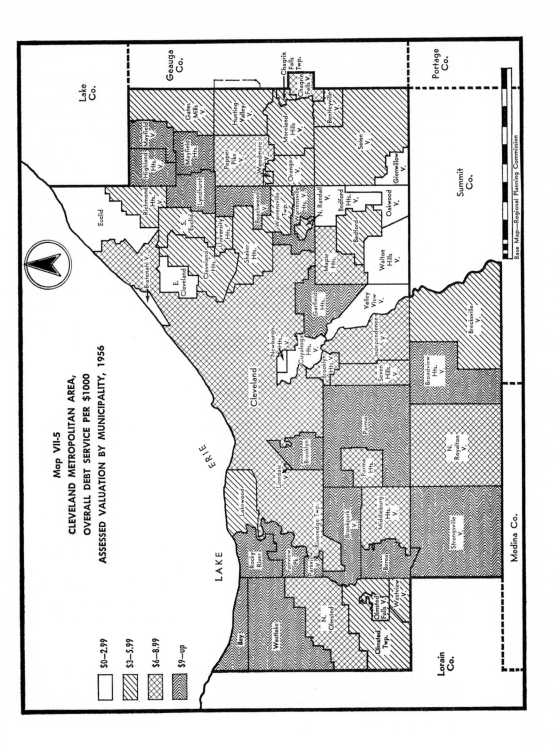

Map VII-5

CLEVELAND METROPOLITAN AREA,

OVERALL DEBT SERVICE PER $1000

ASSESSED VALUATION BY MUNICIPALITY, 1956

$0—2.99

$3—5.99

$6—8.99

$9—up

Base Map—Regional Planning Commission

1956, no jurisdiction had an overall net debt in excess of $154.30 per $1000 of assessed valuation. This, of course, was partially a reflection of the declining of debt from 1940 to 1950, but from 1950 to 1956 when the average increased, the range continued to contract because of the behavior of a few isolated cases.

It would be a mistake to assume from these general patterns that the behavior of all municipalities taken together is representative of the behavior of each of them individually. The growth of debt in the area is reflected in the fact that, in seventeen of the thirty-eight villages the level of overall debt in 1956 was above the level of 1940; however, the overall debt grew in only one city during the same years. It should be noted that generally, in the former case, these were villages that had low debt levels in 1940, and that, in the latter case, these cities and villages which had a very heavy debt in 1950 have by and large experienced significant reductions in debt per $1000 of assessed valuation.

The Cost of Borrowing: Debt Service

The existence of bonded indebtedness places a dual burden upon taxpayers. Repayment will occur over time and an additional expense is incurred for this privilege. Therefore, the payment in any single year, traceable to the incurrence of debt, consists of both repayment of part of the original amount borrowed, the principal, and also the payment of interest. The total of both of these is called "debt service." In any one year, the sum of these two amounts can have any one of a variety of relationships to the original amount borrowed depending upon the nature of the obligation.

There are a great many factors which determine the rate of interest actually paid, or the effective rate of interest on any single bond issue. For purposes of summary, these factors may be placed in five general groups.[5]

---

5. It is not intended that this be an exhaustive listing of factors, nor that all factors apply equally to the borrowing of any particular issue or government. For a further description of the factors influencing the credit standing of a municipality see, Carl H. Chatters and Albert M. Hillhouse, *Local Government Debt Administration* (Prentice-Hall, Inc., New York), 1939, pp. 281-287. This listing is primarily a condensation of this cited reference.

First, there is the amount and nature of the government's debt. This includes the cause, character, and amount of short term borrowing, the amount of net and overall debt, the rate at which debt has grown or been reduced, the character of debt outstanding, and the method of retirement.

Second, there is the market's reaction to an issue which may be influenced by such factors as the size of the unit, its location with respect to large financial centers, the frequency with which it has borrowed, and the degree to which financial officials have made information readily available to potential lenders.

Third, there is the trend which the financial condition of the community is following. This includes the ability of the municipality to live within its budget, the degree to which conservative accounting procedures are followed, the trend of tax rates and assessed valuation, the importance of revenue sources other than the property tax, and the extent to which contingent liabilities such as special assessment obligations or revenue bonds may have to be financed from property taxes.

Fourth, there is the administration and structure of the government and the soundness of the laws under which it operates. This includes the character and legal status of the government, the type of administration, the honesty and intelligence of the administration, the presence of overlapping jurisdictions, the overall tax limitation law, the tax collection machinery, the security of public deposits, and the immediate and ultimate remedies for bondholders in the case of default.

Fifth, there is the economic and social nature of the borrowing government. This includes the compactness of the area, the degree to which it is strategically located in relation to transportation and financial markets, the character of the population, the economic resources of the community, and the stability of the economic life of the community throughout business cycles.

Debt service as related to assessed valuation is a measure of the burden of debt. It differs from the overall net debt as related to assessed valuation. Overall debt as related to assessed valuation is an indication of the burden of debt without regard for time. It

shows nothing, by itself, of the actual degree to which the existence
of debt places a direct monetary burden upon taxable property, but
rather is a general indicator of the amount of debt which must,
over some time period, be redeemed by taxes upon each dollar of
assessed value. Debt service as related to assessed value, by contrast,
is a measure of the amount of this overall net debt burden which
is being paid by taxes upon property in a single year.

While these measures are obviously related to each other, there
is no simple relationship between them. Some communities with
relatively heavy overall debt as of any period may have a very low
burden as measured by debt service if the debt is generally of long
maturity. On the other hand, there are communities which have a
relatively low burden in terms of overall debt but a high burden in
terms of debt service due to the fact that the debt is either being
amortized very rapidly or is of short maturity.

The measure of debt service used most extensively is parallel to
the measure of overall debt in that it represents the debt service
imposed upon any single municipality by each of the three overlapping governments—the county, school district, and city, village
or township. When governments borrow and repay within a single
year, frequently in anticipation of subsequent long term borrowing,
there is not really any additional burden upon taxable property
except interest charges. As in the case of debt, we have attempted to
net out short term borrowing and repayment so that the resulting
debt service figures represent a close approximation of the funds
collected in the form of property taxes and paid to bondholders.
Data are presented for the 1956 and 1950 years in Table VII-11.

Table VII-8—Total Debt Service, All Governments, Cleveland Metropolitan Area, 1956

	Interest	Principal	Total
All Governments *	$9,791,000	$32,906,000	$42,697,000
County	496,000	2,047,000	2,543,000
Cleveland	5,828,000	11,066,000	16,894,000
Others	3,467,000	19,793,000	23,260,000
Cities and Villages	7,248,000	24,493,000	31,741,000
School Districts	2,047,000	6,367,000	8,414,000

* This debt service was applied to a debt of $377,627,000 which includes public utility debt.

Table VII-9—Distribution of Overall Debt Service Per $1000 Assessed Valuation, by Classes of Municipality Cleveland Metropolitan Area, 1950 and 1956

GOVERNMENTAL UNIT	MEDIAN	
	1950 (Dollars)	1956 (Dollars)
Cities	9.73	8.75
Villages and Townships	4.60	5.73
All Municipalities	5.25	5.98
	RANGE	
Cities	4.07-22.30	2.01-13.76
Villages and Townships	1.61-21.28	.55-12.22
All Municipalities	1.61-22.30	.55-13.76

THE PATTERN OF DEBT SERVICE—1956

Overall debt service per $1000 of assessed valuation in 1956 was generally higher in the cities than in the villages and townships. For cities the median was $8.75 per $1000 of assessed valuation for overall debt service, and for villages and townships it was $5.73.

Generally, municipal debt service was below school district debt service, with the median for municipal debt being $2.51 per $1000 of assessed valuation while for school districts the median was $3.58, a result which is consistent with debt levels. Debt service for cities generally was much higher than for villages and townships as a class. While the median for cities was $4.81 per $1000 of assessed valuation, it was only $.60 for villages and townships. This was in part due to the fact that fifteen in this latter class had no municipal debt and, consequently, no municipal debt service. If those villages and townships without debt are excluded, the median for those having to pay debt service rises to $3.02 per $1000 of assessed valuation, but this is still below the median for cities as a class. In the case of school districts, the distribution of debt service in both city school districts and local and exempted school districts as classes is nearly identical. The median for city districts was $3.59 per $1000 of assessed valuation and for local and exempted districts $3.58.

In summary, then, in 1956, the following pattern emerges: For overall debt service, cities generally had higher debt service costs

Table VII-10—Overall Debt Service by Muncipality, Cleveland Metropolitan Area, 1956 (In Dollars Per $1000 Assessed Valuation)

Governmental Unit	Municipal	School	County	Total
Cuyahoga County			0.55	0.55
Cities				
Bay Village	5.60	4.87	0.55	11.02
Bedford	4.27	1.09	0.55	5.91
Berea	7.18	2.89	0.55	10.62
Brooklyn	9.34	3.87	0.55	13.76
Cleveland	6.40	0.06	0.55	7.01
Cleveland Heights	1.64	2.84	0.55	5.03
East Cleveland	0.71	0.75	0.55	2.01
Euclid	1.96	1.49	0.55	3.00
Fairview Park	7.13	5.04	0.55	12.72
Garfield Heights	8.39	3.59	0.55	12.53
Lakewood	2.36	1.43	0.55	4.34
Lyndhurst	6.86	5.79	0.55	13.20
Maple Heights	4.20	4.00	0.55	8.75
Mayfield Heights	4.75	5.06	0.55	10.36
North Olmsted	7.18	0.91	0.55	8.64
Parma	6.41	5.17	0.55	12.13
Rocky River	4.87	3.71	0.55	9.13
Shaker Heights	4.49	4.52	0.55	8.56
South Euclid	2.65	5.79	0.55	8.99
University Heights	1.68	2.84	0.55	5.07
Villages				
Beachwood	6.75	2.05	0.55	9.35
Bedford Heights	0.27	1.09	0.55	1.91
Bentleyville	0.00	2.83	0.55	3.38
Bratenahl	0.00	0.00	0.55	0.55
Brecksville	1.05	4.06	0.55	5.66
Broadview Heights	6.21	4.06 †	0.55	10.82 †
		4.56 ‡		11.32 ‡
Brooklyn Heights	5.12	0.62	0.55	6.29
Brook Park	7.33	2.89	0.55	10.77
Chagrin Falls	2.83	2.83	0.55	6.21
Cuyahoga Heights	0.86	0.62	0.55	2.03
Gates Mills	0.21	5.06	0.55	5.82
Glenwillow	0.00	3.06	0.55	3.61

Table VII-10 (Continued)

Highland Heights	4.31	5.06	0.55	9.92
Hunting Valley	0.20	4.72	0.55	5.47
Independence	2.06	3.58	0.55	6.19
Linndale	0.00	0.06	0.55	0.61
Mayfield	6.42	5.06	0.55	12.03
Middleburg Heights	3.41	2.89	0.55	6.85
Moreland Hills	0.41	4.72 §	0.55	5.68 §
		2.83 **		3.79 **
Newburgh Heights	0.20	0.06	0.55	0.81
North Randall	0.00	5.22	0.55	5.77
North Royalton	3.49	4.56	0.55	8.60
Oakwood	0.00	1.09	0.55	1.64
Olmsted Falls	0.23	3.12	0.55	3.90
Orange	0.00	4.72	0.55	5.27
Parkview	6.63	5.04	0.55	12.22
Parma Heights	1.17	5.17	0.55	6.89
Pepper Pike	0.79	4.72	0.55	6.06
Richmond Heights	3.70	2.15	0.55	5.85
Seven Hills	3.02	5.17	0.55	8.74
Solon	1.79	3.06	0.55	5.40
Strongsville	3.08	6.07	0.55	9.70
Valley View	0.00	0.62	0.55	1.15
Walton Hills	0.00	1.09	0.55	1.64
Warrensville Heights	4.46	5.22	0.55	10.23
Westlake	4.12	4.37	0.55	9.04
West View	0.00	3.12	0.55	3.67
Woodmere	0.00	4.72	0.55	5.27
Townships				
Chagrin Falls	0.00	2.83	0.55	3.38
Olmsted	0.00	3.12	0.55	3.67
Riveredge	0.00	2.89	0.55	3.44
Warrensville	0.00	5.22	0.55	5.77

† Portion of Broadview Heights in Brecksville School District.
‡ Portion of Broadview Heights in North Royalton School District.
§ Portion of Moreland Hills in Orange School District.
** Portion of Moreland Hills in Chagrin Falls School District.

than villages; school debt service was higher generally than municipal debt service, and was equally as high for city as for local and
exempted school districts; municipal debt service of cities was much
higher than municipal debt service of villages and townships, and in
the case of cities as a class, municipal debt service exceeded city
school debt service.

Table VII-11—Median Debt Service by Classes of Government, Cleveland Metropolitan Area 1956 (In Dollars Per $1000 Assessed Valuation)

Debt Service	Class of Government	Year	
		1956	1950
Overall	All Municipalities and overlying governments	5.98	5.25
	All Cities and Overlying Governments	8.97	9.73
	All Villages and Townships and Overlying Governments	5.73	4.60
Municipal	All Municipalities Only	2.51	N.A.
	All Cities Only	4.81	N.A.
	All Villages and Townships Only	.60	N.A.
	Villages and Townships with Debt Only	3.02	N.A.
School	All School Districts Only	3.58	N.A.
	City School Districts Only	3.59	N.A.
	Local and Exempted School Districts Only	3.58	N.A.

N.A.—Not Available

In 1950, the median overall debt service cost for all municipalities was $5.25 per $1000 of assessed valuation. Overall debt service
cost for cities as a class was, however, much greater than for all
municipalities, being $9.73, while for villages and townships, it
was only $4.60.

The outstanding feature of a comparison of debt service patterns
for all municipalities between 1950 and 1956 is that while there
was a small increase in the average debt service there was a marked
shrinkage in the range of variations between municipalities. This is
seen by the fact that in 1950 the higher 30 per cent of the
municipalities had debt service costs between $9.00 and $22.30 per
$1000 of assessed valuation, while in 1956 the highest 30 per
cent ranged between $9.00 and $13.76. Contrary to the trend for
all municipalities, the median overall debt service cost for cities
as a class decreased from 1950 to 1956. The overall increase was the

result of an increase in the median overall debt service cost for villages and townships as a class.

Interest Rates and Maturity Patterns

Due to many limitations deriving from the variety of factors that influence the credit standing of a government and, consequently, the interest rate it must pay, and because a government may pay different rates at different times, depending upon the general state of the market for municipal bonds, it is difficult to meaningfully compare interest rates. Some very general observations, however, may prove useful. In order to establish a basis for comparison, an "average effective interest rate" was computed for each class of government. This was done by dividing the interest paid on all debt during 1956 by the average amount of net debt plus public utility debt [6] outstanding during the year, including short term debt, for the entire class. This, then, is a measure of the actual percentage paid in the form of interest on the net debt plus public utility debt outstanding. It should be noted that this is an aggregate computation and does not, therefore, necessarily reflect the interest rate paid by any single jurisdiction. However, it was felt that similar computations on a government-by-government basis would be of little analytical value because of the variety of factors influencing interest costs.

As may be seen from the table, the effective interest rate paid by the more heavily indebted school districts is slightly higher than the rate paid by cities and villages, with the county paying a rate appreciably lower than the other classes and the City of Cleveland paying a slightly higher rate than the average of other municipalities. But the City of Cleveland's debt structure has no counterpart elsewhere in the county.

No attempt has been made to ascertain maturity patterns of existing debt within the county by governments because data are not readily available for all governments. However, an indication

---

6. It was necessary to include public utility debt in this computation because interest payments excluding public utility debt were not available.

**Table VII-12—Average Effective Interest Rates, and Average
Number of Years to Maturity, Selected Classes
of Government, Cleveland Metropolitan Area, 1956**

Class of Government	Interest Rate (Per Cent)	Average Number of Years to Maturity
All Cities excluding Cleveland	2.33	3.39
All Villages	2.42	4.18
All Cities and Villages excluding Cleveland	2.34	3.54
City School Districts	2.51	10.70
Local & Exempted School Districts	2.54	24.10
All School Districts	2.52	12.26
Cleveland City	2.72	8.79
Cuyahoga County	1.73	13.53
All Governments	2.59	7.62

of the rate at which debt is maturing by classes can be easily determined. Under Ohio law, most bonds must be of a straight serial nature, that is, the principal repaid in equivalent annual or semi-annual amounts. Therefore, by dividing the year-end debt of each class by the amount of principal paid in that year, an indication of the rate at which existing debt matures is obtained. This measure indicates the number of years necessary to eliminate existing debt provided that the payment of principal is the same amount each year as was paid in 1956.

Clearly the most significant feature shown by this measure is that the debt, recently incurred, of school districts is of longer term generally than the existing debt of municipalities. It is also evident that the debt of the City of Cleveland and of the County is of longer maturity than other non-school governments. In the case of Cleveland, this is a reflection of substantial quantities of long term public utility obligations, and in the case of the County, large long term borrowing in the very recent past is responsible for the relatively long maturity period.

Credit Ratings

Potential investors in municipal bonds are greatly influenced by the credit rating of the borrowing government. Moody's Investor Service, for instance, rates many municipalities, i.e., local governments, but not all who have borrowed or are in the process of borrowing. Not all local governments are rated. In some cases, a lack of rating may be due to insufficient information in the hands of the rating service or, in other cases, to a lack of borrowing of amounts sufficient to warrant the investigation necessary in the assignment of a credit rating.

Currently, fifteen of the twenty cities in the county have Moody's credit ratings, none of the villages is rated, sixteen of the seventeen city school districts are rated and five of the local and exempted school districts are rated. The cities' ratings in 1957 ranged from Ba to Aa, but in 1950 ranged from Caa to Aa, and in 1940 from Ca to Aa. In no case has a rating declined since 1940 and in most cases there has been improvement since 1940. This is primarily a reflection of the unusually low ratings in 1940 which were due in many cases to heavy refunding and in some cases defaulting in the 1930's. The ratings of the school districts also ranged from Ba to Aa in 1957, but with a single exception have shown a much better historical record than was the case with cities. In 1940, school district ratings were generally higher than city ratings due primarily to the fact that there was much less refunding in the case of school districts. Currently, a slightly greater proportion of rated cities have ratings above Baa than is the case of rated school districts, and of the total of thirty-seven rated governments, only four fall below the Baa rating. By contrast, in 1940, of the forty governments rated, twenty-nine were below the Baa level.

VIII

The Outlook for 1965

LIKE OTHER MAJOR METROPOLITAN AREAS IN THE United States, the Cleveland Metropolitan Area is expected to continue evolving in the manner that has characterized its behavior since the end of World War II. Not only is an increase in population and economic activity expected, barring some major change arising from world conditions, but the redistribution of people and commerce and industry between the older central area and newer suburbs is also expected to continue. The already very heavily urbanized Cuyahoga County will be almost completely urbanized by 1965, except in those areas where population and industrial growth is restricted by natural or legal barriers. The overflow to other counties will render the restriction of the metropolitan area to a single county, as in the case of this study, or to two counties as in

310

the case of the Cleveland Standard Metropolitan Area, artificial. As people and industry move to the surrounding counties and as such large urbanized areas as those of Youngstown, Akron and Lorain-Elyria are drawn closer to Cleveland, the relevant area for analysis may increase tremendously in size and the metropolitan concept itself may have to be revised to accommodate these new problems.

However, for the period up to 1965 our fiscal forecasts and projections will still be restricted to that area which has been defined as the Cleveland Metropolitan Area because of the hazardous nature of any forecasts of the pattern of economic activity beyond boundaries of Cuyahoga County, and because of the absence of any basic fiscal information concerning the counties, municipalities, school districts, and other governments which in many cases are just beginning their development or are still to be born.

As was indicated in Chapter II, the population growth in the Cleveland Metropolitan Area will take place outside of Cleveland and the older inner-ring municipalities in the decade to come. There will also be a redistribution of population within governmental boundaries of the older inner-ring communities as a result of new land use patterns and urban renewal in the decade to come. School age population and school enrollment will probably continue to increase until 1965 in all school districts either as a result of increased population or changed age distribution, if the experience of the period immediately past is duplicated.

The effects of economic activity and prices on local finances are more hazardous to forecast or project than population; however, they are essential for the formulation of meaningful projections. In particular, this means the formulation of assumptions in terms of national trends and local conditions, and their effects on the level of economic activity and prices. Nationally, it is assumed that economic growth continues at an average rate of about 3 per cent per year and that 1965 is a year of relatively high economic activity and that there will be neither any severe depressions nor a transition to an entirely defense-oriented economy, consumer prices are assumed in 1965 to be a) at 1956 levels and b) at 20 per cent above the 1956 level. The latter figure is equal to the average annual rate of increase in the consumer price index for the period 1950-56 extrapolated to 1965. The price of providing local governmental services is assumed to go up at a more rapid rate, 20 per cent in the first instance, and 40 per cent in the latter case, corresponding to the actual annual rate of increase in the local government price index for the period 1950-56.

Assumptions concerning local developments in the Cleveland Metropolitan Area must be superimposed on the above-mentioned national patterns. It may be noted that the local and specific projections are more hazardous to formulate than projects of national and aggregate developments. However, a number of points concerning local developments seem quite evident at this time (1959). First, that the rate of growth in economic activity in the Cleveland Metropolitan Area, i.e., Cuyahoga County, will probably not equal that of the most recent period (cf. Census of Manufacturers material in Chapter II). Second, that the greatest rate of economic growth will probably take place on the periphery of an expanded Cleveland Metropolitan Area where there are large enough tracts of land to build the low level plants that are becoming increasingly characteristic of large industrial establishments. Third, that there will be no basic changes in the location of industry and commerce other than those presently evidenced within the Cleveland Metropolitan Area such as the decentralization of shopping centers and certain forms of industry, by 1965. Fourth, that changes in local fiscal policy in the Cleveland Metropolitan Area will have relatively little effect on the level of local economic activity.

The aim of the projections contained in this chapter is to show what would happen if existing trends affecting governmental finance were to continue. Their function is to provide a sound basis for critical thought. Two kinds of projections have been formulated, pure and modified. A pure projection would show what would happen if past trends were extrapolated without modification. However, certain changes are already known to be taking place or it is known that past behavior does not provide a reliable guide to the future. To take account of these circumstances, the projections were modified in accordance with the best available information which is presented later in this chapter. Finally, it is possible to forecast where the connection with the past is broken and the aim is to state explicitly as possible what is expected to happen. To summarize: pure projections show what would happen if existing trends (linear, logarithmic, etc.) were maintained; modified projections show what would happen if existing trends were altered. Where account is taken of all departures known or expected to take place, forecasts are an attempt to show what will be true as of a future date or time period and may or may not be related to the projections.

Projections are presented for consideration of two interrelated but distinct problems that are to be faced in the decade ahead. The first may be called the problem of the "fiscal gap," that is, what is going to be the relationship between the fiscal needs and resources of the governments collectively and individually comprising the Cleveland Metropolitan Area. Given assumptions concerning world conditions, national and local economic growth and activity, what would be the relationship between total receipts and disbursements?

The second set of projections involves an analysis of each of the sectors that make up local finance; current operating expenditures, capital expenditures, revenues, and debt. Although each of these sectors is obviously related to the others and to the over-all problem of the "fiscal gap," the aim of these projections is to analyze the several components of each sector in detail. The sources of changes and/or the lack of change will be determined by class of government and by class of fiscal activity, whether it be expenditure, revenue, or debt.

The "fiscal gap" analysis will not reflect the problem of the individual governments—county, municipalities, school districts, and library districts—equally. Depending on their individual requirements and resources, the problems faced by individual governments in the metropolitan area will be either reduced or intensified, but their individual positions will reflect the position of the metropolitan configuration itself.

Current operating expenditures are projected on an aggregate and per capita basis based on a variety of assumptions applied to the trends from 1950 to 1956. The pure projections were modified to account for known changes in trends since 1956 or for conditions which were not considered as representative. In the case of capital outlays, pure projections provided a starting point, but nothing more, because of the arbitrary nature and the irregularity of outlays for capital construction. In like manner, revenue and debt projections were only initially based on mechanical methods and were modified to take into account known changes or more probable circumstances than purely mechanical methods would permit.

The exact basis for each set of projections will be presented in its appropriate section below. In general, they are all the result of evaluating the effects of present trends operating within the Cleveland Metropolitan Area, rather than the evaluation of the effects of profound upheavals internationally, nationally, or locally.

The Fiscal Gap

Between 1956 and 1965, total disbursements of local governments are expected to increase from $297 million to $585 million, or by almost 97 per cent. Under existing tax rates anticipating "normal growth" of revenues, total receipts are expected to increase from $301 million to $500 million, or by 66 per cent. This would leave a gap between expected receipts and expected disbursements of $85 million. To understand the meaning of this gap and to determine the manner in which this gap may be bridged, we will turn first to the period between 1950 and 1956 and then to a detailed analysis of the expected developments between 1956 and 1965. The "fiscal gap" will be applied first to the Cleveland Metropolitan Area as a whole and then to the selected important and/or typical areas we noted earlier.

PROJECTING 1956 IN 1950

In 1950 total disbursements by all governments in the Cleveland Metropolitan Area, exclusive of public service enterprises, were $162 million. Total receipts were $172 million. Cash balances grew by $10 million in 1950.

On a current basis, that is including all revenues except those dedicated to capital outlay, and including current operating expenditures, interest, and debt retirement (viewed as the approximate equivalent of depreciation), there was an increase in cash balances of $20 million. On capital account, outlays exceeded borrowing and

Table VIII-1—Actual and Projected Cash Flows, All Governments, Cleveland Metropoitan Area (In Millions of Dollars)

Account	1950	1956	1965 *
Receipts			
Revenues	155	250	385
Borrowing	17	51	115
Total	172	301	500
Disbursements			
Current	135	240	455
Capital Outlay	27	54	130
Total	162	294	585
Change in Cash Balance	+ 10	+ 7	...

* Projected.

dedicated revenues by $10 million. This was probably paid for by drawing down existing cash balances which were built up by the current surplus or earlier borrowing to the extent of $10 million.

Confronted in 1950 with the problem of predicting the financial position of the governments in the Cleveland Metropolitan Area in 1956, one would have to predict the level of prices and the level of economic activity as well as the real value of governmental expenditures in 1956. Suppose that one predicted with accuracy not only the current cost of operating government, but also interest payments and debt retirement as well. It would also have been necessary to predict total capital outlays of $55 million. The current account would have shown expenses of $242 million, or an increase of $107 million between 1950 and 1956. If the $20 million cash balance of 1950 were applied wholly to 1956, this would still have left a final gap of $87 million in terms of the 1950 revenue structure to be filled. The gap was filled between 1950 and 1956 and it is the manner in which the gap was filled that is of the greatest interest.

Apart from a reduction in expenditures, which has been excluded by assumption and fact, the gap could have been reduced by resource to local sources or the increased availability of governmental aid. Other possible solutions would have been either temporary borrowing or shifting responsibility to the state or federal

Table VIII-2—Actual and Projected Current and Capital Accounts, All Governments, Cleveland Metropolitan Area

CURRENT ACCOUNT
(In Millions of Dollars)

Account	1950	1956	1965 *
Current Income			(minimum)
Revenues for Current Expenses	155	244	370
Current Expenses			
Current Operating	119	205	380
Interest	4	7	17
Debt Retirement	12	30	58
Total	135	242	455
Effect on Cash Balance	20	2	—85

CAPITAL ACCOUNT
(In Millions of Dollars)

Account	1950	1956	1965 *
Receipts			
Earmarked Revenues	†	6	15
Borrowing	17	51	115
Total	†	57	130
Capital Outlay	27	55	130
Effect on Cash Balance	— 10 †	2	0

* Projected (1965 in 1956 consumer dollars).
† Probably some earmarked revenues.

government. As a matter of fact, intergovernmental sources of revenue increased between 1950 and 1956, but borrowing was restricted primarily to capital outlays. Thus, the largest part of the increase in revenues was the result of the expansion of local revenue sources, principally the property tax, and there is strong reason to believe that up to 1965 it will continue to be the principal source of increased revenues in the Cleveland Metropolitan Area.

The net expansion of the property tax base between 1950 and 1956 was the result of a number of forces operating simultaneously: growth in the value of property subject to taxation, reassessment and reappraisal of existing property values upwards, and, on the

minus side, a decrease in the average millage or property tax rate
for local purposes. The result was an increase of local property taxes
levied of $58.6 million between 1950 and 1956 of which a small
proportion was earmarked for capital outlays.

To be more specific, the increase in the yield of the property tax
between 1950 and 1956 was the result of the following:

	Increase in Yield
Growth ($1,098.8 million)	$ + 33.8 million
Increase in Value as a Result of Reassessment and Reappraisal of Real Estate ($824.4 million)	+ 25.4 million
Decrease in Tax Rates from 30.82 mills in 1949-50 to 30.49 mills in 1955-56	− 0.6 million
Total Property Tax Change	$ + 58.6 million

During this period other local revenues increased by an additional
$14 million; at the same time revenues from intergovernmental
sources increased by $23 million. As a result of these changes, less
the amount earmarked for capital outlays, the gap of $89 million was
filled and cash balances were increased by $2 million on current
account in 1956. On capital account, borrowing increased sufficiently
to finance the increased capital outlay, and it may be assumed, apart
from dedicated or earmarked revenues, that capital outlays will
continue to be financed by borrowing.

Not all of the incease in cost of local governmental services
was the result of additional services. Exclusive of debt retirement,
the increase in the cost of local government was $79 million in
1956 dollars as compared to $127 million in current dollars.
At the same time, the increase in the real tax base (i.e., constant
basis of appraisal) and other revenue sources did not increase as
rapidly as expenditures in current dollars, with the result that part
of the fiscal gap was the result of a differential ratio of increases in
the cost of providing services and in the resources to finance them.
A much smaller effort would have had to have been made had

there been parity in movement between the cost of providing the services and the resources available.

Projecting 1965

With this experience, let us ask what is expected of revenues and expenditures in 1965. Here there is no possibility of being omniscient, although we have checked our assumptions by the experience of 1957 and 1958, and by the plans for 1959. These tend to confirm, at least for the time being, our projections. Moreover, the purpose of these projections is to establish an order of magnitude and the nature of the problem rather than to predict precise amounts.

Disbursements in 1965 are expected to be $585 million. This figure is based on the same rate of increase between 1956 and 1965 in operating expenditures as occurred between 1950 and 1956, plus some considered assumptions concerning interest, capital outlay, and debt retirement in the period to come. For our first estimate, it is assumed that inflation will continue to act on the consumer price index and on the cost of providing government services equally, and roughly at the rate of 1.9 per cent per annum (as between 1950 and 1956) for a total of 20 per cent by 1965. Insofar as the cost of providing governmental services rises more rapidly or slowly than the assumed 20 per cent rise in the consumer price index, the estimated gap would accordingly be expanded or contracted. Thus if the cost of governmental services rises by 20 per cent more than the cost of living, total disbursements would be roughly $670 millions.

There are two potential gaps, that on current account, and that on capital account. It is assumed that the latter will be met entirely by borrowing and by earmarked revenues. It is assumed that the electorate will approve and that the governments will be able to sell their obligations in 1965 to finance their capital outlays.

The principal problem involves the gap on current account. It is projected that at a minimum, current expenditures in 1965 will reach $455 million ($519 million if the cost goes up 20 per cent more than the consumer price index). With the 1956 level of current revenues, the gap would be $211 million and it is assumed that revenues will go up $126 million on the basis of projected trends in revenue sources. This would consist of the following:

Table VIII-3—Projected Increase in Current Revenues, All Governments, Cleveland Metropolitan Area, from 1956 to 1965

(In Millions of Dollars)

Revenue	1956	1965	Increase 1965 Over 1956
Property Taxes	142	227	85
Other Local Revenue	52	75	23
State Aid	51	71	20
Federal Aid	5	13	8
Total	250	385	135
Less: Revenue earmarked for capital purposes	6	15	9
Current Revenue	244	370	126
Supporting Data for Property Tax			
Tax Duplicate (Millions)	4,641	6,400	1,759
Average Tax Rate for Local Purposes in Mills	30.48	35.5 *	5.02

* Estimated 1958-1959 rate.

The projection for 1965 assumes the 1957-58 average tax rate and continuation of the recent rate of growth in the tax base. If the estimates are correct the gap between the 1965 disbursements on current account and the 1965 current income will be $85 million. Given the assumed rate of taxation and the projected growth in the tax base, but no reappraisal, revenues for current purposes will be $370 million or $85 million less than current expenditures. This amount implies that a gap equal to about thirteen mills in the property tax rate would have to be bridged. This gap could be even larger, depending on the relative growth in the cost of providing government services, as indicated by the $670 million figure, if the differential is 20 per cent.

In Chapter VI and later in this chapter, a number of alternative revenue sources, in addition to the expansion of property tax collection, are suggested. The excess of 19 per cent of projected current operating expenditures over current revenues for 1965 applies to the entire Cleveland Metropolitan Area. The gap for individual local governments will be relatively smaller or larger depending on the conditions in each jurisdiction.

The increase may be smaller or larger, insofar as some governments are concerned, depending on specialized conditions. Only in exceptional cases can a 100 per cent increase in current expenditures be met with relative ease; however, there may be one such case in the county. On the other hand, most communities will be faced with the problem of raising substantial additional revenues, which would be complicated if substantial additional services are also necessary.

Thus far in this chapter emphasis has been placed on the anticipated "fiscal gap" for 1965. In this and succeeding parts of Chapter VIII, emphasis will be placed on the individual disbursements (outgo) on current operating expenditures, capital outlay, interest and debt repayments on the one hand, and the income from tax and non-tax sources, intergovernmental revenues, and borrowing on the other. A series of projections have been formulated, which are designed to bring out the developments within each of the above categories of governmental income and outgo. But, whereas in the discussion of the fiscal gap the principal aim was to present the overall income and outgo in directly comparable fashion, in this and succeeding parts of this chapter it will be the projected movements within the individual sectors which will be analyzed in a directly comparable fashion. In the case of current operating expenditures and capital outlays, for instance, this means the difference between including the effect of a 20 per cent increase in the local government price level over and above the consumer price level between 1956 and 1965, which was incorporated in the analysis of the fiscal gap, and their presentation in constant (1956) dollars in the analysis of operating expenditures and capital outlays.

It is assumed, in the analysis that follows, that current operating expenditures in 1965 will continue to reflect patterns of growth that have been in evidence since 1946, and most clearly since

1950. Specifically, the growth in operating expenditures between 1950 and 1956 has been chosen as a norm for projecting classes of operating expenditures in 1965. There were differences in relative rates and absolute amounts of growth among classes of expenditures, most of which were noted and explained in Chapter IV; continued differences are expected in the future. A range of projections is presented to illustrate what would happen under different assumptions concerning the future. The projections were tested for consistency and accuracy against historic time series.

In order to place the projections for 1965 operating expenditures in perspective, actual and projected data for interest and capital outlays are shown in aggregate and per capita constant dollars by government for the years 1940, 1950, 1956 as well as for 1965. And it should be noted again that the municipal category includes Cuyahoga County and the Cleveland Metropolitan Park District, as well as all the cities, villages and townships.

This summary table shows the changing relationship of current operating expenditures, capital outlays and interest expenditures, excluding public service enterprises and debt retirement, by major classes of government. The changing importance of current oper-

Table VIII-4—Actual and Projected "Probable" Expenditures, All Governments, Cleveland Metropolitan Area (In Thousands of 1956 Dollars)

Expenditures	1940	1950	1956	1965 *
Municipal operating	111,918	93,685	120,846	182,900
School operating	50,162	51,636	78,511	134,500
Library operating	5,388	5,709	6,364	7,500
Total operating	167,468	151,030	205,721	324,900
Municipal capital	20,862	24,500	36,312	78,500
School capital	1,846	9,800	18,147	32,000
Library capital	27	520	658	500
Total capital	22,735	34,820	55,117	111,000
Total Interest	22,764	6,882	9,791	17,000
TOTAL	212,964	192,732	270,629	452,900

* Projected.

ating expenditures relative to total expenditures and to capital and interest expenditures is interesting.

It is anticipated that the relative importance of municipal operating expenditures both to the total of all expenditures and to school operating will continue to decline as it has for the period

Table VIII-5—Actual and Projected Distribution of Expenditures, All Governments, Cleveland Metropolitan Area

Expenditures	1940	1950	1956	1965 †
(Per Cent)				
Municipal Operating	52.6	48.6	44.7	40.4
School Operating	23.6	26.8	29.0	29.7
Library Operating	2.5	3.0	2.4	1.7
Total Operating	78.6	78.4	76.0	71.7
Municipal Capital	9.8	12.7	13.4	17.3
School Capital	0.9	5.1	6.7	7.1
Library Capital	0.0 *	0.3	0.2	0.1
Total Capital	10.7	18.1	20.4	24.5
Total Interest	10.7	3.6	3.6	3.8
Total All	100.0	100.0	100.0	100.0
Exhibit—Total in millions of constant (1956) dollars	212.96	192.73	270.63	452.90

* Less than .1%.
† Projected.

1940-56. Further, it is anticipated that the decline in municipal operating expenditures will be in part offset by an increase in municipal capital outlays in the decade to come.

If changes in population as well as price levels are taken into account, then a markedly different picture emerges. As shown earlier, the dip in real operating expenditures between 1940 and 1950 is much larger in per capita terms and the increase between 1950 and 1956 much less than the totals alone would indicate. Likewise, the per capita increase in real expenditures between 1950 and 1956 appears much smaller than does the aggregate increase projected as most probable for 1965. A considerable part of the increase in aggregate actual and projected expenditures will continue to be associated with population growth, especially of the school aged and the elderly. The population is assumed to grow 15.8 per cent between 1956 and 1965, and the number of students attending public school by 41.6 per cent.

Table VIII-6—Per Capita Actual and Projected Expenditures, All Governments, Cleveland Metropolitan Area (In 1956 Dollars)

Expenditures	1940	1950	1956	1965 *
Municipal operating	91.94	67.43	76.51	99.95
School operating	41.20	37.16	49.67	73.50
(School operating per ADM)	(301.64)	(315.36)	(347.26)	(423.36)
Library operating	4.42	4.11	4.03	4.10
Total Operating	137.58	108.70	130.22	177.55
Municipal capital	17.14	17.65	22.97	42,90
School capital	1.51	7.05	11.48	17.49
(School capital per ADM)	(11.10)	(59.85)	(88.87)	(100.00)
Library	.02	.35	.42	.27
Total Capital	18.67	25.05	34.87	60.66
Total Interest	18.69	4.96	6.19	9.28
TOTAL	174.97	138.71	171.23	247.49

* Projected.

The growth of operating expenditures in the Cleveland Metropolitan Area since 1950 is a reflection of a number of forces in addition to the growth of and change in the age composition of the population. Other factors of importance include the continuing movement to the suburbs which involved the provision of government services to more widely dispersed industrial and residential property; the change in the demand for government services, particularly education, but other services as well; and finally the increased cost of providing given amounts of government services. In current dollars the figures for 1965 and those for 1940 and 1950 are considerably lower than are indicated by the constant (1956) dollars used in Table VIII-6.

Projecting Operating Expenditures—Detail 1965

Functional breakdowns of projected operating expenditures provide guide lines for projections of individual government expenditures. The functional projections made for governments in the Cleveland Metropolitan Area should be compared in general outline with other projections for approximately the same time period made by others.[1]

From 1950 to 1956 with one minor exception, public health, every category of operating expenditure increased not only in current amounts, but in constant dollars as well. This stands in contrast with the period 1940-50 where conversion into constant dollars reversed a pervasive upward movement into a pervasive downward movement. If the constant dollar totals are converted into

---

1. Mr. Grant Apthorp, Director of Finance of the City of East Cleveland has suggested the following way of analyzing projected expenditures for 1965:

	1950	1956	1965
Estimated Population	1,389,532	1,580,553	1,830,000
Population as % 1950	100.0	113.7	
Population as % 1956		100.0	115.8

1956 estimate provided by Cleveland Regional Planning Commission

Consumer Price Index (C.P.I.)	102.8	116.2	
C.P.I. as % of 1950	88.5	100.0	119.5 (calculated)
1965 = 1956 + 150% * × 13.0% increase (1950-1956)			
Implicit Price Index (I.P.I.)	115.3	146.6	
I.P.I. as % of 1950	78.6	100.0	140.6
1965 = 1956 + 150% * of the 27.1 increase (1950-1956)			

Actual and Estimated Expenditures in Millions of Dollars
   (1965 in 1956 consumer dollars)

			Straight Line	Probable
Current Operating	118.8	205.7	336.0	380
Interest	4	7	11.5	17
Capital	27.4	55.1	96.7	13$
Debt Retirement	12	30	57.0	58
TOTAL	162.2	297.8	501.0	585

* 150% allows for growth over 9 years, 1956-65, compared with the 6 years, 1950-56.

per capita terms the same general picture remains for both periods, but with a sharper decline between 1940 and 1950 and a lesser increase between 1950 and 1956.

The projections of expenditures by function are presented in terms of a high, a low, and a most probable level. Two separate approaches were followed in formulating the projections; the first was based on the observed changes in constant dollar expenditures by functional category between 1950 and 1956; the second approach was based on analysis of constant dollar per capita (or per student) expenditures in 1940, 1950, and 1956. The projections based on the two methods were consistent with each other. The advantage of the former approach is that it provides a basis for determining total amount of expenditures; the advantage of the latter approach is that it provides a basis for evaluating service levels.

The *low projection* for 1965 is consistent with the amount of growth between 1950 and 1956, the *probable projection* for 1965 assumes the same rate of growth as between 1950 and 1956, and the *high projection* for 1965 assumes an increase in the rate of growth over the 1950-56 rate. Specifically, the *low projection* means, in terms of per capita expenditures, a minor improvement in standards and the continuation of the present amount of growth with respect to individual functional categories. It assumes a slightly larger increase in per capita real expenditures than occurred between 1950 and 1956, but of course 1956 to 1965 is a slightly longer period. If schools are excepted, it assumes per capita real expenditures slightly below those that existed in 1940. If public welfare is omitted, the result would be a minor increase in per capita expenditures.

The *probable* projection assumes an improvement and equal-ization of standards consistent with increased urbanization and greater demands on local governments. It assumes an increase in per capita real expenditures above those of 1940 whether or not public welfare expenditures are included and considerably above in the case of current operating expenditures on schools. It is assumed that the major deficiencies in providing governmental services still existing in 1956 will be made up by 1965.

The *high* projection assumes that almost all governments in the Cleveland Metropolitan Area will provide standards of service in

Table VIII-7—Actual and Projected * Expenditures by Function, All Governments, Cleveland Metropolitan Area (In Thousands of 1956 Dollars)

Expenditures	1940	1950	1956	Low 1965	Probable 1965	High 1965	Probable 1965/56 (Per Cent)
General Government	13,930	11,058	14,804	20,423	22,900	23,800	154.7
Police	13,749	13,877	16,542	20,540	22,300	22,900	134.8
Fire	8,658	7,716	9,695	12,663	14,700	15,700	151.6
Other Public Safety	2,287	3,400	4,465	6,063	6,900	7,300	154.5
Public Health	1,560	1,849	1,845	1,839	2,700	3,700	146.3
Hospital	11,121	7,339	12,201	19,494	22,900	26,200	187.7
Public Welfare	32,156	16,636	21,178	27,991	30,400	32,900	143.5
Streets & Highways	15,545	12,510	14,504	17,495	20,100	21,900	138.6
Misc. Comm. Activity	6,530	10,235	12,826	16,712	18,300	20,100	142.7
Recreation & Culture	2,480	3,917	5,071	6,802	7,500	8,200	147.9
Land Use & Development	85	510	521	537	1,100	1,800	211.1
Pensions	2,608	4,159	6,210	9,286	11,300	12,800	182.0
Misc. & Unallocable	1,200	479	982	1,736	1,800	2,700	183.3
Total Municipal Operating	111,918	93,685	120,844	161,581	182,900	200,000	151.4
Total School Operating	50,162	51,636	78,511	118,824	134,500	147,300	171.3
Total Library Operating	5,388	5,709	6,364	7,347	7,500	8,200	117.9
Total Current Operating	167,468	151,030	205,719	287,752	324,900	355,500	157.5
Interest	22,764	6,882	9,791	14,154	17,000	22,000	173.6
School Capital	1,846	9,800	18,149	30,673	32,000	47,600	176.3
Municipal Capital	20,862	24,500	36,312	54,530	78,500	80,500	216.2
Library Capital	27	520	657	400	500	1,800	76.1
Total Capital	22,735	34,820	55,118	85,565	111,000	129,900	201.4
TOTAL ALL	212,964	192,732	270,630	387,659	452,900	507,400	168.9

* Projections: Low—assumes minor improvement in standards. Probable—assumes an improvement and equalization of standards consistent with increased density and greater demands on local governments. High—assumes governments will provide standards of services in 1965 equivalent to those provided by the best units in 1956, or where performance is not recognizably adequate, improvement to some objective standard.

Table VIII-8—Actual and Projected * Per Capita Expenditures, by Function, All Governments, Cleveland Metropolitan Area, (In 1956 Dollars)

Expenditures	1940	1950	1956	Low 1965	Probable 1965	High 1965	1965/56 Probable (Per Cent)
General Government	11.45	7.96	9.37	11.16	12.50	13.01	133.4
Police	11.30	9.99	10.47	11.22	12.20	12.51	116.5
Fire	7.12	5.55	6.13	6.92	8.03	8.57	122.3
Other Public Safety	1.88	2.45	2.83	3.31	3.75	3.98	132.5
Public Health	1.28	1.33	1.17	1.00	1.50	2.02	128.2
Hospital	9.13	5.29	7.72	10.65	12.50	14.32	161.9
Public Welfare	26.42	11.97	13.40	15.30	16.60	17.97	123.9
Streets & Highways	12.78	9.00	9.18	9.56	11.00	11.96	119.8
Misc. Comm. Activity	5.36	7.37	8.11	9.13	10.00	10.98	123.3
Recreation & Culture	2.03	2.82	3.21	3.71	4.10	4.48	127.7
Land Use & Development	.07	.37	.33	.29	.60	.98	181.8
Pensions	2.15	2.99	3.93	5.07	6.20	6.99	157.8
Misc. & Unallocable	.99	.34	.67	.95	1.00	1.47	149.3
Total Municipal Operating	91.94	67.43	76.51	88.30	99.95	108.70	130.0
Total School Operating	41.20	37.16	49.67	64.93	73.50	80.49	148.0
Total (School Operating Per A.D.M.)	(301.64)	(315.36)	(347.26)	(371.32)	(423.36)	(463.64)	(121.9)
Total Library Operating	4.42	4.11	4.03	4.01	4.10	4.48	101.7
Total Current Operating	137.58	108.70	130.22	157.24	177.55	193.67	136.0
Interest	18.69	4.96	6.19	7.73	9.28	12.02	149.9
School Capital	1.51	7.05	11.48	16.76	17.49	26.01	152.4
(School Operating Per A.D.M.)	(11.10)	(59.85)	(88.87)	(95.85)	(100.00)	(148.75)	112.5
Municipal Capital	17.14	17.63	22.97	29.78	42.90	43.98	186.8
Library Capital	.02	.37	.42	.22	.27	.98	64.3
Total Capital	18.67	25.05	34.87	46.75	60.66	70.97	174.0
GRAND TOTAL	174.97	138.71	171.28	211.79	247.49	276.66	145.8

* Projections: Low—assumes minor improvement in standards. Probable—assumes an improvement and equalization of standards consistent with increased density and greater demands on local governments. High—assumes governments will provide standards of services in 1965 equivalent to those provided by the best units in 1956, or where performance is not recognizably adequate, improvement to some objective standard.

1965 equivalent to those provided by the best units in 1956—or where performance is not recognizably adequate, improvement to some objective standard. This would mean no major deficiencies in the provision of local governmental services in Cuyahoga County in 1965.

Specifically, the projections of current operating expenditures assume the following: 1) a growth in population from 1,580,000 in 1956 to 1,830,000 in 1965; 2) no changes in the purchasing power of governments in the Cleveland Metropolitan Area (that is, they are formulated in terms of 1956 dollars); 3) an increase in school age and older people relative to the total population; 4) a continuation of urban-type growth outside Cleveland and other core area communities, and a substantially unchanged population in the core area with 945,000 persons living in the City of Cleveland; 5) no major change in the present functional responsibility from or to governments in Cleveland Metropolitan Area, except in those cases where explicit account is taken of readily foreseeable developments (this assumption is modified considerably in the projections of capital expenditures, especially those for urban renewal in 1965).

As shown in Table VIII-7, the most probable projection of municipal operating expenditures assumes an increase of $62.1 millions or 51.4 per cent; at the same time, it is projected that school operating expenditures will increase by $56.0 or 71.3 per cent. The more rapid increase in school operating expenditures is due to the fact that the school enrollment is expected to rise by 41.6 per cent as compared to an increase in population of 15.8 per cent between 1956 and 1965. This is shown in the per capita estimates which assume a 30.0 per cent increase in municipal operating expenditures and a 49.0 per cent increase in per capita school operating expenditures. However, if the school operating expenditures are analyzed on a per student basis, the increase is 21.9 per cent, or less than the projected increase in per capita municipal operating expenditures. Library operating expenditures both in total and per capita are expected to show little change.

Unlike school operating expenditures where instructional costs predominate, municipal operating expenditures reflect many factors depending on the functions involved, and not all functions are expected to grow equally. Because data are not available individually, all municipal pension contributions have been grouped together instead of being allocated to their respective functional categories, with the result that the increases in several of the functional categories are understated. Municipal pension contributions are expected to continue to grow at an above average rate between 1956 and 1965.

Municipal functions may be grouped together according to anticipated rates of growth—those considerably above average, those below average, and those about average. In the above average expenditure group are included, in addition to Pensions, the Hospitals, Land Use and Development, and the Miscellaneous and Unallocable categories. Each of these categories reflects not only the underlying pattern of growth, but also special conditions governing a more rapid rate of growth. Of these categories, the most spectacular absolute growth is expected to occur in the case of hospital expenditures. However, it should be noted that between 1950 and 1956 hospital expenditures grew by 11 per cent per annum (much of it is due to a single government, Lakewood); while during the period 1956-65 they are expected to increase at a slightly lesser rate of 9.5 per cent. As the county's hospital expenditures increase, this reflects not only the transfer of responsibilities, but the increasing cost of hospital services, especially that resulting from the increase in the number of aged and their special care. In addition, hospital costs are expected to increase more rapidly than the cost of providing other government services by a considerable amount. On the other hand, the increased hospital care of the aged probably will be reflected by lower relief costs for the aged than would otherwise be the case. The introduction of large scale federal housing for the aged, or increased federal grants for the aged, may alter this picture, depending on the nature of the program, its financing, and the responsible agency.

The expected growth in operating expenditures on land use and development is just a minor reflection of the vast expansion that is expected in this expenditure category; this represents the increase in local public planning activities almost exclusively. The large relative increase is partly a statistical illusion, since it represents a small absolute increase; on the other hand, it reflects large increases in capital outlays which are not always discernible, since operating costs associated with land use and planning appear in almost all other operating expenditure categories, in the capital outlay sector, and as costs associated with borrowing. In addition, certain land use and development expenditures are not reported because they are not made by local governments, as, for instance, the operating expenditures of the Cleveland Metropolitan Housing Authority. These expenditure are not reported but neither, on the other hand, are its revenues. There is no doubt, therefore, that the actual expenditures on local land use and planning will be far in excess of the figure projected, but that only more inclusive accounting could account for the total sums to be spent.

The increase in pension contributions by government reflects, as has been stated, the increased cost of providing other services. The increase in pensions has been taking place at a considerably more rapid rate than municipal operating expenditures as a whole. Much of the increase in police and fire expenditures has occurred here, rather than in additions to take-home pay. Since contributions to police and fire pension funds reflects the growth of the tax base, these will increase accordingly. Expected increases in municipal wage levels and in PERS (Ohio State Retirement System) coverage for the period 1956-65 will also contribute to the projected growth in pensions. Major changes in policy such as in the rate of local contributions or inclusion under social security may lead to major differences between the projected and actual expenditures in 1965. The same would hold in the case of school and library operating expenditures.

Local expenditures for the Other Public Safety category represent in part a reduction of what was earlier considered police and fire expenditure to a public safety overhead, as well as the introduction of newer functions, primarily civilian defense. A change in federal policy and responsibility for civilian defense could lead to a vast increase in local expenditure, if for example federal or state expenditures were made via locally administered civilian defense grants through the county or municipalities. The projection does not anticipate such a major change in civilian defense policy, but rather a continuation of the present trends which are primarily overhead in nature.

The growth of the Miscellaneous category reflects the growth of

Workmen's Compensation and/or governmental liability for a variety of circumstances. This trend does not seem to be reversible, and depending on the courts and public policy, may be many times as great as is projected.

Current operating expenditures on Police, Public Welfare, Streets and Highways, and Miscellaneous Commercial Activity are projected as growing at a less rapid rate than the average. Three of the four represent the "older" governmental functions, which are already almost fully developed. The fourth, Miscellaneous Commercial Activity, represents special considerations which are reflected more in capital outlay and interest and debt repayment, than as current operating expenditures. Each represents a considerable absolute increase, and a lesser relative increase.

Police expenditures are expected to show the smallest rate of growth between 1956 and 1965. This partly reflects the fact that the police function is perhaps the most completely developed municipal function in the Cleveland Metropolitan Area, and that part of its growth appears in other functional categories such as Other Public Safety and Pensions. In addition, the rate of increase appears small because of the relatively large base to which it is compared.

For a variety of reasons, operating expenditures on streets and highways are expected to grow less rapidly than the average of all operating expenditures. Partly this is because of the growing importance of state and federal highway expenditures, especially on new construction as compared to maintenance. Again, like police expenditures, street and highway expenditures are a highly developed function, and large absolute increases appear as small relative increases. A number of factors, however, indicate that even the high projection may be on the low side. First, the per capita expenditure on streets and highways, even under the high projection, are still below the per capita real expenditure on highways in 1940. The increased highway construction and usage should be reflected in increased operating cost. Secondly, the maintenance of major arterial and other highways, once constructed, should be far greater than those of the present highway system. The cost of snow removal on arterial systems may be far in excess of existing costs. Third, changes in the financial responsibility for road maintenance which will occur as a result of the reclassification of villages to cities will also result in increased local expenditures. However, the increased capital outlays may still be reflected in lower operating costs at least through 1965, and the projected expenditures on streets and highways may continue to serve as a useful guide.

Expenditures on public welfare differ from all other categories of operating expenditures herein considered in that the absolute amount of expenditure in 1965 is expected to be lower than the comparable amount for 1940, and in per capita terms very considerably below those of 1940. Nevertheless, for the period 1950-56 the trend was generally upward, as it has been for the longer period 1948 to the present, partially as the result of the growth in the number of long term relief clients which are financed to a greater extent out of local funds more than any other welfare program. Even during periods of full employment, the public welfare case loads have been substantial. This is seen in the fact that between 1948 and 1956 the number of general assistance cases rose from 1,000 to 3,800. It is estimated that after full recovery from the economic decline of 1958 the case load will level off at about 4,500.

The current operating expenditures on Miscellaneous Commercial Activities are not expected to grow to the same extent as other functions. This is partly because miscellaneous commercial activity expenditures, unlike other expenditures, grew between 1940 and 1950 and continued to grow between 1950 and 1956, although at a reduced rate. And, like expenditures on streets and highways, growth in this sector is reflected in capital interest and debt repayment expenditures, rather than current operating expenditures. The largest expenditure is and will continue to be sewerage and rubbish collection. A major change in locally operated air transportation facilities or in the lakeport may, however, induce further changes in operating expenditures.

Between the extremes of great and little growth are a number of functional categories whose growth does not distinctly fall into either area. Expenditures of General Government, Fire, Other Public Safety, Public Health, and Recreation and Culture categories fall into the middle category. Of these, expenditures on general government and fire will account for the largest absolute increases.

The slightly greater than average growth in general government expenditures is counter expectation. The considerations in Chapter IV would have indicated a decline or below average growth. The increase in expenditures reflects the increased number of municipalities that will be cities in 1965 as well as the expectation that the general government functions of Cuyahoga County will continue to expand in the decade ahead.

In like manner there may be a major increase in local fire expenditures as full-time fire protection becomes more general throughout an increasingly urbanized Cuyahoga County. This development seems to be an inevitable consequence of increased densities in the outlying sections of the county as well as of an increased number of cities. A few very highly developed volunteer companies may continue to exist, but where there is no strong volunteer tradition and no locally available personnel, there seems to be no alternative to full-time departments by 1965. Nevertheless, it is assumed that the rate of increase will be almost exactly average partly because of the heavy weight of the older built-up areas, especially Cleveland and other core area communities, and partly because part of the increase in fire expenditures will appear also in the Pension and Other Public Safety categories.

Current expenditures on Public Health and Recreation and Culture are expected to grow at about the average rate. Again changes in policy and/or responsibility may render these projections obsolete. However, on the basis of past developments and consultation with experts in the field, this does not seem too likely for the area as a whole, although there may be changes within the area.

Up to this point, only municipal operating expenditures have been considered in detail. Since expenditures on municipal public service enterprises are explicitly omitted, this leaves only school and library projections which were briefly mentioned before to be accounted for, and since the library expenditures seem to be direct reflection of the means of their financing, they may also be set aside at this point. This leaves a single category of operating expenditure still to be accounted for, namely, the most important single category of local operating expenditures—schools.

The growth of school operating expenditures has been the outstanding single development in post-World War II local expenditures in the Cleveland Metropolitan Area as well as elsewhere. For instance in 1940, 30 per cent of the operating budget was devoted to school operating expenditures; in 1956, 38.2 per cent was so allocated; and in 1965, it is projected that 41.5 per cent of current operating expenditures will be so allocated. There is no doubt that, barring some fundamental change in our entire way of life, the local fiscal picture will continue to be dominated by public school expenditures to an even greater extent than it has been in the past. The possible extension of education to the locally supported junior college within the decade would increase the importance of education even further.

Capital Outlays in 1965

Capital outlays in 1965 will continue to be concentrated on a limited number of functions and will continue to affect individual governments unequally. The breakdown of capital outlays which separates those of Cleveland from those of Cuyahoga County, on the one hand, and from the surrounding municipal and school governments, on the other, appears to be losing some of its usefulness as functional responsibilities continue to be reallocated especially to the county government. Decisions concerning capital outlay will determine and will be determined by decisions concerning borrowing, taxes, and operating expenditures of the governments directly and indirectly involved.

Further, because they are contained within one of the major metropolitan areas of the nation, the governments in the Cleveland Metropolitan Area will have outlays that will be quantitatively and qualitatively different from governments in smaller metropolitan areas as well as from the small independent municipality and its overlying governments.

Since the Cleveland Metropolitan Area is sufficiently wealthy to maintain any reasonable standard of public service its citizens establish for it, there is little doubt that, regardless of the particular governments involved, the desired levels of capital outlays could be forthcoming in the future.

Capital outlays in 1965—or in any representative year in the middle sixties—will depend on past capital outlays, capital outlays already planned for, the existing pattern of metropolitan and community growth, and the areas of future growth. Unless there are major unanticipated changes in the location of population, industry, and commerce dictated by national defense considerations, and unless the state and federal governments change their responsibilities drastically, the principal areas in which capital requirements will be important in 1965 can be determined with a great deal of confidence. Although projections are made for the year 1965, it should be recognized that, because of the volatility of capital outlay, the choice of a given year is used primarily to establish a definite framework for viewing projections. Capital outlays have varied and will continue to vary greatly from year to year, although the variation for all governments as a group will be far less than for an individual government.

Using the same breakdown of capital outlays as was used in analyzing operating expenditures, it appears that the functional pattern of capital outlays in 1965 will not differ from the functional pattern of capital outlays existing in 1956 with the possible addition of major sums devoted to urban renewal. However, there will be changes in the amounts and relative emphasis given these functions, and of course different governments will be involved.

Projections are made in constant 1956 dollars under three sets of assumptions, roughly the same as those used in formulating the projections of operating expenditures. The first is a *low* projection which assumes a minor improvement in standards; for the municipalities and schools this means an absolute increase roughly that which occurred between 1950 and 1955, since outlays in 1956 appeared to be definitely on the low side as compared to 1954, 1955, and 1957. The second set of projections are based on the rate of growth between 1950 and 1956 as modified by current information and knowledge concerning the future. The *probable* estimates assume an improvement and equalization of facilities; these would not affect all functions or governments equally. For instance, it assumes that the first upgrading of facilities would have a greater effect on streets and highways and sewer outlays than on school outlays. The *high* estimate assumes that a definite effort will be made to improve the capital plant to a level equivalent to those provided by the best units in 1956. Under this assumption it is projected that school capital outlays would then go up more rapidly than municipal outlays.

If the probable figure is used as in the current operating expenditures then a major contrast between schools and municipalities emerges at the outset. For, where it is projected that school operating expenditures are going to grow at a more rapid rate than municipal operating expenditures between 1956 and 1965, the converse is assumed in the case of capital outlays, where it is projected that municipal outlays will grow at a more rapid rate than school outlays between 1956 and 1965. It is assumed that a peak in school construction will have occurred prior to 1965, whereas it is assumed that peak municipal outlays may or may not have been reached by 1965. Nevertheless, under all three sets of assumptions school outlays are projected as the single most important locally financed capital outlay in the Cleveland Metropolitan Area, although in terms of all levels of government, federal, state, and local, street and highway outlays in the Cleveland Metropolitan Area may be far greater than any other category of outlays in 1965. It is further projected that the rate of increase in school outlays, which characterized the period 1950-56, will not be maintained unless there is a major effort to improve and modernize school facilities by 1965. It should be noted that, in terms of the number of students in average daily membership, the rate of growth in school plant will be much smaller than it appears in the aggregate.

School outlays on new construction and equipment are primarily a function of expected enrollment, existing facilities, and the educational standards of the individual school districts. The expected Average Daily Membership achieves additional meaning when it is viewed in terms of its distribution between school districts. It is estimated, on the basis of population estimates of the Cleveland Regional Planning Commission, that the enrollment (ADM) in 1965 will be approximately 320,000 as compared to 226,000 in 1956. Further, it is assumed that in the increase in public high school will be relatively larger than the increase in public elementary school enrollment between 1956 and 1965. Therefore, it is projected that high

Table VIII-9—Actual and Projected Capital Outlay, All Governments, Cleveland Metropolitan Area
(In 1956 Dollars)

Capital Outlay	1950	1954	1955	1956	Low 1965	Probable 1965	High 1965	Probable 1965/1956 (Per Cent)
General Control *	1,700	5,300	3,600	4,300	3,000	6,000	6,600	139.5
Hospital	3,900	2,000	1,900	1,500	2,700	4,000	4,400	266.7
Streets and Highways	7,200	13,100	18,500	12,300	17,500	25,000	27,000	203.3
Misc. Comm. Activity								
Sewerage	5,100	10,500	7,900	8,400	9,300	16,000	17,500	190.5
Rubbish & Garbage Disposal	1,300	400	1,000	1,600	1,300	2,000	2,400	125.0
Other Misc. Comm. Activity	2,200	5,700	3,300	4,700	4,000	8,000	8,800	170.2
Recreation & Culture	2,900	3,400	3,300	2,300	4,400	7,000	3,800	304.4
Land Use & Development		700	2,000	1,200	2,900	10,000	11,000	875.0
Misc.† & Unallocable	200	100	100	100	500	500	500	1500.0
Total Municipal	24,500	41,100	41,600	36,300	54,500	78,500	85,500	216.2
Total School	9,800	22,200	22,000	18,100	30,700	32,000	42,600	176.3
Total Library	520	200	700	700	400	500	1,800	71.4
GRAND TOTAL	34,820	63,500	64,300	55,100	85,600	111,000	129,900	201.5
Public Service Enterprises Exhibit								
Water	11,400	10,100	8,000	10,900	4,000	7,000	9,000	64.2
Mass Transit	2,600	16,900	9,600	2,300	2,000	3,000	6,000	130.4
Electricity	1,900	1,000	600	700	1,000	2,000	3,000	285.7

* Includes: General Government, Police, Fire, and Other Public Safety.
† Includes: Public Health, Public Welfare, and Pensions.

school construction will be the principal area for new construction and that, except for replacement, the shortage of elementary school facilities will be considerably eased by 1965.

Unless there is a fundamental shift in the American way of life there is no doubt that the principal category of municipal capital outlay in the Cleveland Metropolitan Area, as well as in practically every area throughout the nation, will continue to be on Streets and Highways. Because of the division of financial responsibility between the federal, state, and local governments, only a small part of the total outlays on streets and highways in the Cleveland Metropolitan Area will be financed out of local sources and reflected in local totals. Should any change in financial arrangements occur among the various levels of government this might be reflected in a vast increase in reported local capital outlays.

It appears that the low figure of $17 million represents an almost irreducible minimum for arterial and local highway construction financed out of local funds in 1965. It is in fact lower than the level of outlays on streets and highways attained in 1955. A more probable figure based on past behavior and existing plans would be $25 millions divided as follows:

City of Cleveland	$ 9 million
Other Municipalities	10 million
Cuyahoga County	6 million

Changes in the pattern of responsibility might change not only the distribution as between governments, but the total amount of new construction as well. The same would be true if the pattern of state and federal aid were also changed.

As it has been in the past, so it is assumed in the future that outlays for the construction of Storm and Sanitary Sewers will follow street and highway construction in importance. In contrast to street and highway outlays, however, the figure is a good measure of the total amount of outlays on storm and sanitary sewers because they are almost entirely locally financed. The low projection of $9.3 millions seems to represent an irreducible minimum for 1965. In real terms, it is slightly larger than the outlays in 1956, but smaller than those of 1954. The probable figure of $16 million would seem to be far more in accord with the increasing density and distribution of population in Cuyahoga County.

Although outlays for Public Service Enterprises are explicitly excluded from the major body of this study the close connection between expenditures on sewerage with those on water supply should be noted. A major increase in the expenditures on sewerage systems would have important consequences on the outlays on water.

As was noted earlier in this section, local outlays on Urban Renewal will probably undergo the most spectacular growth in the decade to come. It is assumed in the low projection that no new federal legislation has been enacted and that urban renewal is carried on at a level slightly greater than it has been during the latter 1950's. On the other hand, if federal moneys are forthcoming at a new and higher level, then local outlays on urban renewal, especially in the city of Cleveland, will grow considerably. The figure of $10.5 millions is primarily designed to show an order of magnitude because of the absence of any real relevant past experience. However, the figure is consistent with the announced plans of other governments.

Outlays on Recreation and Culture represent another category in which a major relative and absolute increase is probable. Further, it should be noted that the amount of new construction devoted to recreation and culture is understated insofar as new recreational and cultural facilities are included in school outlays. A low figure of $4.4 millions would be slightly higher than the figure for 1954 and would represent a low figure considering the increase in population, its distribution, and its changing age distribution. However, in view of the very extensive plans for recreation facilities, it is assumed that the $7.0 million is more probable.

Outlays for the Other Miscellaneous Commercial Activities category may exceed those for recreation and culture, but they will reflect a variety of functions rather than a single function. For this category not only includes expenditures on airports, lakeports, and other commercial ventures, but off-street parking which will probably loom very large in the future. Although it is assumed that the probable figure will be $8.0 million, a minimum might be half as much. A major effort to improve the Port of Cleveland might conceivably raise the figure considerably above the high figure, but as of the present there seems to be no reason to make such an assumption.

The General Control category like the Other Miscellaneous Commercial Activities category includes outlay for a number of functions. Unlike the latter, the general control category, however, includes the older, more established functions, general government, police, and fire, rather than the newer functions. It is assumed that outlays will continue to grow on general control at a lower rate than in the past, because they are so well established. At a minimum it is assumed that outlays for general control purposes might be lower than the amounts spent in 1954, 1955, or 1956. Even the probable figure would be only a few hundred thousand dollars greater than the actual real expenditure in 1954. Again a major building program by Cuyahoga County, the City of Cleveland, or a major civil defense effort, might make the figure many times as large as is currently projected.

Responsibility for Hospitals except for debt incurred in the past has just undergone a major change in the Cleveland Metropolitan Area as the City of Cleveland has shifted its major responsibilities to the County. Exactly what impact this will have on outlay for hospitals, if any at all, is difficult to say. However, it appears that the increase may be large compared to the outlays in 1956, although not to 1950, when a large hospital plant was constructed by Lakewood.

METRO, in its report *Refuse Collection and Disposal in Cuyahoga County* (1958) noted that at least fifteen cities will require incinerators by 1963. Also at least nine municipalities now classified as villages will be requiring incinerators in the not too distant future. If account is taken of projected urbanization of the County it appears that $1 million would be in the neighborhood of an irreducible minimum outlay on rubbish and garbage disposal. This would, in fact, be lower than the outlays in 1956. A figure of $2 million seems more probable.

Based on past history or existing plans there is no way of formulating any realistic projection of outlays on Libraries. There appears to be no large scale construction or purchase of capital

equipment in the foreseeable future, especially since the purchase
of the old Cleveland Plain Dealer building by the Cleveland Public
Library. An average figure of $0.5 millions would not seem out
of line as a probable figure.

Debt in 1965

The level of debt in any particular year is determined by two
factors: first, the amount of borrowing which accrues in that year
and, second, the debt still outstanding from previous borrowing.
The amount of borrowing which occurs in a given year depends
mainly upon the quantity of capital outlay which is financed
during the year under consideration while the debt outstanding
from previous years is determined by the borrowing which has
taken place in the past and the rate at which previous borrowing
is being paid off.

The projection of debt levels, therefore, requires the combining
of a known factor, existing debt, with a predicted factor, future
borrowing. The projection of future borrowing requires first a projection of capital outlays and, second, an assumption of the extent
to which capital outlays will be financed through borrowing. The
difficulty in projecting capital outlays was considered earlier in
this chapter, and it should be stressed that the reliability of the debt
projections crucially rests upon the projection of capital outlays.
Projections are made for just two broad classes of governments,
municipalities (cities, villages, townships, and the County) and
school districts.

MUNICIPAL NET DEBT—1965

Certain explicit assumptions must be made in projecting debt
for municipalities in 1965. The first of these is that the net debt for
1956 would be entirely redeemed by 1965 with the exception of
that of Cuyahoga County and Cleveland. This assumption is based
upon the observation that if the rate of redemption which existed
in 1956 continued, net municipal debt would fall to zero by 1961

Table VIII-10—Projected Net Debt for 1965, All Governments, Cleveland Metropolitan Area

Indebtedness Category and Year	Municipal	School	Total
Net Debt in 1956 still outstanding in 1965 (In Thousands of Dollars)	9,276	20,771	30,047
Total Net Debt 1965 (In Thousands of Dollars)	350,645	173,412	524,057
Total Net Debt per $1000 Assessed Valuation (In Dollars)			
1956	37	17	53
1965	56	28	83
Total Net Debt Per Capita (In Dollars)			
1956	109	49	158
1965	192	95	286

or 1962 depending upon the class of municipality, but for the county and Cleveland some of the 1956 debt would still be outstanding in 1965.

The second assumption is that 90 per cent of the locally financed capital outlays would be financed by borrowing. The selection of 90 per cent is somewhat arbitrary but, in light of past trends, appeared to be reasonable.

The third assumption concerned the type of bonds which it was assumed would be issued for the borrowing from 1956 to 1965. Borrowing for different projects invariably results in bond issues of varying maturity patterns, but as a simplification all bonds issued are assumed to be straight serial maturing over fifteen years.

The final assumption is that between 1956 and 1965 the rate of growth of municipal capital outlays would be constant. This assumption is justified primarily on the basis of simplicity and on the fact that if the bulk of capital outlay falls in the later years, the projected debt for municipalities is understated.

On the basis of the assumptions stated above, it is found that net debt for the County, cities, and villages combined will reach a level of $350,600,000 in 1965, or 5.5 per cent of the projected assessed valuation. Comparable net debt for this group was $172,500,000 in 1956 or 2.6 per cent of assessed valuation.

Alternatively, expressed in relation to population, the 1965 projection is $192 per capita (based on the estimated 1965 population), as compared to $109 per capita in 1956.

SCHOOL DISTRICT NET DEBT—1965

The assumptions made in projecting school debt for 1965 are similar to those made in projecting municipal debt but somewhat more complex. The first assumption is that by 1965 neither city nor local and exempted districts would have completely paid off that debt which existed in 1956. As in the case of municipalities, this assumption is based upon the observed maturity pattern which existed in 1956. Because of the differing rates of maturity in 1956 between city school districts and local and exempted school districts, the amount of debt which existed in 1956 and would still be outstanding in 1965 was projected separately for each of these classes.

The second assumption is that 75 per cent of the projected capital outlays in 1965 would be financed by borrowing. The reason that this figure is lower for schools than for municipalities is that, in the past, a greater portion of school capital outlays have been financed out of current revenues. This is a reflection of the historic "no debt" policy followed by some of the larger districts, especially the Cleveland School District.

As in the case of municipalities, it is assumed that the bonds issued would be straight serials, but for school borrowing the term was assumed to be twenty years. This appeared to be justified by the fact that almost all school bonds issued in recent years are of twenty-year maturity.

Finally, in the case of school capital outlays, it is assumed that the pattern of outlay between 1956 and 1965 would be irregular and that the average outlay in the years between 1960 and 1965 would be greater than the average between 1956 and 1960.

It is estimated that by 1965 net school debt for all school districts would reach $173,400,000 in 1956 dollars. If the Cleveland School District (which had no debt in 1956 and will probably have none in 1965) is eliminated, this level of debt represented 3.8 per cent of assessed valuation, in 1956, and will reach 5.6 per cent, in 1965. If the Cleveland School District is included the increase is from 1.7 per cent to 2.7 per cent of assessed valuation or from $49, in 1956, to $95 per capita, in 1965.

In 1956, the net debt of all governments combined in the Cleveland Metropolitan Area was $250,600,000. On the basis of the assumptions stated above, and projected capital outlays between 1956 and 1965, it is estimated that the net debt would increase to $524,000,000, or more than double the 1956 level. This implies an increase from 5.3 per cent of assessed valuation, in 1956, to 8.3 per cent, by 1965. The growth in net debt also exceeds the projected growth in population so that the per capita net debt, in 1965, is estimated to rise to $286 as compared to $158, in 1956.

Finally on the basis of the pattern of debt service costs and interest rates in 1956 it is estimated that in 1965, $55 million would be required for debt redemption and $13.5 million for interest payments.

Revenue Projections

A projection of revenues ahead to 1965 for local governments in the Cleveland Metropolitan Area is a dangerous but necessary task. A projection is not to be confused with a forecast. Instead, a revenue projection is necessary to show what will happen under certain reasonable assumptions. The purpose here is to show the relation of revenue to expenditure projections and to pose to the people of the Cleveland area the financing problems which their local governments are likely to face over the next decade. Knowledge of the spending, revenue, and debt implications of the different courses of action allows more intelligent decisions among the various alternatives.

The projected excess of expenditures over revenues indicates the magnitude and impact of the problem and highlights the choices available to the people and to local government officials. Should certain activities causing expenditures be eliminated or reduced? Should property tax rates be increased? Are other local sources of revenue preferable? Is it more desirable to seek additional state or federal aid? Would a different organization of local governments ease the financial problem?

PROJECTION OF 1965 REVENUES

Each of the major sources of local government revenues has been projected separately. An attempt has been made to go beyond a purely mechanical projection of rates of growth to allow for general economic conditions including the 1957-58 reecssion, the availability of land, transportation facilities, land use and zoning, and the economic and demographic characteristics of the metropolitan area and of different jurisdictions within the area.

Specification of our basic assumptions provides the framework on which these projections are based and allows the reader to substitute his own judgment where he prefers.

The first assumption is that the national economy will grow and prosper over the next decade, with growth approximating that of the 1948-57 period. The Cleveland area is expected to share this growth and prosperity.

Second, these projections assume stable prices at the 1956 level. A variation based on a 2 per cent a year price increase will also be offered to show the differential effect on total revenue and different components of revenue and expenditures of a rising price level.

Third, the projections are based on continuation of present assessment practices and assessment levels for real estate under the property tax. (Appraisals are required every six years by Ohio law and another one would be due before 1965. Reassessments do not necessarily increase the tax duplicate, depending largely on the rulings of the Ohio Board of Tax Appeals. This board aims primarily to make assessments uniform throughout Ohio, in terms of a recent level of costs.) Present state laws on the valuation of tangible personal property will also be assumed to be unchanged. Growth in the tax base in this projection thus depends on improvements to land, new construction, and greater value of equipment and inventories. An alternative projection allows for a 25 per cent increase in the assessed value of real estate due to a reappraisal by 1964.

Fourth, property tax rates are assumed to continue at the level existing during the 1958-59 tax year. Including a state levy of 5/10 of one mill, the weighted average rate in Cuyahoga County was 36.0 mills in 1959. It is most unlikely that this will be the rate in 1965, but projecting on this basis provides an opportunity to see the revenue gap, if present revenue effort in all aspects is continued. The average 1958-59 rate represents an increase of 5.3 mills over the 1955-56 average.

Fifth, the present state programs for aid to local governments by tax sharing and grants will be continued as provided in existing law. This includes the School Foundation program, the Local Government Fund, moneys for roads and streets from the gas tax and motor vehicle licenses, and state support for poor relief. Payments from the State to local governments will rise automatically under most existing programs due to such changes as the continuing increase in school enrollments and the sale of more gasoline. But the initial projections are not so brash as to predict the type and extent of changes in state programs and functions between now and 1965. Present federal programs are also projected to continue through 1965.

PROPERTY TAX REVENUES FOR 1965

Projection of the general property tax base is the most important single step in a study of future revenues. This analysis projects the tax duplicate separately for real estate, public utility property, and tangible personal property.

Real Estate—Assessed value of real estate has increased from $1,925 million on January 1, 1950, to $3,554 million at the beginning of 1958. The 1950 amount is not comparable with recent years for our purposes, however, as two reassessments in 1952 and 1955 raised real estate assessments by an average of 36.5 per cent.[2] With this adjustment, the comparable 1950 figure for real estate is $2,628 million. The real growth in the assessed value of real estate thus was $926 million over an eight-year period, or $116 million a year.

After allowing for a slower growth of realty assessments in

---

2. The 1952 reassessment was a flat 25 per cent increase on every real estate tax value in the County. The 1955 reappraisal, allowing for an abnormally large number of downward revisions the following year, averaged a 9.2 per cent net increase. Each property was appraised separately in the 1955 reappraisal. The 1952 reassessment also increased the real estate portion of the public utility duplicate.

1958-59 due to the recession, the average net increment is estimated at $120 million a year of taxable value during the 1959-63 period. This projection does not allow for any major upward or downward revision in assessed values. The real estate assessed value thus would be about $4,230 million on January 1, 1964, the date for tax valuations against which taxes would be collected during the 1965 calendar year. This projection would represent a 28.5 per cent increase over 1955-56. An alternative projection, shown in Table VIII-11(a), presents the 1965 figure, if real estate is reassessed to 50 per cent of its 1956 true value, against the present actual average 40 per cent assessment ratio.

Public Utility—This part of the tax duplicate has increased from $256 million, in 1950, to $384 million, in 1958. About 25 to 30 per cent of the assessed valuation of utilities is real estate, the rest tangible personal property. Adjusting the 1950-51 assessed value of utility real estate for the increase from the 1952 reassessment, gives a 1950 comparable figure of $280 million.

Over the six years, 1958-63, the addition to public utility property is projected to be about $10 million a year, down slightly from the 1950-56 rate as the public transit systems will no longer be included. The projected increases are expected largely from the telephone, electric, and gas utilities. Allowance for drastic changes, such as the discontinuance of Cleveland Terminal as a passenger station, are not incorporated in these projections. The assessed value for 1964-65 is projected at $445 million, a 23 per cent rise over 1955-56.

Tangible Personal Property—The assessed valuation of this type of property has increased more than seven-fold since 1936-37, compared with a 150 per cent increase for real estate and only a 90 per cent rise for public utilities over the same period. Part of this rapid growth is due to court decisions, allowing property formerly classified as real estate for tax purposes to be treated as tangible personal property. Over the 1952 to 1957 period, which followed the major reclassification of real to tangible personal property, the increase in assessed value has been $95 million a year. The estimates of tangible personal property gave a 1958 figure of about $1,285 million as a base for future projections.

Assuming a high level of economic activity during the 1960's, a projection for calendar year 1964 might indicate $1,760 million as the mid-point of the range. This would include reasonable annual growth for the five years, 1960-64 inclusive, at about $70 million a year, after a larger increase in 1959 to recover from the recession. The most likely 1964-65 figure would represent a 68 per cent increase for 1955-56.

Total General Property Tax Duplicate—A projection of the total tax duplicate to 1964-65 indicates that $6.4 billion (rounded off from $6,435 million) is the most probable figure. Given our assumptions, the possible range of the 1964-65 duplicate is from a low of $6.0 billion to a high of $6.9 billion. The more likely figure of $6.4 billion would be a 38 per cent increase over 1955-56. The range of projections give a low increase of 30 per cent and a high increase of 49 per cent.

Revenue from General Property Tax—Based on a $6.4 billion projection for the 1964-65 tax duplicate, the present tax rate would raise about $230 million, as shown in Table VIII-11. The State of Ohio would receive $3 million and $227 million would go to the local governments in Cuyahoga County. This amount of revenue would be a 61 per cent increase over the property tax receipts of 1955-56, reflecting both the growth in the tax base projected to 1964-65 and the actual 5.3 mill increase in the average tax rate between 1955-56 and 1958-59.

Intangible Property Tax (Local Situs)—The yield from this tax to libraries and other local governments in Cuyahoga County grew from $3,870,000, in 1947, to $7,130,000, in 1956. The increase averaged $384,000 annually over this period. Adjusting for the 13 per cent increase in the consumer price level, the annual increase in constant dollars would be about $300,000. Actual and estimated collections in 1957-59 are about $8.0 million a year.

Projecting increases of $300,000 annually from 1959 would give an amount of about $9.8 million for 1965. This growth seems reasonable under the assumption of economic prosperity and growth, which is usually accompanied by a rising level of dividend and interest payments. The 1965 projected amount compared to 1956 would be about 38 per cent increase in total, and a rise from $4.68 to $5.35 per capita.

OTHER REVENUES IN 1965

Licenses and Other Taxes—Revenues from inheritance and admission taxes, cigarette licenses, and liquor and beer permits brought in $4,180,000 revenue in 1956, against $2,766,000 in 1950. The increases in county and village revenues from these sources more than doubled over this period while cities' collections rose more slowly. The inheritance tax and the admissions tax are somewhat affected by the price level. The most likely projection seems about $5.5 million for 1965, in constant 1956 dollars.

Fees and Miscellaneous Charges—This revenue source has grown from $5.3 million, in 1940, to $12.6 million, in 1950, and to $19.7 million, in 1956. Included here are fines, costs and forfeitures, sewerage charges, recording of land and auto titles, hospital charges, adult education, school lunches and work books, etc. Municipalities, schools and the County all experienced a more than 50 per cent increase in revenue from this source between 1950 and 1956. About $2.5 million was collected for sanitary sewer service and about $6.4 million for hospital charges in 1956.

Projecting recent rates of increase indicates about $30 million of receipts in 1965, divided about $2.5 million to the schools and $27.5 million to the County and municipalities.

Except for hospital charges, the rates for most of these services have not risen with the general price level. But Cleveland City Council voted in 1958 to increase sewer rates on the suburbs substantially, and the 1959 session of the Ohio Legislature raised the schedule of fees and charges for services performed by county officers throughout the State. Thus, if our assumption of constant prices were relaxed, it would be realistic to allow for higher charges by governments, perhaps up by one-third to a total of $40 million by 1965.

Special Assessments—Growth in these charges has been relatively slow from $5.8 million, in 1950, to $6.5 million, in 1956. After correcting for price level changes, all the increase is eliminated. On this basis, special assessments are projected unchanged at $6.5 million for 1965, all for the County and the municipalities.

Interest—Local governments received almost $3.7 million of

Table VIII-11(a)—Actual and Projected Property Taxes, Duplicate, Rate, Yield 1950-65 All Governments, Cleveland Metropolitan Area: (In Millions of Dollars)

Year	Real Estate	Public Utility	Tangible Personal	Total	Weighted Average Tax Rate (mills)	Property Tax Levy Duplicate x Average Rate (In Millions of Dollars)
		ACTUAL TAX DUPLICATE				
1950	...	...	...	2,718	30.83	83.8
1951	2,628 *	280 *	644	3,552 (adj.) (2,826 act.)	33.01	93.3
1955	3,120 †	350	1,008	4,478	31.20	131.5
1956	3,230	362	1,048	4,641	30.68	142.4
1957	3,295	369	1,181	4,846	33.07	160.2
1958	3,436	384	1,293	5,113	34.42	178.7
1959	3,554	384	1,285 (est)	5,223	36.00 (tentative)	190.0 (tentative)
		PROJECTED TAX DUPLICATE				
Nature of Estimate (Estimated 1-year increase)	+76	+11	+125	+212		
1960	3,630	395	1,410	5,435	36.00	195.7
(Estimated 5-year increase)	(120 x 5)	(10 x 5)	(70 x 5)			
	+600	+50	+350	+1,000		
1965 { Most likely	4,230	445	1,760	6,435 (6,400)	36.00	230.
1965 { Low	4,000	400	1,600	6,000	36.00	216.
1965 { High	4,400	500	2,000	6,900	36.00	248.
		ALTERNATIVE TAX PROJECTION ‡				
1965						
Most Likely	4,230	445	1,760	6,435		
25% increase	1,057	33	...	1,090		
	5,287	478	1,760	7,525		

* Actual duplicate of real estate for January 1, 1950 ($1.925 million) multiplied by 1.365 to adjust for 1952 reassessment and 1955 reappraisal. Similar adjustment for real estate portion of 1950 public utility actual valuation. Total actual public utility duplicate was $257 million in 1950.
† Real estate for January 1, 1954 valuation ($2,857 million) multiplied by 1.092 for 1955 reappraisal.
‡ Alternative projection allowing for a 25 per cent increase in assessments of real property only, raising real estate on the average to roughly 50 per cent of its 1956-59 market value:

Table VIII-11(b)—Actual and Projected Total Average Tax Rate All Governments, Cleveland Metropolitan Area, 1956-1965 (In Mills)

Tax Year	County	Municipalities	Schools	Total Local	State
1955-56	3.40	12.3	14.8	30.5	0.2
1956-57	3.8	12.7	15.9	32.4	0.2
1957-58	4.7	12.0	17.2	33.9	0.6
1958-59	5.0	12.6	17.9	35.5	0.5
1964-65 (proj)	5.0	12.6	17.9	35.5	0.5

interest from investments in securities of the United States, state, and local governments, and from bank deposits. The high interest rates available in 1956 and 1957 attracted alert local finance officers to invest all temporarily surplus funds. Projecting future interest income is particularly hazardous, because it requires a guess as to what interest rates on short-term government securities will average in a future year. Average interest rates on three-month Treasury bills since 1950 have varied from a high of 3.27 per cent a year, during 1957, to a low of 0.95 per cent, during 1954. Assuming that balances available to earn interest may be about $175 million in 1965, reasonable in view of the higher projected level of receipts and expenditures, interest revenue could vary from $1.7 million with a 1 per cent interest rate to $5.2 million with rates averaging 3 per cent. For a likely projection, the 2 per cent average rate of the last eight years would suggest a $3.5 million interest revenue.

Other Local Sources—This catch-all heading covers revenues which increased from $4.5 million in 1950, to $10.4 million in 1956. Adjusting to 1956 constant dollars, this represents an increase of about $900,000 a year. Receipts from rent, sale of property, donations, and other miscellaneous transactions are included here. A straight-line annual increase is used to project about $18.5 million revenue for 1965, with about $10.2 million to the County and municipalities, $7.5 million to the schools, and $0.7 million to the libraries.

Local Government Fund—As presently constituted by state statute, this fund consists of $24 million from the Ohio sales tax and all the intangible taxes levied on security dealers, banks, and other financial institutions.

Table VIII-12—Actual and Projected Property Tax Base, and Revenue from the Property Tax, Cleveland Metropolitan Area

A. PRICE LEVEL AND ASSESSMENT RATIOS VARYING

Tax Collection Year	Total Property Tax Duplicate (Millions of Dollars)	Weighted Average Tax Rate (Mills)	Computed Tax Yield (Millions of Dollars)
1956	4,641	30.68	142.4
1957	4,845	33.07	160.2
1958	5,113	34.42	176.0
1959	5,223 *	36.00	190.0
1965 †	6,400	36.00	230.0
1965 ‡	7,000	36.00	252.0
1965 §	7,500	36.00	270.0
1965 **	8,000	36.00	288.0

B. PRESENT REVENUE TRENDS AND EFFORTS

Tax Collection Year	(Dollars) Per Capita Revenue		Population	Total Revenue (Millions of Dollars)	
	All Sources	Property Tax		All Sources	Property Tax
1956	157.94	89.71	1,580,553	249.6	141.8
1965 ††	157.94	89.71	1,830,000	289.0	164.2
1965 ‡‡	189.53	107.65	1,830,000	346.8	197.0

C. PERCENTAGE OF PERSONAL INCOME CONSTANT

Tax Collection Year	Personal Income (Millions of Dollars)	Revenues (Millions of Dollars)		Revenues as Per Cent of Personal Income	
		Total	All Local	Total	Local
1956	4,100	249.6	193.6	6.09	4.72
1965 §§	5,970	363.6	281.8	6.09	4.72
1965 #	7,300	444.6	344.6	6.09	4.72

* Partly Estimated.
† At 1956 prices and estimated 1959 tax rates.
‡ Assuming a reappraisal which allowed for a two per cent per year price increase after 1956.
§ Assuming a reappraisal based on fifty per cent of current value in 1956 Dollars.
** Assuming a reappraisal based on fifty per cent of current value in 1956 Dollars and a two per cent increase after 1956.
†† Same burden per capita as in 1956, in 1956 Dollars.
‡‡ Same burden per capita as in 1956, but allowing two per cent per year inflation.
§§ Constant 1956 Dollars, and assuming a 2.6 per cent increase in per capita income per annum,
# Assuming a 5.5 per cent increase in per capita income per annum allowing for price increases, and a population of 1,830,000.

The sales tax portion of the fund to the counties is allocated 1) 75 per cent on the proportion which the total property tax duplicate in the municipalities in the county bears to the tax duplicate for all municipalities in Ohio, and 2) 25 per cent according to the ratio of the county's population to the state's population, based on the most recent Census. Cuyahoga County had 28.38 per cent of all assessed property values in municipalities in Ohio for the calendar year 1956. Based on the 1950 census, Cuyahoga County had 17.5 per cent of the State's population.

Over recent years, Cuyahoga County has about held its own on the distribution formula, with the county's percentage of the eligible duplicate rising slightly between 1947 and 1956 and its estimated share of the state's population down only slightly from 1940 to 1956.

Over the long run, the present formula will probably mean a declining percentage of the sales tax part of the Local Government Fund for Cuyahoga County and its local jurisdictions. With 98 per cent of assessed value in municipalities already and with only 14.7 square miles remaining in the four unincorporated areas in the county, Cuyahoga County can gain little by new incorporations or annexations. Every other county in the state is likely to gain on Cuyahoga by the incorporation and annexation of township areas and thereby add more municipal assessed valuation which counts in the distribution formula. Increase in the tax duplicate by new construction and additional equipment and inventory is the only path open to Cuyahoga, and this path is open to all the counties. Thus, Cuyahoga County is likely to have a declining percentage of Ohio's total tax duplicate located in municipalities.

On the population side, Cuyahoga County will be approaching capacity by about 1970, based on Regional Planning Commission's estimates. After 1960, it is likely that population growth will be slower in Cuyahoga County (but not necessarily in the expanding Cleveland Metropolitan Area) than in the rest of Ohio. So the county's share of the Local Government Fund is likely to decline from population changes in the long run.

A projection to 1965 indicates Local Government Fund receipts of about $14.6 million, up from $11.8 million in 1956. This 1956 amount is Cuyahoga County's present share (about $6.1 million) of the $24 million appropriated from sales taxes plus the collections expected in the county from the state-situs intangible tax on financial institutions and dealers in securities. From 1950 to 1956, collections of this latter tax rose about $300,000 a year, to $5.8 million in 1956. Projecting this annual increase gives $8.6 million from intangibles plus $6.1 million from sales tax. The sales tax appropriation to Cuyahoga County rose almost 50 per cent since 1950. If the state continues to increase this appropriation, Cuyahoga County would share in the increase.

SCHOOL FOUNDATION PROGRAM

Under present legislation in Ohio, State Aid to school districts varies largely with the number of teacher units in the school district. The number of teacher units depends on the number of pupils and the pupil-teacher ratio. An increase in the number of teacher units tends to mean an automatic increase in State Aid for a school district. Additional State Aid is available to poorer districts.

In 1957, with total average daily membership in the public schools of Cuyahoga County at 240,970 pupils, the Foundation Program paid $17,291,000 to the thirty-two school districts in the county. This aid averaged $74.75 a pupil. Although the distribution formula is much more complicated than on a per pupil basis, this figure gives a rough approximation for the future in this county under the present program.[3] With a school enrollment of about 320,000 by 1965, State Aid at the same per pupil figure would total almost $23 million.

Almost certainly the state program will be revised by 1965, probably both in amount of aid and in the basis of distribution.

STATE AID FROM GAS TAX AND MOTOR VEHICLE LICENSES

The number of licensed motor vehicles has risen every decade in Cuyahoga County since the invention of the automobile. In re-

---

3. For a discussion of the formula for distributing state school aid in Ohio, see Cleveland Metropolitan Services Commission, *Education in Cuyahoga County* (1959).

cent years, the number of passenger cars per 1,000 population has risen from 225 in 1930, to 306 in 1950, and 356 in 1956. A figure of 400 cars per 1,000 population seems reasonable for 1965. The number of other vehicles remained at a constant ratio to population (45 per 1,000 people) between 1950 and 1956. This same ratio is used for 1965. With 1,830,000 population expected in 1965, these ratios of vehicles to population would mean 732,000 passenger cars and 82,250 other vehicles. License fees collected on these vehicles would total about $9.4 million, all of which would be returned to jurisdictions within the county. This compares with $7,551,000 on about 636,000 vehicles in 1956.

Under present legislation, 35 per cent of gas taxes collected in Ohio are returned to counties, municipalities, and townships. Between 1947 and 1957, the taxable consumption of motor vehicle fuels increased 85.9 per cent. If this growth continues until 1965, total state collections of gas taxes then would be $251.1 million, against $141.6 million in 1956. Based on the distribution formula in effect in 1956, shown in Table VI-26, Cuyahoga County's municipalities will receive about $6.6 million, the county would receive about $370,000, and the four townships in Cuyahoga County would receive a total of about $53,000. Distribution to municipalities is based on proportion of vehicles; each of the 88 counties receives an equal share and each of the 1334 townships an equal amount. The total expected thus would be about $7.0 million for local governments in the county, up from $5,158,000 in 1956.

The combined revenue from vehicle licenses and the gas tax under present legislation, allowing for an increase in the number of cars and a slight increase in annual miles per car, is projected at $16.4 million for 1965. This would be a 29 per cent increase over 1956.

OTHER STATE AID

A partial list of these state payments includes public utility excise tax and matching funds for poor relief, health subsidies, aid to police pension funds, and aid to schools for purchase of school buses, vocational education, and classes for physically handicapped children. Of the 1956 total of $12.6 million, most of the money goes to the county and most of the total goes for poor relief.

These forms of State Aid to the county and municipalities rose from $8.1 million in 1950, to $11.8 million in 1956. In constant 1956 dollars, this represents an increase of approximately $430,000 a year. If this average annual increase continues until 1965, the annual amount then would be about $15.7 million. As these payments depend in large measures on the needs and program for poor relief, this amount would be affected by such factors as the level of relief payments, by the amount of unemployment, by changes in coverage of the federal social security programs, by provisions for eligibility in Ohio with large numbers of in-migrants, and by the federal-state ratio for sharing the costs.

The increases in other State Aid to schools has averaged only about $32,000 a year between 1950 and 1956. Projecting this rate of increase gives $1.0 million of other State Aid for schools in 1965.

FEDERAL AID

Local governments in Cuyahoga County received $5.1 million from the federal government in 1956, over $3 million of which went to the county to help finance the programs of aid to dependent children, to the blind, to crippled children, and to the disabled. Other payments include part of the cost of urban renewal and aid to school districts which receive an unusually heavy impact from children of employees at federal installations. Revenues from welfare-type programs have been rising steadily, at roughly $500,000 a year recently. This suggests a projection for 1965 revenues for this purpose of about $7.8 million, against $4.3 million estimated for 1958.

Other federal payment depends largely on programs which now are only temporary, under present legislation. Assuming the federal government continues to pay two-thirds of urban renewal costs, 1965 revenue of $6.7 million for this purpose is consistent with the $10 million of expenditures projected for this purpose. Federal payments under other programs are estimated at a round figure of $500,000, half of which is allocated to the schools. No new major federal aid programs are assumed.

On these assumptions, the projection of federal payments for 1965 totals $15.0 million, almost a 200 per cent increase over 1956 due largely to the expected large urban renewal program.

PROJECTION OF TOTAL REVENUE FOR 1965

Revenues for all government purposes, excluding only water, transit, and electric enterprises, total $387 million as projected for 1965. This represents a 54 per cent increase over the $250 million received in 1956. In these projections, the local property tax and State Aid are both up by 40 to 60 per cent in 1965 over 1956. The property tax would produce about 59 per cent of all revenue and State Aid almost 20 per cent. Federal aid, if realized as projected, would show the most rapid growth between 1956 and 1965 but would still account for only 4 per cent of all revenue in 1965.

An alternative projection, shown in the rightmost column of Table VIII-13, allows for changes in revenue which would be likely to accompany a 20 per cent increase in the consumer price index between 1956 and 1965. This allows for a 25 per cent revaluation upward of real estate subject to the property tax. For other revenues, it extends the 1950-56 revenue projections as if the same annual rate of price increase of that period should continue.

The financial gap is projected at $85 million annually for 1965, but financial gaps can never really occur when governments are required to operate with balanced budgets. By some combination of reduced expenditures, higher rates on existing taxes, new local revenue sources, and more state and federal aid, any prospective gap must disappear before the future year actually arrives. The people of the Cleveland area have voted higher property tax rates on themselves, raising the average rate in the county by more than 5 mills (or about $28 million a year) since 1956. Still higher property tax rates and added revenue from other sources will eliminate the remaining projected gap before 1965 arrives. The policy question is the best choice of the sources of the additional revenue, weighed against the benefits from the expenditures.

Table VIII-13—Projected Revenues, Assuming Population and Economic Growth, Stable Prices, Existing Legislation, and 1958 Tax Rates, Cleveland Metropolitan Area, 1965 (In Millions of Dollars)

LOCAL SOURCES	County and Municipalities	Schools	Libraries	STABLE 1956 PRICES Total	Prices 20% Above 1956 Total
General Property	112.6	114.4	0.2	227.2	240.0
Intangible Property			9.8	9.8	10.6
Licenses & Other Taxes	5.5			5.5	6.8
Total Local Taxes	118.1	114.4	10.0	242.5	257.4
Fees & Misc. Charges	27.5	2.5		30.0	40.0
Special Assessments	6.5			6.5	7.8
Interest	3.2	0.3		3.5	4.4
Other Local Sources	10.2	7.5	0.7	18.5	19.5
Total Local Sources	165.5	124.7	10.7	301.0	329.1
STATE AID					
Local Gov't Fund	14.6			14.6	17.5
School Foundation		23.0		23.0	27.6
Other State Aid	15.7	1.0		16.7	18.4
Motor Veh. License	9.4			} 16.4	16.4
Gas Tax	7.0				
Total State Aid	46.7	24.0		70.7	79.9
FEDERAL AID	14.7	0.3		15.0	15.0
Total Intergovern.	61.4	24.3	0.0	85.7	94.9
Total All Revenues Except P. S. E.	226.9	149.0	10.7	386.7	424.0

Note: Property tax allocated to type of government as shown in footnote to Table VIII-11. Detail may not add to total due to rounding.

The 20% price increase allows most 1950-56 increases to be continued. It allows for a 25% increase in *real estate* assessed valuation for the property tax and a 10% property tax rate reduction.

These projections are comparable with the actual 1940, 1950, and 1956 data presented in Table VI-1.

The other problem besides the need for more revenue is the wide differential in taxable capacity between the many municipalities and school districts in the metropolitan area. To some observers the imbalance is already intolerable. Others find the present situation acceptable, but expect the differentials to widen and require action since they foresee uneven growth, deteriorating property in some sections, and increasing pressure for more government service and service at a minimum metropolitan level in small or poor municipalities.

The major problem municipalities and school districts are the very small jurisdictions, the rapidly growing areas, the poorer ones, and the jurisdictions, such as the county and the municipalities with new city status, which acquire new responsibilities and consequent larger expenditures. The traditional approach has been to let each jurisdiction seek its own solution without consideration of the effects which flow all over the metropolitan area.

One alternative would be to transfer certain metropolitan functions to the county, relieving pressure on local revenue sources and perhaps tapping a new revenue source, such as a metropolitan income or sales tax, to finance the additional county spending.[4]

Another alternative would be a more even distribution of revenue sources within the metropolitan area, assuming at least an average local tax effort by the poorer jurisdictions. Several actions might be taken, with varying degrees of effect, toward intra-county equalization:

1. Equalization could be given much greater emphasis in distribution of the local government fund. This is possible by action of the County Budget Commission. About $12 million a year is available in the local government fund.
2. The local intangibles and inheritance taxes could be allocated to the County Budget Commission for distribution to equalize

---

4. For a general discussion of these and other alternatives see the report of the Study Group on Government Costs, *Government Costs: Questions for Community Decision* (1959).

the tax capacity. The state would have to change present laws to achieve this, as the local distribution is now to municipality of situs. No more than $4 million a year would be available, after most of the intangibles are allocated to libraries.

3. Industrial, commercial, and utility property, real and tangible, might be subjected to a county tax at an average rate, with distribution made on a per person or a per pupil basis throughout the county. Such a move might disrupt the existing local tax base. It would penalize jurisdictions which worked to develop a balanced tax base in favor of dormitory communities. But it would share the rich tax base more evenly throughout the area. Perhaps better would be allocation of a fraction of the tax on business property to a metropolitan area equalization fund for municipalities, schools, or both.

4. A flat rate tax throughout the metropolitan area on the present tax duplicate with distribution on a per person or per pupil basis could be very potent in minimizing imbalance. Alternatively such a tax might finance major traffic arteries, trunk sewers and sewage disposal, public health facilities, and other functions transferred to county or metropolitan operation. Precedent exists in the Cleveland Metropolitan Park District and recent support of transfer of hospital and correctional facilities from Cleveland to the County.

The possible use of a 10-mill county-wide property tax, distributed on a per pupil basis, is shown in Table VIII-14. This tax in effect would transfer about $4 million from school districts with above average valuations per pupil, such as Cuyahoga Heights and Cleveland, to districts whose local tax bases are below average, such as Olmsted Falls and Parma. The tax effort would generally be made more equal, especially by increasing the effort in those districts with lower tax rates.

(Calculations use 1956 assessed valuations and average daily membership)

School Districts	Yield per Pupil from 10 Mills (Dollars)	Difference from County Average per Pupil (Dollars)	Yield from 10 Mills in District (Thousands of Dollars)	Amount from 10 Mills per Pupil (Thousands of Dollars)	Effect of Equalization (Per Cent)	Receipts/Local Collection (Per Cent)
Cities						
Bay Village	130.99	—83.31	307.7	508.4	+195.7	163.6
Bedford	230.55	+16.25	901.7	838.1	—63.6	93.0
Berea	329.62	+115.32	1278.6	831.3	—447.3	65.0
Brooklyn	247.83	+33.53	408.9	353.6	—55.3	86.5
Cleveland	232.49	+18.19	27371.0	25229.5	—2141.5	92.2
Cleveland Heights	178.45	—35.85	2149.3	2581.0	+331.7	120.1
East Cleveland	198.50	—15.80	1075.4	1160.9	+85.6	108.0
Euclid	223.29	+8.99	2326.9	2233.2	—93.7	96.0
Fairview Park	161.63	—52.67	381.6	506.0	+124.4	132.6
Garfield Heights	129.9	—85.01	560.5	926.2	+365.7	165.2
Lakewood	215.96	+1.66	1598.3	1586.0	—12.3	99.2
Maple Heights	128.90	—85.40	625.6	1040.0	+414.4	166.3
North Olmsted	130.50	—83.80	285.9	469.5	+183.6	164.2
Parma	146.23	—68.07	1962.2	2875.5	+913.3	146.5
Rocky River	219.25	+4.95	578.8	565.8	—13.1	97.7
Shaker Heights	260.41	+46.11	1710.9	1408.0	—303.0	82.3
So. Euclid-Lyndhurst	137.91	—76.39	913.6	1419.7	+500.1	155.4
Local & Exempted						
Beachwood	274.85	+60.55	206.1	159.2	—46.9	77.2
Bratenahl	299.39	+85.09	53.6	38.4	—15.2	61.6
Brecksville	144.62	—69.68	274.1	406.0	+132.0	148.2
Chagrin Falls Ex.	108.49	—105.81	130.3	257.4	+127.1	197.5
Cuyahoga Heights	1403.99	+1189.69	1065.6	162.7	—903.0	15.3
Independence	250.95	+36.65	195.5	106.9	—28.6	85.4
Mayfield (City)	143.45	—70.85	428.5	640.1	+211.6	149.4
North Royalton	126.24	—88.06	173.6	294.7	+121.1	169.8
Olmsted Falls	88.09	—136.21	135.0	328.3	+193.3	243.3
Orange	261.31	+47.01	387.8	318.0	—69.8	82.0
Richmond Heights	188.14	—26.16	65.9	75.0	+9.1	113.9
Solon	194.10	—20.20	208.9	230.6	+21.7	110.4
Strongsville	125.61	—88.69	145.8	248.8	+103.0	170.6
Warrensville Heights	175.12	—39.18	259.5	317.6	+58.1	122.4
Westlake Ex.	177.72	—36.58	285.1	343.7	+58.7	120.6
Average or Total	214.30	0.00	48,451.9	48,451.9		

* Result of 10 mills multiplied by assessed valuation per pupil, shown in Table VI-8.
For 1956 ADM see Table II-10.

IX
Summary and
Recommendations

$\mathbb{T}$HE COMPLEX PATTERN OF LOCAL GOVERNMENT finances in the Cleveland Metropolitan Area is a reflection of the more than one hundred independent taxing and spending jurisdictions that comprise the area. The rapid changes in the size and the distribution of population in the urban environment which we have called the Cleveland Metropolitan Area indicate that the increase in the cost of government in the immediate past is the prelude to major quantitative and qualitative fiscal changes in the future.

The fiscal domination of Cleveland, city, school, and library, will be supplanted by an almost coequal fiscal status of the central city and the surrounding communities, with an increasingly important role being played by the County or any successor government.

362

An understanding of the reasons for the growth of local finances is essential if we are to spend more wisely and finance more equitably. In 1956, total expenditures by all local governments in the Cleveland Metropolitan Area, less public service enterprises, were equal to $301 millions; in 1965, they are expected to grow to $511 millions in 1956 dollars. If the ingenuity that has been characteristic of the past is true of the future, then local public opinion and officials will find ways of financing these requirements. The information and analysis of this study of the finances of the Cleveland Metropolitan Area are designed to aid in the solution of the problems by stating what they are expected to be and what alternatives and suggestions for improvements are available.

During the next seven years there will be a continuation of many of the forces that have operated since the end of World War II which have resulted in the real increase in local expenditures nationally as well as in the case of the Cleveland Metropolitan Area. Many factors are responsible for this growth, some of which will continue to be of importance, while others will decline in importance. For the period since 1946 these were:

1. The backlog of deferred maintenance and new construction resulting partly from the war, partly from the depression years just preceding it, and partly from the advancing age of of the central city and its immediate neighbors.
2. The growth and change in age-composition of population within the Cleveland Metropolitan Area with its tremendous effect on public school expenditures.
3. The changing socio-economic characteristics associated with the redistribution of population within the Cleveland Metropolitan Area.
4. The higher level of governmental goods and services that has been created by "the scientific, technological, cultural and social advances" of the most recent past, especially in the field of education, but also in almost every other field of municipal activity.
5. A more liberal political philosophy favoring greater government activity which has "undoubtedly played a part in fos-

tering a higher level of state and municipal activity," although this has not been uniformly important in all areas.

6. The increasing cost of providing local government goods and services which has been especially great since productivity advances have not been as rapid here as in the provision of consumer goods.

7. The ease with which state and local governments were able to raise additional sums of money either by taxation or by borrowing which contributed to past growth and which may contribute to future growth in specific instances, although this factor has certainly ceased being as important as it was in the immediate post-war period.

8. The stimulating effects of federal and state grants on local government expenditures, especially those which carry matching requirements.

9. The extent to which public sentiment and the actions of present and past federal and state administrations have resulted in the decision in favor of having public needs taken care of closer to home, rather than on a state or federal level.

As a result of these factors, governments in the Cleveland Metropolitan Area will face two kinds of problems in the years to come. The first and more basic problem is the problem of fiscal imbalance. This has to be considered because of the existence of the State of Ohio, on the one hand, and more than one hundred governments within an area as wealthy as the Cleveland Metropolitan Area, on the other. For as has been pointed out often: Local governments are *required* by the State to perform a variety of functions, but are *permitted* by the State to raise revenue in certain ways.[1]

Thus unequal fiscal requirements are imposed on governments which are in no way related to their otherwise unequally distributed fiscal resources. The result is that even under the most favorable conditions some governments will find it difficult to meet their fiscal requirements, whereas others will be able to meet almost any rea-

---

1. Report of the New York State-New York City Fiscal Relations Committee, 1956, p. 219.

sonable set of fiscal requirements with ease. The distribution of fiscal resources was considered in Chapters II, VI, and VII, and the fiscal requirements in Chapters IV, V, and VII.

As shown by any analysis of the fiscal gap or fiscal imbalance, it is impossible to separate the expenditure, revenue, and debt operations of governments from each other. Yet each area has problems unique to itself. In Chapters IV and V, the operating and capital expenditures were considered in detail. In Chapter VII debt services charges were considered in detail. And in Chapter VIII these various expenditures or outgos of government were considered together. A number of potential danger spots emerged at each stage of the analysis which may now be brought together.

First, it was shown that as the result of metropolitan-type growth, existing governments will have new demands for government services thrust upon them. These demands may be either the result of persons or industry located within their boundaries, or the result of developments outside their own boundaries. Thus, for instance, the location of a municipality between two other municipalities, one of which is a dormitory and the other an industrial enclave, may create major traffic and police problems for the government which would not in and of itself have either. The existence of industrial enclaves means the concentration of the tax base in communities whose expenditures requirements are low relative to resources, whereas in dormitory communities the expenditure requirements may be great, but the resources very low. The existence of political boundaries will have an increasingly important effect as communities become increasingly specialized in their functions.

Second, as governments change in nature, their expenditure requirements will also change. Some will be able to take advantage of economies of scale, others will be confronted with diseconomies either because they are too big or too little.

In Chapter IV, a number of potential danger areas were considered, the most important of which involved school operating expenditures. Later, in Chapter VIII, it was indicated that school operating expenditures will impose a tremendously increased burden on school districts because of the increase in school population and the increasing concentration on the high school level. With thirty-two separate school districts providing a variety of levels of educational service, the strain of providing a minimum adequate level of service may become increasingly difficult, especially to those school districts that depend almost entirely on a residential property tax base. Another potential danger area arises from the independent nature of schools and municipalities. The implication of their independent existence should be considered more carefully than is generally the case, with respect to operating expenditures for a long period ahead, and capital expenditures especially in the next few years.

Other potential major problem areas include welfare, the responsibility for street and highway maintenance, and some of the operations included under miscellaneous commercial activity.

The principal trouble spot other than that of school operating expenditures in the decade to come seems to lie in the area of municipal capital outlay. Many governments will need funds for capital improvements on streets and highways, sewage, and water but will be without the resources to finance them. These include some very small municipalities, but also some municipalities whose fiscal resources are inadequate because of this economic and social characteristic. What is true for the wealthly Cleveland Metropolitan Area as a whole, namely that it can meet virtually any requirement, is not true for each of the individual governments which comprise it.

In its other studies METRO has considered the governmental problems of the Cleveland Metropolitan Area on a functional basis or on a governmental basis. On a functional basis it has considered police, fire, welfare, recreation, sewage, public health, etc. Also considered were functions which are governmental in nature, namely education and libraries. In addition METRO has also considered the problems of local government within the Cleveland Metropolitan Area, including those of fiscal management, land use, and county government, all of which have fiscal implications.

These various functional studies throw additional light on what might be considered the critical areas of the future. These studies suggest possible solutions to many of the fiscal problems considered here, but they do not show the extent to which the existence of one set of problems for a government, influences the solutions to other problems. The existence of one functional problem area within the boundaries of a government may make the entire government a problem area. This is especially true as a government approaches its tax and debt limits.

The problems raised by the existence of virtually separate library districts, with separate revenue sources, points out another danger spot involving school districts and municipalities even though the over-all amounts of money involved may be very small in terms of total revenue and expenditures.

Most of these potential danger spots have been recognized by the community; what this report has attempted is to bring together all the parts and indicate the magnitudes involved.

In addition to a recognition of the existence of actual or potential danger spots, a number of existing deficiencies in fiscal data and the fiscal processes must be overcome in order to provide the effective fiscal planning that is essential to any orderly growth in the future. Particularly it was found that existing fiscal data were inadequate to accommodate the governments that comprise the Cleveland Metropolitan Area to the future metropolitan age. With respect to the reporting of expenditures it is recommended therefore that:

A. Uniform state-wide rules for reporting at all stages of the budgeting of fiscal process by all governments, including the state government, be established. This would require co-ordination at the state level.

B. These rules be placed in a manual of instructions which will be uniformly applicable to all local governments and if possible the state government. The State Auditor should be made responsible.

C. The reporting of expenditures be made comprehensive; i.e., all expenditures by all local governments and, insofar as possible, state expenditure data should be integrated with those of localities by placing them on a local unit basis (viz. highway expenditures).

D. Local governments be identified by a code or index and put on punched cards for electronic data processing in such a manner as to permit grouping of county, city, village, township, school, library and special districts by metropolitan area, region, etc.

E. The reporting of expenditures be integrated with the planning and performance use of expenditure data. Fund type of expenditure reporting should be made supplementary rather than primary. [Functional classifications, economic classifications, and classifications by organizational unit when used appropriately are valuable tools for recognizing and solving the fiscal problems of the individual governments, classes of governments, as well as of metropolitan areas as wholes.]

F. A central source of expenditure information be provided comparable to that concerning revenue. For immediate purposes this could be done on a county-wide basis by using the facilities of the Cuyahoga County Auditor. Greater co-operation between county auditors on the transmission of expenditure information will be important as metropolitan areas continue to grow beyond county boundaries. Ultimately this responsibility should be given to the State of Ohio, where the fiscal information will be co-ordinated with relevant state and federal fiscal information and with available local and metropolitan economic and social data.

G. Historical and comparative data be made available, preferably by the State. But if funds are not available they should be housed in a central location either in the Cuyahoga County Auditor's Office and/or the State Auditor's Office. A detailed study should be made of metropolitan areas or at least counties comparable to the work done by the State Tax Commission in recent years for sections of the state.

H. Economic and demographic data be kept current. The Cleveland Real Property Inventory and available fiscal data provide an excellent basis for assembling a stock of useful information which will be of value for the individual governments and the entire metropolitan community. The Cleveland Regional Planning Commission preferably, or some other organization, could act as a co-ordinating or depository agency for this information. This will also require closer co-ordination between the fiscal agencies and agencies collecting economic and demographic data.

With respect to fiscal processes it is recommended that:

I. The inadequate local tax budgets, with their emphasis on fund accounting, be expanded and correlated with the State Auditor's post audit forms.

J. Program budgets be designed to plan, and performance

budgets designed to evaluate performance, especially in the case of the larger governments.

County and state governments should make expert assistance available to the smaller jurisdictions for these purposes.

K. The current expenditures and capital outlays be considered in conjunction with each other.

L. The planning of capital expenditures be co-ordinated both within governments and between governments.

M. The work of the Cleveland Regional Planning Commission be expanded and made comprehensive and that its work be co-ordinated with that of an expanded County Budget Commission.

N. The existing fiscal processes be made more open and subject to greater public control and scrutiny.

O. Steps should be taken to permit co-ordination in the fiscal processes, especially at the planning stage of governments that have or may have legal or economic fiscal relations with each other, county, school libraries, and cities.

Revenue: Summary and Recommendations

Two major questions concerning revenue face the people of all metropolitan areas. First, how shall large amounts of additional revenue be provided? METRO projections indicate that about $470 million of revenue for local governments in the Cleveland Metropolitan Area will be needed in 1965, compared with $250 million raised in 1956. About $385 million of revenue can be expected from the 1958-59 system of tax rates and intergovernmental programs applied to the larger 1965 tax base. A gap of about $85 million a year appears in the projection of revenues and expenditures to 1965. How can such an additional sum be raised, equitably and with the minimum adverse economic effect?

The second crucial revenue question is the distribution of the tax base and revenue between the different municipalities and school districts in the metropolitan area. A wide range of local taxpaying capacity exists in the Cleveland area, as in most metropolitan areas with many separate local governments.[2] The State of Ohio through the School Foundation program provides some additional aid to the poorer school districts. What is desirable in the various local jurisdictions, all of which are part of one interrelated and interdependent metropolitan area? Ignore the differences? Shift costly metropolitan functions to a county or other area-wide government? Initiate a program to equalize taxable capacity or revenues between jurisdictions within the metropolitan area? Or equate capacity to need?

The Cleveland area obtains its local revenues in amounts and from sources similar to those of most other metropolitan areas in the United States. Local governments in Cuyahoga County rely more heavily on the property tax, compared to the average local government throughout the United States and elsewhere in Ohio, as indicated in Table IX-1.

Table IX-1—Local Government Revenues, United States, Ohio, Cuyahoga County, 1956

	ALL LOCAL GOVERNMENTS IN		
	UNITED STATES	OHIO	CUYAHOGA COUNTY
	(In Millions of Dollars)		
General Revenue from own sources	23,137	1,209.1	249.6
Intergovernmental Revenue	6,899	407.0	56.0
General Revenue from own sources	16,238	802.2	193.6
Taxes	12,992		153.4
Property	11,282	594.2	141.8
Other	1,711	} 208.0	11.6
			40.2
Charges and Miscellaneous	3,246		
		Per Cent	
General Revenue from own sources	100.0	100.0	100.0
Intergovernmental Revenue	29.8	33.7	22.4
General Revenue from own sources	70.2	66.3	77.6
Taxes	56.2		61.5
Property	48.8	49.1	56.8
Other	7.4	} 17.2	4.7
Charges and Miscellaneous	14.0		16.1

Sources: U. S. Bureau of Census—*Summary of Governmental Finances in 1956* (Washington, 1957); Ohio Department of Taxation, *Ohio State and Local Governmental Revenues, RE-1, 7-58,* Table 8.

---

2. Margolis, "The Variation of Property Tax Rates," *op. cit.,* pp. 326-28.

The property tax has been a strong revenue source. Economic growth has been reflected in additional valuation, especially for real estate and tangible personal property. The real value of the property tax base has apparently kept up with inflation, but this is not reflected in property tax assessments. Since 1940, general reappraisals and reassessments effective in 1946, 1952, and 1955 have raised the valuation of existing real estate only about 50 per cent above their 1940 levels. This increase in the real estate appraisals between 1940 and 1948 compares with a 106 per cent increase in the consumer price index, a 156 per cent increase in the cost index for state and local government expenditures (to 1957), and a 171 per cent increase in the average of construction cost indices. An increase in average assessed value of about 75 per cent in 1959 would restore the 1940 assessment ratio and would approximately equal the price increase in the cost of government services.

The burden of the property tax on real estate in real terms declined between 1940 and 1956. The rise in the value of real estate

Table IX-2—Cleveland Metropolitan Area, Revenue Yield from Several Possible Revenue Sources, 1965 (In Millions of Dollars)

Tax	Size of Base	Rate	Yield
General Property	6,400	1 Mill	6.4
(1956)	(4,600)	(1 Mill)	(4.6)
Income	5,500	1 Per Cent	55.0
(1956)	(4,000)	(1 Per Cent)	(40.0)
Sales	3,000	1 Per Cent	30.0
(1956)	(1,500)	(1 Per Cent)	(15.0)
(1959)	(2,200)	(1 Per Cent)	(22.0)
Value Added	5,000	.5 Per Cent	25.0
(1956)	(4,000)	(.5 Per Cent)	(20.0)
Local Motor Vehicle		$10 Per Car	9.0
License		$20 All Other	
(1956)	(563,685 Cars)	($10 Per Car)	(7.0)
	(72,165 All Other)	($20 All Other)	
Municipally Owned Electric, Water, and Sewer Utilities			
(1956)	(32)	(3 Per Cent)	(1.0)

outdistanced substantially the rise in assessed valuation, on the average, so that the ratio of assessed value to market value (or current cost of construction) fell from about 70 per cent in 1940, to about 40 per cent in 1956. Thus, despite the rise in tax rates, the average ratio of property taxes to market value of real estate actually dropped from about 20 mills in 1940, to about 13 mills in 1956.

The present assessment ratio, low by historical standards, necessitates high tax rates, with the political and psychological effects these may carry. Low assessments keep the yield from taxes within the 10-mill limit small and make referendums necessary in most jurisdictions on additional levies and bond issues. The low assessment ratio also sets a ceiling on the debt which the county, municipality, or school district may incur. The limit, stated as a statutory percentage of the tax duplicate, cannot be exceeded. Municipalities and the county partially sidestep the statutory debt limit by use of revenue bonds, but this is not possible for school districts.

Limits on taxes and debt expressed in terms of the property tax duplicate should be reconsidered since property is only one of several measures of a local government's ability and willingness to raise revenues locally.

The property tax base is large on a per capita or per pupil basis for Cuyahoga County as a unit compared to other counties in Ohio. The distribution of the tax base between taxing districts within the metropolitan area is very uneven. A few jurisdictions find it easy to finance a high level of services with little effort, while other municipalities and school districts are hard pressed to support minimum services with comparatively high tax rates. Cuyahoga Heights, for example, has almost one hundred times as much assessed valuation per person as Oakwood. Assessed valuation per pupil in the richest school district is 15 times that of the poorest school district.

The local property tax in Cuyahoga County is a productive, stable, well developed tax. Administration is efficient. The tax positions of different properties are built historically into their market values. Taxpayers are accustomed to this tax. The property tax is unneutral between different types of economic activity, hitting investments in real estate and business tangible personal property. The tax on land falls on the owner. With residential property the burden in the long run is on the owner-occupant or tenant. With business property, the tax is usually shifted to the consumer. The incidence of the tax is regressive, with the low-income groups paying a larger per cent of their income in tax.

If real tax rates (legal tax rate multiplied by the market value) are high compared to competitive areas with equal availability and costs of resources, markets, labor forces, transportation, and other factors, location of new business and expansion of existing businesses in the high tax area will be discouraged. Manufacturing is more mobile or flexible in choice of location than retail and service industries. The sum of state and local taxes in the Cleveland area indicates a favorable position relative to competitive locations.

The property tax will undoubtedly remain the major local revenue source for decades to come. The open questions are how it can be improved and whether additional local revenue, beyond that generated automatically by economic growth on the property tax base, should come mostly from higher property tax rates.

Other local revenue sources now in use account for about 21 per cent of local general revenues. Admissions taxes, fines, special assessments, interest revenue, fees, charges and miscellaneous local sources can be expected to continue to provide a fifth. Extension of service to areas not now served and wider use of service charges for street lighting, garbage and refuse collection and disposal, sanitary sewers, and other facilities could increase the proportion of revenue from these sources.

Intergovernmental revenue comes mostly from the State of Ohio. State Aid provides about 20 per cent of local revenue and federal aid about 2 per cent. The largest dollar amount of intergovernmental aid is for schools, then highways, local government fund, welfare, and urban renewal.

From the viewpoint narrowly defined of the Cleveland area taxpayer, more state or federal aid is no solution for revenue problems of local governments. More generous state or federal payments to county, municipalities, or schools throughout the state or nation would cause state or federal tax payments in the Cleveland area to increase by more than the amount of additional aid received. As Cuyahoga County is above the national average in income per capita and above the Ohio average in retail sales, inheritances, gasoline consumption, and other bases for state taxes, the Cleveland area should expect to pay more than it will receive for most national and state programs.[3]

Recommendations: Revenues

PROPERTY TAX

A. Require appraisal of all taxable real estate as of a recent year and at a taxable value equal to a reasonable percentage, preferably 50 per cent or higher of true value or market value. Continue to enforce the requirement of reappraisal of each property at least every six years by a physical inspection. This requires state supervision and inter-county equalization, and county planning and financing.

B. Include private automobiles in the property tax base, assessed at a fraction (perhaps 50 per cent) of their "Blue Book" value. This would require legislation by the state.

C. Assess new property every six months or change the tax lien date closer to the year of collection to shorten the period between providing of services by local government and payment of first local taxes. This change would be of special help to rapidly growing communities. This would require state legislation.

D. A higher valuation on real estate increases its tax burden and lightens the tax load on other classes of taxable property. To protect the tax base, achieve equity between owners of different types of taxable property, and to consider the economic effects of a tax shift, the Ohio legislature should re-examine the dividing line between realty and tangible personal property and the statutory percentages at which different classes of tangible personal property are taxed. Ohio is more vague and uncertain and has a less well-defined boundary between real and tangible personal property than other states

---

3. There are many and substantial advantages to the people and businesses of the Cleveland area from programs to assist less prosperous areas to maintain a reasonable level of service for education, highways, health, welfare, etc. But this is not recommended primarily to solve the revenue problems of the Cuyahoga County local governments.

which tax tangible personal property. A clear definition of real estate is needed to prevent disputes and litigation and to maintain the tax base.

E. Provide additional state assistance, such as assessor's manuals and valuation tables. Data to the county auditors and probably to the public on assessment ratios between properties differing by location, use, age, price range, and construction, and dispersion between assessment ratios for comparable properties could and should be provided by the State Department of Taxation. If this is not done by the State, this should be done as part of the research program in the County Auditor's office, or by a metropolitan area research organization.

INTANGIBLES TAX

The present revenue system for the libraries is not satisfactory and, with the growth in the financial needs of libraries, the entire local situs intangibles tax will be inadequate in a few years to cover the budgets of the libraries. But in view of the present demands on property tax, it seems undesirable to recommend that the property tax support the libraries.

In view of the distribution of revenue capacity and revenue need in the metropolitan area, the intangibles tax (local-situs) might best go to the County either to support metropolitan functions shifted to the County from the municipalities, or for distribution among libraries and municipalities on the basis of need without regard to situs.

Distribution of the locally collected intangibles tax to the municipality of origin is generally a case of the rich getting richer and the poor getting poorer. The municipalities with high assessed valuations per capita usually also have higher than average intangibles tax collections per capita, and low valuations usually accompany low intangibles collections. (See Table VI-8.)

LOCAL MOTOR VEHICLE LICENSES

As an alternative to levying property taxes on private cars, the state should either increase the motor vehicle license tax and distribute the additional revenue back to the local governments or authorize local governments to charge a local license tax on motor vehicles, perhaps with provision for state administration at cost. Any revenue from this source would be dedicated to streets and highways. Local revenues from highway users at present cover only about half of local costs of streets and highways.

ADDITIONAL REVENUE

If large amounts—perhaps $85 million a year—of additional revenue beyond the increase generated from economic growth under the present tax system are required by 1965, how can these funds best be raised? If all these funds are raised locally from the general property tax with property assessed on the present basis, an increase estimated at 13 mills in the average county tax rate would be required.

Which of the following methods of raising $85 million of additional funds would be preferable? (Table IX-2 shows the revenue yield from several possible local revenue sources.)

(1) An average increase of 13 mills above the 1958-59 tax rates in the general property tax, to a county average tax rate of about 48 mills.

(2) 1 per cent tax on individual and business income to yield about $55 million and a property tax increase of about 4.5 mills.

(3) A 1 per cent local sales tax on top of the present state 3 per cent rate (yield about $20 million) plus an eight mill increase in the property tax rate.

(4) A value-added tax at a 0.5 per cent rate (yield $25-30 million) and an eight- or nine-mill increase in the property tax rate.

Minor local taxes and fees could increase revenues by perhaps $12 million, the equivalent of almost two mills from the property tax. Local annual motor vehicle licenses at $10 per private car and $20 for other vehicles would raise about $9 million a year in 1965.

IMBALANCE

The variation in revenue capacity between municipalities and school districts is so great that it calls for action now. Several smaller, poorer, or rapidly growing jurisdictions can provide a range and quality of governmental services adequate to maintain minimum standards in the metropolitan area only with a tax effort excessive by area standards. More likely the poorer districts will provide poor or no service with possible adverse repercussions throughout the metropolitan area in such functions as public safety, public health, sewerage, roads, and education.

Several steps with varying degrees of impact might be taken to equalize the differential revenue capacity:

1. Emphasis on below average tax base in distribution of local government fund.

2. State action to give the local-situs intangibles and inheritance taxes to increase the local government fund for distribution on an equalization basis. Libraries would continue to have first claim on the intangibles tax. Distribution of portions of the inheritance and intangible taxes back to municipalities of origin generally aggravates the imbalance from the property tax.

3. Use of county-wide tax on business property with distribution on the basis of population or school enrollment, with safeguards for the revenue position of jurisdictions which have attracted industry.

4. A modest tax on the county tax duplicate with distribution on basis of population or pupils.

5. A new tax, such as a county-wide income tax, sales tax, or value-added tax, with distribution to municipalities and school districts on a flat amount per person or per pupil, or inversely to property valuation. Depending on the amount of revenue and the basis of distribution, the new tax might not only reduce imbalance but also provide some relief for the property tax.

6. Shift of functions of metropolitan-wide concern, such as sewerage, main roads, and public health, to the county with either a higher county property tax rate or a new tax source to finance the newly-assumed county functions. To the extent that present municipal functions are transferred, municipal tax needs would decline offsetting the increased county requirements. A county charter and probably an Ohio Constitutional Amendment would be necessary to allow a county charter provision for more flexible use of the property tax and any county tax other than the property tax.

Problem of Growing Municipalities and School Districts

One problem of special concern to rapidly growing jurisdictions is the present Ohio schedule of real property assessment and tax payment, with the long interval between the construction and occupancy of a new building and the first tax payment. A new house, for example, might be started in March, 1960, completed in June, and occupied in July, 1960. The new residents would begin to receive local municipal services immediately, and the children could attend public schools beginning in September, 1960. The family will be paying federal and state taxes currently on their income and purchases. The county assessor, guided by 1960 building permits, will assess their new home as of January 1, 1961. Based on this assessment, the homeowner will receive his first property tax bill in December, 1961, with the first payment due by mid-January, 1962.[4] If the County is able to meet the statutory schedule, tax settlement by the County Treasurer to the municipality or school district will probably be in March, 1962, almost two years after local government services were first provided.

In stable or slowly growing areas, this lag is a minor problem. But in rapidly growing jurisdictions such as Beachwood and Parma, in which the population growth between 1950 and 1956 was 60 per cent and 20 per cent a year respectively, a lag between the provision of additional services and the receipt of revenues from new property of more than a year is very serious. Parma's real estate duplicate, for example, increased about 10 per cent a year between 1950 and 1957. As of January 1, 1957, the taxable value of real estate in the Parma School District was $174.5 million. Tax collections during 1957, however, were based on real estate assessed as of January 1, 1956, which amounted to $156.7 million. If construction during 1956 occurred

---

4. The statutory deadline for the first half payment on real estate is January 20, but hardly ever do counties get their tax bills prepared and mailed in time to allow taxpayers to meet this date. Cuyahoga County believes itself to be the only one of the 88 counties in Ohio which will meet this deadline on first half payments in the 1958-59 tax year. Cuyahoga County itself had not met this statutory deadline for many years. Later payment would further aggravate the problem discussed in the text.

at a constant rate during the year, a tax lien date of July 1, 1956, would have given a tax base for calendar 1957 collections of $165.6 million. At the Parma school tax rate of 20.9 mills this would have meant about $186,000 or about 4.5 per cent more revenue in 1957. For the entire county, the real estate portion of the duplicate would have been $70.9 million higher by an assessment as of July 1, 1956. At an average tax rate of about 33 mills, this would have provided an additional $2.3 million to support local services, apportioned among the local governments according to the increase in assessed value in their boundaries.

Ohio laws could be changed to shorten the lag between construction and the first tax payment. One approach would schedule the tax lien date on July 1, instead of January 1. This would reduce the lag substantially by getting taxpayers six months closer to current payment of their tax liabilities. No property owner would pay more taxes during his period of ownership than he does now. But payment would begin sooner on many new properties and the present overhanging liability for past unbilled and unpaid taxes would be smaller to the extent of earlier payments.

The county's staff of assessors would be able to spread their work more evenly over the year. At present, in Cuyahoga County, skilled assessors begin appraising new construction in January and are through in August. For about four months in the year the assessors are transferred to the accounting and billing operations. This shift in assignments is a good use of manpower under the present statutory schedule of assessing, budgeting, and billing. But much better would be use of expert assessors at their highest skill for the full twelve months, if possible. Here changes in Cuyahoga County are dependent upon changes in Ohio law. This suggestion is closely related to the recommendation for a change in the budgeting schedule.[5]

DEBT LIMITS

The statutory debt limits are now based entirely on the property tax duplicate. But property values are out of date as the only or

5. See Waldby and Theuer, *Problems in Fiscal Administration*, Part 1 (*op. cit.*).

necessarily the best measure of local revenue capacity. If local governments utilize new major revenue sources, such as income or sales
taxes, definition of the debt limit in terms of local capacity and local
effort under any or a combination of taxes would more accurately
reflect debt servicing capacity and intent. Such a change would
increase local autonomy and encourage local governments to use
revenue sources best adapted to their economic base and revenue
needs.

If the changes anticipated in this study take place, by 1965 the
pattern of finances in the Cleveland Metropolitan Area will be
different from that existing today. And there is little reason to believe that they will not. Therefore, it is essential that any change
introduced by the citizens and their governments alleviate rather
than compound the problems of financing governments in the metropolitan area. To be successful, the changes and modifications in
existing practices will have to take into account the metropolitan-
wide problems and resources, and, at the same time, enhance those
elements and features of government which are viable and desirable
ends in themselves.

Conclusion

If the changes anticipated in this study take place, by 1965 the
pattern of finances in the Cleveland Metropolitan Area will be
different from that existing today. And there is little reason to believe that they will not. Therefore, it is essential that any change
introduced by the citizens and their governments alleviate rather
than compound the problems of financing governments in the
metropolitan area. To be successful, the changes and modifications
in existing practices will have to take into account the metropolitan-
wide problems and resources and, at the same time, enhance those
elements and features of government which are viable and desirable
ends in themselves.

Bibliography

Adrian, Charles R., *Governing Urban America: Structure, Politics, and Administration*, New York, McGraw-Hill Book Co., Inc., 1955.

Alexandersson, Gunnar, *The Industrial Structure of American Cities: A Geographic Study of Urban Economy in the United States*, Lincoln, University of Nebraska Press, 1956.

American Academy of Political and Social Science, *Metropolis in Ferment, Annals* of the Academy, November 1957.

Berolzheimer, Josef, "Influences Shaping Expenditure for Operation of State and Local Governments," *National Tax Association Bulletin*, May 1947, pp. 237-244.

Bird, Frederick L., *The Municipal Debt: A Description, Analysis and Appraisal of Debt Policy and Administration of the City of New York*, New York, Mayor's Committee on Management Survey, 1952.

Bogue, Donald J. (ed.), *Needed Urban and Metropolitan Research*, Oxford, Ohio, Scripps Foundation, Miami University, 1953.

—— and Harris, Dorothy L., *Comparative Population and Urban Research via Multiple Regression and Covariance Analysis: A Methodological Experiment, with an Illustrative Application to the Study of Factors in the Growth and Suburbanization of Metropolitan Population*, Scripps Foundation, Miami University, and Population Research and Training Center, University of Chicago, 1954.

381

Bollens, John C. and Scott, Stanley, *Effect of Inflation and Growth on City Costs and Services: Case Study of Berkeley, California*, Berkeley, University of California, Bureau of Public Administration, 1949.

Bolton, Dale L., "Some Aspects of Equalizing Educational Opportunity and Taxation Burden," *National Tax Journal*, December 1958, pp. 354-361.

Brazer, Harvey E., "The Role of Major Metropolitan Centers in State and Local Finance," *American Economic Review*, May 1958, pp. 305-316.

——, *City Expenditures in the United States*, New York, National Bureau of Economic Research, Occasional Paper 66, 1959.

Brecht, Arnold, *Expenditures in Their Relation to Density of Population*, Cambridge, Harvard University Press, 1941.

Burkhead, Jesse, *Government Budgeting, Economic Character Classification*, New York, John Wiley & Sons, Inc., 1956.

Campbell, Alan K., "Taxes and Industrial Location in the New York Metropolitan Region," *National Tax Journal*, September 1958, pp. 195-218.

Chatters, Carl H., "The Economic Classification of Cities and Its Fiscal Implications," *National Tax Journal*, June 1948, pp. 111-116.

—— and Hillhouse, Albert M., *Local Government Debt Administration*, New York, Prentice-Hall, Inc., 1939.

Citizens Research Council of Michigan, "Summary Digest of Michigan Tax Study," *Staff Reports*, Detroit, 1958.

Cleveland Chamber of Comerce, "93 Governments or 1?" *A Report of the Committee on City Finances*, 1925.

Colm, "Why Public Finance," *National Tax Journal*, September 1948.

Crouch, Winston W., and others, "Metropolitan Los Angeles: A Study in Integration," *Finance and Taxation*, v. 14, Los Angeles, Haynes Foundation, 1954.

Cuyahoga County Regional Planning Commission, "Our Citified County: A Study of Cuyahoga County and Its Land Use Now, and for the Future," Cleveland, 1954.

Due, John F., *Government Finance* (2nd ed.), Chicago, Richard D. Irwin, 1958.

——, *Sales Taxation*, Urbana, University of Illinois Press, 1957.

Esser, George H., Jr., *Greensboro Suburban Analysis*, Chapel Hill, Institute of Government, University of North Carolina, 1956.

Ferber, Robert, *Statistical Techniques in Market Research*, New York, McGraw-Hill Book Co., 1949.

Fisher, Robert Moore (ed.), *The Metropolis in Modern Life*, New York, Doubleday, 1955.

Fitch, Lyle C., "Metropolitan Financial Problems," *Metropolis in Ferment, Annals* of the American Academy of Political and Social Science, November 1957.

——, "Financial Problems of New York City," *Proceedings of the 45th Annual Conference on Taxation of the National Tax Association*, Toronto, 1952, Sacramento, 1953, pp. 379-387.

——, "Trends in Federal, State, and Local Government Expenditures Since 1890," *American Economic Review*, May 1953, pp. 216-233.

Goldfield, Edwin D., *Statistical Abstract of the United States*, 1957, U.S. Dept. of Commerce, Bureau of the Census, 78th Annual Edition.

Green, Howard Whipple, "Real Property Inventory of Metropolitan Cleveland," *Sheet-A-Week,* Sept. 6, 1956.

Gronouski, John A., "State Supervision of Property Tax Administration," *National Tax Journal,* June 1957, pp. 158-170.

Groves, Harold M., *Financing Government* (5th ed.), New York, Henry Holt, 1958.

Haig, Robert M., "Toward an Understanding of the Metropolis," *Quarterly Journal of Economics,* 1926, pp. 179-208.

———— and Shoup, Carl S., *The Financial Problem of the City of New York: General Summary Volume of the Finance Project,* Report to Mayor's Committee on Management Survey, New York, 1952.

———— and McCrae, Roswell C., *Regional Survey of New York and Its Environs,* v. 1; *Major Economic Factors in Metropolitan Growth and Arrangement: A Study of Trends and Tendencies in the Economic Activities within the Region of New York and Its Environs,* Regional Plan of New York and Its Environs, 1927.

Hansen, Alvin H., and Perloff, Harvey S., *State and Local Finance in the National Economy,* New York, Norton, 1944.

Harris, Britton, "The Economic Aspects of the Metropolitan Region," *University of Pennsylvania Law Review,* 105, February 1957, 467-471.

Harvard University, Graduate School of Public Administration, Bureau of Research in Municipal Government, "Comparative Status of 83 Cities and Towns in the Boston Metropolitan Census District: Population, Assessed Valuation, Assessed Valuation per Capita, Tax Rates, Direct Tax per Capita, Amounts, Increases or Decreases, Indices, Rank Orders, Distributions, 1930 to Date," Cambridge, Mass., December 1943.

————, "Metropolis in Maps; Graphic References for the Boston Area," Cambridge, Mass., 1946.

Hatt, Paul K., and Reiss, Albert J., Jr. (eds.), *Reader in Urban Sociology* (rev. ed.), Glencoe, Free Press, 1957.

Hawley, Amos H., *Human Ecology,* New York, Ronald Press, 1950.

————, *The Changing Shape of Metropolitan America: Deconcentration Since 1920,* Glencoe, Free Press, 1956.

————, "Metropolitan Population and Municipal Government Expenditures in Central Cities," *Journal of Social Issues,* 1951, pp. 100-108.

Hirsch, Werner Z., "Measuring Factors Affecting Expenditure Levels for Local Government Services," *Metropolitan St. Louis Survey,* St. Louis, Mo., 1957.

Institute for Training in Municipal Administration, *Municipal Finance Administration,* 5th ed., Chicago, International City Mgrs. Assn., 1949.

International City Managers' Association, *Municipal Year Book.*

Isard, Walter, and Coughlin, Robert E., "Municipal Costs and Revenues Resulting from Community Growth," Federal Reserve Bank of Boston and the American Institute of Planners, Wellesley, Mass., Chandler-Davis Publishing Co., 1957.

Kneier, Charles M., *City Government in the United States,* New York, Harper, 1947.

Kramer, Eugene, "The Scope of Chicago Area Fiscal Activities: A Process Approach," Chicago Area Transportation Study, 4812 Madison, Chicago 44, Ill. No. 119 (12/10/57), 3. 7. 2.—Chicago Area Fiscal Activities 37, 200—VIII.

Lambie, Morris B., "Experiments in Methods of Municipal Analysis with Special Application to the 351 Cities and Towns in the Commonwealth of Massachusetts," Bureau for Research in Municipal Government, Harvard Graduate School of Public Administration, No. 5, December 1941.

———, "Status of the Property Tax 1945 and 1949 in 43 Cities and Towns within the Boston Metropolitan Area: An Experiment in Methods of Municipal Analysis," Bureau for Research in Municipal Government, Harvard Graduate School of Public Administration, No. 19, January 1950.

Leland, Simeon E., "Financing Metropolitan Government," *Symposium Conducted by the Tax Institute*, Chapter XXIV, Princeton, 1954.

Margolis, Julius, "Municipal Fiscal Structure in a Metropolitan Region," *Journal of Political Economy*, LXV, No. 3, June, 1957, 225-236.

———, "On Municipal Land Policy for Fiscal Gains," *National Tax Journal*, September 1956, pp. 247-257.

———, "The Variation of Property Tax Rates within a Metropolitan Region," *National Tax Journal*, December 1956, pp. 326-330.

Mayor's Committee on Management Survey of the City of New York, Finance Project Staff, "Revenue and Expenditure Trends in the City of New York No. 7," (rev. ed.), 1952; No. 12, May 1952.

McKenzie, R. D., *The Metropolitan Community*, New York, McGraw-Hill, 1933.

Michigan Tax Study, *Staff Papers 1958*, Lansing, Michigan, 1958.

Miller, Donald C., "Sales Tax Progressivity Attributable to a Food Exemption," *National Tax Journal*, June 1951.

Mills, Frederick C., *Statistical Methods*, New York, Holt, Rinehart and Winston, Inc.

Musgrave, R. A., and others, "Distribution of Tax Payments by Income Groups: A Case Study for 1948," *National Tax Journal*, March 1951.

——— and Culbertson, J. M., "Growth of Public Expenditures in the United States, 1890-1948," *National Tax Journal*, June 1953.

Neff, Philip, "Government Services and Costs as Affected by Rapid Growth in Population," *Proceedings of the 41st Annual Conference on Taxation of the National Tax Association*, Denver, 1948. Sacramento, 1948.

Netzer, Dick, "The Outlook for Fiscal Needs and Resources of State and Local Governments," *American Economic Review*, May 1958, pp. 317-327.

Newcomer, Mabel, "Decline of the General Property Tax," *National Tax Journal*, March 1953, pp. 38-51.

Northern Virginia Regional Planning and Economic Development Commission, *Northern Virginia Fiscal Survey*, Alexandria, 1957.

Ohio Department of Taxation, "A Study of the Tax and Revenue System of the State of Ohio and Its Political Subdivisions," *Report of the Tax Commissioner to the Governor and the 97th General Assembly*, Columbus, 1947.

Ohio Legislative Services Commission, Columbus, Ohio, *Staff Research Reports: Local Government Financing Problems in Ohio*, #33, 1959; *Selected*

Metropolitan Area Problems, #34, 1959; *School Finance Equalization in Ohio*, #38, 1959.

Pennsylvania Economy League, Inc., Western Division, *The Relative Cost of Manufacturing Industry: A New Comparison of Pennsylvania with Several Other States* (1957 rev.), Pittsburgh, 1957.

Phillips, H. S., "Municipal Efficiency and Town Size," *Town Planning Institute Journal*, May 1942, pp. 139-148.

Reed, Thomas H. and Doris D., *Financing a Postwar Public Improvement Program for Greater Cleveland: A Report of the Cleveland Bureau of Governmental Research and the Metropolitan Cleveland Development Council*, Sponsored by the Consultant Service of the National Municipal League, Jan. 29, 1946.

Reed, Thomas H., *Cleveland at the Crossroads*, Cleveland, 1945.

Regional Government Committee of "400," *Hearings*, Fact Finding and Policy Committee, Cleveland, 1928.

————, *Report*, Fact Finding and Policy Committee, January 1929.

Reiss, Albert J., Jr., "The Community and the Corporate Area," *University of Pennsylvania Law Review*, February 1957.

Report of the Governor's Minnesota Tax Study Committee, Minneapolis, 1956.

Report to the Governor of the State of New York and The Mayor of the City of New York, New York State, New York City Fiscal Relations Committee, 1956.

Rockefeller Report on the U.S. Economy, "The Challenge to America: Its Economic and Social Aspects," Special Studies Project Report IV, Rockefeller Brothers Fund, America at Mid-Century Series, Report of Panel IV of the Special Studies Project, 1958.

Sacks, Seymour, Egand, Leo M., and Hellmuth, William F., Jr., *The Cleveland Metropolitan Area: A Fiscal Profile*, Cleveland, Cleveland Metropolitan Services Commission, 1958.

Schauffer, Mary C., *The Suburbs of Cleveland*, Chicago, 1945.

Schultz, W. J., and Harriss, C. L., *American Public Finance*, New York, Prentice-Hall, 1954.

Scott, Stanley, and Feder, Edward L., *Factors Associated with Variations in Municipal Expenditure Levels*, Berkeley, Bureau of Public Administration, University of California, 1957.

Sigafoos, Robert A., *The Municipal Income Tax: Its History and Problems*, Chicago, Public Administration Service, 1955.

Simon, Herbert A., *Fiscal Aspects of Metropolitan Consolidation*, Berkeley, University of California, Bureau of Public Administration, 1943.

Sloan, Allan K., *A Metropolitan Government for Cleveland: A Case Study in Local Politics*, Princeton, Princeton University, April 15, 1952.

Tablemen, Betty, "Governmental Organization in Metropolitan Areas," *Michigan Governmental Studies #21*, Ann Arbor, University of Michigan Press, 1951.

Tax Foundation, *Facts and Figures on Government Finance* (9th ed.), New York, 1956-1957; (10th ed.), New York, 1958-1959.

Tax Institute, *Financing Metropolitan Government: A Symposium*, Princeton, 1955.

Thomas, Carol J., *Distribution of the Cost of Public Services in Metropolitan Boston,* Boston, Boston University.

Tiebout, Charles M., "A Pure Theory of Local Expenditures," *Journal of Political Economy,* October 1956.

University of Pennsylvania Law Review, *A Symposium on Metropolitan Regionalism: Developing Governmental Concepts,* February 1957.

Urban Land Institute, "Urban Land Use and Property Taxation," Technical Bulletin, No. 18, Washington, D. C., 1952.

U.S. Congress, Joint Economic Committee, "National Economic Accounts of the United States," *Hearings* before the Subcommittee on Economic Statistics of the Joint Economic Committee, 85th Congress, 1st Session pursuant to Sec. 5 (a) of Public Law 304, 79th Congress, Oct. 29 and 30, 1957, pp. 41-42-43, 178, 184, and 232.

U.S. Department of Commerce, Bureau of the Census, *Compendium of City Government Finances in 1955.*

U.S. Department of Commerce, Bureau of the Census, *Compendium of City Government Finances in 1956.*

U.S. Department of Commerce, Bureau of the Census, "Historical Statistics on State and Local Government, 1902-1953," State and Local Government Special Studies No. 38, Washington, D. C., 1955.

U.S. Department of Commerce, Bureau of the Census, "Local Government Finances in City Areas in 1953," State and Local Government Special Studies No. 39, Washington, D. C., 1955.

U.S. Department of Commerce, Bureau of the Census, *1957 Census of Governments,* Washington, 1957, 1958; especially the following: Vol. I, No. 2, Local Governments in Standard Metropolitan Areas; Vol. II, No. 3, Local Government Employment in Standard Metropolitan Areas; Vol. III, No. 1, Finances of School Districts.

U.S. Department of Commerce, Bureau of the Census, *1957 Census of Governments Advance Releases;* especially the following: State and Local Government Finances in 1957 (February 1959); Governmental Finances in the United States, 1902 to 1957 (March 1959).

U.S. Department of Commerce, Office of Business Economics, *Survey of Current Business, National Income Number,* Vol. 37, No. 7, Govt. Printing Office, July 1957.

Vernon, Raymond, *The Changing Economic Function of the Central City,* New York, Committee for Economic Development, January 1959.

Walker, Mabel L., *Municipal Expenditures,* Baltimore, Johns Hopkins Press, 1930.

———, "Fiscal Aspects of Metropolitan Regional Development," *University of Pennsylvania Law Review,* February 1957.

———, "Local Tax Competition within Metropolitan Areas," *Proceedings of the 50th Annual Conference on Taxation of the National Tax Association,* Columbus, 1957. Harrisburg, 1958, pp. 431-437.

Wessel, Robert H., "Cincinnati's Income Tax—An Emergency Financing Device," *National Tax Journal,* March 1956, pp. 84-90.

Wheaton, Wm. L. C., and Schussheim, M. J., *The Cost of Municipal Services in Residential Areas,* Washington, U.S. Department of Commerce, 1955.

Williamson, C. C., *The Finances of Cleveland*, New York, Columbia University Press, 1907.

Wood, Robert C., *Metropolis against Itself*, New York, Committee for Economic Development, March 1959.

Woodbury, Coleman (ed.), *Urban Redevelopment: Problems and Practices*, Chicago, University of Chicago Press, 1953.

———— (ed.), *The Future of Cities and Urban Redevelopment*, Chicago, University of Chicago Press, 1953.

Zimmer, Basil G., "Differential Property Taxation in a Metropolitan Area," *National Tax Journal*, September 1958, pp. 280-286.